Shelley's Goddess

For Jerry and Elizabeth,
with love and gratitude,
from Barbara

November 4, 1992

SHELLEY'S GODDESS

Maternity, Language, Subjectivity

BARBARA CHARLESWORTH GELPI

New York   Oxford
OXFORD UNIVERSITY PRESS
1992

Oxford University Press

Oxford   New York   Toronto
Delhi   Bombay   Calcutta   Madras   Karachi
Kuala Lumpur   Singapore   Hong Kong   Tokyo
Nairobi   Dar es Salaam   Cape Town
Melbourne   Auckland

and associated companies in
Berlin   Ibadan

Published by Oxford University Press, Inc.,
200 Madison Avenue, New York, New York 10016

Oxford is a registered trademark of Oxford University Press

Library of Congress Cataloging-in-Publication Data
Gelpi, Barbara Charlesworth.
Shelley's goddess : maternity, language, subjectivity /
Barbara Charlesworth Gelpi.
p.   cm.   Includes bibliographical references and index.
ISBN 0-19-507383-5(cloth).—ISBN 0-19-507384-3 (pbk.)
1. Shelley, Percy Bysshe, 1792–1822—Criticism and interpretation.
2. Mother and child in literature.   3. Psychoanalysis and literature.
4.   Subjectivity in literature.   5. Motherhood in literature.
6. Infants in literature.   I. Title.
PR5442.M67G45   1992   821′.7—dc20   91-35901

2 4 6 8 9 7 5 3 1

Printed in the United States of America
on acid-free paper

For Albert,
Christopher,
and Adrienne

Preface

The writings of Percy Bysshe Shelley take on significant new meaning when read through two intersecting ideologies: the ideology of the maternal, which underscored the necessity of mothers' constant, immediate, and personal care of infants and young children; and the ideology of the aesthetic, as it has been defined by Terry Eagleton. With the Greek meaning of *aisthesis* (pertaining to sense perception) as his warrant, Eagleton gives "aesthetic" its widest possible meaning. The word establishes a distinction not between "art" and "life" but between "the whole region of human perception and sensation, in contrast to the more rarefied domain of conceptual thought" (13). He theorizes that the aesthetic, in this inclusive sense, takes on the significance it had during the eighteenth century (and later) as a way of mollifying the rigors of bourgeois individualism: "In economic life, individuals are structurally isolated and antagonistic; at the political level there would seem nothing but abstract rights to link one subject to the other. This is one reason why the 'aesthetic' realm of sentiments, affections and spontaneous bodily habits comes to assume the significance it does" (23).

Eagleton does not make an explicit connection between the importance placed on the aesthetic and the segregation of women into a domestic realm of "sentiments and affections," where they were charged with the task of instilling their children with "spontaneous bodily habits." The omission is rather surprising, since the point has been made by a number of feminist scholars that middle-class women's function within a capitalist system was—and is, since the "thousand points of [volunteering] light" are gendered—recuperative and thus conservative in two senses of that word (Gallagher 119; Newton 19; Poovey 10; B. Smith 10). While availing myself of Eagleton's phrase and the ideas it signifies, my thinking is actually closer to that of Alan Richardson, who argues that "in moving from an 'Age of Reason' to an 'Age of Feeling' male writers drew on the memories and fantasies of identification with the mother in order to colonize the conventionally feminine domain of sensibility" (13). My reading of what is involved in that identification and of the range of its effects is somewhat different from Richardson's. Using broader terms than he does, I would say, that the the role assigned to mothers, with its attendant effects on the construction of subjectivity and the acquisition of language, has consequences for every possible area of human activity, including literature.

Thus, much material in the first two chapters of this book is relevant to a consideration of other nineteenth-century writers and has benefited from earlier work in this field. My study provides a sociological context, together with a broader psychological schema, for Barbara Schapiro's pioneering but overly narrow analysis of Shelley, Keats, Coleridge, and Wordsworth, and dovetails with Anne Mellor's discussion of the signal importance of the domestic in the writings of Mary Shelley. Jerome McGann suggests the possibility that the poetry of Byron also reflects the workings of this dual ideology. Paul Sawyer writes that "Wisdom [Athena in Ruskin's *Queen of the Air*] is Ruskin's name for what Eagleton calls the 'ideology of the aesthetic,' the introjection of the social law experienced as consensus" (139).

My area of interest overlaps in a number of ways that of Nathaniel Brown, though we come to precisely opposite conclusions. Brown holds that the eighteenth-century doctrine of sympathy offered a "psychological alternative to the traditional polarization of the sexes into separate spheres," whereas I see the two as part of a cultural whole, with the doctrine not implying "the dissolution of sex roles" but reinscribing them. I most emphatically do not subscribe to the view that Shelley was a feminist, much less "the first major writer to experiment in literary consciousness-raising" (Brown 3).

My work is perhaps most constantly in dialogue with *Shelley's Process* by Jerrold Hogle. The chiming of our two titles, while unplanned in that we were working completely independently, is appropriate. In defining the centrality of "radical transference" to Shelley's creativity, Hogle writes: "Indeed, his self-reproducing and self-altering transference is the otherness-of-self-from-self long consigned to 'woman' by patriarchal discourse and recently revived in French theory as the feminine 'unconscious' on which the construct 'man' (including the Freudian version) is actually based without realizing the fact" (18). In a note Hogle adds that "Jardine's notion of *gynesis* striving toward *gynema* is very close to what I mean by Shelleyan transference" (347). As will become clear in the first chapter, Hogle and I use the same phenomenon—the mirrored maternal at the core of subjectivity—as our starting point. We subsequently move in different, though not antithetical, directions, our differing methodologies steering us toward different areas of interest. Both of us, however, can be numbered among those critics employed in exploring what Coppélia Kahn has described as "that gray, shadowy region of identification, particularly male identification with the mother" (88).

Although I endow the maternal ideology, as implementation for the ideology of the aesthetic, with very broad relevance, distrust of generalization has led me to focus on a single subject—Percy Bysshe Shelley. That the relation to the maternal of virtually all writers since the mid-eighteenth century bears careful investigation seems to me incontrovertible, yet in each case the nature of that relation will vary according to the circumstances, the personalities, and the historical moment. In the second chapter, therefore, I limit myself to the version of the maternal ideology disseminated at the time of Shelley's infancy and childhood, and in the third I link it to the interactions that characterized the Shelley family. I then read only one work by Shelley—albeit a long and significant one—in order to track the presence of the maternal, with the explicit understanding that this deeply ambivalent relationship, while present in many other places, will not manifest itself in the same way even in different works by the same poet.

The specificity needed for such a task justifies my concentrating on only one nineteenth-century poet. But why Shelley should be my choice requires further explanation. My reading of Shelley's poetry as part of an academic apprenticeship aside, I first took an interest in his work—a negative interest, to be sure—while I was considering the viability of androgyny as a feminist concept. When an "androgynous" pair, Laon and Cythna, is first presented to us, Cythna is curled up beside Laon "like his shadow" (*Laon and Cythna* I.lx.534 [*CW* I, 274]), but the Jungian term "anima" would describe her more appropriately: "None else [besides Laon] beheld her eyes—in him they woke / Memories which found a tongue, as thus he silence broke" (I.lx.539–40). An analysis of this and similar fantasies in works by other authors underlies my caveat (in "The Politics of Androgyny") against androgyny as historically misogynist; its ambition is to "transcend" relationships with actual women by subsuming "the feminine" into the subjectivity of the male. More generally, one could say that Shelley's obsession with finding "a soul within our soul that describes a circle around its proper Paradise which pain and sorrow and evil dare not overleap" ("On Love," *SPP* 474) expresses a desire for unity of being that denigrates and seeks to escape the actualities of human dependence and interdependence. There were other cogent reasons for abandoning androgyny as a feminist project, but this—at least in my own case—was the primary one.

My notations on incest as, so to speak, an androgynous metaphor in Shelley's work drew my attention to the fact that the incestuously paired sister and brother Cythna and Laon functioned like figures painted on a theatrical scrim, at once revealing and concealing their true stage presences as mother and son. Kenneth Cameron's insights into the biographical significance of Shelley's relationship with his mother (*Young Shelley* 3–5) had not received further scholarly attention, and a study of that bonding caught my interest as a possible project.

Contextually, I had as models the brilliant feminist analyses of mothering that appeared in the mid-1970s: Adrienne Rich's *Of Woman Born*, a break-through conceptualization of motherhood as an institution, a constructed and therefore not a "natural" experience; Nancy Chodorow's *Reproduction of Mothering*, an analysis of the ambivalence created through sons' separation from and daughters' identification with the mother, constructed to be their primary—and often sole—care giver; and Dorothy Dinnerstein's study *The Mermaid and the Minotaur*, which theorizes that the ambivalence toward maternal power created by infant dependence on a female caretaker produces in both genders a fear of experiencing empowerment in women. Incidents in

Shelley's life as well as situations and locutions in his work give evidence of such ambivalence—*true* ambivalence in that fascination with and fear of feminine power are equally manifest.

I found that my essentially biographical method uncovered a wealth of material, but it proved unsatisfactory: the underlying Freudian theory needed better historical grounding, and the study's descriptive rather than analytical character lacked theoretical interest and complexity. I turned to other projects. Through these I had a further opportunity to learn about the construction of motherhood as a historical phenomenon as well as an ongoing process. With the influx of Lacanian, and specifically Kristevan, thought into American feminist theory in the late 1970s and early 1980s, I became more conscious of the problematic relationship between the maternal and the acquisition of language, which led me back to Shelley. Also, since acquisition of language occurs along with acquisition or, according to another theory, increase of conscious subjectivity, I found that my dialogue with Shelley engaged concerns that had motivated me as far back as the writing of *Dark Passages*.

In that book I traced the angst experienced by central figures of the Pre-Raphaelite, Aesthetic, and Decadent movements to an epistemology that encloses the perceiving consciousness in a separate house/room/prison cell haunted by Other(s) that—there being no sure knowledge of an external reality—take on the character of projections from the self. My analysis took these writers to task with a stern moralism that I now smile over because I see that, as the "hypocrite auteur," I was finding morally unacceptable a philosophic position that the epistemological theory I shared with the writers in question made intellectually compelling. Shelley, it turns out, has all along been "mon semblable, mon frère" because he, too, found the axioms of the Humean "intellectual system" inescapable ("On Life," *SPP* 476) but its conclusions productive only of a "vacancy" (477).

Similarly, I have understood very well what Kaja Silverman means when she writes that the Freudian and Lacanian dicta about the nature of subjectivity "seduce" by their "very rigors" (*Subject of Semiotics* 192). The Lacanian model apparently turns the Humean on its head in that the perceiving subject, deluded by imagined notions of its unity and coherence, is in actuality split in such imponderable ways by the unconscious that it might be conceived of as a vacancy mirroring Other(s) whose "space" creates its experience of being a conscious subject (Lacan, *Four Fundamental Concepts* 144). But the common idealist source of the two theoretical positions (Nye, "A Woman Clothed" 681; Borch-Jacobsen, *Lacan* 62) makes the *experiential* result the same: a subjectivity haunted by/mirroring Other(s) who have the character of specters. This shared epistemology, along with shared fascination in the links between subjectivity and language, makes Lacanian theory particularly applicable to Shelley's work (Fry 451).

One could say that the intellectual box I once labeled "decadent consciousness" is the one from which, like Shelley, I wished to escape. But the question remains: Why look to Shelley when there are present-day feminist writers who can act as much better instructors and models than he? I have in mind here writings by women of color who address the problem of the split and inscribed—or haunted—subjectivity experientially and thereby, in Michelle Cliff's superbly paradoxical phrasing that serves as title to her book, *claim* "an identity they taught me to despise."

The distinction between "identity" and "subjectivity" is crucial here, positing as it does a conscious and constant agency that many exponents of Lacanian theory have suggested is delusory. The paradox, however, in using "identity" as signifier lies in the fact that the term, traditionally conveying the notion of a single, unified consciousness (*OED* VII, 620), here designates a consciousness that asserts and accepts—even claims—divisions as uniquely its own. This identity takes as its ongoing and laborious work the transformation of the nothingness or invisibility assigned to it by dominant Other(s) into the verbalized and thereby experiential ground of its being. One sees this process movingly described in works such as Moraga and Anzaldúa's *This Bridge Called My Back* and, more recently, Anzaldúa's own *Making Face, Making Soul*. It is also the theme central to Bulkin, Pratt, and Smith's *Yours in Struggle* and Evelyn Beck's *Nice Jewish Girls*.

The power of human consciousness makes it possible to say "As we conceive ourselves, so we are"—a process of self-conception and self-birth that is the specific topic of Adrienne Rich's poem "Necessities of Life" and the theme of all her work. Furthermore, as we conceive and thus transform the self, we simultaneously conceive and transform the world. Phrased in this way, the revolutionary potential of our self-conceptions would sound limitless, were it not for the dialectical meaning that lies in the conjunction "as," where it signifies not "while" but "in the way that." According to the second interpretation of the phrase, others' conceptions of us impinge upon, mold, and inform our self-conception throughout life. Since this impingement is particularly strong and formative during the first years of life, and since mothers and mother surrogates have traditionally been assigned the task of socializing and caring for infants, one could say that as our mothers or mother surrogates conceive us (their conceptions bearing the stamp of the culture's fiat), so we are. Democratizing Shelley's statement about "Poets . . . philosophers, painters, sculptors and musicians," one can, then, make us all "in one sense the creators and in another the creations of [our] age" (*SPP* 135).

The structure of the foregoing argument makes the maternal conception appear a restraint or baffle; yet this is not necessarily the case. The positive function of the mother-infant relationship has this lyrical expression in the prose of Mikhail Bakhtin:

> The child receives all initial determinations of himself and of his body from his mother's lips and from the lips of those who are close to him. . . . The child begins to see himself for the first time as if through his mother's eyes, and begins to speak about himself in his mother's emotional-volitional tones. . . . Thus, he uses affectionate-diminutive terms in the appropriate tone of voice in referring to himself and the limbs of his own body——"my footsies," "my tootsies," "my little head," "go night-night," "nightie-night." (49–50)

But Bakhtin, at least in this passage, averts his gaze from the negative side of the process: the hushed, hissed, or shouted words "Don't touch!" "That's dirty!" with verbalizations expressive of this "dirt" transmitted and learned along with those of the pleasurably permitted "tootsies."

"Inscription" is one of the favored metaphors used as signifier for this process—and rightly so—for verbalizations about oneself cannot be separated from the experience of self: they *are* the experience. But insofar as the metaphor of inscription carries the suggestion of an indelible mold or press, it fails to convey the complexity of the actual (and ongoing) process. The paradigmatic interaction with the first care giver functions not only as an initial stamp but as a subterranean molten essence (if I may mix volcanic and alchemic metaphors) infusing all later interactions. Thus, all experience—as a reenactment but not, or not *necessarily,* a repetition of the primary experience—shares with those first interactions the potential for changing our self-concepts. By verbalizing the primary experience—recalling "our sensations as children," in Shelley's phrase (*SPP* 477)—we can reconceive it, ourselves, and the world.

This is the feminist project that most deeply engages me; in my pursuit of it, truth to my own experience has nonetheless made me take Shelley rather than a contemporary feminist writer as my dialogical companion. "Shelley"— signifier for the cultural tradition that has inscribed me and that, as one inscribed but aware of and thus resistant to inscription, I both cherish and reject—is the given with which I must work. "He" acts as my subject/object/ alter ego because, while steeped in that tradition and reveling in it—indeed, made an avatar of it by his Victorian worshipers—he, too, resisted and sought to change its unjust, violent institutions, though from a different perspective and with different priorities. Moreover, he also looks to the relationship between mother and infant as the locus for imagining a new experience of subjectivity, a just and nonviolational exchange through language. One can learn from him.

Each section of this book is written with the understanding that Shelley's is the particular subjectivity and body of writing under consideration. Yet in each I also take up a topic for its own sake and with reference to other concerns. Thus, in Chapter 1 I examine the relevance of certain theories about infants' acquisition of language to Shelley's thought and work. But I am also interested, first, in critiquing the dichotomy set up in Freudian paradigms between speechless bonding with the maternal and release into language through the paternal and, second, in exploring the connection between acquisition of language and "mirroring" of the maternal. This chapter, therefore, presents two versions of the story about each human infant's acquisition of speech: that of Freudian analysis and that of Daniel Stern, who adapts the findings of developmental psychologists to plot the maturation of infants through certain observable phases.

While an analysis of motherhood's meaning to one in Shelley's social class during the years of his infancy, childhood, and youth is the focus of the second chapter, I am also interested in exploring, through a detailed look at contemporary texts, aspects of the maternal ideology during the process of its inception. This subject—specifically, the eroticization of the maternal and the emphasis placed on the mother as educator—has not received the attention it warrants. The third (biographical) chapter has something of its own agenda as well. For reasons that will become apparent, much significant documentation on the relationship between Shelley and his mother has received surprisingly little attention. While not attempting a full-scale biography of either mother or son, I do cover all the available evidence in an attempt to set that record straight.

The second part of the book focuses on the first three acts of *Prometheus Unbound* as a Shelleyan text whose meaning unfolds through the context provided in the first part of this study: through psychological awareness of the maternal mirror, sociological insights into the uses to which that mirroring was put, and biographical information about the "plots" that structured interactions within Shelley's family. But I am interested as well in the related but somewhat separate plots that structure *Prometheus Unbound*—the revised Aeschylean plot and the pastoral plot of Venus and Adonis—in order to provide a full interpretation of the play's first three acts. For *Prometheus Unbound* is the Shelleyan work most involved with restructuring language and subjectivity through remembering, but also re-membering, relationship with the mother. Shelley's impulse to search there for a new understanding of subjectivity that would radically alter all human institutions strikes me as admirable and as revelatory even at its points of failure—even, that is, when the understanding of subjectivity that was his cultural given impeded or vitiated the attainment of his purpose.

Acknowledgments

The Marilyn Yalom Research Fund enabled me to spend the summer of 1987 doing research in England at the British Library, as well as the Fawcett and Bodleian Libraries. I am deeply grateful for the fellowship, the library resources it made available to me, and the help of librarians, particularly David Doughan and Catherine Ireland at the Fawcett. I am also indebted to the British Library, the Bodleian, and the Bettmann Archive for permission to use several of the illustrations that, to use the nineteenth-century word, "embellish" this book, as I am to the San Francisco Museum of Art for the reproduction on its cover.

Through the kindness of The New York Public Library, my book also includes a portrait of Elizabeth Shelley; I am grateful for that and for the resources both of the library and of the Carl H. Pforzheimer Collection housed there. My thanks go most especially to the director of the collection, Donald Reiman, for focusing with such instant courtesy on whatever questions I brought to him and then answering them in such generous detail. Several sections of this book appeared earlier as a contribution to *The New Shelley: Later Twentieth-Century Views,* edited by G. Kim Blank and published by St. Martin's Press © 1991. Reprinted with permission of St. Martin's Press and Macmillan. I am grateful to both the editor and the publishers for permission to reproduce those passages.

Above all, I am grateful for the resources and the staff of Green Library at Stanford, which has been not simply a base but a home base. Librarians in all its departments—but particularly in Reference and in Special Collections—have helped me in countless ways. My special thanks go to Joanne Hoffman, James Knox, William McPheron, and Michael Ryan. Boyd Murphy, in the course of my entrances and exits, took an unfailing and heartening interest in the progress of the book.

Elizabeth C. Traugott, dean of Graduate Studies at Stanford, gave me both material help and scholarly encouragement by making research funds available. Material help and encouragement in another form came from Hillary Trivett May's unstinting work as my summer research assistant in 1991. Constantly I have received fresh ideas and been exposed to new ways of thinking by my students, particularly those working with me on related dissertations: Doree

Allen, Mary Favret, Kelly Hurley, Joseph Lew, Ira Livingston, Rebecca Mark, Judith Raiskin, Hilary Schor, Stacey Vallas, Bernadette Ward, and Mary Wood.

A number of people read the whole of this manuscript in draft form and gave me invaluable advice and encouragement. Ronald Davies, my computer editor, helped in countless ways in the preparation of my text. I feel deeply indebted to Elizabeth Maguire, my editor at Oxford University Press in New York, for her immediate and full understanding of my book's purpose and potential. I am grateful also for the careful attention Susan Chang, Henry Krawitz, and others at Oxford University Press gave the book as it was in preparation, as well as for its thoughtful editing by Amanda Heller, for the learning and diligence Louise Herndon brought to reading its page proofs, and for Cecil Golann's perceptive index. The press's anonymous reader provided one of the most helpfully detailed reports I have ever seen—and I have read a great many. Other readers— Donald Gelpi, John L'Heureux, Herbert Lindenberger, Edward Socola, and Adrienne Rich—also took on the burden of reading and offering suggestions about the penultimate draft. Their encouragement, as well as that of Terry Castle, Jill Conway, George Dekker, Anne Mellor, and Diane Middlebrook (who all read the final draft) have sustained and cheered me.

But the list does not end here, for many colleagues read parts of the manuscript and, on that basis, offered insights that I found enormously helpful: Susan Groag Bell, Michelle Cliff, Clark Emery, Jane Emery, Estelle Freedman, Regenia Gagnier, Jana Kiely, Robert Kiely, Joyce Moser, Thomas Moser, Marjorie Perloff, Robert Polhemus, and David Riggs. Still others took time—often many hours—to bring their learning to the aid of my ideas: John Bender, Anne Fernald, René Girard, David Halperin, Marsh McCall, Stephen Orgel, Joseph Perloff, William St. Clair, and Helen Tartar. I have also been much encouraged and my project fostered by Martin Evans and Ronald Rebholz, who, *seriatim,* have chaired the English Department while I was working on the book, and by Carolyn Fetler, the department's administrator.

Support comes in many forms. I have been aware for some time that the ability to think long and hard about anything needs to have as its base the gift of other people's love. My gratitude goes out to those who have created and daily re-create that base for me: to my children, Adrienne and Christopher Gelpi; my parents, Lionel and Ardelle Charlesworth; my sister, Joan Wichmann; my mother-in-law, Alice Gelpi; and my brother-in-law, Donald Gelpi. John and Marion Oldfield were also unfailing in their encouragement and interest.

I have saved for last among the book's benefactors the name that should also stand first: Albert Gelpi. The book was written within my life's constant and sustaining dialogue with him, but such dialogue is no simple matter. Adrienne Rich has described it in "Like This Together" when she writes that "only our fierce attention / gets hyacinths out of those / hard cerebral lumps, / unwraps the wet buds down / the whole length of the stem"—except that the word "fierce" is inapplicable here. Inapplicable.

Stanford, Calif.   B.C.G.
August 4, 1991

Contents

Abbreviations

CW	*Complete Works*
L	*Letters*
PS	*The Poems of Shelley*
PU	*Prometheus Unbound* (Unless otherwise noted, all citations from *Prometheus Unbound* refer to *SPP.*)
SHC	*Shelley and His Circle*
SPP	*Shelley's Poetry and Prose*
SPU	*Shelley's "Prometheus Unbound"*
V	*Prometheus Unbound: A Variorum Edition*

I

The Nurse's Soul

Men had to do fearful things to themselves before the self, the identical, purposive, and virile nature of man, was formed, and something of that recurs in every childhood.

Max Horkheimer and Theodor W. Adorno
The Dialectic of Enlightenment

If language is as old as consciousness itself, and if language is a practical consciousness-for-others, and, consequently, consciousness-for-myself, then not only one particular thought but all consciousness is connected with the development of the word. The word is a thing in our consciousness . . . that is absolutely impossible for one person, but that becomes a reality for two. The word is a direct expression of the historical nature of human consciousness.

Lev Semenovich Vygotsky, *Thought and Language*

1

Infancy Narratives

After the birth of his first child, Ianthe, the story goes, Shelley was beside himself with anxiety because Harriet Shelley refused to nurse the baby herself and insisted on hiring a wet nurse. In the account recorded by Newman Ivey White, Shelley's concern was that "the nurse's soul would enter the child." Walking up and down the room with the infant in his arms, he crooned nursery songs to her, expostulating with Harriet at the same time about her decision. "At last, in his despair, and thinking that the passion in him would make a miracle, he pulled his shirt away and tried himself to suckle the child" (I, 326).[1]

White suggests that Thomas Trotter's *View of the Nervous Temperament* (1806), which Shelley had ordered from his bookseller Thomas Hookham only a few months earlier (in December 1812), put this notion in his mind. Trotter warns: "Much pretended refinement often takes place about selecting a nurse free of disease: but what scrutiny can secure the suckling against the bad effects of her passions; these must frequently sow the seeds of future indisposition, that may not be discovered till too late" (93).

Actually, another book that White cites elsewhere as a very strong influence on the youthful Shelley's thinking, George Ensor's *Independent Man* (1806), uses phrasing more dramatic than Trotter's, more suggestive of the nurse's "soul" entering with her milk: "A wet-nurse should be chosen with great caution; much depends on the parents, much also on the nurse. It has been remarked, that children not unfrequently assume the character of their nurses . . . which is not strange, as beasts of mild natures are said to become fierce by sucking the ferocious" (I, 6). It was an idea abroad in the culture. *The Nurse's Guide,* first printed in 1729 and continuing throughout the century as a household staple, argues that a mother who puts her child out to nurse is "unnatural" because the infant that "she has carry'd Nine Months in her Womb, and nourish'd with the purest Part of her Blood" is "her own Living Image." The strong suggestion is that this "Image" will bear all the more resemblance to the mother if she performs the function of nurse; if not, the image is overlaid by another's: "Without doubt, just as a Plant by being transplanted to a foreign Soil, quite changes its Nature, so a child by being put to Nurse, quite alters his natural Genius and Inclinations" (23).

These admonitions came as part of a medical campaign, conducted throughout much of the eighteenth century, in favor of maternal breast-feeding, which I shall discuss in the next chapter. They also show a typical strategy in disturbing motherly consciences about putting infants in the care of servants. But the language conveys a bizarre, almost gothic perception of the passage of "soul" as well as milk between nurse and infant. Or I should say that in this early phrasing the idea *sounds* bizarre. It much resembles the now familiar Lacanian theory about the way in which an infant's primary care-taker, usually the mother, serves as the "mirror" for the formation of its sense of a coherent and bounded subjectivity.

The parallel is not coincidental. If one allows a single essentialist statement about the nature of subjectivity—that it is produced mimetically—then the two theories are describing the same process. I am not thereby saying that the human subject constructed through mimesis is essentially or universally the same in both views. On the contrary, the different ways in which the process is understood, and thus the different ways in which it is implemented, construct different subjects, as is seen in the differences among signifiers used to describe the "product": member of the Mystical Body of Christ, one integer of Universal Man, a human individual, a mirroring split subject, to give a few examples drawn only from the so-called Western cultures. The determinism and material-ism implied in the word "construct" make the word appropriate in that it reflects the inevitability of mimesis and its material base in human interactions. The volitional component in mimesis, however, must not be overlooked. We may have no choice but to mirror; but choices about who or what we mirror present themselves constantly as possibilities for willed change. The mixing of this volitional element with the unique combination of each subject's develop-mental circumstances gives every human identity the distinctness made typo-logically manifest in finger- and voice-prints.

The common mimetic base means that the narratives constructed within four different fields of inquiry can be brought to bear upon the Shelley anecdote: the Lacanians' analysis of the process whereby the infant acquires language; Daniel Stern's description of the stages observable in infant devel-opment; Eagleton's philosophical treatise on the process whereby the "aes-thetic" becomes the source of "the subject's self identity" (23); and histori-ans' accounts of those changes in family structure underlying the emphasis in Shelley's time on maternal breast-feeding. The four narratives are not the same. My conviction, nonetheless, is that taken together, they speak to a mother-centeredness in Shelley that makes him effectively an early practitio-ner of that "gynesis" described by Alice Jardine as characteristic of French theory in the past two decades. That is to say, the spiral movement of Jean-Joseph Goux's world's plot as described by Jardine could also serve to out-line the action of *Prometheus Unbound:* "For Goux, history has been the history of Man and men, but now we are entering a new historicity, the End of History, the Death of Man: a true *jouissance* as we move beyond the fear of falling back into the original maternal abyss and toward a 'new access to the feminine' " (33). Yet the question raised by Jardine about the relationship between these speculations and feminist theory also has relevance to Shelley's work:

> It is always a bit of a shock to the feminist theorist when she recognizes that the repeated and infinitely expanded "feminine" in these theoretical systems often has very little, if anything, to do with women. If everyone and everything becomes Woman—as the culture obsessively turns itself inside out—where does that leave women, especially if, in the same atmosphere, feminism is dismissed as anachronistic along with Man and History? (35)

Jardine's question seems much more urgent than my redirection of it to an interest in Shelley, since she is writing about theories still in process that might conceivably be formulated or reformulated in ways that would serve feminist aims. Shelley's version of gynesis is long past. Moreover, in practical terms it was considerably less than helpful to the women who loved him, and there is no evidence that its poetic (and theoretical) formulation in *Prometheus Unbound* has in any way advanced feminist aims. Still, what motivates me is a feminist purpose, even an urgency. Shelley's obsession with the maternal grew out of a social milieu that still dominates the industrial West. To analyze that maternal ideology both psychologically and historically, as I propose to do in this chapter and the one that follows, and to come thereby to an understanding of why that ideology failed in practical and theoretical ways to relieve the oppression of women may also aid in the feminist analysis and reformulation of ideas that will succeed where it failed.[2]

As the opening anecdote reveals, I am unweaving a human experience in which the psychological cannot be entirely separated from the historical. Shelley's faith in maternal breast-feeding, created through a complex of ideas that can be traced historically, may not have activated his mammary gland, but it did infuse his thinking about the nature of human experience and thereby shaped that experience itself. Born of the same historical matrix as Shelley's, contemporary understandings of infancy produce faith narratives that shape our present experience and our histories, and have relevance for his as well. I shall begin, then, with these overarching constructs, then move back to their specific manifestations at the time of Shelley's birth.

The Lacanian-Kristevan Narrative

In *The Subject of Semiotics* Kaja Silverman begins her account of the Lacanian narrative on how we arrive at subjectivity with a quick summary of Aristophanes' amusing tale in *The Symposium* explaining the nature of love: the original humans were round, happy, and vigorous, with four arms and four legs, but were cut in half by Jupiter when, in their energy and arrogance, they tried to storm heaven. Like Aristophanes, Jacques Lacan traces the first in a series of losses in the history of the human subject to a splitting or division at the moment of birth. In Lacan's thinking, as Silverman points out, that moment actually serves only as epiphany or manifestation of the intrauterine splitting that had occurred earlier at the moment of sexual differentiation (152). This moment, itself preordained by the structure of the chromosomes, seals for the subject a life of dependence in a body whose sexuality expresses its mortality: "The real lack is what the living being loses, that part of himself *qua* living being, in reproducing himself through the way of sex. This lack is real because it relates to something real, namely, that the living being, by being subject to sex, has fallen under the blow of individual death" (Lacan, *Four Fundamental Concepts* 205). It is worth noting here, for its significance later, the stress Lacan's statement places on "individual." Lacan's phrasing places him, despite all the questions his theory raises about the coherence of the divided subject, within the idealist Lockean tradition of "individuality."[3]

The first reintegration that the infant attempts is with the mother, her breast, writes Lacan, representing "that part of himself that the individual loses at birth, and which may serve to symbolize the most profound lost object." Lacan calls such objects "objets petit autre," which he shortens to "objets petit a" (Silverman, *The Subject of Semiotics* 156). The way in which Lacan's formulations chime with Shelley's surfaces in this originary myth. In the summer of 1818, a few months before he began writing *Prometheus Unbound,* Shelley translated Plato's *Symposium;* Donald Reiman, using manuscript evidence, dates Shelley's prose fragment "On Love" to a time immediately after that translation (*SPP* 473). There the Aristophanic theory about humans searching for completion by finding their correspondent half fuses with an image of the nursing infant as one who enjoys such fullness of being, the breast a "petit a" possessed momentarily. Shelley writes: "We are born into the world and there is something within us which from the instant that we live and move thirsts after its likeness. It is probably in correspondence with this law that the infant drains milk from the bosom of its mother" (*SPP* 473).

In the very first month after birth, as Lacan's story continues, the infant does not really distinguish between self and other. Consciousness has no edges. That part of what we are and feel that Lacan calls the *moi* is forming, nonetheless, through the infant's introjections and projections in relation to its primary caretaker—usually its mother or a female mother substitute. Abstractions like "introjection" and "projection" give very little sense, however, of what actually occurs. Lacanian theorists clarify the significance of identification when they describe the way in which the infant in the first six months of life, unable to position itself or control its movements because of human helplessness at birth, orients itself and begins its organization of perception (and also of an identity or subjectivity) by fusing itself with disconnected impressions. Ellie Ragland-Sullivan explains:

> Perception begins with the linking of the corporal being that *is* the infant to
> the signifying or meaningful material outside it: i.e., images and language
> (part-objects) in tandem with their effects on sensory-perceptual being. . . .
> The visual-verbal impact may cause confusion, but it also forms what Lacan

has called "letters" (abstract signifiers) of the body in the pre-mirror stage. These are the effects of touch, sound, the gaze, images, and so forth as they intermingle with sensory response. In this way, the human body becomes eroticized in relation to its earliest experiences of the outside world. (20; my emphasis)

Ragland-Sullivan's enumeration of "touch," "sound," and "the gaze" as eroticizing the infant's interactions with "the outside world," as that world is epitomized by the mother in a pre-mirror stage, does not sufficiently highlight the way in which the maternal voice itself acts as mirror for an emerging subjectivity. In her discussion of this phenomenon, Silverman reviews several of the metaphors for the sound of the mother's voice: a "sonorous envelope" (Rosolato 81; Doane 44); "a mobile receptacle" (Kristeva, *Desire in Language* 282); a "bath of sounds" (Anzieu 173); and "music" (Bailblé 53). But the one she chooses as most appropriate for describing the process is Guy Rosolato's phrase "acoustic mirror." Rosolato writes: "The voice [has the property] of being at the same time emitted and heard, sent and received, and by the subject himself, as if, in comparison with the look, an 'acoustic' mirror were always in effect" (80; Silverman's translation). From this observation Silverman takes the more explicit point that voice, heard in both an interior and exterior way by both sender and receiver, "can spill over from subject to object and object to subject, violating the bodily limits upon which classic subjectivity depends, and so smoothing the way for projection and introjection" (*The Acoustic Mirror* 80).

Didier Anzieu's description of the way in which the mother's voice functions for the infant suggests that the voice is not only the medium for intersubjectivity but also a mirror that functions as an acoustic wall or baffle, defining the bounds of subjectivity itself. He notes that the four types of physiologically based cries emitted by an infant—responses to hunger, anger, pain, and frustration—all call forth from the mother a response that will quiet the cry. And the surest way of doing so is with her voice: "By the end of the second week, the sound of the mother's voice stops the baby's cry much better than any other sound whatsoever or than the sight of the human face." After only one more week this interaction has a further result: the baby gives a fifth kind of cry, the false cry of distress used to attract attention, which has a quite different physical character from the four basic cries. Anzieu comments, "This is the first intentional sound signal, in other words, the first communication" (168; my translation). In sending forth that sound the infant is asking for attention, to be sure, but also for the reassurance of a responding voice that provides a sense of boundaries.

My last point is an extrapolation from Anzieu, not a statement he makes explicitly, but one legitimated by the conflation of his commentary on the fifth cry with Elaine Scarry's description of voice as "a final source of self-extension; so long as one is speaking, the self extends out beyond the boundaries of the body, occupies a space much larger than the body" (33). In making it I am writing from the fantasized situation of the infant and giving that situation a positive character not present by any means in all descriptions. My calming space, refuge from the abyss that would open up if the call simply echoed endlessly, becomes in Michel Chion's *Voix au Cinéma* the site of paranoid enclosure:

> In the beginning, in the uterine night, was the voice, that of the Mother. For the child after birth, the Mother is more an olfactory and vocal continuum than an image. One can imagine the voice of the Mother, which is woven around the child, and which originates from all points in space as her form enters and leaves the visual field, as the matrix of places to which we are tempted to give the name "umbilical net." A horrifying expression, since it evokes a cobweb—and in fact, this original vocal tie will remain ambivalent. (quoted in Silverman, *The Acoustic Mirror* 74)

Silverman links this ambivalence to the imagined point of view from which the "fantasy of the maternal-voice-as-sonorous envelope" takes place. By calling it a fantasy, she is making the point that all these "descriptions" are of an irrecoverable situation but does not thereby mean to label them untrue. At the same time, the nature of the truth changes depending on the perspective toward the imagined situation being described: "Viewed from the site of the unconscious, the image of the infant held within the environment or sphere of the mother's voice is an emblem of infantile plenitude and bliss. Viewed from the site of the preconscious/conscious system, it is an emblem of impotence and entrapment" (73).

Even development in the very earliest months thus involves forms of mirroring; but beginning at around six months of age, as the infant gains greater control over its movements and thus different conceptualizations of spatial relationships, it fully enters the "mirror-stage," so called by Lacan not primarily because the infant can now recognize its mirror image (although that occurs) but because "the identification with a *Gestalt* of [the infant's] own body is paralleled in the infant's relating to the mother's *imago* as if it were his own" (Ragland-Sullivan 24).

Most important here is the infant's identification with the mother's gaze. Lacan notes: "What determines me, at the most profound level, in the visible, is the gaze that is outside. It is through the gaze that I enter light and it is from the gaze that I receive its effects" (*Four Fundamental Concepts* 106). The point, then, is not so much that the infant sees itself as the mother; rather, the infant reflects the way in which it "sees itself be seen" (Silverman, "Fragments of a Fashionable Discourse" 143). Otherness is thus from the beginning the mirror in which subjectivity finds itself. This response means that in humans subjectivity is necessarily split; the experience of self as a unity, even before the further division into conscious and unconscious, is delusory (Ragland-Sullivan 26). And the first two "layers" of that internalized Otherness are made up of sensory impressions associated with the primary caretaker: "There is never a period of prefusion or defusion from the m(Other) . . . since she is psychically represented at first (zero to six months) in relation to fragmented images or objects of Desire, and then—as a whole object—

becomes the source of one's own body image" (Ragland-Sullivan 26). These are now psychoanalytic truisms, lending themselves to the fairly brisk enunciation Ragland-Sullivan gives us, but their extraordinary significance deserves special emphasis: the material forming the bases of subjectivity in *both* genders is created through identification with a feminine imago in any culture in which women are infants' primary caretakers.

Meanwhile, through her absences and returns, the mother also makes the infant aware of alienation. The passionate desire to be *everything* not so much *for* the mother as *with* her is rebuffed by the mother's absence, and then, through the intervention of the father, must be denied altogether. Putting the case another way, one can say that the infant, whether male or female, wants to be the phallus for the mother—the phallus here serving as signifier for "fullness of being" (Silverman, *The Subject of Semiotics* 183). But the father bars the way to that fulfillment. *He* is the phallus, now the signifier for power as well, and is thereby the lawful object of the mother's desire.

If frustrating, this proclamation of the incest taboo and of patriarchal dominance phylogenetically and ontogenetically propels human beings into the uses of symbol—into language—and after language into thought, culture, history, social order. Without that bar on incest made by a dominant masculinity, none of those human goods, according to the account given in this narrative, would ever come into being.

Why this should be so and how the process actually occurs is explained by yet another story, that of Freud's infant grandson's game with a stringed reel. "O-o-o-o" (meaning "Fort"/"gone"), the little fellow would crow as he allowed the spool to disappear outside his crib, and "Da" ("there") he would exclaim as he caused it to reappear (XVIII, 14–15).

Freud (who is addressing himself to the question of why adults in their dreams and children in play as well as dreams often repeat experiences that are actually traumatic and painful) does not focus on the infant's acquisition of language as a way of mastering drives. He is making the point that his grandson, by using the icon of the spool and then the verbal symbols "Fort" and "Da" to represent his mother, is able to transform loss into *his* loss, a gain that cancels the initial loss and thus achieves the state of equilibrium that Freud defines as pleasure (i.e., *jouissance*).[4]

Lacan would not entirely disagree but makes two further points. First, the reel is not the mother but "a small part of the subject which detaches itself from him while still remaining his, still retained." It is, then, another example of an "objet petit a" (*Four Fundamental Concepts* 62). But also crucially important is the fact that Freud's grandson, by differentiating between the sounds "o" and "a," has entered into recognition of the paradigmatic and syntagmatic relationships that constitute language. He has added to what Lacan calls the "unary signifier," "Fort"—a meaningless utterance by itself— the binary signifier "Da." In doing so he has acquired the sense of meaning and can think; he has excluded and controlled the drives, particularly the drive toward union, reunion with his mother; that exclusion has formed the unconscious; he has entered as a subject into the symbolic order—that is, into language—where he is an "I"; and is now bound into desire for a literally unspeakable and forever unattainable freedom from lack (*Four Fundamental Concepts* 218–19).

The child, in symbolizing her or his separated self as "I," in having the signifier "I" *stand in* for the self, loses that self into the unconscious; or, if you will, that self is murdered just as all immediate experience is murdered through the symbolic mediation of language. For, as Anika Lemaire writes with the succinctness and drama that this situation demands, "We know that the word is the murder of the thing and that this death is the condition of the symbol" (85). Julia Kristeva's expression for what occurs is that "what is violent is the irruption of the symbol, killing substance to make it signify" (*Revolution in Poetic Language* 75).

The murdered self of the subject's being that is sacrificed for the sake of the subject's meaning is not dead, however; it continues to exist in the unconscious, where Lacan characterizes it as the "unary signifier," nonsensical within the symbolic order of meaning but reverberating with the subject's lost being. Silverman explains:

> Because it is not assimilable to the closed system of meaning inaugurated by the binary signifier, the unary signifier might be conceptualized as the trace of the repression suffered by the drives—as the mark of the subject's rupture with its being. Indeed, Lacan refers to it as embodying a "traumatic" nonmeaning, suggesting that it is there that the reverberations of the conflict between being and meaning are registered. This nonsensical signifier attests too fully to the terms upon which the subject enters the symbolic order to be available to the conscious subject, and it is hidden away in the unconscious. (*The Subject of Semiotics* 172)

To sum up the chronicle thus far: Freud's description of the Oedipal transaction, Lévi-Strauss's pronouncements on the incest taboo, and Saussure's concept of the symbolic all fuse in the Lacanian judgment: "The primordial law is therefore that which in regulating marriage ties superimposes the kingdom of culture on that of nature abandoned to the law of mating. The prohibition of incest is merely its subjective pivot. . . . The law is revealed clearly enough as identical to an order of language" (*Écrits* 16). Glossing this text, Lemaire writes: "Accession to the symbolic order of the family (Alliance and Kinship) alone allows everyone to know who he or she is, what his or her exact position is, what limits are placed upon his or her rights in the light of respect for others; in total promiscuity and in the absence of a minimal organization of the group life, no one can situate himself or herself in relation to everyone else" (84).

But Lemaire's application of this necessary "placing" to both genders is imprecise, for the young woman's situation, her "exact position," is fluid, undefined, changeable in that it depends on her (dependent) relation to men. As Carole Pateman points out, "Women, unlike sons, never emerge from their 'nonage' and the 'protection' of men; we never interact in civil society on the same basis as men" (94). Meanwhile, men interact with one another through an individuality established in the capacity of their bodies as their own bounded property to possess the "permeable," unbounded bodies of women (96). This historico-political fact has psychological repercussions; it creates one of the paradoxes mentioned earlier, in which the maternal mirror of a boundaried soma, and the assurance it gives of a coherent and unified psyche, is simultaneously the Medusa's head, the ultimate terror, the abyss of abjection—unbounded, permeable, not clearly individual, yet a person.

My phrasing deliberately echoes Kristeva's discussion of the mother's fearsome liminality in *The Powers of Horror,* published in its original French in 1980. In *Revolution in Poetic Language*—which appeared in France in 1974—and other early works Kristeva addressed the topic of this maternal fluidity more positively. Though not differing in essentials from Lacan in the separation she makes between the mother and the acquisition of language, she places much more emphasis than he on the function of language at a time in the infant's life *before* words become arbitrary signifiers for concepts but when they are "signs" of presence and are introjected as such. With special attention to the glossolalia of the crib, she notes that infant play with language, infant enjoyment of sounds and rhythms for their own sake, is as essential to poetic discourse as is acquiescence to language as an arbitrary system of signs. Moreover, Kristeva is of the opinion that without the continuing trespass of this "semiotic" into the symbolic, we would all be bound without recourse to an unchanging social order established by a shared but unchangeable discourse. The potential and all the experience of the unconscious, where each subjectivity bases itself in a different layering of semiotic material, would be utterly lost. For while the mimetic process is universal, the mimetic *experience,* distinct for every human subject, is an important factor in the creation of unrepeatable difference among subjectivities. Also lost would be that pleasure in language for its own sake so essential to the creation of poetry. And because this pleasure is so closely fused to the state of the "semiotic chora," in which infant being is experienced as the maternal presence, the writing of poetry is by its very nature an incestuous pleasure, an incestuous play (*Desire in Language* 136).

The relation between motherhood and language remains highly problematic nonetheless: "mother" is the "archaic, instinctual, and maternal territory," appropriated by a conscious subjectivity (which is identified with the masculine, if not necessarily a man) for its own cultural purposes, from which the feminine as "instinctual" is by definition excluded. Erich Neumann told this story in *The Origins and History of Consciousness,* as did Joseph Campbell in *The Hero with a Thousand Faces.*

This is not, however, Kristeva's more recent thinking on the relation between the semiotic chora and the symbolic. In a talk titled "Histoires d'Amour—Love Stories" that describes the thesis of *Tales of Love,* she changes her metaphor for the semiotic or presymbolic period. She speaks of "sexuality" (conflated here, one gathers, with subjectivity) as "an effect of spaces, more or less amorous." The infant's intense relationship with the parents must not be "too erotic, too sexual" but rather must be somewhat distanced by a "certain benevolent interdiction," which Kristeva, following Freud, identifies as a "father of individual prehistory":

> a sort of conglomeration of the two parents, of the two sexes, which is nevertheless to be considered as a father—not one severe and Oedipian, but a living and loving father. Why father and not mother, when one knows the mother to be she who first attends to us, giving us our first kisses, our first loves? Because we are thereby permitted to pose an intrapsychic instance that is not the physical envelope of the mother, which exists in too great proximity to the infant and risks provoking short-circuits leading to inhibition and psychosis. (21)

In an interview with Kristeva about the talk, the Marxist feminist Rosalind Coward questioned her about this "fatherly" psychic space necessary to speech: "You're not referring to a real father or a real man. You're actually referring to the mother's desire being elsewhere as a necessary precondition for that kind of primary separation to take place. . . . [You] seemed to repeat some of those classic Freudian divisions of father and mother, even in maintaining those terms, even in maintaining the paternal metaphor which is something that very much comes from Freud and Lacan" (23).[5]

In replying, Kristeva said that to her the words "mother" and "father" were not "absolutely necessary": "What is necessary is to have three terms, if you prefer to call them X and Y, why not? But I'm not sure that changes much. What is necessary for what I call the psychic space to acceed [sic] to language is the existence of this distance and I cannot imagine another organisation but the one of the three terms" (23).[6] Thus, while shrugging off a need to speak in terms of gender, Kristeva actually restores gender through the seemingly abstract terms X and Y, since the Y chromosome determines masculinity. As Andrea Nye has demonstrated in " 'A Woman Clothed with the Sun': Julia Kristeva and the Escape from/to Language," the idealist assumptions of the metaphysical tradition within which Kristeva writes make it impossible for her to use any other terms.

Nye explicates those presuppositions through a metaphorical reading of certain incidents described in the Book of Revelation: "a woman clothed with the sun" brings forth a male child; the child is "caught up to God and to his throne," and the woman flees to the wilderness (12:1–6). In the philosophical tradition extending back to Plato and still operative in the thinking of Wittgenstein, Lévi-Strauss, Derrida, and Lacan, the sun, as "rational order, the systematic arrangement of concepts reflected in logical form, or, more recently, semantic theory," is by definition masculine. The woman can be "clothed" in these attributes, but her true dwelling place is necessarily a speechless wilderness where there are only "groans, glossolalia, cries, only the rhythms of her body, instinctive drives, expressible in snatches of melody and scraps of song" (665).

A telltale Kristevan word, "glossolalia" moves Nye into the center of her argument: a description and critique of the strategies Kristeva as thinker and woman uses to shuttle between the dualities of sun and wilderness. Important among these is the disruptive function of the cries, rhythms, and urges of the semiotic in unbalancing the rational equilibrium of the symbolic order: *temporarily* unbalancing but not, finally, overthrowing, since that order, however tyrannical, is essential to holding the line between animal and human. "The contribution that the analyst or linguist can make . . . is the negative one of sapping the power of the established order, of drawing attention to its frailty as well as to the always threatening abyss of psychotic fusion with the mother" (680).

This essentially nihilist position is inescapable, given the terms in which Kristeva conceives of subjectivity. I quote Nye's analysis of those terms at some length because it also bears on the Humean philosophy to which Shelley accedes:

> The split in Kristeva's subject that corresponds to the split between sun and wilderness is a variant of the familiar philosophical distinction between what is subjective and what is objective. But for Kristeva, what is objective is not so because it refers to some independent reality. Rather, what is objective represents an internalized patriarchal order to which all are expected to conform. Patriarchal objectivity is then contrasted with subjective drives, the expression of which is identified with a child's fusional relationship to its mother. The "I" of logical order confronts the feeling, out-of-order, maternally identified "me" whose "pulsions," according to Kristeva, are also formalizable, although in a different logic. . . . Conflict and process remain subjective, a matter of conflict within a subject, between a feeling self and the internalized logic of social order. (681–82)

Nye uses the term "idealist" to describe the concept of consciousness that she analyzes as producing the Kristevan bind. That term is appropriate for her because she is tracing this philosophical mode back to Plato. My plan, however, is not to take so long a view but to consider Shelley specifically within the post-Cartesian and Lockean context that created the notions of "subjectivity" in which he was raised. For this the word "liberal" in its philosophical meaning may be more useful than "idealist." Although they have other serious sources of disagreement, both Descartes and Locke postulate a subject as an individual consciousness in a body which Locke describes as its "*Property*" (*Two Treatises* 287). Hume, taking the same bounded, individual consciousness as axiomatic, adds the philosophically acute recognition that the boundedness is total: there can be no "feedback" by which one individual can ascertain the "objective truth" of his or her impressions and the resultant ideas, because those impressions, in Walter Pater's plangent phrase, belong to "the individual in his isolation, each mind keeping as a solitary prisoner its own dream of a world" (*Renaissance* 235). Or, in Shelley's words, "Nothing exists but as it is perceived" (*SPP* 476).[7]

This is Shelley's starting point in the prose fragment "On Life," which Reiman dates "sometime late in 1819" (*SPP* 474)—a few months after Shelley's completion of *Prometheus Unbound*. It is, however, only a starting point, for Shelley continues: "What follows from this admission? It establishes no new truth, it gives us no additional insight into our hidden nature, neither its action, nor itself" (477). Searching for further insight into "our hidden nature," he turns to recollection of "our sensations as children." In phrasing that suggests a universal human phenomenon, he writes: "We less habitually distinguished all that we saw and felt from ourselves. They [sic] seemed as it were to constitute one mass." Then, apparently moving from the universal to the personal, Shelley describes the experience of "some persons who in this respect are always children": "[They] feel as if their nature were dissolved into the surrounding universe, or as if the surrounding universe were absorbed into their being" (477).

Shelley posits two possibilities: one that the boundary around the perceiving consciousness is dissolved, the other that the boundary expands to include all that it perceives. In either case the experience sounds euphoric. Then two things appear to happen: the recognition that the bounded perceiver can also be taken as an Other's perceived reverses the meaning of "nothing exists but as it is perceived" so that it makes the bounded individual's existence problematic; and, as a result, euphoria changes to terror:

> The difference is merely nominal between those two classes of thought which are vulgarly distinguished by the names of ideas and of external objects. Pursuing the same thread of reasoning, the existence of distinct individual minds similar to that which is now employed in questioning its own nature, is likewise found to be a delusion. The words, *I, you, they,* are not signs of any actual difference subsisting between the assemblage of thoughts thus indicated, but are merely marks employed to denote the different modifications of the one mind.

Shelley's next paragraph explicitly states that this reasoning leads him not into solipsism but into the possibility of shared life; still, the sharing he imagines invades the sense of individual existence in a terrifying way:

> Let it not be supposed that this doctrine conducts to the monstrous presumption, that I, the person who now write and think, am that one mind. I am but a portion of it. The words *I,* and *you,* and *they* are grammatical devices invented simply for arrangement and totally devoid of the intense and exclusive sense usually attached to them. It is difficult to find terms adequately to express so subtle a conception as that to which the intellectual philosophy has conducted us. We are on that verge where words abandon us, and what wonder if we grow dizzy to look down the dark abyss of—how little we know. (477–78)

Interestingly, the strangely shifting signification of pronouns that Shelley finds so disturbing is to Nye the basis for a positive linguistics of "interpersonality" which can serve as an escape from the dichotomous thinking that brings Kristeva—and Shelley—to the brink of the abyss:

> All languages contain the interrelations of the pronominal system that are the framework on which semantic structure hangs. These pronouns are not only

the subjective "me" and "I," but also constitute a complicated system of subtle and shifting relationships between I's, you's, they's, we's, she's, and he's. Kristeva's idealism reduces all to the "I" and the "me"; "you's" and "they's" are seen only as projections of an otherness first discovered within the subject. What the myth of the sun and wilderness represents as the necessary banishment of the expressive woman to the wilderness depends on a prior banishment, the myth's own banishment of interpersonality. (682–83)

In arguing for interpersonality from the nature of pronouns Nye makes no mention of the work of Émile Benveniste. The omission is, I take it, political, in that Benveniste's linguistics enter into Lacanian and Kristevan theorizing about the nature of subjectivity. A key passage for this theory is Benveniste's question "What then is the reality to which *I* or *you* refers? It is solely, 'a reality of discourse,' and this is a very strange thing. *I* cannot be defined except in terms of a 'locution,' not in terms of objects as a nominal sign is. *I* signifies the 'person who is uttering the present instance of the discourse containing *I*'" (218).

That insight brings validation to the Lacanian view that the subject is a construction of the discourse into which he or she is inserted, or, in another formulation, that the subject is constructed "in the space of the Other" (*Four Fundamental Concepts* 144). That Other is, in one way of considering the matter, the "Name of the Father," the necessarily masculine realm of the social order. But, given the crucial importance of mirroring, it is also the introjected m(Other). So it is at least possible to interpret Lacan's statement that "the supreme Being, which is manifestly mythical in Aristotle, the immobile sphere from which originate all movements . . . is situated in the place, the opaque place of the *jouissance* of the Other—that Other which, if she existed, the woman might be" (*Feminine Sexuality* 153).[8]

Considered from the second perspective, when women are the "nonexistent," mirroring creates the constant danger that one will come to the edge of Shelley's abyss. Thus, while the coherent subjectivity conferred by acceptance of one's social "place," that designated by the "Nom/Non du Père," is a delusion, it is the delusion needed to hold off psychotic disintegration, the Néant de la Mère. And (Nye's point) that subjectivity remains more Cartesian than Lacanian theory admits: "I am perceived, therefore I am" retains the binary divisions of "Cogito, ergo sum."

But in the same essay about the peculiar nature of pronouns, Benveniste formulates another thought that can serve as linguistic underpinning to a different philosophical understanding of the nature of subjectivity:

> If each speaker, in order to express the feeling he has of his irreducible subjectivity, made use of a distinct identifying signal (in the sense in which each radio transmitting signal has its own call letters), there would be as many languages as individuals and communication would become absolutely impossible. Language wards off this danger by instituting a unique but mobile sign, *I,* which can be assumed by each speaker on the condition that he refers each time only to the instance of his own discourse. (220)

Benveniste shows the Cartesian axioms present in his own thought when he equates a sense of "irreducible subjectivity" with possession of distinct individuality. Thus he takes solipsism to be a logical but undesirable effect that must be warded off by language. Similarly Shelley, though he asserts as "merely nominal" the distinction between subjective "ideas" and "external objects," maintains the binary split between subject and Other axiomatic to his philosophical system. As a result the subject becomes invaded by a "you" and a "they" whom its bounded nature cannot help but enclose. Yet if we posit subjectivity as relational in its essence, posit it *as* relation, the peculiar fluidity of pronouns takes on a much more positive character, offering insights into the interpersonal nature—split and vulnerable yet ongoing and unified—of each human's "identity."

In the next section of this chapter I turn to a psychological description of the interactions between infants and their caretakers that might offer a material base on which to construct a different philosophical understanding of the speaking subject. And though Shelley's thinking in this area is mythic and poetic rather than rationally philosophical, the impulse behind *Prometheus Unbound* has a similar exploratory purpose. My analysis so far has given the word "abyss" as Shelley uses it in "On Life" a negative valence, but that "multistability" of language that Stephen Behrendt rightly finds so noticeable in Shelley's writings operates in this instance as well. The sublimity evoked by the signifier "abyss" offers the possibility of breathtaking vistas, sudden expansions of knowledge and understanding, as well as of horrific descents into nonbeing. Shelley's poetic practice in *Prometheus Unbound* suggests that his thinking about the nature of subjectivity in relation to language is "multistable" in this way.

Explaining his term, Behrendt points out that "multistability enables images, words, or other constructs to alternate between, usually, two different schemata or significations. The most familiar multistable image is the two-dimensional picture that alternately discloses an urn and two face-to-face profiles" (2). On the principle that "nothing exists but as it is perceived," one might add that urn or profiles are there when seen there; the viewer's perception brings either possibility into existence. In the iconography structuring *Prometheus Unbound*, multistability alternates between a Jupiterean and a Dionysian perception of the way in which speech creates thought. Lacanian theory works as a remarkably apt gloss for the Jupiterean. The subject, driven by the desire to fill a loss of something, a lack, and thus experiencing subjectivity as emptiness, finds itself at the same time filled, inscribed—and simultaneously annihilated—because it helplessly mirrors an Other.

In the blink of a moment's perception, which Shelley constantly insisted was the one thing necessary for revolutionary change, the Jupiterean vision of subjectivity can become Dionysian. The very etymology of Dionysus' name is interesting in this connection. While it is still a matter for scholarly dispute, the etymology given it in antiquity, the one Shelley would have known and accepted, was Dios Dionysos: Zeus' son Dionysus (Burkert, *Greek Religion* 162, 412).[9] So the Shelleyan shift is from focus on the father to focus on the son. With that change, fluidity, the lack of boundaries—incompleteness itself—instead of being painful becomes an experience of shared life expressing itself in the play of shared, if slippery, signifiers. And the maternal, fearful to the Jupiterean perspective both because of the mother's abjection through association with lost being and because of her own subjection to and consequent administration of paternal law, changes into the first experience of shared "soul."

The infancy narrative told by Daniel Stern, especially in its emphasis on synesthesia, more adequately captures Shelley's positive understanding of the link between the experience of being mothered and the acquisition of language than does the Freudian version. Both narratives, even though they differ in marked ways, are applicable to Shelley's own thinking because, while he shows at times an extraordinary prescience about Freudian concepts, he was speculating on these matters before the infant psyche had been mapped by Freud or infant behavior had been observed by developmentalists. He was under no intellectual obligation, then, to adhere to one version of the story so consistently that he would be forced to deny the other.

The Interpersonal Narrative

Nye concludes her argument with the suggestion that a truly different kind of social interaction becomes possible "as soon as interpersonality is rehabilitated" (683). In that context the title of Daniel Stern's study of infant development seems especially promising: *The Interpersonal World of the Infant*.[10] Trained in both psychoanalytic theory and the observational methods of developmental psychology, Stern notices striking ways in which the "clinical infant" of the psychoanalytic narratives differs from the "observed infant" whose behavior is studied by developmentalists as it occurs. Yet neither approach really grapples with the infant's experience of subjectivity. Developmentalists, working within traditionally empiricist boundaries, "choose not to make inferential leaps about the nature of subjective experience" (4), while the inferential leaps of the psychoanalysts, based on patients' reconstructions as well as on "older and outdated views of the infant as observed" (5), lack full credibility. Stern's purpose is to bring the two together in order to ascertain the nature of infant experience; his project clearly has applications as well to the wider topic of human subjectivity as experienced throughout life.

Stern divides the first fifteen months of life into four "domains," using that term instead of "stages" in order to make the point that the experiences in each remain permanent aspects of subjectivity. These are the domains of (1) emergent relatedness, (2) core relatedness, (3) intersubjective relatedness, and (4) verbal relatedness. His strong emphasis on development as a process involving self and Other (with its axiomatic given that such a thing as an infant subjectivity exists) makes his account very different from the Lacanian one, in which subjectivity itself is an illusory construct. In describing the first three months of life—the period in which, according to Lacanian theory, the infant's body is being "territorialized" into different erogenous zones, or in which, in Margaret Mahler's account, the infant is experiencing "normal autism" (44)—Stern focuses on the infant's extraordinary and active power to perceive and organize experience across different sensory modalities, a capacity he calls "amodal perception" (47), using "cross-modal" and "trans-modal" as synonymous terms. Nor are infants "lost at sea in a wash of abstractable qualities of experience. They are gradually and systematically ordering these elements of experience to identify self-invariant and other-invariant constellations" (67). This combination of an ability to organize the sensate, cognitive, and affective aspects of experience, along with the cross-modal perceptions of intensity, shape, and temporal patterns, functions as the matrix of both subjectivity and language:

> This global subjective world of emerging organization is and remains the
> fundamental domain of human subjectivity. It operates out of awareness as
> the experiential matrix from which thoughts and perceived forms and identi-
> fiable acts and verbalized feelings will later arise. It also acts as the source
> for ongoing affective appraisal of events. Finally, it is the ultimate reservoir
> that can be dipped into for all creative experience.   (67)[11]

This ability to organize perceptions makes it possible for an infant of two or three months to distinguish between a "core self" and other core selves with whom he or she interacts. Well aware that this description of infant experience flatly contradicts the "fusion" theories of psychoanalysts, Stern offers as proof the changes created in the behavior of infants during observed incidents such as peekaboo games or a spiraling exchange of smiles. In an "I'm gonna getcha" game, for instance, "the mutual interaction generates in the infant a self-experience of very high excitation, full of joy and suspense and perhaps tinged with a touch of fear. This feeling state, which cycles and crescendoes several times over, could never be achieved by the infant alone at this age, neither in its cyclicity, in its intensity, nor in its unique qualities" (102).

Stern's point is that changes in the infant's behavior produced by but not simply imitative of the actions of another demonstrate that what is occurring is interaction and not identification. When play starts, the infant may be calm and simply watchful, while the companion is at least pretending to be actively mischievous. The infant responds by becoming suspenseful and incipiently joyful, and so on. At each stage of the cycle, the infant's emotions are being "regulated" by the caretaker/playmate, but that regulation presupposes the interaction of a self with an Other: "The infant is with an other who regulates the infant's own self-experience" (102). And of course the play he describes is not the only type of "self-experience" that depends for its existence on the presence of another but could not occur were the infant experientially fused with the Other:

> Cuddling or molding to a warm, contoured body and being cuddled; looking
> into another's eyes and being looked at; holding on to another and being

held—these kinds of self-experiences with another are among the most totally social of our experiences, in the straightforward sense that they can never occur unless elicited or maintained by the action or presence of an other. (102)

While each of these experiences has its own unique character, quality, and rhythm, they all, of course, are repeated in some general pattern countless times—repeated and remembered so that in each new yet renewed experience the infant gathers a store of expectations based on a generalized past. An important element of those memories is the "evoked companion," the remembered presence from past interactions who is now once more (but with slight differences) the self-regulating Other of this one. Moreover, this evoked companion may be activated within the memory even when the actual person is absent, and so from as early as three months—the age at which "cued memory" begins (117)—the infant's subjectivity is peopled by other presences, as it will be throughout the rest of life: "In fact, because of memory we are rarely alone, even (perhaps especially) during the first half-year of life. The infant engages with real external partners some of the time and with evoked companions almost all the time. Development requires a constant, usually silent, dialogue between the two" (118).

The term "evoked companion" sets up a key psychological and philosophical difference between Stern's analysis of what is occurring and either the Jupiterean version of Shelley's thought or the theory of the Lacanians. Shelley's phrase—"the nurse's soul would enter the child"—has the potential to create an interior ghost or spook; in Lacanian theory, similarly, the introjected mother imago is simultaneously the (delusory) guarantee of coherent identity and the threat of boundaryless abjection. Stern's locution calls up by contrast a separate individual, remembered rather than introjected, with whom one interacts both in fantasy and in a shared external reality, asserting also that it is possible to distinguish between the two. This Dionysian "nurse's soul" acts as the first medium for the experience of human connectedness.

The next developmental leap, beginning around the age of seven months—the Lacanian "mirror" stage—is in Stern's account the point at which the infant has built up sufficient self-experience (through interaction with an Other) and sufficient sense of the Other *as* another to achieve "intersubjectivity." "Affect attunement" is the intersubjective behavior between mothers and infants that Stern emphasizes at this point; he sees it as closely related to what clinical theory calls mirroring, but he thinks his own term less misleading. His discussion has particular relevance to the relation between motherhood and the acquisition of speech because affect attunement is, in his opinion, a stepping stone toward language.

Affect attunement builds on the infant's extraordinary capacity for amodal perception. It involves the mother's showing the infant that she shares the feeling of a moment, such as sudden joy or slight bewilderment or disappointment, not by mimicking the infant's acts or facial expressions but by a virtually instantaneous response in another sensory modality. (This behavior, it should be noted, is not ordinarily conscious on the mother's part, but through video-tapes of interactions between mothers and infants, Stern and his colleagues were able to record multiple instances and then discuss the tapes with the mothers participating in the experiment.) Stern gives a number of examples of affect attunement, from which I select only one:

> A nine-month-old boy bangs his hand on a soft toy, at first in some anger but gradually with pleasure, exuberance, and humor. He sets up a steady rhythm. Mother falls into his rhythm and says, "kaaa-*bam,* kaaaa-*bam,*" the "*bam*" falling on the stroke and the "kaaaa" riding with the preparatory upswing and the suspenseful holding of his arm aloft before it falls. (140)

While not a shared system of arbitrary verbal signs, affect attunement functions as a language in that it involves communication about a common referent—the infant's experience at that moment. Also, as Stern points out, this change from imitation of the infant's overt behavior (which often occurs in play during the first few months) to another form of expression is significant in that it makes the sharing specifically of "affect" the point of the interchange. If the mother simply imitated the infant's acts, she would convey the message that she saw what the infant did, but her response would not speak of her sharing the same *inner* experience. Stern therefore avoids the term "mirroring" because it allows insufficient distinction between imitation per se and affect attunement. The two exist along a spectrum of interaction and thus are related, but the focus and the socializing effect of each is very different:

> True imitation does not permit the partners to refer to the internal state. It maintains the focus of attention upon the forms of external behaviors. Attunement behaviors, on the other hand, recast the event and shift the focus of attention to what is behind the behavior, to the quality of feeling that is being shared. It is for the same reasons that imitation is the predominant way to teach external forms and attunement the predominant way to commune with or indicate sharing of internal states. (142)

Although Stern offers little explicit discussion of the differing sociological consequences that result when infants are reared with the emphasis either on imitation or on attunement, he does mention that societies differ in the relative weight they give to the need for intersubjectivity. Societies which assume that all members have "essentially identical, inner subject experiences," and which stress this homogeneity of felt life, tend to develop few strategies to foster intersubjectivity. In their child-rearing practices such societies will cluster at the imitative end of the spectrum. By contrast, societies that value highly the existence and the sharing of individual subjective differences—as Stern notes ours does (137)—will look when socializing infants for ways to facilitate that intersubjectivity. Affect attunement is one important way. Guides to mothering in the late eighteenth and early nineteenth centuries, while not using the phrase, express the concept through their reiterated stress on the affective and intellectual life shared by mother and infant, as we shall see in Chapter 2.

Although Stern himself does not go further into the matter, his contrast between the different effects produced by an emphasis either on imitation or on attunement makes it possible to understand why a society desiring to foster a strong sense of the male as an individual while subsuming female individuality under the male would nonetheless stress the individuality of its girl children as well as its boys. One can, for instance, see why Locke put his influential imprimatur on the coeducation of young children; for girls must have a sense of themselves as individuals, a sense made ambiguous by simultaneous ideological training in their social function as women, if they are to raise the individualistic children of the succeeding generation—each gender, again, "individualistic" in a different way.[12]

While the phenomenon of affect attunement has historically been subject to this and other forms of manipulation, Stern's descriptions of it give a potentially much more positive understanding of how "introjection of the mother" functions than do those of Lacanian theory. The process involves not the introjection of an Other into a split consciousness but rather the creation of a "space" in which two (or more) separate subjectivities interact. This is a very different and much more liberating space than the paternal one provided by Kristeva. The difficulty is that Stern does not argue for it explicitly enough to overcome, perhaps even in his own mind, a traditional identification of the maternal with the nonsubjective.

There are two major ways in which attunement acts as a stepping stone to the next domain—that of "verbal relatedness"—which marks the boundary between infancy and childhood. First, since an attunement is an analogue, a nonverbal metaphor which recasts a subjective state into different terms, it helps create the concept of symbolization necessary to language use. (The fact that its recasting involves the crossing of sensory modalities makes affect attunement relevant also to nineteenth-century poets' fascination with synesthesia.)[13] Second, the intersubjectivity produced through attunement yields, in Stern's judgment, that sense of mutuality, of "we," that L. S. Vygotsky has shown to be crucial to the acquisition of language.

Vygotsky, Stern notes, took as his preliminary question how "mutually negotiated meanings (*we* meanings)" for the arbitrary symbols that are words make their way into the child's mind (170). Stern gives this topic only brief mention, but because of its relevance to the stress laid by the maternal ideology on the mother as educator, I must turn to Vygotsky's *Thought and Language* for a closer look. Despite his emphasis on speech as an "interpsychic" phenomenon at its inception (228), Vygotsky makes no specific mention of the mother or female caretaker as the person most involved in producing the interchanges that will result in the ability to speak. Thus his work does not explicitly create a balance righting what Silverman describes as Kristeva's "massive disavowal of the tutelary role the mother classically assumes with respect to the child's linguistic education—of her function as language teacher, commentator, storyteller" (*The Acoustic Mirror* 105). The omission may be particularly striking in Kristeva's work because she associates the maternal so firmly with the non- and preverbal; but in fact it is characteristic of Lacanian thought generally, and logically so if one conceptualizes mother and child as a speechless dyad with a masculine third term as agent of both speech and consciousness. Vygotsky's objection to the Freudian model underlying Jean Piaget's theory about language acquisition serves, therefore, to create a different sense of what the mother's presence means for the child, even if that presence remains in the shadows.

Piaget sees a developmental pattern from infant autism to the outwardly directed, logical, and social speech of a five- or six-year-old as having an intermediate stage, "egocentric speech," the audible but not always intelligible vocalizations made by the child as he or she plays. But when Vygotsky placed the little, supposedly egocentric speakers in experimental situations where listeners were either deaf, totally inattentive, or absent altogether, the verbalizations became very noticeably fewer and even stopped. These reactions proved that, however difficult it might be actually to understand the children's language, they thought of themselves as engaged in a social act: "Three- to five-year-olds while playing together often speak only to themselves. What looks like a conversation turns out to be a collective monologue. But even such a monologue, being the most spectacular example of the child's 'egocentrism,' actually reveals the social engagement of the child's psyche" (232). Vygotsky, therefore, posits that at its inception speech is "for others" and that Piaget's "egocentric speech" is actually a way station toward "speech for oneself," the quick interior verbalizations with which the adult thinks (235).

Vygotsky reiterates again and again the complex and necessary association—though not identification—between all speech, including this "inner speech," and thought: "The relation of thought to word is not a thing but a process, a continual movement back and forth from thought to word and from word to thought. . . . Thought is not merely expressed in words; it comes into existence through them" (218). But behind thought and therefore behind words is an intensely social process: "Thought is not begotten by thought; it is engendered by motivation, i.e., by our desires and needs, our interests and emotions. Behind every thought there is an affective-volitional tendency. . . . A true and full understanding of another's thought is possible only when we understand its affective-volitional basis" (252). "Desire in language," in a Kristevan context, expresses the idea that language results from the rupture of the original mother-child dyad; in Vygotsky's analysis the phrase would convey instead the deep impulse to communicate that exists between two separate but attuned humans.

In his discussion of language acquisition, Stern makes no specific mention of Mikhail Bakhtin, although he does refer to an essay by Bakhtin's biographer, Michael Holquist, on dialogism (169). Bakhtin, whose linguistic theory has strong affinities with Vygotsky's (Emerson 251–52; Morson and Emerson, *Mikhail Bakhtin* 205–8, 214–15), has a similar understanding of language as necessarily and constantly produced by and in relationship that merges (but does not fuse) subjectivities. In Bakhtin's formulation:

> Everything that is said, expressed, is located outside the "soul" of the speaker and does not belong only to him. The word cannot be assigned to a single speaker. The author (speaker) has his own inalienable right to the word, but the listener also has his rights, and those whose voices are heard in the word before the author comes upon it have their rights (after all, there are no words that belong to no one). (Morson and Emerson 129)

Bakhtin's concept of *vzhivanie,* "live entering" or "living into," as he sets it out in "Toward a Philosophy of the Act," also has a bearing on Vygotsky's "affective-volitional basis" and on Stern's "affect attunement." Bakhtin is at pains to distinguish *vzhivanie* from *Einfühlung* (empathy), for he defines the latter as a fusion or identification, which is different from "live entering": "I *actively* enter as a living being [*vzhivaius'*] into an individuality, and consequently do not, for a single moment, lose myself completely or lose my singular place outside that individuality" (Morson and Emerson 54).

Bakhtin notes elsewhere, "Just as the body is initially formed in the womb of the mother (in her body), so human consciousness awakens surrounded by the consciousness of others" (Todorov 96). Bakhtin shears away from the recognition that his parallel is closer than his statement concedes. Indeed, the structure of his sentence suggests that he intends a dichotomy, not a parallel: the feminine/body(animality)/the unconscious versus the masculine/humanity/consciousness. The old dichotomy. But read within Stern's narrative and Vygotsky's observations, Bakhtin's sentence is more than a parallel or an analogue. It describes an actual continuum.

Bakhtin moves from the mother's womb, in which the infant's physical body is formed, to generalized and plural consciousnesses, which form the environment for the emerging infant awareness. Granted, the mother is not the only subjectivity with which the infant interacts. But in cultures in which women, whether mothers or mother surrogates, are infants' primary caretakers, the intersubjectivity experienced through attunement between a female caretaker and an infant is, as Stern suggests, the principal matrix of language. He therefore makes the point that those who stress only "the separation and individuation" acquired through language lose sight of the fact that "the opposite is equally true, that the acquisition of language is potent in the service of union and togetherness. Indeed, every word learned is the by-product of uniting two mentalities in a common symbol system, a forging of shared meaning" (172). That is to say, to those struck by the alienation that Freud's grandson shows as he plays his sad little "Fort"/"Da" game, Stern would point out that it is through and with his mother (for mother's and infant's are the two mentalities to which Stern refers) that the boy learned "Fort" and "Da," and indeed her attunement made her the first to be aware of his meaning. In Nye's formulation, "When language is seen dialogically, the goal is not the subversion of always reconstituted rationality but, rather, the achievement of understanding and commonality" ("Woman Clothed with the Sun" 683).

Also, the mother's voice—its pitch, its intonation, its evocation of her presence and of the emotions that presence creates—gives a physicality to words that is experienced along with the physicality, hers and the infant's, of breath, tongue, palate, teeth, and throat shaping each sound. In addition to this "presence," there is the presence of the word as in itself an object. As Vygotsky notes in *Thought and Language,* "The data on children's language (supported by anthropological data) strongly suggest that for a long time the word is a property, rather than the symbol of the object; a child grasps the external structure of a word-as-object earlier than the inner symbolic structure" (92).

A child, then, would find it conceptually impossible to agree with Hegel's statement that "the first act by which Adam made himself master of the animals was to impose a name on them; that is, he annihilated them in their existence as beings" (Bruns 191). The word "giraffe," for instance, is not conceived of or experienced as an arbitrary sign standing in for what in any case is the concept of an animal and not the animal-in-itself. Rather, the word is evocative, calling up and rounding out the image of "giraffe." It may well be filled with the humor experienced because of the way the animal looks, a pleasurable humor shared intersubjectively when we hear the voice of the person who says the word while pointing to the pictured or the zoo-penned animal. Also the word carries the pleasure experienced in the physical act of forming it: the "mother tongue" is imbued with physicality because it is learned in the mother's company, while one watches her tongue, teeth, and lips use the cavities of her mouth, throat, and nostrils as instruments of sound and experiments with analogous noises to be made within one's own. And this, the infant's and the child's experience of language, necessarily remains central to both the writing of all poetic language, in the broad sense of that term, and to hearing or reading it.[14]

Although Stern emphasizes the mutuality of speech in what seems a deliberate attempt to balance the psychoanalytic stress on its alienating effects, he does begin his discussion of language by describing it as a "double-edged sword" (162). Moreover, one of the points he makes in arguing for the nonalienating aspects of language comes fairly close to the Lacanian interpretation of the "Fort"/"Da" game. He includes as an interesting possibility John Dore's speculation that language begins as a form of "transitional phenomenon," in D. W. Winnicott's sense of the phrase. Stern explicitly interprets Dore's thought in positive and Bakhtinian terms: a word "occupies a midway position between the infant's subjectivity and the mother's objectivity. It is 'rented' by 'us,' as Holquist puts it" (172). The example he then gives, however—the "crib talk" of a little girl comforting herself after her father's departure at bedtime—makes language a transitional object in the more negative sense: it takes the place of or stands in for what it thus forever alienates. (Stern may, by the way, have consciously used this father-daughter example as his way of critiquing the Lacanian emphasis on castration anxiety as the necessary prerequisite to language and the phallus as primary signifier. No Oedipal allusion of any kind ever enters his text in any case.)

Stern's very silence dismisses the idea that language, ironically, arises as a strategy for the subjugation of a desire for the mother which it actually makes from then on the subject's master. Nonetheless, he, too, recognizes elements of loss and alienation involved in the acquisition of language. What concerns him specifically is the loss to creativity that occurs when the infant's global and amodal perception is replaced by language and cannot again be experienced in an unmediated way. And, though Stern does not make this point, if one remembers that the period of amodal perception was spent above all in the company of the mother, then the fading of that relationship as an unmediated rather than a mediated experience becomes paradigmatic of all other losses.

Stern uses as his example of transmodal loss, the one to which he gives most attention, the difference between what an infant experiences when watching a yellow patch of sunlight on a wall and what happens to a child in the same situation:

> The infant will experience the intensity, warmth, brightness, pleasure, and other amodal aspects of the patch. . . . To maintain this highly flexible and omnidimensional perspective on the patch, the infant must remain blind to those particular properties (secondary and tertiary perceptual qualities, such as color) that specify the perceptual channel through which the patch is experienced. The child must not notice or be made aware that it is a visual experience. Yet that is precisely what language will force the child to do. Someone will enter the room, and say, "Oh, *look* at the *yellow* sunlight." (176)

The "someone" has no assigned gender in Stern's imagined account of what occurs, but in our society the likelihood until quite recently has been that the someone will be a female caretaker, very probably the mother. Thus the surrounding and supportive consciousness in which, through intersubjectivity, the infant comes to the use of language is also the agency that brings about the "death" of both the infant amodal experience and the nonverbal affect attunement necessary for the birth of linguistic capacity.

Stern's conceptualization of what occurs at this point of crossover is different from Lacan's in that it involves no Oedipal crisis, but it carries the same sense of lost potential conveyed by Lacan's concept of the "unary signifier." There, out of reach of consciousness, inexpressible in the symbolization of language, is a total experience that language strives to recapture. Stern writes: "The paradox that language can evoke experience that transcends words is perhaps the highest tribute to the power of language. But those are words in poetic use. The words in our daily lives more often do the opposite and either fracture amodal global experience or send it underground" (176–77).

The scholarly context in which Stern writes makes it inappropriate for him to describe the paradoxes surrounding language in more impassioned tones. His thought, though, much resembles that which is by general agreement of fundamental importance in Shelley's work:

> A man cannot say, "I will compose poetry." The greatest poet even cannot say it: for the mind in creation is as a fading coal which some invisible influence, like an inconstant wind, wakens to transitory brightness: this power arises from within, like the colour of a flower which fades and changes as it is developed, and the conscious portions of our natures are

unprophetic either of its approach or its departure. Could this influence be durable in its original purity and force, it is impossible to predict the greatness of the results: but when composition begins, inspiration is already on the decline, and the most glorious poetry that has ever been communicated to the world is probably a feeble shadow of the original conception of the poet. (*SPP* 503–4)

The subjunctive mood of "Could this influence be durable . . . " admits defeat ahead of time. Nonetheless, I take it that in *Prometheus Unbound* Shelley is striving to imagine a scenario in which this influence makes itself felt for long enough and with strength enough to create not only artistic but political changes that the "conscious patterns of our natures" would consider impossible. The search for the source of that creativity and revolutionary power brings him necessarily into the presence with which it was originally experienced and the relationship out of which came language, Prometheus' gift to humankind: the state of being-with-the-mother. Shelley and Stern agree in a number of striking ways on how that state can be described. And both see as in some way alienated the "finished" subjectivity that appears at the conclusion of Stern's infancy narrative and is Shelley's point of departure at the opening of *Prometheus Unbound*.

In writing "On Life" Shelley drew back from the dark abyss that the concept of introjection opened beneath his philosophical feet. But when engaged in the creation of *Prometheus Unbound*, he headed down into that abyss, convinced that it contained the revelation of how to render powerless the tyrannical political, social, and religious institutions that so enraged him. His aim was to replace a Jupiterean-Lacanian language with a Dionysian-Bakhtinian one. Relation to the primary caretaker has crucial significance in both—whether in Freudian terms it creates the possibility of symbolic communication only through the experience of loss or in Bakhtinian ones it establishes the capacity for dialogue through "live entering" or (in Stern's phrase) "affect attunement."

Language takes the place of or stands in for the state of being-with-the-mother. By metonymy the idea of the mother in turn stands in for that state. And in societies in which motherhood is taken as women's essential function, "woman" stands in for the mother. Therefore, language takes the place of "woman." "Woman," then, no longer exists, and women, while visibly existing in some fashion or other, are put in highly problematic relation to language. These are well-known dicta of Lacanian discourse, and I rehearse them here only because Stern's narrative (linked to Bakhtinian linguistic theory) arrives at a similar end: language, made possible within the primary relationship, kills the transmodal nature of experience in that relationship.

It is possible, nonetheless, to think either positively or negatively about this "death." While it is an oversimplification to associate the negative view with the Lacanian narrative and the positive with Stern's, I think it is true to the overall tone of each to say that the former places emphasis on the more negative, the latter on the more positive.

The negative statement: because language stands in for the mother, the mother has no relation to language. At the same time, paradoxically, as the object of desire shadowed behind the phallus, the mother becomes one with the phallus. So, by the metonymical processes I have just described, women have not the right to language but are, along with language, possessed as signs of phallic power. Phallic power, ownership of language (along with control over all the human institutions language creates), and control over the exchange of women are all male prerogatives. One way of demonstrating women's exclusion from language is to make the use of a "dead" or "learned" language—a language that is no longer a "mother tongue" anywhere in the world—purely a male prerogative (Ong 25–27).

The positive statement: because language stands in for the mother, it, as that which the relationship with the mother has become, constantly dis-covers that relationship in other forms. Language, as the product of relationship, can continue to draw from behind the veil that is the death of the primary association new conceptualizations of relationship—in both the aesthetic and the social meanings of the word—that are the essence of creativity in every aspect of human life: politics, religion, the arts, scientific thought, philosophy, and so on. High in esteem among expressions of this creativity are works in the "mother tongue." But when this position, like the more negative one, lacks full recognition of the mother's subjectivity (as it did in Shelley's time and does to this day), women's creativity as mothers remains associated with the prerational and preconscious "wilderness," while their potential for creativity in politics, religion, and so on is constantly in question. Woman is object, and woman is muse.

While I am associating Stern's narrative with the second of these positions, I should make clear that Stern himself does not carry the argument to this conclusion. His analysis takes the separate subjectivity of the mother for granted, as the title of his book shows, and understandably so, since he is writing as a psychologist, not a philosopher. Since, however, as Nye points out, "the linguistic that would describe . . . [an interpersonal] language has not yet been developed" ("Woman Clothed with the Sun" 686), and since women's full subjectivity is still functionally denied, the subjectivity that nurtures the infant up to and across the threshold of language can easily become the mother-in-the-mind, the first of many phantoms haunting the split consciousness, once that threshold is crossed.

Because historically, as I shall show in the next chapter, that nurturant task was being assigned to mothers with special emphasis around the time of Shelley's birth, it is not surprising that he himself experienced women in these two ways—as possession and as muse. The drama of *Prometheus Unbound* involves his repudiation of the first and his exploration of the liberating potential of the second, but it does not transcend those categories. It is in the mother's immanence in language, not in women's own fulfillment through the use of language, that his consuming interest lies. Understandably also, given these circumstances, Shelley's struggle to reach the core point where the "influence" streaming from the primary relationship is "durable in its original purity and force" (*SPP* 504) puts him, as "Alastor" records, at constant risk of abjection in the face of the maternal experienced as dissolution, death, non-being. It is a risk he continues to take, nonetheless, for the sake of a renewed subjectivity to be found where the maternal and the linguistic coexist.

Shelley's search for a "regenerate speech" is the theme of Susan Brisman's essay on the problem of voice in *Prometheus Unbound*. The bases of our arguments differ, since she does not use a psycholinguistic approach; but her analysis of the contrast between what she terms "Hermetic" and "Promethean" conceptions of language has parallels deserving of attention with what I have described as the negative and positive ways of thinking about the fact that language takes the place of the mother.

Brisman describes the Hermetic as "a language of reference, where words are assumed to have stronger relations to the objects and thoughts they represent than to one another" (59). While this Hermetic view separates thought from the words that clothe it, as Saussure's linguistic theory does not, it is nonetheless close to the Saussurean view of language as an arbitrary system of signs used for the exchange of the conceptualizations they symbolize. And, although Brisman does not allude to Lacanian theory, the Hermetic as she describes it functions as the "symbolic" does in Lacanian theory to maintain the systems of power instituted through language: "The world governed by Hermetic speech—Earth, Jupiter, and the Furies—behaves as if the spoken word had drawn into itself and inscribed in its own fibre the intention to which it once referred" (60). Prometheus' struggle in act one is to free his own thought—and its attendant speech—from the presuppositions of this viewpoint, while acts two and three dramatize the search for a "Promethean utterance," in Brisman's phrase, that will "bring word and world into being simultaneously and . . . make their single presence the ground of all signification" (58).

The difficulty with Brisman's argument arises only from the fact that, whereas her exposition of the ways in which Hermetic language functions and of the Promethean strategies for undoing its power has clarity and vigor, her description of the Promethean alternative lacks the specificity that would make it convincing. Her emphasis finally is on the way in which Shelley "deconstructs his fiction of the power of voice to confer presence" (80). The Shelley described in her conclusion has not the modernist faith in language as that which actualizes what would otherwise be transience and mere drift but rather reflects the postmodernist deflation of language into lack: "The commonplace—all things are subject to time but eternal love—is imageless, because Shelley knew such truth to be fulfilled only in presence, between friends and lovers, without the mediation of pictures or even words" (84). Her analysis rightly points up the shakiness of that modernist faith, resting uneasily as it does on the thought that an alienated and divided subjectivity produces the integrated and coherent work of art. Thus in an eye blink modernism deconstructs into postmodernism. But writing, it would seem, from within the theory of subjectivity common to both, Brisman can offer no alternative.

More recently William Keach has argued convincingly through a careful study of Shelley's many discussions of or comments on language that "Shelley's attitude towards language is deeply divided" and thus that one cannot come to any single pronouncement about its nature. But Keach does succeed in extracting the element common to Shelley's distrust of language as the ossification of "symbols of domination and imposture"—his description of it in *A Philosophical View of Reform*—and his celebration of language in act four of *Prometheus Unbound* as "a perpetual Orphic song": "In both cases it is the power of language to constitute and rule thought that is at stake." Keach continues:

> As Richard Cronin observes, for Shelley a situation in which speech creates thought and "the limits of speech are defined as the limits of language" is often a cause "not for celebration but for dismay." Only in the paradoxical myth of an original "infancy of society" when "language itself is poetry" (paradoxical because Latin *infans* means "unable to speak," as Shelley certainly knew), or in the complementary myth of an ideal future when "Language is a perpetual Orphic song," is Shelley momentarily able to celebrate the power of words over thought. (40–41)

Among my purposes in this book is to unravel the paradoxical idea that it is to the state of being *infans* that we must look for a language that "itself is poetry," for that renewed and cleansed "Promethean" language which apprehends and expresses the relation "first between existence and perception, and secondly between perception and expression" (*SPP* 482). That task involves an attempt to reconstruct, insofar as possible, Shelley's experience of infancy and childhood.

The reconstruction has, however, my own historical context. I return to Jardine's question: "If everyone and everything becomes Woman—as the culture obsessively turns itself inside out—where does that leave women?" Glossing her arresting words, one might say that the way in which a culture constructs the experience of infancy always creates an "inside" or "core" patterning of experience. Constructors of and constructed by a specific maternal ideology, both the infancy narratives outlined in this chapter create a situation central to the culture in which infants' introjection of a maternal care giver means that "everyone or everything becomes Woman." When, at the same time, women's subjectivity continues to be conceived as essentially relational to men's, then relationship between and among subjects becomes problematic while "Woman" is Goddess/Demon of an unattainable unity. Everyone and everything, but particularly women, miragelike, promise "Her" fullness, then disappoint.

Because the Lacanian narrative acquiesces more explicitly and more deeply in a conflation of the feminine with nonbeing, I find it less promising than Stern's for a feminist reconstruction of all social processes, beginning with the process by which infants are socialized within the human community. Not explicitly, but at least potentially, Stern's understanding of the way in which infants enter community through language allows the possibility that the "Goddess" is not one's lost "being," the opposite of one's social subjectivity, but is relationship itself, the core of human being and meaning. But "She" will not have a gender, it being understood that the task of establishing and grounding such relationship for each infant is shared by the whole community.

That imagined future situation is far from Shelley's historical one. Shelley's Goddess is emphatically gendered. She rises within a particular cultural sea and is more often wafted on the sighs of Lacanian desire than on the breath of mutuality. In Chapter 2 we watch her form take shape within the texts on and about motherhood long pooled in microfilm collections and in brackish estuaries of the British Library, but once a torrential spate foaming from English presses.

Among all these sources I have looked with particular care at the volumes of *La Belle Assemblée* because we know that Shelley saw at least one issue of that journal: volume 6, number 41 (January 1809). In notes to line 765 of "The Wandering Jew" and to book seven, line 67, of *Queen Mab,* Shelley quotes at length from a monologue imagined as spoken by Ahasuerus, the Wandering Jew. Shelley's brief commentary in both instances gives the (false) impression that he himself translated the piece from a German original. As a further mystification he adds in the note: "I picked it up, dirty and torn, some years ago, in Lincoln's-Inn Fields" (*PS* I, 395).

The search for that scrap, the labor of scholars for more than a toiling century, is summarized by the editors of *The Poems of Shelley,* who conclude with the editorial judgment that the passage, a translation of C. F. D. Schubart's "Der ewige Jude: Eine lyrische Rhapsodie" (1783), derives from "*La Belle Assemblée* with greater or less deliberate embellishment by S. according to requirement" (I, 392). They also conclude that "The Wandering Jew," where the passage first appears, was composed between September 1, 1809, and March 5, 1810 (I, 38); Shelley was looking, then, at an issue only a few months old of a journal so sturdily bound that its volumes in the British Library are in excellent condition to this day. I think it likely, therefore, that he saw the translation from Schubart not in Lincoln's Inn Fields but in Field Place. It was not a torn scrap but a selection in the glossy pages of a journal to which his mother may well have subscribed (certainly she would have been precisely the sort of reader targeted by the publication) and which Shelley, the omnivorous reader, had often picked up before.

Feminist scholarship has used these materials over the past twenty years to transform our understanding of women's history and women's writing. In specifically literary study, Mary Poovey has drawn on them to describe the "Proper Lady" who casts her shadow over the writings of Mary Wollstonecraft, Mary Shelley, and Jane Austen (3–47). Nancy Armstrong places eighteenth-century conduct books in juxtaposition with the rising genre of the novel to analyze the new subjectivity created through both. The focus of both these scholars, then, is the novel, particularly the novel as a genre in which women excelled. Closer in some ways to my project is Friedrich Kittler's chapter "The Mother's Mouth" in *Discourse Networks, 1800/1900;* there he uses the works directed to women as mother-educators to interpret "the system of equivalents Woman = Nature = Mother" as a central tenet of Romanticism (28). His study comes, however, as part of a sweeping analysis of discourse with a specifically German focus of interest. My use of texts on mothering as context for a reading of an English male Romantic's poetry is thus an entirely new departure, though adumbrated by Armstrong's statement that "by the end of the eighteenth century . . . the program aimed at producing the domestic woman offered a form of social control that could apply to boys just as well as to girls" (21).[15] Behind the form of social control in which Shelley came to experience himself as a subject stands a particular conceptualization of the mother.

NOTES

1. Peacock, who did not put this anecdote into his memoir of Shelley, told it to Lady Shelley, who believed it and told it in turn to Stopford Brooke. White's source, then, is an entry in Brooke's diary for March 27, 1899, which appears in Lawrence Pearsall Jack's *Life and Letters of Stopford Brooke* (White I, 326, 666). Like Lady Shelley, I believe it; even the language attributed to Shelley, though in indirect discourse, echoes statements in the contemporary literature about breast-feeding in a way that corroborates its authenticity.

2. My analysis of motherhood as an institution is indebted to more than a decade of feminist scholarship, beginning with Adrienne Rich's *Of Woman Born*. Marianne Hirsch's review essay in *Signs,* "Mothers and Daughters," covers research up to 1981; a very partial list of relevant work that has appeared since then would include Barbara Schapiro's *Romantic Mother,* Margaret Homans's *Bearing the Word,* and Marilyn Massey's *Feminine Soul,* as well as *The (M)other Tongue* (edited by Shirley Nelson Garner et al.), and essays by Alan Richardson and Laurie Langbauer in *Romanticism and Feminism* (edited by Anne Mellor).

3. In Paul Smith's opinion, "Lacan leaves room for a consideration of subjectivity as contradictory, as structured in divisions and thus as never the solidified effect of discursive or ideological pressures. Far from being such an *in-dividual,* the 'subject' is a divided and provisional entity" (22). I agree that Lacanian theory may leave room for this thesis, but it subscribes as well to a contradictory Cartesian view of subjectivity. Borch-Jacobsen makes this point more emphatically and specifically than Nye:

> We could go so far as to say that the theory of the mirror stage and of paranoid knowledge not only does not call the essentials of the modern problematic of the subject into question but even reintroduces . . . a previous motif, a strictly Platonic one. Indeed, we recall that Heidegger, referring to the Cartesian *cogito,* spoke of a "rescendence" of the Platonic Idea into a subjective representation: from being transcendent and "metaphysical" in Plato, the Idea was progressively transformed into the *perceptum* of a *perceptio,* into the "perceived" of a human "perceiving." Now Lacan, for his part, and under the various names of "image," "form," and "ideal identification," proceeds toward an astonishing "reascendence" of the *perceptio* into *idea.*" (*Lacan* 61–62)

4. Freud's "pleasure principle" alludes to orgasmic pleasure only after the fact, as it were; he considers it that surcease of excitation that fulfills the deepest human desire. The meaning of the French Freudians' more positive term *jouissance* slides between "ownership" and "orgasm" and is interpreted so variously among these theorists that its import must be understood contextually.

5. I am grateful to Barbara Freeman for bringing this article to my attention.

6. For a brilliant analysis of the different (and contradictory) significations of the "chora" in Kristeva's work, see Silverman, *The Acoustic Mirror* 101–6.

7. This sentence is Shelley's encapsulation of what he refers to as the "intellectual system" or "intellectual philosophy," citing Sir William Drummond's *Academical Question* as the best exposition of it (*SPP* 476). C. E. Pulos, who sees this as the philosophy most central to Shelley's thought—a position now widely accepted among Shelley scholars (*SPP* 475–76) but critiqued in important ways by Ulmer (11–15)—writes: "By the 'Intellectual Philosophy' . . . Shelley must have meant the philosophy attacked by the Common Sense school—the philosophy that reached its fullest development in the criticism of Hume" (*Deep Truth* 35). Compare Shelley's statement in the fragmentary tale "The Coliseum" (1818): "The internal nature of each being is surrounded by a circle, not to be surmounted by his fellows; and it is this repulsion which constitutes the misfortune of the condition of life" (*CW* VI, 303).

8. Judith Butler glosses this passage in her beautifully succinct explication of the difference between "having" and "being" the Phallus: "For women to 'be' the Phallus . . . means to reflect the power of the Phallus, . . . to supply the site to which it penetrates, and to signify the Phallus through 'being' its Other, its absence, its lack, the dialectical confirmation of its identity" (44).

9. Walter Burkert, describing the name Dionysus as "a conundrum," uses Euripides' *Bacchae* for his source when he adds, "The first element of Dionysos—also found as Deunysos, Zonnysos—must certainly contain the name Zeus, and this is how it was construed in antiquity: *Dios Dionysos,* Zeus's son Dionysos" (*Greek Religion* 162).

10. I am grateful to Anne Fernald for bringing Stern's work to my attention.

11. Coleridge, functioning himself rather like a developmental psychologist as he observed the behavior of his infant son Hartley, saw a similar developmental continuum from amodal sensory perception to the acquisition of language: "Hart[ley] seemed to learn to talk by touching his mother" (*Notebooks* item 838). Elsewhere in the *Notebooks* Coleridge muses over the tongue's significance as an instrument of cross-modal perception: "Babies touch *by taste* at first—then about 5 months old they go from the Palate to the hand—& are fond of feeling what they . . . taste / Association of the Hand with the Taste—till the latter by itself recalls the former" (*Notebooks* item 924). For these references I am indebted to Margery Durham's essay in *The (M)other Tongue* (170). Augusta Bonnard's analysis of the tongue's significance also draws attention to its cross-modal functions:

> We must remember that the tongue has the richest direct supply of cranial nerves, and is the single operator of more varied skills than is any other muscular organ or part of the body. Thus it is that, as our major "scanner" in all senses of the word, it discriminates by being our most exquisitely accurate and actively engaged proprio- and exteroceptor. Furthermore, as well as being the mediator of taste, it is an organ of speech. . . . [And] its assessments are *non-visual.* . . . Through its explorations and sensations, it establishes the outside of the self as well as the attractiveness of external objects, contrasting them with the familiar inside boundaries of the "primal cavity." (304)

Bonnard builds on René A. Spitz's essay "The Primal Cavity," which also describes the cross-modal nature of intraoral sensations: "The sensations of the three organs of perception—hand, labyrinth [of the ear], and skin cover—combine and unite with the intraoral sensations to a unified situational experience in which no part is distinguishable from the other" (225).

See also Lawrence E. Marks, *The Unity of the Senses,* in which he writes: "The senses of hearing and of vision, it has been hypothesized, both evolved from an earlier touch sense. That there is presently a close kinship between hearing and the modern touch sense is clear. Both modalities are excited by mechanical energy, that is by changes in patterns of pressure at the receptors, and both show phenomenological as well as psychophysical similarities. . . . [L]ess obvious is the possibility that vision too may have evolved directly from touch. Yet just such a phylogenetic history was suggested by [R. L.] Gregory [in "Origins of Eyes and Brains"], who proposed that the earliest visual system—the first eyes—emerged out of a tactile system, then developed independently as a means to process information about objects at a distance" (182–83).

12. The editors of *Victorian Women* discuss this point when describing the transition from the "positional" to the "personal" family (Hellerstein et al. 4).

13. Lawrence Marks points out that "the poetry of nineteenth century England—especially the poetry of the so-called Romantics—reveals some of the finest examples of synesthetic metaphor in literature" (236). Shelley is the poet most often cited among Marks's examples. My hypothesis is that the family structure in which affect attunement rather than imitation plays the most significant function will create the greatest sensitivity to cross-modal imagery in its children and thus in its artists.

14. In the introductory chapter of *Bearing the Word,* Margaret Homans's distinction between "figurative" and "literal" language takes up this element of corporality within signification through the connection with the mother's body, but with a line of argument different from mine. Homans uses the Lacanian psycholinguistic narrative sketched out earlier in this chapter in associating the figurative use of language with a masculine symbolic order predicated on the differences among arbitrary signs for the creation of a discourse based on absence, specifically the absence of the mother (6–7). In the Lacanian account the renunciation of the mother which is prerequisite to language applies to infants of both genders. Homans uses Nancy Chodorow's theory about the girl child's continued and condoned—even culturally demanded—identification with the mother to make the point, however, that the Lacanian version of the story, while applicable to boys, does not adequately describe a daughter's situation. A daughter can keep her connection to the "literal"—that is, the presymbolic, unmediated relationship with the mother—in a way that a son cannot: "The daughter therefore speaks two languages at once. Along with symbolic language, she retains the literal or presymbolic language that the son represses at the time of his renunciation of his mother. Just as there is for the daughter no oedipal 'crisis,' her entry into the symbolic order is only a gradual shift of emphasis" (13). I agree that there may be two languages, or rather two ways in which language functions, but Homans's acceptance of the Lacanian "myth," in her term, as it applies to men along with her substitution of an alternative Chodorowian myth for women fails to gain my assent. One can, for instance, synthesize observational data on infant behavior with Bakhtinian linguistic theory, as Stern does, to arrive at another version of the psycholinguistic narrative, in which infants of both genders move into language in the company of their mothers. In that process for both genders a particular, unmediated, and cross-modal relation to the mother is lost, becomes absent; but it also remains in the "feel," the "taste," the "pulse" of language, and remains with particular strength in those who are writers. Working simply from my reading across a spectrum of authors, I find it impossible to say whether women retain more of this connection than men. That varies from writer to writer, irrespective of gender. But no one can write effectively without a good measure of it.

15. Dorothea von Mücke's *Virtue and the Veil of Illusion,* published when my book was already in press, does not give the same attention I do to the role of the mother because its focus is generic. She summarizes her central question as follows: "How does the cultural program for the formation of a new type of subjectivity become attached to the production of new literary genres?" (14) Our common interest in "a new type of subjectivity" nonetheless puts our two projects in a fruitfully dialogic relationship.

I regret that Jessica Benjamin's *The Bonds of Love* came to my attention too late for me to have the benefit of her analysis of the "intrapsychic" and the "inter-subjective" approaches to subjectivity. She contrasts, as I do, the psychoanalytic model and Stern's intersubjective one (20–21), but stresses also the necessary "coexis-tence" of the two views (131).

2

Her Destined Sphere

The beautiful Elizabeth Pilfold Shelley could hardly have been pregnant with her first child at a more auspicious time. With admirable competence she had conceived only a month after her marriage to Timothy Shelley, thus proving herself a good breeder; moreover, the necessary changes in her figure would not necessarily have caused injury to her vanity. Quite the contrary. It was her good fortune to be pregnant when that condition was so desirable that women, regardless of age or marital status, were pretending to be so by wearing a garment called "the six-month pad" (Werkmeister 328–30).[1] The pad is one of those humble material objects made numinous by the ideological significance with which it is informed. It serves as a visible sign of the domestic ideology established only within the century before Shelley's birth in 1792. True to its ideological nature, however, this new domesticity was firmly in place as a newborn's natural, inevitable, immutable, and self-explanatory environment.

Historians are aware, of course, that domestic relationships underwent a change, but they have difficulty reaching consensus even in a description of what that change involved, freighted as such descriptions are by the describers' ideological givens. Thus, while historians can agree that a transformation in domestic relations more dramatic than any that has occurred since (with the exception, perhaps, of the one taking place at present) had established itself in England by the late eighteenth century, and while they can come to rough agreement on its social manifestations, they describe *what* occurred very differently.

The dominant voice in the discussion is still Lawrence Stone's. His data convince him that changes in family relationships "first became predominant in wealthy merchant and professional households in the city in the last third of the seventeenth century. From there they spread to the upper landed classes, gathering strength rapidly in the early eighteenth century, and reaching a climax towards 1800" (222). These changes he links to the growth of "affective individualism" and a trend away from authoritarian, patriarchal family rule and "toward greater freedom for children and a rather more equal partnership between spouses"; an increasing separation of the nuclear family from other kin and from the community; the development within that nuclear family of "much warmer affective relations between husband and wife and between parents and children"; and children's emergence as a "special status group, distinct from adults" (221).

Stone has been taken to task by Marxist critics for his dismissive and inaccurate projections of working-class life and for his universalizing of the middle-class family as *the* family.[2] Similarly, a feminist will notice instantly that the "individual" experiencing this growth in affect has a particular gender: "What is involved is a change in how the individual regarded himself in relation to society (the growth of individualism) and how he behaved and felt towards other human beings, particularly his wife and children on the one hand, and parents and kin on the other (the growth of affect)" (222).

Stone is describing the same historical process as that analyzed by Carole Pateman in *The Sexual Contract* as a move "*from Status to Contract*" (9).[3] The change, radical in the sense that it goes to society's roots but also in its potential for cataclysmic social consequences, is from a hierarchically ordered society built on a concept of patriarchal control of a kin group to a contractual society in which the individual is the fundamental unit (9–10). Stone's awareness of the civil disorder made possible by this shift matches Pateman's. In his judgment, "anarchy lay only just below the surface" of eighteenth-century England. "But," he continues, "authority held, for, as Burke pointed out, political liberty was—and is—bought at the price of internalized respect for social discipline." Stone's use of the passive, however, enables him to glide over the fact that the political liberty of one group is paid for not by that group but by others, though his next sentence makes the terms clear enough:

> Individual autonomy—contemporaries called it "freedom" or "liberty"— therefore, was a new luxury which now could safely be indulged in by the well-to-do, and which modified and mitigated the rigidities of a society whose fundamental cohesion was preserved by habits of obedience to legitimate authority, two of the most important aspects of which were the subordination of children to parents and of women to men. (223)

Again, Stone's use of the ungendered phrase "the well-to-do" blurs the fact that the actual referents are men, and his emphasis on the modifications wrought by the concept of "individual autonomy" diminishes the impact of his concluding point: the fundamental cohesion of society *continued* to depend on "the subordination of children to parents and of women to men." His remarks serve as commentary on Locke's classic phrasing of the contract theorists' rationale for a distinction between a public civil contract formed between autonomous male individuals and a private marital contract in which a naturally weaker female "freely" surrenders her autonomy in exchange for male protection. As Stone points out, Locke argued in *Two Treatises on Government* that conjugal society (unlike civil society) "was formed by voluntary contract for the purpose of bearing and rearing children. There was no need for absolute sovereignty in marriage to achieve these limited ends but merely leadership by the stronger and wiser of the two, namely the men" (Stone 265). In Pateman's rephrasing, "Conjugal power is not paternal, but part of masculine sex-right, the power that men exercise as men, not as fathers" (22).

Such phrasing carries a brutal truth that the new domestic ideology took great pains to veil through an elision made possible by the concept of contract. Equated were a Rousseauist original contract struck between free, autonomous, and equal individuals for the sake of mutual help and safety, and actual contracts, such as marriage, between groups having unequal power—with both taken as proof and continuing guarantee of individual freedom.

One may well ask why such a fiction of equal partnership within the marital contract surfaced at all. Why not admit the difference openly and clarify the point that only property-holding males are included in the original contract based on equal rights? The answer, Pateman argues, lies in the fact that those interested in creating the shift from status to contract can do so only by declaring equality to be the universal right of all humans. At the same time, as I have just noted, they have no intention of creating a social situation in which they themselves stand to lose political and social control.

Another factor—an emotional one—may enter as well into the swathing of actual power relations in veils of affect. Stone's research persuades him that a new kind of personality type, one with "steep gradient affect," predominated among the upper bourgeoisie and the squirearchy during the eighteenth century. Assigning no particular gender to this personality, Stone writes that those possessing it had a greater capacity for intimate relationships and were much more closely bound to "spouses and children" than had been the norm earlier. He adds, "The cause of this personality change is not known, but it seems plausible to associate it with a series of changes in child rearing which created among adults a sense of trust instead of one of distrust" (268).

Randolph Trumbach is somewhat more tentative, but he too argues that changes in child-rearing methods bred a new personality. The revision of the male code of honor that eventually put a stop to dueling is the example that he brings forward, pointing out that the opponents of dueling, such as Addison and Steele in *The Spectator,* were at the same time proponents of the new domesticity: "In the course of the nineteenth century, duelling disappeared—not, I would suggest, because the aristocracy had turned bourgeois, but because male aggression had lessened" (235).

To make differences in child-rearing practice the answer to a perceived change in personality traits only carries the question back one stage further. True, no other area of human life can serve as better evidence of an ideological shift; but the way children are socialized is precisely the manifestation of an ideology at work, not the force creating the ideology. I have problems also with the characteristics that Stone and Trumbach ascribe to this personality: how is it possible to think that a society embarked on England's industrial, mercantile, and colonial course in the nineteenth century was made up of more trusting and less aggressive individuals than those of earlier generations?

Still, the change in methods of child rearing discussed by Stone and Trumbach does seem to have occurred and does deserve attention, especially since it was taking place during the shift from status to contract—and, indeed, Lockean theory figures importantly in both. When discussing Locke's *Thoughts Concerning Education,* Trumbach makes a comment that reaches to a nodal interest among the proponents of new methods in infant care and socialization: "Locke wrote his *Education* largely to persuade parents to take their children out of the hands of untrustworthy servants" (130). First among these suspects, as the opening anecdote of the previous chapter suggests, is the wet nurse, and so in fact Trumbach's sentence needs to be amended to say, more specifically, that the advocates of changes in child rearing sought to remove responsibility for the feeding, toilet training, and socialization of upper- and middle-class children from servants and to place it squarely upon mothers.

Alice Ryerson, when describing and analyzing these changes, takes them as symptomatic of a transition from an extended to a nuclear family structure. She therefore ascribes the injunctions about maternal breast-feeding, the emphasis on strict and early toilet training, and the increased concern over any manifestations of infant sexuality to a situation in which the mother had less help from kin than in an extended family (thus the need for earlier toilet training) and in which the intimacy of a very small family group aroused concerns about incest. Even if one takes the controversies about dating the actual emergence of the nuclear family into account, however, servants *could* have functioned in nuclear families as surrogate extended family members. Perhaps, if Alan Macfarlane is correct in seeing the nuclear family pattern as the norm from the late Middle Ages on (70), they in fact did so for a couple of centuries.[4] The injunctions of Locke and many others make such reliance morally reprehensible, enclosing mother and her infants, children, and older daughters (but not older sons) in a circle, a sphere where the mother's power, described as different from the father's and in no competition with his, is "equal" to his.

To keep the centrality of the mother's presence in mind slightly shifts the emphasis of Ryerson's analysis but does not diminish its usefulness. Her study compares books of advice on child rearing from 1550 to 1900.[5] In it she divides the works into two major periods: the first from 1550 to 1750, the second from 1750 to 1900. Her rationale for this division is "a dramatic change in the character of the advice given about child-rearing" that occurred "rather abruptly" in the middle of the eighteenth century (305).

Ryerson's study concludes that infants in the second period had a considerably decreased amount of oral gratification compared to those in the first. The advice about anal training also becomes much more repressive after 1750: toilet training began at a much earlier age, as did the expectation that the infant stay dry through the night, and "cleanliness was on its way to becoming an obsession" (312).[6] Silence in the first period with regard to sexual training provides Ryerson with only negative evidence, but it does seem significant that the prohibitions against masturbation, nudity, and sex play among children and the sexual stimulation of children by adults, which are emphatic and explicit after 1750, receive no mention in earlier advice books (307). Finally (*pace* Trumbach), she notes that the tolerance for aggressive behavior in the second period was actually much higher than in the first (307, 317).

These findings suggest that the person whom Stone would describe as "the affective mother" also had the task of being the disciplinary and intrusive mother. That is, the intimacy between infant and mother, now much greater and more constant than in the earlier period, becomes the site for a number of different and conflicting emotions masked by the blandly noncommittal term "affect": rage, fear, and frustrated sexual passion as well as joy, love, and unguarded dependence.

As the passages I have quoted from Stone and Trumbach show, but as my own analysis betrays as well, it is extremely difficult to keep one's attempt to write an impartial historical account free from any tincture of one's own attitude. But the material facts, however differently imbued by their interpreters, remain constant. The palpable evidence of books of conduct and medical advice, essays in women's journals, paintings, imaginative literature, and hymns yields the certainty that from around the middle of the eighteenth century, women were being barraged with admonitions about remaining in the sphere of the home in intimate and constant contact with their infants and young children: breast-feeding them; supervising and participating in their play; guiding them in the use of language; socializing, cleansing, amusing, and instructing them. Grudgingly it was allowed that the mother's tasks might to some extent be supervisory in that she could delegate some of them to servants some of the time—but never to the point where a servant's relationship with the child would have anything of the immediacy, importance, or power of her own.

This amassed evidence cannot, of course, serve as a historical record of women's actual ideas or actions. In a certain way it serves as negative evidence. If women were conforming totally to the model considered so desirable by those dominating the society's media of communication, what need would there be to continue spending resources—time, money, human energy— urging them so to conform?[7] At the same time, an ideology this powerful can create in the minds of those immersed in it something real in that it exists, even when it exists in contradiction to other social realities. For the child so immersed this is particularly true, and Shelley, by virtue of his class and his date of birth, was such a child. In other words, no matter how particular mothers around him (including his own) were acting, Shelley necessarily grew up within a fairly recently established but very strong ideology of motherhood. Also, if the injunctions laid down by that ideology for physical, emotional, and intellectual bonding between mother and children were even imperfectly obeyed, the mother-nurse's soul would indeed enter the child.

In describing women's allocation to a maternal sphere through this ideology, I have so far emphasized its constrictions. And I have suggested, following Pateman, that the process by which maternal breast-feeding and instruction of children become the locus of woman's separate but supposedly equal power, her partnership in a supposedly egalitarian marriage, serves in part as a rationale for her continued subordination, in part as a screen covering the fact that any subordination exists. But obviously, if women are without overt coercion to step mildly into their sphere and remain there, its restrictions can best be experienced as liberating, and the subordination as, indeed, superiority.

The line that the argument must take, then, becomes a tightrope across what Leonore Davidoff and Catherine Hall describe as "the contradictions between the claims for women's superiority and their social subordination" (149). The power ascribed to women within their sphere could be made so great that it threatened the masculine dominance it was designed to maintain.

The contradiction manifests itself in the very metaphor contained in the signifier "sphere." When used to define, indeed restrict, women's social position, "sphere" has the sixth meaning given it in the *OED:* "a province or domain in which one's activities or faculties find scope or exercise, or within which they are naturally confined; range or compass of action or study." The words "domain" and "scope" suggest full control, while "confined" and "compass" carry seemingly opposed notions of restriction. Behind this contradiction lies the ancient "signified" of this signifier, the *OED*'s second definition: "one or other of the concentric, transparent, hollow globes imagined by the older astronomers as revolving around the earth and respectively carrying with them the several heavenly bodies" (XIV, 205). These separate spheres are those Ptolemaic globes that rise concentrically above Earth—Moon, Mercury, Venus, Sun, Mars, Jupiter, Saturn—each of which serves as both domain of and containment for its guiding Intelligence, the source of its "influence."

Thomas Gisborne consciously uses the word with the restrictive possibility of the *OED*'s sixth definition when warning young women against excessive ambition as part of his *Enquiry into the Duties of the Female Sex* (1797). There are, he laments, female malcontents who "are occasionally heard to declare their opinion, that the sphere in which women are destined to move is so humble and so limited, as neither to require nor to reward assiduity" (11). Even in his sentence, however, the resonant juxtaposition of "sphere" with "destined to move" calls up the possibility that this sphere to which a woman is "limited" is also the one in which and from which she acts as a tutelary deity. For along with ancient astronomy, the signifier "sphere" trails the ancient belief in those divinities named as ruler of each. The planets, as C. S. Lewis points out, "had, after all, been the hardiest of all the Pagan gods." He adds:

> Modern readers sometimes discuss whether, when Jupiter or Venus is mentioned by a mediaeval poet, he means the planet or the deity. It is doubtful whether the question usually admits of an answer. Certainly we must never assume without special evidence that such personages are in Gower or Chaucer the merely mythological figures they are in Shelley or Keats. They are planets as well as gods. Not that the Christian poet believed in the god because he believed in the planet; but all three things—the visible planet in the sky, the source of influence, and the god—generally acted as a unity upon his mind. I have not found evidence that theologians were at all disquieted by this state of affairs. (104–5)

Lewis's use of the reductive phrase "merely mythological" assumes that Shelley and Keats cannot participate in medieval Christianity's complex appropriation of pagan worship. I question that assumption and hold rather, with Donald Reiman, that "there is still room for further exploration of the relationship of Shelley's mythmaking to the tradition of allegorizing ancient religions and mythologies" (*Intervals of Inspiration* 392). Specifically, I hold that the language used in Shelley's formative years to describe the maternal function and influence, including the concepts implied by the term "sphere," fostered a mythology centered on a maternal deity and that Shelley was drawn to the subversive potential in this mythology.

In examining the literature produced by the same ideological configuration in eighteenth-century and early nineteenth-century Germany, Marilyn Massey makes the point that the feminine "soul" constructed to suit society's purpose "began to refer to a female God. At that point, belief in the feminine soul ceased to serve as an ideological force to shape women for their place in the social order and flickered with the promise of subverting and transforming that order" (43). Massey describes the social function of novels such as Johann Pestalozzi's *Leonard and Gertrude* in ascribing to women those "angelic" qualities of soul that would make them devoted and nurturing wives and mothers. I share that interest but want to investigate as well the slippage across genders that occurs, through mirroring, when this maternal soul becomes the chief instrument for the socialization of infants and children. Eagleton's language, when he describes the aestheticized subject of the new contractual social order, is filled with words and phrases associated with domestic angels:

> The ultimate binding force of the bourgeois social order, in contrast with the coercive apparatus of absolutism, will be *habits, pieties, sentiments* and *affections*. And this is equivalent to saying that power in such an order has become "aestheticized." It is at one with the *body's spontaneous impulses, entwined with sensibility and the affections,* lived out in *unreflective custom.* (20; my italics)

Within the same context Eagleton compares the bourgeois subject to a work of art in that it is "autonomous and self-determining, acknowledges no merely extrinsic law but instead, in some mysterious fashion, gives the law to itself" (23). Since women, in the society Eagleton is describing, were by definition and in legal status "relative creatures," his "autonomous and self-determining" subject is male, but the "mysterious" process that endows him with a soul free in its own internalized law involves his imbibing that soul from his mother.

Alan Richardson's analysis of the "story" behind the cultivation of sentiment described by Eagleton—an analysis consonant with my own put forward in "The Politics of Androgyny" and so one that it would be churlish of me to deny outright—makes the imbibing an active, appropriative, even "cannibalizing" (21) process. In his analysis "Reason," overvalued in the Augustan period, lost its primacy in a pendulum swing toward "sympathy in ethics and empathy in art criticism" (14). In consequence, "where male writers had relegated sympathy and sensibility to their mothers, wives, and sisters, they now sought to reclaim 'feminine' qualities through incorporating something of these same figures" (15). In similar terms Diane Hoeveler writes, "The Romantics cannibalistically consumed these female characters [mothers, sisters, lovers, femmes fatales, muses], shaped them into ideal alter egos, and most of the time destroyed them by the conclusion of the poem" (9).

My difficulty with this argument is that it works from the same premises as those it critiques. That is, it accepts the presumption that the male ego is a boundaried whole, capable of making aggressive, penetrative raids on the weak-boundaried feminine and encapsulating those attributes it desires while not in itself being vulnerable to any such penetration. Now, insofar as this version of what was occurring reflects the attitudes of the male Romantics discussed in Richardson's and Hoeveler's wide-ranging analyses, I think it is the truth, but not the whole truth and not even—or at least not always—the male Romantics' own whole truth. For the initial presumption is incorrect: *all* human psyches are permeable to external "impressions," and the body along with the psyche, since any psychic impingement, positive or negative, becomes inscribed on the body as, respectively, well-being or malfunction.

Working from an incorrect assumption of male invulnerability, men assigned to women the inculcation of a sensibility that would produce "whole," self-regulating bourgeois men. There were, however, unforeseen consequences, as I wish to show through consideration of Shelley's "case." Phrasing Massey's point somewhat differently, I would say that the maternal ideology proved to be an Aladdin's lamp out of which rose the Mother Goddess, that Shelley was one of the many under her influence, and that the effect of that influence shows the way in which the imbibing of feminine "soul" created the possibility of subverting and transforming the social order it was designed to maintain.

In calling this force abroad in the culture a Mother Goddess, I appear to be thinking in the very sort of reified, external absolutes that, as Jerrold Hogle well argues, Shelley deplores and resists (54). For Shelley, human subjectivity and creativity flow from a constant transaction or sharing; using the term "transference," Hogle describes this as "any 'bearing across' between places, moments, thoughts, words, or persons" (15). While the associations of the word "transference" are Freudian, this dialogic concept of subjectivity is also Bakhtinian, as Hogle himself suggests when he notes that Shelley "prefigures Bakhtinian concepts of 'heteroglossia' and the process of self-composition" (346). As I suggested in the last chapter, both infancy narratives are therefore applicable to Shelley's understanding of the formation and activity of a human subject, and in his poetry the Mother Goddess functions as mythic representation of that inner psychological process and not as a reified external deity. Yet as such a representation and also as a force that is real in that "her" effects are real and operative, Shelley's goddess manifests herself constantly in his poetry.

Because she is specifically a Mother Goddess, her manifestations bear obvious relation to ideas about the nature of mothering current in Shelley's time. Thus both the cultural milieu as a whole and the constellation of relationships within the Shelley family in particular will need further description as I pursue my argument. The second of these is the subject of Chapter 3. I turn now to the first. In the ensuing sections of this chapter I wish to establish an eroticization of the maternal, particularly of the maternal breasts, that gives preparation for the resurgence of "Venus" as an operative if not an acknowledged cultural force. Meanwhile, the language and imagery used in the discourse defining the mother's role as educator creates a metaphorical and potentially mythological connection between the maternal and the providential, the topic addressed in the final two sections of this chapter. So both the pagan and the Christian traditions fuse in the Shelleyan goddess.

Reiman makes the point that in 1816–17 Shelley and his close friends "played at being religious Pagans" as a protest "against the established trends in British social and political life" (*Intervals of Inspiration* 215). I would say rather that a force to which I am assigning the code name "Venus" was abroad in the society and that Shelley experienced its effects; he was not, then, as much in control as Reiman's word "play" implies. At the same time, his protest or revolutionary plan in *Prometheus Unbound* does consciously involve using "Venus" to sabotage the institutions that the social trend or pressure for maternal care of children had intended that force, that "Venus," to contain. But one further circle: as an ever-present but unfulfillable alternative and thus as play, as fantasy, "Venus" serves as a conduit for revolutionary energies, containing them in two senses of that word.

Maternity Eroticized

In his introduction to a reissue of William Buchan's *Domestic Medicine,* William Nisbet quotes a striking passage from Rousseau's *Emile:* "Should mothers condescend to *nurse their own children,* manners would form themselves; the sentiment of nature would revive in our hearts; the state would be repeopled; the principal point, this alone would reunite everything" (xxiv; Nisbet's emphasis). Rousseau's language, as Richardson points out, is "almost millennial" in its view of breast-feeding (18). Indeed, if one sees breast-feeding as paradigmatic of the sympathetic interchange that will both construct and characterize the subjectivities who will repeople the state—who, that is, will people a renewed state—one can drop the modifier; the statement *is* millennial.

Rousseau's primary interest, heard in the somewhat hectoring tone, is in co-opting women's physical and emotional powers for the construction of a system in which they will possess no political or economic power. Still, the paradigm of the nursing mother as image of the fully responsible human subject has further consequences. First, as Irving Babbitt expostulates, on his own terms most astutely, "By subjecting judgment to sensibility, Rousseau may be said to have made woman the measure of all things" (132; quoted in Richardson 23). What is more, Rousseau's emphasis on mother power transforms the husband, whatever his legal, political, and social status, into only a slightly older child when in the presence of his nursing wife. Nisbet's quotation from Rousseau continues: "When a family is all lively and animated, domestic concerns afford the most delightful occupation to a woman, and the most agreeable amusement to a man" (Buchan xxiv).

The suggestion implied by the language here—that woman is the maturely occupied adult and man the agreeably amused child—reflects an attitude already widespread in the culture. William Cadogan in 1750, for instance, had infantilized the husband even more outrageously than Rousseau: "The Child, was it nurs'd in this [maternal] way, would be always quiet, in good Humor, ever playing, laughing, or sleeping. In my Opinion, a Man of Sense cannot have a prettier Rattle (for Rattles he must have of one kind or other) than such a young Child" (27). The ongoing presence of the idea can be seen in Wordsworth's grotesquely serious depiction of Vaudracour, seeking, as Richardson notes, "spiritual restoration at one of Julia's breasts while their infant sucks from the other" (18):

> Oftener he was seen
> Propping a pale and melancholy face
> Upon the mother's bosom, resting thus
> His head upon one breast, while from the other
> The babe was drawing in its quiet food.
> (*Prelude,* 1805, 9.811–15)

For all three of the men I have quoted, this nursing fantasy is a peaceable one, with husband and babe receiving full measure of solace or pleasure according to their need. In real life, however, a situation in which father and infant are siblings makes them in the nature of things rivals as well as companions.

If the mother serves as chief implementer of this new family ideology, she is only acting in ways similar to those in which she is being acted upon. Her own body is invaded, zoned, and manipulated both literally and figuratively. Attention, of course, is focused most particularly on the breasts: prurient, intrusive, and obsessive attention from medical advisers and concerned family members; narcissistic and complicatedly, masochistically pleasurable attention from potential or actual mothers. Consider this passage from James Nelson's *Essay on the Government of Children.* I quote it at some length, partly because it serves as a good example of what Michel Foucault describes as "the great process of transforming sex into discourse" and partly because it also exemplifies specifically the zoned eroticization of the maternal body, the maternalizing of the erotic.

Nelson, in discussing the proper timing for the infant's first breast-feeding, gives this account from Dr. Hunter, one of the "Men-Midwives of the Lying-in Hospital" when that charity institution first opened. The subjects of this experimentation, then, were poor women, but the addressees are women of the upper and middle classes, who are invited to share in a fascinated "scientific" eroticism:

> The Child was not put to the Breast till the Milk came freely, or run out of itself; and as the Breasts commonly began to fill in about eight and forty Hours after Delivery, soon or later, they were allowed to fill more and more, perhaps as much longer, 'till the Milk began to discharge itself: to forward this, the Breasts were frequently embrocated with warm Oil; to invite the Milk both the Softness of the Oil, and the Motion given the Breasts by rubbing it in with the Hand. This Method was adhered to pretty generally, 'till they found by Experience that it was wrong. (51)

One senses that the discovery took longer than was necessary because the doctors had become so mesmerized by the process of "embrocation" itself and with observing these breasts fill to bursting that they took insufficient note of the procedure's purpose.

Elsewhere in the essay, with an insinuating suggestiveness in his turn of phrase, Nelson mentions the pleasurable sensations of breast-feeding as one of its major inducements. Within the same context also, through his juxtaposition of the word "Innocence" with "Cunning" and "Tricks" to describe the infant at the breast, he creates an aura of seduction, a buzz and hum of sexual fantasy surrounding both participants in this intimate process. Held forth is the promise that the mother's ministrations will both deploy her own sexual power and serve as the vehicle for her "innocent" seduction by her sexualized infant:

> All Mothers who experienc'd it, whose Minds are temper'd with natural Affection, assure us, that there is an inexpressible Pleasure in giving Suck, which none but Mothers know; for besides that the Sensation itself is said to be mighty pleasing; to behold the Innocence, the Cunning, the Tricks, and the various Whims of a Child; to observe likewise the early Sentiments they discover; must doubtless give a Pleasure which no Words can describe. (48)

Underlying a tone at once crisp and wheedling in Sarah Brown's *Letter to a Lady on the Best Means of Obtaining the Milk* (1777) is an appeal to an erotic mixture of sensations and emotions: feelings of rivalry about the size and shape of breasts, of sexual arousal through them, of masochistic fascination with their possible destruction:

> I have heard many ladies give, as a reason for not suckling, that they never had any nipples at all; that is impossible, (I am convinced,) for nature is always formed perfect: so far I will allow, that children will pick them off by degrees for I will take on me to say, that not one woman in ten has perfect nipples, and it is that which occasions the violent pain in attempting to open the milk tubes. . . . I therefore flatter myself no lady . . . will scruple to put either herself or daughter under my care, particularly as there are many sorts of nipples. (7–8)

In his *Essay on the Management, Nursing, and Diseases of Children* (1794), William Moss gives just as much attention to women's misshapen or damaged nipples, but he does not entertain the ghoulish thought that young women have picked them off. He places the blame, rather, on tightly laced stays. The problems in breast-feeding experienced by upper-class mothers who want to suckle their infants but cannot do so because of "unfavorable nipples" rarely trouble those in "the laborious and inferior stations." The sole cause of the difference is "tight lacing over the breasts" so much practiced by "those in the better life." The lacing "not only destroys the natural beauty, shape, and proportion of the breasts, but depresses and flattens the nipples, and sinks them into the breasts, so much that they are not without difficulty, and sometimes cannot be got out at all" (375–76).

The publication date of Moss's work just precedes one of the most radical changes in the design of women's garments, including undergarments, in all English history. In their *History of Underclothes,* Willet and Phillis Cunnington point out that at this time "the Englishwoman of the fashionable world succeeded in reducing the total weight of her clothing to a couple of pounds. Such a thing had never previously been attempted in this country" (97). Analysis, as opposed to fairly straightforward description of such changes, is only in its beginnings and is still largely speculative. The close link between women's clothing and the contemporaneous emphasis given to motherhood leads me to offer some speculations of my own on what the new fashions signified.

We must begin with the fashion that was displaced, following Valerie Steele's sensible caveat in *Fashion and Eroticism:* "Whatever connections they might have with wider culture and with social change, styles of dress are clearly and more directly related to earlier styles and to the internal process of fashion change" (23). The London *Morning Herald* on July 5, 1793, ran a description of fashionable dress that could serve in all but a few details as a verbal picture of the ensemble worn by Elizabeth Shelley to have her portrait painted by George Romney in 1795 (fig. 1):[8]

> The hair is still dressed flat upon the forehead and temples, but the ringlet begins to yield its charms to the *queue renversée.* On one side, a *turban cap* is brought very low down upon the temple;—on the other, the hair is drawn through an opening in the cap, and is so suspended till it falls gracefully on the shoulder. Two or three long feathers, chiefly white, or straw-coloured, are placed in front.
>
> The *handkerchief* is pinned low, and the tucker raised high; but not so high as to entirely hide the neck.
>
> *Pads* continue to be worn; and on account of these the dress is still a loose gown of white muslin flounced in front, appearing to be put on with the negligence permitted to the supposed situation of the wearers. A narrow sash ties it at the waist.   (quoted in Werkmeister 329)

By 1795 "padding" was no longer fashionable, but one can see that in other respects Elizabeth Shelley's Directoire gown has the simplicity and "negligence" that the columnist in 1793 associated with the garb of pregnant women. In other words, although so excessive a sign of motherhood's prestige as the pad had lost its éclat, fashions through the 1790s showed a high degree of consideration for the health and comfort of pregnant women, and contem-

Fig. 1. Portrait of Elizabeth Shelley by George Romney, May–June 1795. (*Collection of The New York Public Library, Astor, Lenox and Tilden Foundations, gift of The Carl and Lily Pforzheimer Foundation*)

porary analysis offered the same rationale for the next step: the abandonment of stays altogether.

In May 1800 the *Lady's Monthly Museum* reprinted an edict published "throughout the German empire a few years ago," offering it as proof that "one, at least, of our fashions originated in Germany":

> Whereas the dangerous consequences arising from the use of stays, are universally acknowledged to impair the health, and impede the growth of the fair sex; when, on the contrary, the suppression of that part of the dress cannot but be effectual in strengthening their constitutions, and above all, in rendering them more fruitful in the marriage state: we hereby strictly enjoin, that in all orphan-houses, nunneries, and other places set apart for the public education of young girls, no stays, of any kind whatever, shall be made use of, or encouraged from henceforth, and from this instant. . . . We also hereby command, that it be enjoined to the college of physicians, that a dissertation, adapted to every one's capacity, be forthwith composed, shewing how materially the growth of children of the female sex is impaired by the use of stays. ("Edict Against the Use of Stays" 393)[9]

The same issue of the *Lady's Monthly Museum* begins the translation of a story by Baris de Galitzin described as "imitated from the German of Wieland" (i.e., in the softly pornographic, pseudoclassical mode) titled "Diogenes and Glycere." Its narrator, while walking in Athens, meets "a young nymph from sixteen to seventeen years of age. . . . She was only thinly clad; and her bosom, which might vie with that of Hebe herself, as well as the other parts of her person, were half open to my view" (347). She appears to be highly agitated and faints in his arms. After covering her bosom with his mantle, he revives her. But as she tells him her story, "the mantle which I had thrown around her by degrees unloosed itself, and you are well aware that a like bagatelle on certain occasions, is not a *bagatelle!*" (350).

Although the diaphanous clothing of the "nymph" is supposedly Greek, the descriptions of it could apply equally well to the dress worn by an Englishwoman in 1800. Galitzin's emphasis on the erotic attraction of her breasts suggests, however, that my prosaic analysis so far of the connection between the abandonment of stays and the concern for women's prepartum health shows too much of the midwife's viewpoint and not enough of the gallant's. In contrast, for example, the Cunningtons attribute this new fashion to a "wartime method of sex attraction" (*History of Underclothes* 97), an analysis in line with Willet Cunnington's general principle as a historian of fashion: "I [regard] the instinct of sex-attraction as the principal motive force in feminine fashions. . . . It has always been the claim of fashion that it is attractive. What, then, is to be attracted but man?" (*English Women's Clothing in the Nineteenth Century* 24).

Cunnington's phrasing of the question, while simplistic (and heterosexist), expresses nonetheless the "sex appeal" theory that in Steele's analysis is still "the single most influential explanation of fashion" (34). Another proponent of it is James Laver, who sees women's fashion as reflective of the way in which the male gaze shifts its attention to the different erogenous zones of the female body. The Galitzin fantasy would thus serve Laver as evidence that the male gaze in 1800 was riveted on female breasts and that in response women and their dressmakers at once veiled and exposed those objects in order to take the best possible advantage of this masculine obsession, it being "the business of fashion to pursue [the shifting erogenous zone], without actually catching it up" (97).

Putting to one side for the moment the question of who—or who all— were enjoying the fashionable emphasis placed on breasts, I should take note of the fact that this was scarcely a *newly* attractive erogenous zone. Anne Hollander traces a shift in erotic interest from the abdominal region to the breast as far back as the 1690s. Before that time, she notes, "fashionable posture had suppressed the bosom and swung bellies forward, even under the longest and stiffest boning." Late seventeenth-century fashion, with its very long, straight bodice and a shallow décolletage that pushed the breasts to prominence above it, meant that "the body tilted forward, for the first time leading with the bust. . . . This particular stiff-backed, forward-tilted posture, with its new kind of erotic emphasis, had not been fashionable before" (110).

As Hollander's description continues, however, one sees that while the source of the erotic charge (i.e., the female bosom) remains constant throughout the eighteenth century, the erotic focus shifts. The provocatively exposed bolster, cleft but held by stays into a single form, changed in the last quarter of the century; the waistline was compressed instead of the entire rib cage, "and the breasts were separated, outlined, and moulded into hemispheres by the shape of the bodice" (112). The "noncorseted, Greco-Roman look" adopted in the very last years of the century exposed even further the full shape of breast and nipple. Hollander's analysis of these changes limits itself pretty well to the sexual attraction theory, without discriminating among erotic priorities: "In any case, at the turn of the eighteenth century, breasts were supposed to be likely to pop out of clothes without warning, if given the least chance, but especially under the influence of male lust" (211).

Although I realize the impossibility of proposing a single explanation for what present analysts surmise is the overdetermined nature of fashion change, I suggest that these differently presented breasts do mirror the changing emphases discussed by Pateman in a society moving from status to contract. In a status period, organized along lines of patriarchal power, contemplation of the female abdomen, as vessel for the sperm that guarantees the continuity of male dominance, can in itself arouse desire. As the society changes to one of contract, female vulnerability, for which the exposure of women's breasts becomes a sign, continues to ensure male dominance; the penetrability so encoded makes it necessary for women to live under the protective coverture of "individuals." Considered this way, the exposed bolster of the early eighteenth century, cleft while held by the stays in a unitary form, functions as a displaced image of the defenseless vagina. Breasts at the end of the century still serve as signifiers of women's defenselessness, but the fascination they invite in proffering their own specific shape and texture to the eye and to the imagined or actual touch parallels the shift to an eroticization of the maternal that we have seen in the medical literature previously discussed.[10]

Yet surely a typical emphasis such as Galitzin's on Glycere's youth calls my maternity-oriented theory into question. If fashions in the early 1790s were well suited to the mature and even the pregnant figure, the light and revealing garments of the turn of the century demanded a full-breasted but lithe, slim, and young body if they were to look attractive (fig. 2); cartoon humor of the period makes that graphically clear. As a number of fashion historians have pointed out, such clothing suggests that the culture of the time placed an especially high value on youth.

Fig. 2. "Mme. de Richemont," painting by Baron François Gérard. (*Courtesy of the Bettmann Archive*)

That value, however, is not at odds with an attraction to virginal breasts as capable of lactation in the future and as at least subliminally reminiscent of the maternal breast open to the infant's gaze in the past. Hints of both these attitudes appear in Erasmus Darwin's *Plan for the Conduct of Female Education in Boarding Schools.* Published in 1797, it was being written just as the dress revolution occurred. Thus, Darwin appends a note to his warnings about the nature of stays: "A wise fashion of wearing no stiff stays, which adds so much to the beauty of young ladies, has commenced since the above was written; and long may it continue!" (77–78). There is more than a little of Humbert Humbert mixed in with the concerned pedagogue who pens that ejaculation. At the same time, Darwin elsewhere in the *Plan* notes: "The supposed origin of our ideas of beauty acquired in our early infancy from the curved line, which forms the female bosom, is delivered in *Zoonomia,* vol. I, sect. 16.6 . . . but it is too metaphysical an investigation for young ladies" (27).

Darwin's careful notation of the scholarly source—his own—available if one is interested in further discussion of the question, and his roguish suggestion that the subject is too "metaphysical" for the young, sends the adult, scientific, and inquiring reader instantly, of course, to *Zoonomia.* [11] Part six forms one of the subsections taken up with the subject of instinct, Darwin's larger topic in section sixteen. It begins with a discussion of the way in which the superiority of humans' sense of touch gives them an advantage over other species—even though they lack similar competitive primacy in other areas—because of the close connection between touch and sight (106–7). His point, then, bears interestingly on the present-day analysis by developmental psychologists of the importance of an infant's transmodal perceptions and parallels Eagleton's linkage of the aesthetic, the sentimental, and "that which is bound up with our creaturely life" (13). Superior sensitivity of touch creates a superior vision, which makes possible a "sentimental" appreciation of female beauty transcending "animal passion." But here we need Darwin's own formulation:

> Now as the images, that are painted on the retina of the eye, are no more than signs, which recall to our imaginations the objects we had before examined by the organ of touch, as is fully demonstrated by Dr. Berkeley in his treatise on vision; it follows that the human creature has greatly more accurate and distinct sense of vision than that of any other animal. Whence as he advances to maturity, he gradually acquires a sense of female beauty, which at the same time directs him to the object of his new passion.
>
> Sentimental love, as distinguished from the animal passion of that name, with which it is frequently accompanied, consists in the desire or sensation of beholding, embracing, and saluting a beautiful object. (I, 144)

The heterosexual male is so singly the norm of human subjectivity in Darwin's analysis, the female so completely an object, that the possibility that women are capable of experiencing "sentimental love" becomes decidedly moot. Thus Darwin offers another corroborative piece of evidence in support of Pateman's argument that women do not participate as fully human "indi-

viduals" in a contract society. No more than Freud's early theorizing about the
centrality of the Oedipal crisis in human development does Darwin's discussion of the human delight in beauty address itself to women, even though
Darwin makes the female breast an object of love for infants of both sexes.
That recognized, one can note with interest how closely Darwin aligns all
"human" appreciation of the beautiful and "human" capacity for sentiment
with the (male) infant's pleasure in the possession of his mother's breast.

His premise makes Darwin's a kinetic aesthetic. "The characteristic of
beauty therefore is that it is the object of love," he writes, and goes on to aver
that many objects called beautiful—such as a Greek temple, music, or
poetry—should rather be termed "agreeable" because "we have no wish to
embrace or salute them." Strictly, he would associate the experience of beauty
with a recognition through the sense of vision, first, of those objects that have
given pleasure to the other senses of smell, taste, and touch; and second, of
those "which bear any analogy of form to such objects."

As it turns out, the objects to which all others arousing the experience of
beauty are merely analogous are the maternal breasts:

> When the babe, soon after it is born into this cold world, is applied to its
> mother's bosom; its sense of perceiving warmth is first agreeably affected;
> next its sense of smell is delighted with the odour of her milk; then its taste is
> gratified by the flavour of it; afterwards the appetites of hunger and thirst
> afford pleasure by the possession of their objects, and by the subsequent
> digestion of the aliment; and, lastly, the sense of touch is delighted by the
> softness and smoothness of the milky fountain, the source of such variety of
> happiness.
>
> All these various kinds of pleasure at length become associated with the
> form of the mother's breast; which the infant embraces with its hands,
> presses with its lips, and watches with its eyes; and thus acquires more
> accurate ideas of the form of its mother's bosom, than of the odour or
> flavour or warmth, which it perceives by the other senses. And hence at our
> maturer years, when any object of vision is presented to us, which by its
> waving or spiral lines bears any similitude to the form of the female bosom,
> whether it be found in a landscape with soft gradations of rising and descend-
> ing surface, or in the forms of some antique vases, or in other works of the
> pencil or the chissel [sic], we feel a general glow of delight, which seems to
> influence all our senses; and, if the object be not too large, we experience an
> attraction to embrace it with our arms, and to salute it with our lips, as we
> did in our early infancy the bosom of our mother.   (I, 145–46)

Radical transference is clearly operative here, as is the continuum described by Eagleton from bodily sensations to emotional states to aesthetic
perceptions to formal self-discipline linked with general benevolence: the
matrix creating the citizenry of Rousseau's renewed state. Darwin's own
terms are somewhat different, however, in that they suggest a version of the
ancient doctrine of correspondences. The aura emanating from these "waving
or spiral lines," whether in landscape or artwork, makes them into signs, not
of a transcendent deity precisely but of a sentiment or feeling—a complex or

node of sensation fused with its associated emotion and consequent idea—permeating but also thereby transcending time. These objects are one jagged half of a symbol, the "antitype" to the "type" provided by an incorporation of breast-as-infant's-experience-of-breast. They come, then, under the category of what Keats calls "Things semireal such as Love, the Clouds &c which require a greeting of the Spirit to make them wholly exist" (*Letters* I, 243). In that moment of "greeting," type and antitype rush together, completing the round of the symbol, round of the breast, round of the infant head mirroring breast.

I have used the typological language of Shelley's "On Love" deliberately in reading the Darwin passage because the subject matter in both has decided parallels and because typological thinking, while much more explicit in Shelley's essay, suffuses both pieces. The effect and even the meaning conveyed by the two is quite different, however.

When Darwin describes the human being produced through memory traces of drafts from the mother's "milky fountain," his language suggests that he writes from within the state that Blake terms "Innocence," or, in the terms discussed in the last chapter, with Bakhtinian "live entering." Like Blake's "Jocund Day" or "Infant Joy," this personality has arms outstretched in an expectation that past delights in shared life are the source of constantly renewed connectedness and so need never be mourned. The author of "On Love," on the contrary, is a Lacanian desirer, in the Blakean state of "Experience." The interior type—"a mirror whose surface reflects only the forms of purity and brightness: a soul within our soul that describes a circle around its proper Paradise which pain and sorrow and evil dare not overleap" (*SPP* 474)—is a desired ideal, a "thirst," and not a source of continuing joy, because its antitype, sought obsessively as a "meeting" with an "understanding," "an imagination," "a frame" that would create this imagined unity, is in fact "unattainable."

This seems the narcissism in its negative form—the narcissism that finds all others inadequate through projection of one's own feelings of inadequacy—that destroyed or endangered all of Shelley's intimate relationships. But Shelley's description and Darwin's are both "sentimental," and both contain the same potential for good or ill. Also, as the fragment moves toward the point at which it breaks off, Shelley writes in terms closer to Darwin's about the "correspondence" between natural beauty and its psychic type and connects this moment of the spirit's greeting with what appears to be a memory trace from infancy:

> There is eloquence in the tongueless wind and a melody in the flowing of the brooks and the rustling of the reeds beside them which by their inconceivable relation to something within the soul, awaken the spirits to a dance of breathless rapture, and bring tears of mysterious tenderness to the eyes like the enthusiasm of patriotic success or the voice of one beloved singing to you alone. (*SPP* 473–74)

Indeed, in the very last sentence of "On Love," Shelley describes the "something within us" as "a want *or power*" (my emphasis) central to the very experience of subjectivity; without it, "man becomes the living sepulchre of himself." The image of suckling infant joined to a full breast—and thus, through metonymy, the female breast itself—has multistability in its correspondence now to desire for unity of being, now to the experience of that unity, but in both cases to a "something" basic to the structure of the human subject.

As a phenomenon reflecting the cultural obsession with breasts, the discarding of stays at the end of the century placed even more emphasis than had existed earlier on the *difference* of women's bodies, specifically on their exposed defenselessness in contrast with the sartorially armored male: *The Lady's Magazine* in 1803 notes that "with the ladies, it is the object to shew how little will do for a dress; with the gentlemen, how much they can carry without fatigue. Hence the total disuse of silk, linen and cambric, and the substitution of broad-cloth and leather" ("On Modern Taste and Style" 375). Similarly, in 1807 *La Belle Assemblée* dictates that "the dress of women should differ in every point from that of men. This difference ought even to extend to the choice of stuffs; for a woman inhabited in cloth is less feminine than if she were clothed in transparent gauze, in light muslin, or in soft and shining silks" ("Fashion" 196).

This concern with difference gave special éclat to women's breasts. Consider, for instance, the "written clothing" (in Barthes's phrase) of this 1806 passage from *La Belle Assemblée* describing the fashionable ideal:

> Her elegant and delicate figure charms the eye while it awakens desire; and the bosom of this new Hebe, agitated by a sentiment which she cannot define, fills the soul with involuntary perturbation. Tell me, what art is capable of embellishing this celestial perfection? Would you cover it with diamonds? Would you load it with parasitical luxury? O, no!—every ornament would conceal a grace, would rob it of a charm. (79)

The fashionable stress laid on women's physical exposure and on sexual difference offers substantiation not only to the theory that women's fashions are created to attract men but also on the zeitgeist theory that fashions in clothing mirror social and cultural change (Steele 20–21)—in this instance a social interest during wartime in promoting both masculine machismo and female reproductiveness and nurturance. Important also in this contract society was the explicit segregation of women in the private sphere.

For all these purposes Hebe, the goddess singled out for admiring comparison when there is discussion of beautiful breasts, perfectly fills the ideological bill. Allusion to her carries its own erotic frisson, since it recalls the story that most clearly links her to turn-of-the-century fashion: she preceded Ganymede as cupbearer to the gods but lost that position because as she went about her duties one day, she tripped and in the fluster bared her bosom. Hebe, then, acted out what the fashions of the day continually promised.

Yet in another account Hebe was not relieved of her duties in disgrace after this incident. Ganymede took her place, but only because she, daughter of Zeus and Hera, was bestowed upon the apotheosized Heracles as the heavenly reward for his labors: maiden youth and delicate beauty given into the keeping of ultimate macho. And she is maiden youth in its most submissively domestic form. An angel in the Olympian house, she acts as attendant upon her mother, Hera, and her brother Ares as well as upon her father and all his court (Barthell 30–31).

Hebe can nonetheless serve to signify as well a complexity in the nature of fashion's signs missing from both the sex appeal theory and the zeitgeist theory. As a system of signs, fashions can simultaneously communicate different, even contradictory, things to their wearers and their viewers. A simple version, a variant on the sexual attraction theory, is that women, while using a variety of fashions to lure men, make them serve at the same time as signals of dominance over other women (Steele 27). While not denying the presence of this motivation, I suggest that the fashion code can communicate to its wearer a very different message about herself from the one signaled to others. Besides dressing for men and against other women, besides *seeming* to dress for herself as a Girardian strategy for attracting the narcissistic desire or envy of both sexes (for I am by no means discounting these motives), a woman can simultaneously use dress in self-celebration. The same signal, the exposed breast—sign of the goddess Hebe—can carry totally different messages.

As we know, the household of Hera and Zeus was not that of a domestically affectionate nuclear family. According to one account, Hebe was born not through a union between Hera and Zeus but through parthenogenesis (Hera conceived her after eating wild lettuce), and Barthell describes her as "a sort of female fountain of youth" (30). Thus Hebe is not necessarily or simply the archetypal daughter; she is also archetypal projection and expression of the Mother Goddess's power, her eternal youth, and her self-sufficient, ever-abundant creativity.

Two images, with their accompanying commentaries, taken from the opening pages of *La Belle Assemblée* for the successive months of August and September 1808, serve as evidence of the way in which the Hebe archetype infiltrated maternal ideology. The first is of Anna Maria Stanhope, Marchioness of Tavistock, placed socially by the commentary as "the eldest daughter of the Earl of Harrington," though in the paragraphs that follow the earl gets no further mention. Stressed early, as it is in virtually all these biographical memoirs, is her seclusion within the domestic sphere: "Because of the delicate privacy of her education, she is as yet not known to the public." That education is also characterized as "in the extreme cautious and skilfully conducted" so as to provide her with "those more solid acquisitions of taste and judgment which augment the dignity, without impairing the amiable softness of her sex." These remarks build toward the fourth and central paragraph of the little account, which turns upon the formative power behind this paragon: "Her Mother, the Countess of Harrington, who has educated, principally under her own maternal control and inspection, a very numerous family, has paid a more particular attention to her elder daughter" ("Anna Maria Stanhope" 1).

The accompanying engraving of her image (fig. 3), in which her large eyes

Fig. 3. "The Most Noble Marchioness of Tavistock." Engraving from *La Belle Assemblée* 5 (1808). (*By permission of the British Library, London*)

are raised in an expression at once submissive and titillating, underscores the written message. Here is an eclectic secular icon: the drapery, the coronal of roses, the seated cherub give the image a vague iconographical relation to representations of the Virgin Mary; but the cherub bears the quiver of Eros, the classical key design adorns the drapery, and that material swirls around to enhance but not to conceal the central focus of the design—the white breasts lifted out toward the viewer by the scalloped lily of the bodice—not Mary but Hebe.

The portrait embellishing the subsequent issue of *La Belle Assemblée* similarly combines voluptuousness and submission in its youthful charm; it depicts the Countess of Harrington, the mother who had exerted such a formative influence on the Marchioness of Tavistock (fig. 4). After a paragraph-long list of her "numerous and illustrious family," the text returns to the importance of that role: "Her own talents and accomplishments are admirably reflected in

Fig. 4. "The Right Honourable Countess of Harrington." Engraving from *La Belle Assemblée* 5 (1808). (*By permission of the British Library, London*)

those of her numerous and amiable offspring, principally educated under her superintendence" ("Countess of Harrington" 1).

I will consider shortly the stress laid on the mother as educator; here my interest is rather in these images of the divinized feminine. The text and the pictured expressions do nothing to call male dominance into question, but the extreme décolletage can be read as the triumphant display of a "petit a" in the possession of women and denied to men: breasts, sign of their power to mother, to nurture, to shape an ever-recurring cycle of physical and social life which gives them, as its presiding officiants, a participatory eternal youth.

I am describing, let me stress, a fantasy conveyed by these images, not the actualities of women's lives. But such fantasies wield a power of their own, attested to by the evidence of men's uneasiness with these fashions. Women's clothing carried another message besides signaling a vulnerability and a sexual dependence designed to call forth male interest and protection.

The Cunningtons' comments on women's discarding of underwear at the turn of the century do not fully analyze this dual message. When they ascribe the new fashion to "a war-time method of sex attraction," they make an explicit point of the fact that these Regency modes were not "an expression of physical emancipation" and thus differed from "similar experiments in modern times." So ends their paragraph on this matter, but earlier in the same paragraph they state, "Feminine underclothing was reduced to a point where it almost ceased to express either class distinction or sex attraction" (97). Insofar as it did not express "sex attraction"—that is, women's admission of a dependence on men that through compulsory heterosexuality maintained the given order within social institutions—what did it express?

Since the veiling of a woman's body has been associated in both the Islamic and the Judeo-Christian traditions with a male "owner's" exclusive sexual rights (Steele 15), this *un*veiling can signal defiance of that prerogative, and was indeed read in that way during the Regency period. A man writing from Paris in late 1801, for instance, has these comments on waltzing: "As to the waltz, I was astonished at the decency with which that very indecent dance was danced by the young Parisians; who placing their arms around the uncovered persons of the handsomest women in the room, yet had sufficient command of themselves not to shock either their partners or the company, by being guilty of the slightest impropriety." When he mentions to an elderly lady his surprise at the men's "extraordinary forbearance," she replies, "Croyez-moi, monsieur . . . nos jeunes gens voient tout cela avec l'indifférence la plus parfaite." ("Believe me, sir . . . the young see all that with total indifference" [my translation].) The author draws his moral: "That female is not less deficient in coquetry, and in the art of commanding the attentions of men, than in every principle of decency, who wantonly exposes to the common gaze of passing curiosity those attractions *which are only valuable as long as the sight of them is the exclusive privilege of a favored lover*" ("Letter from Paris" 631; my emphasis).

In the following year *The Lady's Magazine,* while continuing to serve as verbal and iconic publicist of the new fashions, ran long excerpts from John Bowles's *Reflexions Political and Moral at the Conclusion of the War.* The final selection from the book treats women's self-exposure not as a strategic mistake in a laudable plan to gain masculine attention but as a revolutionary act: "He must have a very superficial knowledge of human nature—he must be consummately ignorant of the structure of the social machine—who does not see in this disposition [to sacrifice decency at the shrine of fashion] a much more formidable enemy than Bonaparte himself, with all his power, perfidy, and malice" (585). Bowles is of the opinion that "female modesty is the last barrier of civilized society" because without it, a "torrent of licentiousness and profligacy" is let loose. Women must show "extreme delicacy, bashfulness, and reserve" in order to hold in check violent male aggressions (585). His, in other words, is another version of the not-so-veiled threat that women enjoy protection from male violence only through submission before male dominance. Sensibly (on his terms) he does not bring up the possibility of women's *self*-possession as a catalyst that could dissolve existing social institutions; but the thought is implicit in his warning that the immodest woman "disturbs the order and endangers the safety of civil society itself" (587).[12]

Admittedly, since breasts were an erogenous zone that strongly attracted the attention of the eighteenth- or nineteenth-century man, their unveiling can serve as at best an ambivalent declaration of a woman's independence. Better evidence that women were using fashion (in part) to signal their sense of possessing their own fecund bodies lies in their adoption of the six-month pad, since big bellies, the focus of male eroticism in earlier centuries, had ceased to fascinate European men (Hollander 97–98). Significantly also, the outcry from male columnists and cartoonists against the revival of the pad was immediate. The sexual politics involved can best be understood through a reading of yet another vehicle for masculine protest, Robert Woodbridge's one-act farce *The Pad*.

Men, not women, dominate the action of this play: Sir Simon Meagre, who hopes for an heir but is unhappily married to a shrewish wife; Captain Credulous, who imagines himself happily married but returns from sea to find his wife apparently pregnant; and Lovejoke, the wit whose plotting undoes the "indecent" practice of padding.

Lovejoke realizes instantly that the Captain's wife is padded but leads the Captain on in his fears and arranges a rendezvous between the two for further discussion. Meanwhile, he persuades Sir Simon that his lady is pregnant and has both of them come to the same meeting, called, in Sir Simon's mind, so that he can give the assembled company the joyful news of his expected heir. When he makes the announcement, his wife is enraged, while Mrs. Credulous suffers the embarrassment of public disclosure of her husband's marital fears. The husbands, of course, are made to look fools as well. The Captain expostulates with Lovejoke:

But, Sir, we are all then your jest.

Lovejoke

Be calm.—The whole of my conduct has been a well-meant satire on so indecent a practice—not guided by any desire of uselessly tormenting you, but by a wish of being instrumental in exploding a custom, at which nature and reason equally revolt.

Captain

You might have effected this, I think, Sir, without thus publicly exposing us all.

Lovejoke

NO, PUBLIC RIDICULE IS EVER MORE EFFECTUAL FOR REFORMATION THAN PRIVATE ADMONITION.

. . .

I am sure none of the *ladies present* [in the audience] will hereafter offend in the same point; well convinced that *Confusion* and *Shame* must ever attend those, who "*outstep the Modesty of Nature.*"

(35–37; author's emphasis)

Words like "nature" and "reason" flag the presence of ideology. Interestingly, the play never for a moment examines the practice of padding from the

women's point of view; it never asks *why* they pad. But it does take up the fact
that padding exacerbates male fears about the indeterminate nature of paternity. Men cannot allow the sly pad to call into question, even symbolically,
their control over women's reproduction. Like Bowles, Woodbridge chooses
to ignore the possibility that women strapped on their pads as a way of
mocking that control. To verbalize it as such a revolt would give it a reality it
never attains when left unspeakable.

Thus the contradiction enunciated by Davidoff and Hall between "claims
for women's superiority and their social subordination" informs the significance of Regency fashion: women's flimsy, revealing garments encode a sexual vulnerability and socioeconomic dependence prescribed by a contractual
system arranged among men; yet by their allusion to the drapery outlining or
declining from the forms of goddesses in antique statuary, these garments also
serve as exhibitions of female autonomy and fertility. They are power clothes.

The Mother-Educator

Another version of the same contradiction, here between women's powerless-
ness as "relative creatures" and their apparently autonomous power as mothers, complicates the abundant literature on the theme of the mother as educator. On the one hand, the exhortations that women, confined to a domestic
sphere, serve the needs of men, infants, and children have as their rationale
women's presumed incapacity for all the important work of the world that the
superior intelligence and stronger will of men must be given freedom to do.
But on the other hand, such negative reinforcement of the argument for
separate spheres, while always present as an undercurrent, gets less actual
articulation, particularly through the fantasies conjured up in stories written
for a female readership, than does a flatly contradictory view: women, men's
moral superiors—and that necessarily involves superiority of will and of the
intellectual perceptiveness directing will—function as the true guiding force in
a social system constantly put at risk by men's irresponsibility at best, depravity at worst.

A good example of the negative statement of the case is an essay signed
"Clementina" in the July 1803 issue of *The Lady's Magazine,* titled "On the
Difference Between the Sexes." The essay begins, as is customary in such
polemics right up to those appearing at present over the signature of Pope
John Paul II, with the assertion that the differences between the sexes are so
great as to make moral comparisons irrelevant: "The female sex has always
been considered the weaker; but it is no imperfection in a dove to want the
strength of an eagle." The following sentence, thesis for the whole essay, then
sets up a moral comparison detrimental to women: "There are certainly many
actions becoming of women which would greatly disgrace a man" (341). Moreover, the source of women's inadequacy is their motherhood: "Our wise
creator having destined women to be the mothers of mankind, they are hence,
in general, more subject to infirmities, accidents, and diseases than men,

whose structure of body is robuster than theirs." This physical liability, this lack of bodily integrity, betrays a corresponding mental slackness. And as, by the law of nature, the mind generally corresponds with the body, the minds of men are in general stronger than those of women, "though Nature sometimes produces prodigies of both sexes" (342).[13]

Two issues earlier, in May 1803, the same magazine ran a selection, "On the Female Character," from the redoubtable Thomas Gisborne's *Enquiry into the Duties of the Female Sex,* which arrives at something like the same conclusion but by a more circuitous route—so circuitous, indeed, that we must survey a considerable expanse of it:

> Examine the domestic proceedings of savage tribes in the old world and in the new, and ask who is the best daughter and the best wife. The answer is uniform. She who bears with superior perseverance the vicissitudes of seasons, the fervour of the sun, the dews of night. . . . [S]he who stands dripping and famished before her husband, while he devours, stretched at ease, the produce of her exertions; waits his tardy permission without a word or look of impatience; and feeds, with the humblest gratitude and shortest intermission of labour, on the scraps and offals which he disdains: She, in a word, who is most tolerant of hardship and of unkindness. When nations begin to emerge from gross barbarism, every new step which they take towards refinement is commonly marked by a gentler treatment, and more reasonable estimation of women; and every improvement in their opinions and conduct respecting the female sex, prepares the way for additional progress in civilization. (254)

In essentials, Gisborne's argument resembles Rousseau's in *Emile;* women's physical vulnerability makes them dependent on men, who will inevitably abuse their superior position. Revolt is not feasible, and so the "best" woman is the one who acquires the most stoicism and patience (*Emile* 333). So, even in the evocation of a barbaric past, Gisborne equates hardships resulting from natural phenomena with those created by male selfishness, sloth, and violence. Still, this anthropological excursus becomes so dramatic and so potentially relevant to an ongoing reality rather than to a past or distant one that he runs the danger of stirring up revolt among his women readers rather than the masochistic submission he intends to inspire. Part of his difficulty lies in his readers' imagined viewpoint: we are watching these noble savage women as they go about their daily tasks, but we are also seeing the lolling, voracious men through the women's eyes. So Gisborne switches abruptly to the position of males (i.e., "nations") and returns to their hands, though without explanation, a superior moral responsibility demonstrated through their courtly concern for women. Gisborne's tightrope walk, then, maintains women as social subordinates through their dependence on masculine recognition of their moral worth—a recognition that also reestablishes men's moral superiority.

Although one can fairly generalize that maintenance of the status quo between genders, Gisborne's desideratum, is also an overarching purpose manifested in each particular item of journals such as *The Lady's Magazine* and *La Belle Assemblée,* the entries do not all adopt Gisborne's strategy. In place of his implied scenario in which a man provides courtly protection in return for women's obedient service, a very different one emerges: a blameless wife and mother, morally superior to her scapegrace husband, finally distances herself from his ribald and irresponsible practices in order to devote total, loving attention to her child, usually a daughter. The husband, moved to repentance by her example, returns to a domestic life ordered under her direction.[14]

The "plots" are similar in that both successfully remove women from the public sphere, but in the second case women's moral superiority manifests itself through their repudiation of public power and its attendant temptations. Also it is clearer that the task of child rearing *must* be women's not because men have sloughed off tedious duties but because men are incapable of the selfless sense of responsibility it demands. So, paradoxically, the more bullying, rapacious, irresponsible, and ungrateful men are represented to be, the stronger the argument for women's life of dedicated, self-abnegating service.

Gisborne is one of Nancy Cott's sources for her analysis of women's constructed "passionlessness." Interestingly, the quoted passage from Gisborne also bears the dim outline of a matriarchal theory that would become much more sharply focused in the nineteenth century and that persists to the present day. Phylogenetic and anthropological in its earlier formulations by Johann Bachofen and Jane Harrison, it gathers an ontogenetic component through Freudian descriptions of pre-Oedipal bliss. In a prehistoric (i.e., unrecorded and unrecordable) past of which we have only traces, the human race as a whole, and each human infant in particular, has passed through a period of noncompetitive, peaceful, and joyous existence under the aegis of a maternal care giver. Like passionlessness, this concept has a history of "serviceability" (in Cott's word) to feminist thinking and strategizing, but its surfacing here in Gisborne bolsters the argument that, far from being an alternative to male dominance, this dream of a mother realm assuages *and thus maintains* the hierarchicalized gender and social system firmly in place.[15] Shelley was one of those drawn by the power of this fantasy, and its formulation within *Prometheus Unbound* will come up for much further discussion; thus its adumbration in a work such as Gisborne's demands this brief notice.

While ideologically canny—as one can tell from its long life right up to the present moment—the strategy that constructs the maternal feminine as more caring than the paternal has a telling circular effect on the "family romance" already created by strengthening the bond between mother and infant. Like the fantasy in which husband and infant are co-participants in the act of breast-feeding, focus on the mother as sole agent and inculcator of sentiment sets up a rivalry between the two in which they compete for both her sexual notice and her maternal nurturance. I think, then, that Shelley's exposure to fantasies of this sort should be kept in mind when we turn later to biographical specifics about his feelings toward Timothy Shelley. And here I am also thinking of Shelley as "typical"; the tyrannical husband/father of these fantasies simply does not offer masculinity as a model for moral action, whereas the mother is a reservoir of moral power.

"The Libertine Reclaimed" in the April 1795 issue of *The Lady's Magazine* can serve as type for the plot I have in mind.[16] A dissipated man of fashion, Mr. Fairfax, marries a beautiful and virtuous heiress. She gives birth to a daughter, but shortly thereafter Fairfax returns to his debauched life. His wife, on a small annuity, moves to "a romantic part of Derbyshire . . . endeavouring to forget her faithless husband in her admiration of the beauties of nature, and her attention to the education of her child" (159). She is engaged in precisely this task—"having her child, the lovely Charlotte, read"—on a fine summer morning when a man comes to the door urgently seeking help for someone badly wounded in a duel. The "someone" is, of course, Fairfax, embroiled in a quarrel over his mistress. His wife tends him ceaselessly and restores him to physical health. Finally appreciative of her, he begs her forgiveness (in terms I will discuss shortly), and both rejoice in his reclamation.

This trite little fantasy takes on a certain prophetic solemnity when one considers its context, or at least it offers another small piece of evidence in corroboration of the Wildean view that life imitates art. Just preceding "The Libertine Reclaimed" is the opening article of the issue, "Account of the Arrival, and Ceremony of Nuptials of Her Royal Highness, the Princess of Wales," which describes the marriage of Caroline of Brunswick to George, Prince of Wales. The juxtaposition was an editorial commentary that would not have been lost on even the most sequestered country reader, since the prince had for years been England's most conspicuous libertine (Hibbert 104–32). But no one at the time could have foreseen that Princess Caroline would give birth within the next year to a daughter named Charlotte, and that within two years, separated from the prince—but also, unlike Mrs. Fairfax in the story, from her daughter—she would live in comparative seclusion in a small house outside London.

Princess Caroline was not, to judge by the historical evidence, such a paragon of gentleness and irreproachable virtue as Mrs. Fairfax; but the way in which the key elements of her story paralleled the fantasy spun out in different versions of this common plot may well have contributed to the strong popular sympathy for her in the press, coupled with execrations against the "incorrigible" prince and his "most disgraceful connections" (Hibbert 155). In 1800 the *Lady's Monthly Museum* described her in terms that made her a domestic model: "What may have influenced her Highness's choice of this kind of seclusion, we cannot be expected to know, but this truth is very extensively known and felt,—that her time there is principally devoted to deeds of benevolence, which give additional lustre even to her exalted rank" ("The Princess of Wales" 3). She was the subject in March 1806 of *La Belle Assemblée*'s lead memoir, accompanied by a portrait. The editors rather cleverly got around the problem of offering personal commentary about a situation that demanded the greatest possible editorial discretion by translating from the German certain passages of Joachim Heinrich Campe's *Travels in England,* which had been published in 1804.

In Campe's account, Princess Caroline is the very paragon of the mother-educator. Emphasized early are her thrift, practicality, and nurturing management: she shows him her vegetable garden, whose produce, she notes, annually brings in "a handsome sum." But the bulk of the extract is given over to discussion of her mothering. Campe first exclaims over the interest and personal attention she gives to the raising of "eight or nine poor orphan children, to whom she has the condescension to supply the place of a mother. Her own is the child of the State, and according to the constitution of the country, must not, alas! be educated by herself" (67). By a certain twist in the argument, however, even the intrusion of her real separation from her daughter becomes proof of her supremely educative role during the one day of each week in which they are together: "Such tender attachment, and such fervent love as this child, only seven years old, manifests to her Royal Mother, is assuredly seldom seen in persons of that rank. Her eyes are incessantly fixed on the beauteous countenance of her tender mother; and what eyes!" (68).

In the very next issue of *La Belle Assemblée* the editors make an explicit statement about the ideological purpose behind these "Biographical Sketches": they are "proposing as examples those who are naturally looked up to as superior in station, and whose pre-eminence in virtue thus entitles them to a double distinction" ("Editors' Note" 121). The timing of their essay on Princess Caroline suggests either that the editors believe that upper-class women must be used as such exemplars no matter what their actual conduct or that they wished to make a positive statement about her when her conduct was under particular scrutiny. Rumors suggesting that one—or perhaps more—of the orphan children receiving her generous care was in fact her own child had become so widespread that a Commission of Enquiry into the matter was in the process of being formed (Hibbert 205–19). Although these accusations were spitefully motivated and remain unproven, Princess Caroline was certainly no Mrs. Fairfax. My point, however, bears not so much on her actual resemblance to the model as on the power of the model in making her exemplary.

A further instance of this dichotomy between a villainous, powerful, and irresponsible husband and an aggrieved, virtuous wife and mother merits discussion, in part because again its (at least putative) veracity adds to its power, allowing for a possible basis in fact to the many admitted fantasies, and in part because the foreign setting makes it possible for the narrator to be more forthright in drawing moral contrasts than when discussing English royals.

In March 1808 *La Belle Assemblée* recounts at some length the sad history of Queen Caroline Matilda, youngest sister of George III, who was married in 1766 at the age of fifteen to Christian VII of Denmark. He is characterized (not unfairly, one gathers) as sexually depraved, foul-tempered, and irreligious, intellectually and physically lazy, spineless and cowardly, and careless of family obligations. The queen's moral integrity, strength, and social responsibility stand out all the more vividly by comparison, and the narrative consistently shows them as operative through her mothering. Much is made, for instance, of the fact that she first met Struensee, the personality most potentially damaging to her reputation, when he came to the court as a physician; she grew to depend on him through their mutual care for her son, the Prince Royal, after his inoculation for smallpox ("Memoir" 106). (His father, it goes without saying, felt no concern at all.)

In 1772 Struensee was charged with having an adulterous affair with the queen, under torture confessed to the charge, and was executed. The queen was then forced to sign a confession of her own, but the power of her brother made it possible for her to escape with her life to the palace of Zell in the electorate of Hanover—but without her two children, the point the narrative most stresses: "It was not the crown that she regretted; her children alone employed her care. The feelings of the sovereign were absorbed in those of the mother; and if she wept the day when she quitted the isle of Zealand, it was because she was bereft of the dear objects of her maternal fondness" (107). (The narrative, consistent with its insistence on maternal virtue, maintains her innocence, though the biographical record suggests that Caroline Mathilda may in fact have had a liaison with Struensee [Wilkins II, 149–50]).

The scoundrel fathers in these stories have so little parental feeling that the children seem totally, virtually parthenogenetically, to belong to their angelic mothers. An interesting, even more parthenogenetic variant appears in the occasional story in which the selfish and tyrannical father disappears altogether, and a young woman cares for an adopted infant girl (I shall discuss later the appeal that this particular fantasy had for Shelley). For instance, in "The Abandoned Infant: A Tale," which ran in *The Lady's Magazine* in March 1794, an unmarried young woman, Lucinda Harvey, finds an abandoned female infant; with her mother's help and consent she nurtures it, but the resultant suspicion throughout the neighborhood that the child is her own leaves her still unmarried ten years later. A Mr. Horton, who has returned from India after a long absence, courts her until he gets wind of the gossip and then grows cool. Now, the narrator has already made the bland statement that Lucinda was initially drawn to Mr. Horton by "the resemblance there was between his features and those of the portrait she had found on the deserted Laura." We can take it, then, that she is not totally surprised when, aware of his change in attitude, she finds the occasion to tell him of the adoption, show him the portrait, and thus learn—or confirm—that he is Laura's father: "In a short time after, Lucinda was married to Mr. Horton, and, triumphing over every scandalous suggestion, became, by law, the mother of the adopted child" (120).

Stories like "The Abandoned Infant" are as unabashedly freighted with ideological messages when directed to their middle-class women readers as were Hannah More's *Tracts,* designed for the working class. The conjunction made between marriage to Mr. Horton and the legality of Lucinda's motherhood grants male dominance in the public sphere. Also, after a return from whatever tasks were assigned to him in the business of conquering India, Mr.

Horton, through the agency of Lucinda, confesses and repents his irresponsible conquest of Laura's mother—which is to say that it is women's assigned social function to assuage, as far as possible, the injuries caused through the doctrine of individualism precisely in order to keep its political, social, and economic practices in place. Still, a possible countermessage could get through. The young woman's name, Lucinda, calls up aurally if not etymologically the goddess Lucina, Diana's appellation when she presides over childbirth (Barthell 221). So if "by law" Lucinda needs Mr. Horton to become a mother, the unspoken antithesis is that she needs him in no other way. As avatar of the powerful virgin patroness of motherhood, she triumphs within her own mothering sphere.

As my discussion of the Countess of Harrington and her daughter suggested, aristocratic women were singled out to serve as models of the mother-educator. In *La Belle Assemblée* Queen Charlotte herself receives special admiration for being a mother who carefully superintends the education of her many daughters—with no mention of what might have gone awry with the sons ("Her Majesty" 1). But if middle-class women do not carry the name recognition of the "star" system set up in these magazines along socially hierarchical lines, their fictional counterparts, as we have seen, get much attention. Also, with the hierarchies still in place, middle-class women were addressed explicitly in conduct literature such as Anne Taylor's *Practical Hints to Young Females, on the Duties of a Wife, a Mother, and a Mistress of a Family* (1816) as themselves models in turn for those in the lower ranks. The image, if not the precise phrase, is "trickle down": "And although the influence of good example in the middle ranks can be but small upon those which are more elevated; yet it descends like a kindly shower upon such as are beneath them, and gives fertility to many a spot which would otherwise have remained sterile and unsightly" (iv–v).

The hierarchic thinking of a passage like this reflects the conditioning it also promulgates; it illuminates the conservative social function of the mystique of the mother-educator. Women's acceptance of a domestic role that subordinates them to men in that it involves them in the performance of given, not chosen, tasks and establishes the site of those tasks as one without access to political power at once creates, models, and indoctrinates a structured social system. Yet the radical potential of the doctrine lies precisely in its creation of a sphere in which "outside" political and social hierarchies are irrelevant, and only mother's law orders life.

What was that ordering supposed to involve? What were the specifics of the mother-educator's tasks? What were these paragons supposed to be doing when, in retirement, they devoted themselves to the education of their infants and children? First of all maintaining a system of surveillance: the Princess Sophia is described as having been educated "under the eye of her Majesty" ("Princess Sophia" 3), and while we may take it that the royal eye in such a case is metaphoric as well as metonymic, the exhortations to mothers usually insist that children should literally be constantly watched. Such a thought is implicit in Maria Edgeworth's comment that "a dame school . . . should, as much as possible, resemble a large private family, where the mistress may be considered as the mother. The children should never be out of the sight of their mistress, and their plays, as well as their tasks, should be equally an object of her care" (*Continuation of Early Lessons* I, xxviii). To read such a passage is to observe, in Eagleton's phrasing, "power . . . shifting its location from centralized institutions to the silent, invisible depths of the subject itself" (27). But note that in those depths power is experienced as the internalized maternal gaze.

Simply observing the children to keep them from physical harm—as well as moral, particularly sexual, wrong, *bien entendu*—is only part, perhaps even the lesser part, of the task. The mother is to involve herself in the children's activities, both passively as a model for behavior, and actively as one who uses the countless incidents of the day to inculcate intellectual curiosity and moral awareness. Lady Eleanor Fenn introduces her *Rational Sports,* a compendium of dialogues based on such imagined incidents, by saying: "It is the province of the mother to tincture the mind. She has the opportunities of infancy and early childhood—she has those of the vacations from school—she must seize every occasion of leading her son gently and insensibly to a taste for *rational amusement*" (vii; author's emphasis). Thus the process by which, during lactation, the nurse's soul enters the infant continues during an education when the mother's influence serves as a dye permeating the childish mind.

The precise topics to be engaged in this ongoing and constant discussion between the mother and her charge or charges will be taken up shortly, but the difficulties involved need immediate attention. After Fenn has given a few examples of ideal interactions, she imagines a dialogue between herself and a mother-reader who is just taking in the fact that she, as mother-educator, must absorb herself totally and constantly in the child's experience as part of this molding process. The mother exclaims:

> "She must sacrifice everything!"
> And do you call it a sacrifice?—Is it not her first *duty?*—ought it not to be her first *pleasure?*—nay, it *is* her first pleasure; for I write for *real moth-ers,* not ladies who leave their offspring to imbibe the follies of the kitchen, whilst they roam to places of diversion. (ix)

The emphases are all Fenn's; with them she pretty well bludgeons a recalcitrant mother into acceptance of her role. Others take a more positive approach. The author of "An Essay upon Female Education," which appeared in the July 1798 issue of the *Lady's Monthly Museum,* addresses "those mothers who are, either by nature or on principle, inclined to resist the allurements which dissipation offers"; in return for a "private method of instruction" they are rewarded by the "infantine caresses of their children" and receive therefrom "a refinement of felicity, to which the gay and the frivolous are utter strangers" (52).

Hannah More disdains a sentimental—and erotic—appeal of this kind and offers instead mother power: "But the great object to which *you,* who are or may be mothers, are more especially called, is the education of your children.

If we are responsible for the use of influence in the case of those over whom we have no immediate control, in the case of our children we are responsible for the exercise of acknowledged *power:* a power wide in its extent, indefinite in its effects, and inestimable in its importance" (III, 44; author's emphasis). Edgeworth makes the same point, though less emphatically, when she writes: "A little praise or blame, a smile from the mother, or a frown, a moment's attention, or a look of cold neglect, have the happy, or the fatal power of repressing or exciting the energy of a child, of directing his understanding to useful or pernicious purposes" (*Practical Education* III, 229).

In fact it is unusual for power to be as nakedly asserted as the basis of the relationship between mother and children as it is in More's remarks; writers of the conduct books usually insist that the mother's power must be muffled; her moral teachings will be most effective when they come not as commands but as the counsels of a trusted, constant, and intimate friend. The author of "An Essay upon Female Education" asks: "If a child is in the habit of considering its mother, or governess, as a *rigid judge,* rather than as a *tender friend,* how can it be supposed to act with that ingenuous confidence which it so essentially necessary to its future welfare?" (54). Actually, More's straightforward recognition of what is occurring in the socialization process as she conceives it seems preferable to an injunction like that of John Moir that it be concealed. Addressing mothers about the education of their daughters, he writes: "Bind them to your purposes by every possible expedient; but your influence will be rather a curse than a blessing, unless you can make them in love with their chains. They should have no will but yours. And the great secret of using it with discretion is, to make them obey from choice, not from compulsion" (*Female Tuition* 117–18).

All the discussion so far turns upon the socializing aspect of education; children's insertion into a milieu structured through gender and class was women's, particularly mothers', responsibility. But mothers ideally were to offer intellectual training as well. So *La Belle Assemblée* holds Madame de Genlis as exemplary in that, before writing about the education of children generally, she functioned as teacher to her own. And again the text hammers away at the contrast between an uncaring, irresponsible socialite mother unworthy of the name and the secluded mother-governess: "At the age of thirty years, an age at which most females of her rank and pretension are desirous only of figuring in the fashionable world, Madame (then the Countess) de Genlis shut herself up in the convent of Bellechasse, that she might complete the education of her daughters, and initiate into the rudiments of science, infants who were still in their cradles" ("Madame de Genlis" 230).

The "rudiments of science" would eventually involve the three R's, but only as the culmination of a process beginning literally in the cradle. Elizabeth Hamilton writes with scorn about the mother who has "never assisted her child in the acquisition of a single idea during infancy" and then "expresses the utmost anxiety for its learning to read" (II, 47). While Hamilton does not explicitly discuss the importance of infants' cross-modal perceptions as Erasmus Darwin does, she implicitly draws connections still made by developmental psychologists between the infant's interaction with the mother-caretaker in sharing varied and interesting sensual experiences on the one hand and the acquisition and use of language on the other. And her ideas had wide dissemination. *Letters on the Elementary Principles of Education* went into multiple editions, and large portions of it were reprinted in *The Lady's Magazine,* among them this passage: "Every distinction which the mind can make you may reckon a new idea acquired. It is in your power to multiply these ideas at a very early period. It is likewise unfortunately in the power of a foolish nurse to retard the natural progress of the mind by perpetually interrupting its attention" (II, 52; *Lady's Magazine* 33 [1802]: 81).

Earlier in the *Letters,* Hamilton demurred on paternalistic and practical grounds at Edgeworth's unqualified prohibition of all intercourse "between the children of the family and domestics of every denomination" (I, 106), but in this instance she calls up the bugaboo of the "foolish nurse" with the very strong implication that an infant left much in the charge of servants will not make the same intellectual progress as one who is mother-reared. When she describes stages in the infant's progress toward speech, she thus makes its acquisition not the moment of separation from the mother but the mother's gift. In other words her scenario is much closer to Stern's and Vygotsky's than to Lacan's or Kristeva's, involving as it does shared "ideas" as preliminary to the shared use of signs.

Hamilton's emphasis on "distinct articulation" (II, 54) as an aid to proper discrimination among sounds also necessarily involves attention to the mother's voice and to her enunciation as the very medium for such discriminations. Like the creators of "Sesame Street," Hamilton considers it useful that children, even before moving from verbal to written signs, hear the letters of the alphabet: "Children are greatly assisted in this process [of distinguishing among articulated sounds] by teaching them, as soon as they acquire the use of speech, distinctly to pronounce the letters of the alphabet. This is seldom thought of, till children are taught their letters; their articulation is consequently seldom distinct till that period; and it may be observed, that the articulation of those who never learn to read, is seldom distinct through life" (II, 57).

Again, since servants are the more likely to be nonliterate, comes the veiled threat that the child's welfare is at risk unless the articulate voice calling forth the child's own is the mother's. And so Hamilton can be read as giving an importance analogous to that which Darwin places on the sight of the mother's breast to the "acoustic mirror" of the mother's voice. She writes: "The impressions made upon the mind through the medium of the sight are, I believe, the chief source of ideas in the period of infancy. That they are not, however, the only source, is obvious from the attention which children pay to sound" (II, 57–58).

The objection can well be made that a discussion of Hamilton's ideas, while edifying in itself perhaps in that it draws deserved attention to the work of a neglected writer, is not of special relevance to *Shelley's* acquisition of language, since Hamilton's work was published when he was eight. But I use Hamilton only because she is an explicit and articulate expositor of ideas already abroad in the culture. Books in which the same ideas are implicit had been pouring off the presses and running into multiple editions for years. Hamilton places herself in the pedagogic tradition of Locke and Edgeworth, but along with those theoretical treatises go the practical reading, spelling, story, and hymn books such as those by "Mrs. Lovechild" [Lady Eleanor Fenn], Anna Letitia Barbauld, Hannah More, Mary Wollstonecraft, and others.[17]

Typically such books, though written and illustrated so as to appeal to very young readers, include a preface directed specifically to mothers, exhorting them and encouraging them in their task as educators, while also suggesting possible uses for the little text. Such a preface to Lady Eleanor Fenn's *Infant's Friend* presupposes an interaction between mother and child in which every physical movement of the mother's lips, teeth, tongue, and throat serves as the child's visual model and oral guide:

> There is seldom sufficient attention paid to a very obvious method of leading on the Learner; namely that of giving him the vowel or diphthong in that particular word; for instance, I will suppose the Child to hesitate at *trace:* ask a,c,e; then r,a,c,e; then prefix *t.* Suppose him to be at a loss for the sound of *cheat;* only ask him *e,a,t;* then *h,e,a,t;* then *c,h,e,a,t:* thus he feels his way, and discovering, or rather recognizing the sound (for I suppose this to be the second time of going through the words) he retains a clearer idea than direct information would give him.   (x–xi)

True, the physicality of this process is only implied, but it is impossible to follow the suggested exercise without the mother's mouth and the child's mirroring each other in the way I have described. Also the author's very presentation makes it obvious that she conceives of the learning process as functioning through a constant dialogue between mother and child. Thus in *The Infant's Friend* her exposition on the teaching of syllables is constructed as an imaginary conversation initiated by the mother: "—Well! now you think you know every letter, meet with it where you may:—I have a mind to try you:—Shew me *m*—Very well!—Now shew me *a*—*m* and *a* spell *ma. . . .* I believe I may indulge you with a lesson of syllables. —We will begin.—Now take your pointer" (6).

Again, the child's sounds, produced through the manipulation of tongue, teeth, and lips, are both instituted and echoed by the mother's voice. Also the crossover from verbal to written signs is made with the mother's voice as bridge, while at the same time her voice creates an affective content that is constantly relational: the child's pride in achievement and thus pleasure in receiving the mother's notice gets recognition and response in the opening statement, though accompanied with a new challenge and a demand for further effort. The reward—"I believe I may indulge you with a lesson of syllables"—is the mother's further interest and attention along with the chance for future praise.[18] Significantly, one of the few recorded interactions between Shelley and his mother during his very early years turns upon her encouragement of his precocious linguistic power: the special notice she gave to his memorizing Gray's "Ode on the Death of a Favorite Cat" (Hogg, *Life* I, 23).

In *Parsing Lessons for Young Children* (1798), Fenn makes it clear in her preface that she is actually addressing only female parents, and again the infusion of breast milk becomes a trope for the infusion of knowledge: "Certainly Providence has designed our early youth should be under the guidance of Females; they must supply milk; they must support the tottering steps of infancy in a figurative, as well as a literal sense. Men of learning are incapable of stooping sufficiently low to conduct those who are but entering the paths" (vi).

Involved in this "stooping" is the mother's participation in the child's "prattle": "Children, if you expect them to read with spirit and propriety, must be supplied with lessons suited to their taste; that is, *prattle,* like their own" (vii). Her use of that word serves as an allusion to one of her early successes, *The Rational Dame; or Hints Towards Supplying Prattle for Children* (1784), a book that uses the incidents and observations of a supposed walk to educate children in beginners' botany and zoology, all in the context of a dialogue between an attentive mother and a curious child.

That maternal presence and attention, expressed through the dialogic voice, is in Fenn's opinion the medium or ambience surrounding the acquisition of all early knowledge. So, after the usual warning against the mother's delegation of her duties to servants ("Infants learn much before they speak, and would learn much more than they do, were they not nursed in the lap of Folly"), she insists that "the watchful eye of *maternal* tenderness is needed to descry the moment when attention awakens or flags; *maternal* affection alone can supply assiduity, patience, and condescension for unremitting infusions of simple, clear, and just ideas" (xi–xii; author's emphasis).

Edgeworth is writing, then, within a well-established tradition in the stress she too places on oral communication in the opening "Address to Mothers" of *Continuation of Early Lessons* (1815), but she admits that the unremitting energy that children can bring to the acquisition of knowledge creates difficulties:

> How to fill up, from day to day, the aching void in the little breasts of children, is a question, that cannot easily be solved. When I recommend teaching, as much as possible, by oral instruction, I have this grand difficulty full in my view; but I hope to point out, that means may be found, by which, in some degree, it may be obviated. There is scarcely any object, which a child sees or touches, that may not become a subject for *conversation* and *instruction*.
>
> For instance, is the mother dressing?—the things on her dressing table are objects of curiosity to the child. The combs are of different sorts—horn, ivory, box, and tortoiseshell.   (xxi–xxii; author's emphasis)

Edgeworth's example suggests that her stress on oral communication is utilitarian, not psychological or metaphysical. Neither Wertherian angst nor Lacanian desire seems what she consciously means to convey through the startling phrase about "the aching void in the little breasts of children." Still, the very overstatement in the phrase suggests that the no-nonsense Edgeworth was influenced by a strong tendency in the discourse on mothering to move from a pedagogical to a theological dimension, the topic to be addressed in the next section.

The Mother God(dess)

The writers of educational treatises and texts whose work I discussed in the previous section—principally Edgeworth, Fenn, and Hamilton—might all be characterized as epistemological Lockeans, but none had taken a further step into Humean skepticism. On the contrary, authors of books for or about the education of children, though with differing degrees of fervor, saw the inculcation of religious values as virtually inseparable from the fostering of secular learning (Quayle 53). The close link between the two meant that the mother educating her children was serving also as an agent in the providential design for their salvation, and allusions to God's Providence feature largely in the little prefaces of exhortation directed to mothers.

I shall take up a few examples shortly but wish to call attention first to an interesting effect of the close association made between providential and maternal care. Involved is a comparison in which the mother's selfless and constant attention to the child's needs acts as a figure or sign of God's benefi-cent watchfulness. But at the point of explicit or implied comparison—mother/God—the unstated difference always present in metaphor can easily lose its impact before the resonance created between the two terms. A virtu-ally contradictory factor should possibly be considered as well: in a religious tradition that conceives God as an emphatically masculine Person, the ele-ment of difference is so strong in a mother-God comparison that the trope functions more effectively in conveying an idea about mothers than it does in describing the nature of God. It adds incalculably to the aura surrounding the idea of mother, lending it a divine numinosity. Any weakening of religious faith has a similar possible result: the God term of the trope fades, while the mother term transforms into the reified divine. What is more, in the general dismissal of men as possible care givers, the providential mother shares power with no masculine consort.

For instance, in the extended simile that makes up the fifth hymn of Anna Letitia Barbauld's *Hymns in Prose for Children,* one can see the mother's likeness to God shifting toward God's resemblance to her. And since the God term in the comparison lacks (for most of the book's readers) the experiential reality of the mother term, the metaphor tends to reify into something ap-proaching the deification of the human maternal: "As the mother moveth about the house with her finger on her lips, and stilleth every little noise, that her infant be not disturbed; as she draweth the curtains around its bed, and shutteth out the light from its tender eyes; so God draweth the curtains of darkness around us; so he maketh all things to be hushed and still, that his large family may sleep in peace" (38–39).

Let us come at the point from a slightly different direction: this literature calls up "the fantasy of the perfect mother," in the phrase used by Nancy Chodorow and Susan Contratto (54), both as a way of inspiring religious devotion to God and as a further inscription on women's subjectivities about their "nature" as mothers. But by bringing submerged recollections of infancy closer to the surface, the image can have more effect on the way mothers perceive themselves and are perceived by others than on people's experience of the nature of the Divine. So an edifying passage from Samuel Richardson, anthologized in both Wollstonecraft's *Female Reader* (1789) and Barbauld's *Female Speaker* (1811), uses, again, an extended simile to describe Providence as a fond mother, but the affect lavished on motherhood as the initial and extended term of the simile is so strong that the passage can be read as the comparison of Providence to an ideal mother: "See a fond mother encircled by her children. . . . [T]o these she dispenses a look, and a word to those; and, whether she grants or refuses, whether she smiles or frowns, it is all in tender love. Such to us, though infinitely high and awful, is Providence" (Barbauld 14–15).

The language used both by and about Mrs. Mason, the "mother-educator" of Wollstonecraft's *Original Stories from Real Life* (1791) makes her seem avatar of rather than medium for the Divine. True, Mrs. Mason is not the biological mother of the two spoiled girls put under her care; Wollstonecraft's recent experiences as a governess, their effect compounded by her ambivalent relationship with her own mother, led to this negation of the doctrine that the biological mother is the ideal educator. Mrs. Mason is, nonetheless, presented as a mother ideal, and one unencumbered by any Mr. Mason.

The book as a whole has the character of a little gospel, with the two girls as disciples instructed by Mrs. Mason through the parables to be found in the small incidents of everyday life. (There is, however, much closer surveillance of these pupils than of Jesus' disciples; Mrs. Mason "never suffered them to be out of her sight" [viii]). Space allows discussion of only a few out of many possible examples. At one point the children come to Mrs. Mason asking "in what manner they were to behave, to prove that they were superior to animals?" The answer involves, first of all, being tenderhearted to all the animal life encountered in this country setting. Such Shaftesburyian pedagogy is common to virtually all these hortatory works, and a poignant "abandoned baby bird" sequence is de rigueur in them. *Original Stories* is no exception, but Mrs. Mason carries the point even further than usual, linking natural sentiment to the evangelical moral counsels and using herself as supreme example of their fulfillment: "I, who never wantonly trod on an insect, or disregarded the plaint of the speechless beast, can now give bread to the hungry, physic to the sick, comfort to the afflicted, and, above all, am preparing you, who are to live forever, to be fit for the society of angels, and good men made perfect" (16–17). One hears similar scriptural echoes when Mrs.

Mason asks, "If I then am so careful not to wound a stranger, what shall I think of your behaviour, Mary?" (65)

As even these brief examples demonstrate, Mrs. Mason is strongly judgmental, but, like God, she is "never in a passion" (52). Her wrath directs itself to acts of injustice, and before her gaze the sinner simply comes to self-recognition. On one occasion, when the girls have misbehaved, Mrs. Mason leaves them for the night with "a kiss of peace," saying that she will instruct them in their fault in the morning: "I declare I cannot go to sleep, said Mary, I am afraid of Mrs. Mason's eyes—would you think, Caroline, that she who looks so very good-natured sometimes, could frighten one so?" (53).

Finally, at its conclusion the book becomes Mrs. Mason's gospel: "I now, as my last present, give you a book, in which I have written the subjects that we have discussed. Recur frequently to it, for the stories illustrating the instruction it contains, you will not feel in such a great degree the want of my personal advice" (175–76).

Wollstonecraft's text is particularly marked by this biblical allusiveness, but in numerous instances an image used in the Bible to illustrate the nature of God serves to describe the nature of motherhood. The flow of affective energy in such tropes transforms deific power into maternal charism. For instance, a story titled "Maternal Antipathy, Contrasted with Filial Piety," while describing the antithesis of the loving mother (and in the process displaying the fear of mother power also aroused by this emphasis on its strength),[19] characterizes the ideal mother through allusion to the text on God's love as shining on the just and the unjust: "The maternal affections ought to be displayed in an equitable proportion, and their invigorating influence disseminated like the rays of the sun, whose enlivening beams are in an equal manner shed upon the unworthy and the good" (264).

Fenn's *Mother's Grammar* contains a section devoted to readings in which the last entry is titled "The Tenderness of Mothers." In it a homely barnyard comparison between maternal care and the solicitude of a mother hen resonates with Jesus' lament over Jerusalem: "How often have I longed to gather your children, as a hen gathers her chicks under her wings, and you refused!" (Matt. 23:37–38). The passage she has excerpted from Percival's *Father's Instructions* begins:

> Mark that parent hen, said a father to his beloved son, with what anxious care does she call together her offspring, and cover them with her expanded wings. . . . Does not this sight suggest to you the tenderness of your mother? her watchful care protected you in the helpless period of infancy when she nourished you with her milk, taught your limbs to move, and your tongue to lisp its unformed accents; in childhood she has mourned over your little griefs, has rejoiced in your innocent delights, has administered to you the healing balm in sickness, and has instilled in your mind the love of truth, of virtue, and of wisdom. (*The Mother's Grammar* 94–95)

In the text that serves as source for the passage, a father is the moral instructor (as opposed to the physical caretaker) in the way that would have been deemed appropriate in a status society. Also, the situation imagined—a "father" in colloquy with his "beloved son"—makes the barnyard serve as mirror of the Heavenly City, with Father and Son in benediction over the maternal labors that are the sign of their constant presence in the world. But lifted by a woman author into a book called *The Mother's Grammar,* the passage carries a rather different message. For one thing, the father seems distanced from all aspects of child care, including socialization and the child's acquisition of language. Father and son are mere witnesses and beneficiaries of maternal actions transcending their capacities. Read that way, the associations called up by the image of the mother hen do not so much feminize the concept of God's Providence as deify the maternal.

The scriptural echoes at the conclusion of "The Libertine Reclaimed" have a similar effect of transferring the domestic sphere into the empyrean. When Mr. Fairfax, nursed by his wife back to bodily health and spiritual repentance, can at last speak, he says: "Most amiable and best of women, whom Providence seems to have bestowed on me to be my guardian angel . . . receive to your arms the returning and truly repentant prodigal" (160). The last phrases call up the parable of the Prodigal Son, image of sinful humankind, who learns at last the depth of his father's love and care for him, as Jesus would have the disciples learn the endlessness of God's love. But the image of selfless and bottomless love built up in this story's revision of the parable is conveyed through a woman, and very specifically a mother. So, while the apostrophe to her describes her as an "angel," the sentence by its conclusion has surrounded her with the divine aura. A passage in Barbauld's *Female Speaker* gives a similarly divine rather than merely angelic control to a mother within her sphere: "There is a world where no storms intrude, a haven of safety against the tempests of life. A little world of joy and love, of innocence and tranquillity. . . . This world is the well ordered home of a virtuous and amiable woman" (9).

The transition from angel to providential deity receives specific discussion in Nisbet's 1809 edition of Buchan's *Domestic Medicine,* discussed earlier, which also contained the revered doctor's *Advice to Mothers.* In his introduction to the *Advice,* William Nisbet includes this quotation from Buchan about the mother's social significance: "The more I reflect . . . on the situation of the mother, the more I am struck with the extent of her powers, and the inestimable value of her services. In the language of love, women are called angels; but this is a weak and silly compliment; they approach nearer to our ideas of the Deity: they not only create, but sustain their creation and hold its future destiny in their hands" (xiii).

The phrasing of all these passages offers yet more evidence, if such be needed, of an earnest Christianity already at work in Regency England to create the mores we call Victorian. The clothing imagined on these providential mothers, however, would not at this point have been the many-layered costume of the "passionless" Victorian angel but rather the fluttering draperies modeled after those worn by the nymphs and goddesses decorating the "antiquities" that were pouring into England, particularly from Italy. Lifted thence, they became incarnate in representations such as those by George Romney of Emma Hamilton. So in the ideology of motherhood permeating the upper and middle classes at the time of Shelley's birth, one finds the possibility of an eclectic fusion of Christian providential imagery with the classical evocations of the Mother Goddess under her many different names and forms of worship.

A major depository in England of Greek and Roman antiquities was the British Museum, which acquired Sir William Hamilton's collection (for a handsome sum) in 1772; that rapidly expanding establishment was also filling up with "Oriental" texts and artifacts such as the thirty-two volumes acquired in 1796 "as trophies of our Egyptian expedition" (*Synopsis of the Contents of the British Museum* xxiii). Meanwhile, English scholars and English merchants along with English soldiers and English adventurers were taking possession of Middle Eastern and Far Eastern territories, politically and economically, but also textually—both through the texts they collected at sites and by the transformation of sites into texts (Said 94). The knowledge they were gathering was extraordinarily diverse, complex, and arcane, and it also had extraordinarily wide dissemination to an interested public, including the readers of women's magazines. These publications carried reviews and digests of Oriental materials as a matter of course, and the tone of the reviewers suggests that they knew themselves to be addressing a well-educated readership. A single issue of *La Belle Assemblée* (3.34 [1808]), for example, contains a learned discussion of Zoroastrianism and an "Account of the City of *Palmyra*. Collected from Various Authors" (154–59)—among them Volney, Wood, and Bruce. The readers' acquaintance with those works is assumed, but the author also directs those interested in yet more information to the sources themselves. Since, as I noted earlier, Shelley may well have been one of those readers, this medium within popular culture takes on the dignity of a scholarly source.[20]

In 1806 the twenty-one-year-old Thomas Love Peacock made "Palmyra" the title poem of his first published volume. He could thereby hope to catch the interest of both men and women in a middle- and upper-class readership; even the quotations in his learned notes were from widely familiar sources: Wood and Volney as well as Gibbon, Ossian, Isaiah, and the Royal Society's *Philosophical Transactions*.[21] His "ruins" poem is a completely traditional working through of the memento mori theme and concludes with a paean to a strongly male deity:

> *Bow then to Him,* the Lord of All,
> Whose nod bids empires rise and fall,
> Earth, Heav'n and Nature's Sire:
> To Him who, matchless and alone,
> Has fix'd in boundless space his throne,
> Unchang'd, unchanging still, while worlds and suns expire!
> (VI, 22)

The rewritten version of "Palmyra"—so much altered as to be virtually a different poem—which Peacock published six years later concludes with a gendered dictotomy that consigns the desert wasteland, with its shattered remnants of former power, to the rule of masculine Time: "His mantle dark oblivion flings / Around the monuments of kings." In contrast, the last stanza hymns the feminine figure of virtue as a sky goddess, guide, and care giver:

> But ne'er shall earthly time throw down
>   The immortal pile that virtue rears:
> Her golden throne, and starry crown,
>   Decay not with revolving years:
> For he, whose solemn voice controlled
>   Necessity's mysterious sway,
> And yon vast orbs from chaos rolled
>   Along the elliptic paths of day,
> Has fixed her empire, vast and high,
> Where primogenial harmony,
> Unites, in ever-cloudless skies,
> Affection's death-divided ties;
> Where wisdom, with unwearying gaze,
> The universal scheme surveys,
> And truth, in central light enshrined,
> Leads to its source sublime the indissoluble mind.
>   (VI, 175)

Shelley's response, when Thomas Hookham sent him the volume, was that "the conclusion of 'Palmyra' [is] the finest piece of poetry I ever read" (*L* I, 325). Enthusiasm for Peacock's topic may have influenced his literary judgment. In the same letter to Hookham he mentions that he has begun "a little poem," *Queen Mab,* enclosing what he has written and adding that he probably has "matter enough for 6 more cantos" (I, 324). That would mean that he sent the first three cantos, in the second of which comes his own apostrophe to Palmyra.

When Queen Mab carries the spirit of the sleeping Ianthe to a celestial palace, the first thing she points out on the tiny, circling orb of Earth is "Palmyra's ruined palaces" ([*SPP*] II.110); Shelley thereby acknowledges his debt to Volney's *Ruins,* since the "scaffolding" in the latter text for an overview of world history is a dialogue which begins in the ruins of Palmyra. Volney's male narrator, who has come there to brood over why "*empires rise and fall*" and to discover "*on what principles . . . the peace of society and the happiness of man* [*can*] *be established*" (Volney 13; author's emphasis), is visited by a male phantom who carries him to a similarly celestial perch for a vision of universal history and a prophecy of its future course.

The change Shelley effects in Volney's scenario by putting two feminine presences into colloquy over the evils of past history, the lamentable state of the world at present, and the hope for a better future has in itself some feminist potential, even though the imagined future is so visionary from its description that no one could draw specific agenda items toward the restructuring of social and political policy. Moreover, close to the end of *Queen Mab,* in verse paragraphs that share Peacock's gender politics at the conclusion of the latter's revised version of "Palmyra," Shelley pictures a renewed world very different indeed from Volney's remodeled patriarchy, a "community of citizens who, united by fraternal sentiments . . . make of their respective strength one common force, the reaction of which on each of them assumes the noble and beneficent character of paternity" (Volney 209). Like Peacock, Shelley gives Time, "the conqueror," a masculine gender and makes him the patriarchal destroyer of destructive patriarchal rule. When "the morn of love" gradually dawns, he flees (whereas in Peacock's poem Time's power remains, powerless only before virtue), and the earth comes under the sway of a force given a feminine gender:

> Reason was free; and wild though passion went
> Through tangled glens and wood-embosomed meads,
> Gathering a garland of the strangest flowers,
> Yet like the bee returning to her queen,
> She bound the sweetest on her sister's brow,
> Who meek and sober kissed the sportive child,
> No longer trembling at the broken rod.
>
> ([*SPP*] IX.49–56)

The language describing passion's movements "through tangled glens and wood-embosomed meads" calls up associations with the maenads, frenzied votaries of Dionysus. But passion's devotion is to a mother/sister. Moreover, Shelley's bee simile makes the figure of Reason elide into that of the Mother Goddess, and it seems to me not only possible but likely that he was using that ancient iconography consciously. He would have found a fairly extended discussion of it in Jacob Bryant's *New System,* one of Peacock's source books, as one might expect, and therefore in all likelihood familiar to Shelley. Bryant's discussion, like every other topic addressed in his book, grows out of an *idée fixe* on the unity of the biblical and the Greek religious traditions.[22] So he associates Noah's Ark with "Seira, or *the hive of Venus*" alluded to by Natalis Comes: "*Let us celebrate the hive of Venus, who rose from the sea: that hive of many names: the mighty fountain, from whence all kings are descended; from whence all the winged and immortal Loves were again produced*" (II, 371–72; author's emphasis). Bryant, noting that "Seira . . . signified Melitta, *a bee,*" adds: "We may perceive that Seira was no other than Damater, the supposed mother of mankind; who was also styled Melitta, and Melissa; and was looked upon as the Venus of the east. . . . The priests of the Seira were called Melittae, and Melissae, from this Deity, whom they worshiped" (II, 372–73).

Reiman links Peacock's concluding vision in the revised "Palmyra" to the passages in the first and twelfth cantos of *Laon and Cythna,* which describe "the Temple of the Spirit," adding, in words that could be modified also to apply to *Queen Mab,* "But, of course, neither Shelley nor Peacock believed literally in such a pacific Valhalla. Rather, they were indulging in conscious mythmaking, creating (in I. A. Richards' terminology) 'pseudo-statements' that reflect their desires that virtuous actions and great artistic achievements be somehow preserved beyond the flux of mutability" (*Intervals of Inspiration* 219).

Peacock shows a similar bent for "mythmaking" in a letter to Thomas Forster written in August 1813: "I have engaged a very beautiful place in Radnorshire, where I purpose to devote myself to the muses of history and philosophical poetry; not altogether renouncing the worship of the Cyprian deity, provided I can discover some young, amiable, unsophisticated mountaineer, who will sacrifice with me to the Æneadum genitrix [mother of the race of Aeneas, i.e., Venus], and enable me to say *vetus ara* multo Fumat *odore* [the *ancient altar* smokes with much *odor*]!" (Joukovsky 32).

Peacock's jaunty tone in the letter gives added justification to Reiman's use of the word "indulging" to describe this kind of myth making. Still, something more complicated is occurring than the generation of "pseudo-statements." Peacock and Shelley both live with a sense of "the Cyprian deity" as a psychological reality because, for different reasons and in different ways, both had experienced with extraordinary force the power of a mother myth permeating the family and social structures in which they passed their infancy, childhood, and youth. Thus, the significance the myth had for them (but of course, in the project here at hand, its significance particularly for Shelley) deserves further study. Writing from a different context, Reiman has noted that "there is still room for further exploration of the relationship of Shelley's mythmaking to the tradition of allegorizing ancient religions and mythologies in such works as Francis Bacon's *The Wisdom of the Ancients* and other Renaissance works discussed, for example, by Don Cameron Allen in *Mysteriously Meant*" (*Intervals of Inspiration* 392).

By the same token, awareness of the social history of motherhood opens up an investigatory space for considering Shelley's fascination with the Aphrodite myth. The ideology of motherhood, in the air everywhere in English upper- and middle-class life during Shelley's infancy and childhood and thereby creating a lifelong framework or context for his creative energies, would have reached him from any number of sources: the primers in which he was taught to read, the storybooks read to him, the attitudes of his caretakers as they were shaped by different kinds of advice books, the popular literature—stories, novels, poems—that he quickly learned to read for himself. I have examined a cross-section of these different ideological media with the hope of catching certain quintessential characteristics of the idealized feminine, the ensphered goddess or goddesslike figure who offers an alternative to the violence and injustice of the patriarchal given of the world.

By its emphasis on maternal breast-feeding and on the mother's constant interaction with her infants, followed by her equally constant involvement in the education and socialization of her children, the maternal ideology sets up a continuum between the mother's "lettering" of the infant through "the effects of touch, sound, the gaze . . . as they intermingle with sensory response" (Ragland-Sullivan 20), the mother's teaching of letters, and the introjection of the "aesthetic" as the grounding of identity. The stimulus from an external source fused with the interior response to that stimulus, a fusion conveyed through the very words "feeling" and "sentiment," functions as "forma informans," in the Coleridgean phrase, not only to the infant's but to the child's experience of subjectivity. Ragland-Sullivan writes that through this lettering "the human body becomes eroticized." It becomes the medium of and for "soul," permeable through all its sensory processes to an influence experienced as feminine but also inseparable from its experience of self.

The domestic situation within the Shelley household would have made its first child and male heir particularly receptive to these influences. Elizabeth Shelley, it is generally agreed, was a much more charismatic figure than her husband. Her dominance within the domestic life of their Sussex manor, Field Place, could only have been strengthened by Timothy Shelley's absences when fulfilling his duties as a member of Parliament. Shelley spent an extraordinarily long time within that closed, feminine circle presided over by a strong mother. Records of his years there before he went to boarding school are rare, but the much more plentiful evidence dating from his late adolescence suggests that Elizabeth Shelley followed contemporary exhortations that she fuse her maternal presence with that of "a *tender friend*" ("Essay upon Female Education" 54) and thus give it even greater strength. Hers was also, to judge by Shelley's own explicit responses, a presence in which the maternal and the erotic mingled as they do in some of the hortatory literature. I am not suggesting anything so brutally reductive as an equation between Elizabeth Shelley and the Mother Goddess, but I think it fair to say that for her son she was the avatar of the goddess who emanated from the prolific literature on motherhood throughout his formative years.

NOTES

1. I am grateful to Mary Favret for bringing Lucy Werkmeister's work to my attention.

2. The first two chapters (1–61) of Linda Pollock's *Forgotten Children,* while focusing specifically on the history of childhood, also serve as an excellent review of the controversies surrounding the history of the family and as a critique of Stone's work (58–59) on a number of different grounds.

3. Pateman's source for the phrase *"from Status to Contract"* (9) is Sir Henry Maine's *Ancient Law* (Maine 100).

4. A number of scholars in addition to Macfarlane now place the inception of the "nuclear family" much earlier than Ariès, Stone, or Trumbach. Pollock, for instance, notes: "Ariès . . . is one of many authors who believe that, prior to industrialization, the family was extended, consisting of several generations living together, and open to the outside world so that children mixed with adults from an early age. . . . [But] Hanawalt . . . found that although the extended family did exist in the middle ages, the nuclear type was most common." She points out also that Laslett and Wall's *Household and Family in Past Time* "conclusively" demonstrates that "for as far back as we have records . . . the simple family was the standard situation . . . the nuclear family was the most prevalent type" (54).

5. A serious drawback to Ryerson's analysis is the admitted paucity of the sources forming her data base. She used only printed materials, and for her first time

span in the comparison (1550–1650) was working from only four sources (305). The list of all her source materials contains only thirty-nine items (320–23).

6. Involved in the strictures about cleanliness and the emphasis on early toilet training is the change from the practice of swaddling to the use of diapers. Ryerson takes it that the swaddled infant demanded more attention from the caretaker—"he could not even brush a fly off his own nose" (313)—but, in fact, the infant's freedom from swaddling bands could well have called for more rather than less watchfulness and concern (cf. Hellerstein et al. 9–10).

7. Judith Lewis's study, which covers the century from 1760 to 1860, suggests that women did not conform. Working from diaries and correspondence, Lewis examines the attitudes of fifty aristocratic women toward childbearing experiences. Her findings show that for such a group, maternal breast-feeding, for instance, was perhaps more common by 1780 than it had been earlier, but "it had become by no means a uniform practice, contrary to the suggestions of Stone and Trumbach" (209). William St. Clair, in *The Godwins and the Shelleys,* wonders also whether the number of hortatory works may not indeed signal women's defiance of their prescriptions (506).

8. The Cunningtons date such discussions of fashion to "about" 1786 (*History of Underclothes* 96).

9. Frederick the Great of Prussia used the more direct instrument, legislation, rather than trusting entirely to hortatory literature to inscribe the maternal ideology. He was able thereby to avoid at the same time any possible diminution of patriarchal power. Article 67 of the 1794 Prussian legal code stated: "A healthy mother is required to breast-feed her child." Article 68 added: "It is, however, the father's right to decide on the length of time she shall give her breast to the child" (Bell and Offen I, 39).

10. An example of this insistence on the visible outline of the breasts is a diatribe against shawls in *La Belle Assemblée,* 1.1 (February 1806): "It [the shawl] is the very contrast to the flowing elegance of the Grecian costume, whose light and transparent draperies so admirably display the female form; and it restores something almost as disgusting, in the upper part of the female dress, as *the doubly fortified hoop, and the nine-times-quilted* petticoat of the last century" (64; author's emphasis).

11. We know from the *Letters* (I, 342) that Darwin's *Zoonomia* was a text familiar to Shelley. He ordered it from Thomas Hookham on December 17, 1812, and Hookham crossed out the title to signify that he had acquired it for Shelley.

12. St. Clair, in *The Godwins and the Shelleys,* shows the connection between fears about disaster to the state and projection of such fears as concern over women's possible dominance by graphing the fluctuations in the price of government stocks along with the yearly publication figures for books of advice for women. He finds that after the early 1790s "the advice book curve rises as the gilts curve falls, worry about women recognizably correlating with wider worries even reflecting the interregnum of the Peace of Amiens" (509).

13. Mary Wollstonecraft, by accepting this argument in *Vindication of the Rights of Woman* (59), increased its power and longevity.

14. This "plot" was used to maintain class as well as gender hierarchies. A classic rendition of it, Johann Heinrich Pestalozzi's *Leonard and Gertrude,* which was translated into English from the German in 1800, treated and addressed itself to the working class. (For further discussion, see Massey 50–63.) Similarly, Hannah More's *Tracts* (see More, *Works)* look to feminine influence to establish those traits in the working class that the middle class wished to foster.

15. I am influenced here by Juliet Mitchell's argument in "Femininity, Narrative,

and Psychoanalysis": "You cannot choose the imaginary, the semiotic, the carnival as an alternative to the symbolic, as an alternative to the law. It is set up by the law precisely as its own ludic space, its own area of imaginary alternative, but not as a symbolic alternative" (428). Judith Butler makes a related point in *Gender Trouble:*

> The self-justification of a repressive or subordinating law almost always grounds itself
> in a story about what it was like *before* the advent of the law, and how it came about
> that the law emerged in its present and necessary form. . . . The story of origins is
> thus a strategic tactic within a narrative that, by telling a single, authoritative account
> about an irrecoverable past, makes the constitution of the law appear as a historical
> inevitability. (36)

16. Other examples are "The Triumph of Patience and Virtue"; "The Unfeeling Father"; and "Three Years After Marriage".

17. For discussion and bibliography, see Gaull (50–80).

18. Work such as Lady Eleanor Fenn's clearly sets the pattern for the "elaborated" speech of a family controlled through the "personal" as opposed to the "positional" mode of interaction, as described by Basil Bernstein (*passim*) and further analyzed by Mary Douglas (Douglas 21–32).

19. The best analysis of the pervasiveness of "mother fear" in our culture is still, to my mind, Dorothy Dinnerstein's study *The Mermaid and the Minotaur.* I fully concur with her argument that the emphasis on mother power (but only within domestic confines) and infants' resulting dependence on a female caretaker create a situation in which both genders resist feminine authority. As Dinnerstein points out, however, these feelings about the mother are truly ambivalent, involving as they do the desire to reexperience maternal care, and my analysis focuses on the positive side of that ambivalence.

20. The reviewer of Fra Paolino da San Bartolomeo's *Voyage to the East Indies* in the *Lady's Monthly Museum* also takes it for granted that the readers are aware of the scholarship compiled in *Asiatic Researches* and not only know Sir William Jones's *Works* but will agree that they have been imperfectly edited ("Review" 477).

21. Gibbon's appearance signals Peacock's acknowledgment of the historian's importance to his mother. The "Biographical Introduction" to Peacock's *Works* notes that "Mrs. Peacock was a great reader of history, and . . . Gibbon was never far from the arm of her chair" (I, xx).

22. Stuart Curran describes Bryant as "the acknowledged patriarch of the Noachian mythographers" and numbers Shelley among those who supported his thesis, "at least for poetical purposes" (*Shelley's Annus Mirabilis* 64).

3

Queen of the Field Place Hive

Information about Elizabeth Pilfold Shelley is so sparse, anecdotal, and badly documented that such a careful Shelley biographer as Newman Ivey White can put the sum of his painstaking research into a single paragraph. By examining histories of Sussex and Surrey, he concludes that Elizabeth Pilfold's people were "country gentry of local importance somewhat less than that of the Shelleys before Sir Bysshe elevated the family" (I, 14). Since this particular branch of the Shelley family had no social eminence before Bysshe Shelley distinguished it with the money gained through eloping, seriatim, with two heiresses, White's meaning is that they do not appear in such records at all.

White next states that "Timothy Shelley's wife was a woman of unusual beauty, and of strong good sense" (I, 14). For the first attribute he has the visible evidence of the Romney portrait (fig. 1) and the eyewitness testimony of Thomas Jefferson Hogg, who describes her as "a lady of rare beauty" (Hogg I, 19). "Strong good sense" is actually Edward Dowden's phrase (I, 5), based in turn on Thomas Medwin's quotation from an unnamed "popular writer" that Mrs. Shelley was "if not a literary, an intellectual woman, that is, in a certain sense a clever woman, and though of all persons most unpoetical, was possessed of strong masculine sense" (104). Medwin's anonymous source is also White's basis for characterizing her as "an excellent letter writer"; in Medwin she is described as a potential "Madame de Sévigné or a Lady Wortley Montague [sic], for she wrote admirable letters" (104).

For the sentence that follows White quotes out of context a letter from Shelley to Hogg: "Her son regarded her in 1811 as 'mild and tolerant, yet narrow-minded.' " White, however, goes on to suggest a personality in which neither mildness nor tolerance figures largely: "Her idea of the son's early training was to fit him for the position of country gentlemen held by his ancestors. Accordingly she was disappointed when he preferred reading to the fishing and hunting she thought more appropriate" (I, 14).

One of White's sources for this opinion may be Mathilda Houston, quoted several times in other contexts in the same opening chapter. Houston met the Shelley parents about twelve years after Shelley's death in 1822, but her memoir, written many years later, dates after the construction of the Victorian "poetical" Shelley:

> To me it soon became abundantly clear that Percy Bysshe Shelley had mo-
> nopolized all the powers of the imagination, which, if divided amongst a
> family of five, would have provided ample provision for all. Both Sir Timo-
> thy and his wife—excellent persons both—were, of all imaginable parents,
> the very last from whose union a looker-on would suppose that a "child of
> fancy," such as the youthful author of "Queen Mab," would be likely to
> spring. The former, clad in his yeoman-like garb, and his tanned leather
> gaiters, was, like the rest of his family (with the exception of Percy) thor-
> oughly practical and prosaic. All were endowed with a fair amount of "good
> sense," and the elder unmarried daughter [Hellen] possessed great quick-
> ness of perception, and a very powerful and autocratic will.   (I, 100–101)

Maddeningly, Houston finesses any specific description of Elizabeth, by now Lady Shelley, at all, moving from the father to the daughter, but by a process of associative osmosis something of Sir Timothy's leather gaiters gets transferred to Lady Shelley's general aura as well.

Dowden's *Life of Shelley* appears to be another of White's sources for this contrast between a squirearchical mother and a bookish son. In an order followed by White, Dowden juxtaposes Shelley's adjectives about his mother— "mild" and "tolerant"—with sentences on her expectations regarding her son. Linking the two is the clause "but there were times when her mildness disappeared." Dowden then gives several vignettes which seem to come from unnamed eyewitnesses:

> She had a special grievance against the boy because he was little of what
> every country gentleman ought to be—a follower of field sports. He must
> fish from the boat while she looked on; or she would send him forth with the
> gamekeeper to bring in a bag of game. Shelley, it is said, would sit poring
> over a book while the gamekeeper was engaged in slaying his fellow-
> creatures, and the birds would be presented to Mrs. Shelley, by an innocent
> fraud, as the spoil of Master Bysshe.   (I, 5)

White modifies this commentary considerably, making only the comparative statement that Shelley "preferred reading to fishing and hunting"—a fair enough statement since reading, to judge by the evidence, was an activity that Shelley preferred above most, perhaps all, others. White has reason to be cautious: Hogg describes Shelley when the two first met at Oxford as "tanned and freckled by exposure to the sun, having passed the autumn, as he said, in shooting" (I, 47), and he later mentions Shelley's delight in long walks straight across country "as is usual with sportsmen in shooting" (I, 76–77).[1] The seeming contradiction can be resolved by allowance for change over time. If Shelley's mother was indeed the strong personality described, the sporting activities she demanded of Shelley in his childhood may by his youth have evolved into pleasures enjoyed primarily because he achieved her approval in pursuing them. Still, White's emphasis on Mrs. Shelley's disappointment coupled with the earlier mention of her lack of interest in literature creates the strong suggestion of incompatible personalities.

The paragraph's penultimate sentence somewhat mitigates that implicit judgment through a statement, based on the evidence of extant letters, that "she tried hard, and more sensibly than the others, to reconcile father and son," but moves quickly on to the point that "after a reconciliation seemed impossible she concurred in her husband's attitude toward the poet" (I, 14). White rounds off the paragraph by implicitly accepting Mark Antony Lower's judgment, set down in *The Worthies of Sussex,* that whatever genius Shelley inherited came from his mother's rather than his father's side of the family (White I, 14); but in the context he appears to be thinking only of genetic and not of personal influence.

White's dismissal of Elizabeth Shelley from serious consideration follows a pattern common to all Shelley's biographers, with the important exception of Kenneth Neill Cameron, who finds the neglect "extraordinary" (*The Young Shelley* 4). Perhaps not so extraordinary, though, when one recalls that Shelley's biography—quickly his legend—was in significant ways the creation of Mary Shelley and then of her daughter-in-law, Lady Jane Shelley. One would never know from the *Shelley Memorials* published by Lady Jane in 1859 that Shelley had a mother. The book opens with the statement that Shelley was "the eldest son of Timothy Shelley, Esq., subsequently, the second baronet; and was christened Bysshe after his grandfather." With no further family information the account continues, "At six years of age, the boy was sent to a day school" (1).

Lady Jane may well have been following the social dictum requiring silence when one is unable to say something "nice"; her devotion to Mary Shelley and her consequent espousal of the latter's opinions would have made it difficult for her to find anything nice to say about Elizabeth Shelley. So at least one can gather from the nature of Mary Shelley's comments about her mother-in-law as they appear in her letters during the years between Shelley's death in 1822 and his mother's in 1846.

Through most of those years, until Sir Timothy's death in 1844, Mary Shelley was in an almost intolerably humiliating position, obliged to beg and keep begging for assistance for herself and her son, Percy Florence, from in-laws who did as little as possible for their son's heir and nothing for her, while they worked in every way to erase from common memory the very existence of Percy Bysshe Shelley. I use the plural because there is no sign that Lady Shelley opposed Sir Timothy's desire to remove his son's name from all spoken or written record, but the evidence itself suggests that the decision was the father's, not the mother's. Houston writes that at her first meeting with Hellen Shelley she was "strictly enjoined . . . never to mention within her *father's* presence the name of his son" (I, 99; my emphasis); and White makes it Sir Timothy's injunction that omitted from the epitaph of Percy and Harriet Shelley's son, Charles, the names of both his parents (I, 13).

But in virtually all the allusions to the Shelley parents that one finds in

Mary Shelley's letters, the real foe is not Sir Timothy but Lady Shelley. For example, she writes to Leigh Hunt in 1835:

> I wish I could look with the indulgence you do on Shelley's relations. Sir Tim indeed, were he alone, I could manage—did I see him—violent as he is—he has a heart & I am sure I could have made a friend of him. It is Lady S—who is my bitter enemy—and her motive is the base one of securing more money for herself and her terror was great lest I should see Sir Tim at one time now there is no fear since the old Gentleman never comes to town. Besides the sacra auri fames (is that the right syntax—I wager not) her conduct having been very open to censure, she naturally attacks me—because those kind of women love detraction.   (II, 219)

In an 1837 letter to Hunt, Mary Shelley shows a similar contrast in attitude toward the Shelley parents: "At Easter I went on a visit to a friend of mine in Sussex—the gentry there are very willing to be civil to me—Every one hating the Shelley's [sic] so much—not Sir Tim exactly—who though something of a fox, is more of a fool—but Lady Shelley is so illnatured, the girls so arrogant & disagreeable, that they are generally disliked" (II, 286). Describing the Shelleys to her cousin Elizabeth Berry in 1843, Mary Shelley writes: "My husband's family are strange people. Sir Tim himself is enclined to be kind but is held back by his wife who is fearful that her second son should not get all that it is possible for him to have" (III, 66).

After Sir Timothy's death Mary Shelley continued to feel that her mother-in-law resented Percy Florence's accession to the title at the expense of Shelley's younger brother, John. To Claire Clairmont she writes, "Lady Shelley will never leave a *sous* to Percy—her money will go to her daughters—& some perhaps to John's children" (III, 141), and she comments in the same vein to Peacock: "Percy is unfortunately considered far richer than he is—coming after Sir Tim—while a thousand things have curtailed his patrimony by half—& so large a surplus of Sir Tims possessions go to Milady & John—" (III, 159). In the event, Lady Elizabeth Shelley's death on August 21, 1846, left Percy Florence "some what richer," as Mary Shelley admits (III, 309), but the story of these relationships as transmitted through Lady Jane Shelley still emphasizes Elizabeth Shelley's partiality toward John. Jane Shelley commented in an interview with Maud Rolleston that Sir Timothy burst into tears when he saw his grandson, Percy Florence, adding: "His wife used her influence after that to keep the boy away from his grandfather, for she was anxious that the title and property should go to her youngest son, John" (97).

That may well have been true, and in time Jane Shelley was in a position to take the most appropriate possible revenge against the woman whom she, with Mary Shelley, held to be more responsible than Sir Timothy for the attempt to wipe out Shelley's memory. While she set up a literal shrine to the memory of Shelley, she also, just through silence, helped create an impression among his later biographers, that, in A. M. D. Hughes's words, "the record [of Elizabeth Pilford] is singularly small, and she played in the drama of her son's life a minor and unavailing part" (5).

Hughes' implied logic is that the paucity of documentation about Elizabeth Shelley registers her comparative unimportance. Other reasons, as I have suggested, may explain her absence from the record, but the biographical problems created by that absence remain. How, out of a vacancy, does one invoke her presence in order to answer questions about her actual relationship with her son in his infancy and his youth? The task would be impossible if the vacancy were total, but wispy strands of information in it begin to coalesce.

Through the rest of this chapter I shall use this information to reconstruct Shelley's relationship with his mother. In doing so I am not working with materials unavailable or unknown to Shelley's modern biographers, but I am turning interpretive attention on existing evidence that has not so far received it. Cameron, though aware in 1950 of the need for work of this kind, had a different focus when writing *The Young Shelley.* Twenty-five years later Richard Holmes, returning to the position of earlier biographers such as Dowden (I, 5), White (I, 14), Blunden (17), and Hughes (5), writes that "we know nothing directly of [Shelley's] relationship with his mother during his first fifteen years, and Shelley rarely mentioned her in later life" (11). He thereby elides seven years about which we do have considerable documentary information, dismissing or radically misinterpreting those records when he suggests that Elizabeth Shelley was "increasingly distant and unresponsive" from the time Shelley went to school and that the rejection Shelley felt in being sent away characterized all his later interactions with his mother (11). That does not correctly state the case. A new attention to evidence long available, therefore, does tell a hitherto untold story.

Strategies of Infant Desire

Begin, then, with a shred of gossip: Medwin's statement that Elizabeth Shelley was "brought up by her aunt, Lady Ferdinand Pool, the wife of the well-known father of the turf, and owner of 'Potooooooooo,' and the equally celebrated 'Waxy' and 'Mealy'" (13). White ignores this information, perhaps because Medwin is such an unreliable source. Yet since Medwin's relationship to Elizabeth Pilfold was actually a degree closer than his cousinship on the Shelley side (13), he would have had access to such family information, and there seems no reason for him to have invented it. At this point facts about the then "well-known father of the turf" Sir Ferdinando Poole are very hard to come by— much harder than records about the feats of Waxy, winner of the Derby in 1792—but even knowledge of Waxy's fortunes around the time of Shelley's birth gives some insight into Elizabeth Pilfold's life before she married Timothy Shelley.

We must, though, place these turfy chronicles in juxtaposition with the fact of Elizabeth Pilfold's age at the time of her marriage. When Hughes writes that "she came to Field Place a young woman—much younger than her husband" (5), his sentence structure suggests a greater equivalence between the simple and the comparative forms of the adjective "young" than is actually the case. True, in 1791 Elizabeth Pilfold at twenty-nine was much younger than the forty-year-old Timothy Shelley, but we have *Persuasion*'s Elizabeth Elliot as evidence that twenty-nine was at this period older than an unmarried woman wished to be. By 1791 Elizabeth Pilfold's sister, Charlotte Grove, had already been married nine years and had produced five of the eleven children she eventually bore to Thomas Grove. True, Charlotte may have been older than Elizabeth; but since the birth date of Thomas Grove precedes that of Elizabeth by only four years, and since Charlotte probably was about his age or younger, she was not likely to have been a *much* older sister (*SHC* II, 495–97). Also, to judge by the evidence of Romney's portrait of Charlotte, painted in 1788, she was then still a young and, like Elizabeth, a very beautiful woman (Ward I, 76).

In 1788 Charlotte must have been living much of the time with her husband at Fern, the Groves' Wiltshire estate, in the domestic retirement so lauded by the prevading ideology. But she undoubtedly figured as well as one of the many ladies of fashion passing through Romney's studio, since he was then at the height of his popularity and prestige as a portrait painter. And, of course, presence at the many sittings a portrait demanded also meant participation during that time in the social life of the London season (Ward I, 116).

As ward of the childless Pooles, however meager her personal dowry, Elizabeth may have moved in these circles much more constantly than Charlotte—at least until the death of Lady Poole in May 1786 (*Complete Baronetage* IV, 94). As a "father of the turf" Sir Ferdinando was one of a small aristocratic clique who were in the process of establishing the institution of horse racing in its modern form. The prominence of the Prince Regent in this group serves as reminder that high breeding should not be equated with high morals. The betting among its members involved extravagant amounts of money, and the gentleman's code by no means prevented the fixing of races. A surviving anecdote about Sir Ferdinando suggests, however, that he stood aloof from such activities. When a proposal was brought to him that he race his famous Waxy against Gohanna, he is said to have replied, "No, gentlemen, you know I never do these things, but if any gentleman wishes to borrow Waxy for the occasion, I will lend him." The Duke of Grafton, Waxy's later owner, took him up on the offer (Taunton I, 214).

However slight, the story gives a certain amount of insight into the Pooles' social milieu. Also, Sir Ferdinando's possession of Waxy as one of a large stable of horses carries the information that, while not a man to risk money on wagers, he was very wealthy indeed. The yearly upkeep of a single horse matched the income of an upper-middle-class family.[2]

Elizabeth's connection with the Pooles may have led to her acquaintance with Timothy Shelley. Lady Poole was the daughter of a Horsham resident, Thomas White (Burke 240); one of the Poole family seats was near Lewes in Sussex (Debrett I, 472), and in 1789–90 Sir Ferdinando was sheriff of Sussex (*Complete Baronetage* IV, 94). Once their acquaintance was made, her acceptance of his proposal of marriage suggests that this beautiful and socially well-connected young woman feared that she had run out of better options.

Decent if unexciting good looks, his position as first son and heir to Bysshe Shelley's considerable fortune, and thus a "settled" social position for the wife of such an heir were about the sum of what Timothy Shelley could offer. (The added éclat of a baronetage would not come until 1806, when the Duke of Norfolk, leader of the Whig party, secured that politically useful honor for Bysshe Shelley [White I, 9].) He had attended University College, Oxford, without distinguishing himself there and made the Grand Tour of the Continent considered appropriate for the "finishing" of a young squire without gaining from it much more than a thin cultural veneer, if one can believe Medwin's acid account (12–13). Otherwise he seems to have lived a life without incident in the forty years prior to his marriage. The calm of that long interval creates the impression that when at last he made the decision to marry, he did so primarily to continue the newly established family line into the next generation.

Holmes, like other Shelley biographers, describes the union of Timothy and Elizabeth Shelley as a reasonable, not to say pedestrian one, but adds: "Timothy Shelley was proud enough of her to have both their portraits painted by George Romney" (11). Even there, however, the timing of the portraits suggests a more complex marital story. Timothy had his *own* portrait painted by Romney in 1791, perhaps—though this is pure speculation—in celebration of his entry into a marriage that would make him paterfamilias (Ward II, 141). Since Romney had already painted Elizabeth's sister and brother-in-law, she might well have liked, even expected, the flattery of having her portrait commissioned as well. But that did not occur. Romney did not paint her until 1795, and his diary takes note of an unusual circumstance: she paid for the portrait herself (Ward II, 142). The money, of course, was Timothy's, but the project of having her portrait painted may have been her own.

Cameron has traced a note of condescension in Shelley's responses toward his father to an attitude general among "his mother and his sisters" (*Young Shelley* 5). Its originator within that small circle, however, would have to have been his mother—though, as we shall see, it seems to have extended to others in the Pilfold clan. The picture that begins to emerge is of a woman "racy" in the positive, English usage of the term: lively, spirited, full of energy for her life and with a sharp interest in the lives of those around her—perhaps too sharp for the comfort of potential suitors. After enjoying many—then too many—London seasons, she accepted the proposal of a dull but "appropriate" suitor. She thereby gained a settled position in life and a sphere of her own, but one that confined her to the duties of wife and mother.

The evidence, if circumstantial, suggests fairly strongly that Elizabeth Pilfold made a marital bargain along these lines. Much less clear is the way or ways in which it affected her later attitudes. A woman in her situation could become a mother whose dissatisfaction with her husband's ineptitudes and incapacities extended itself to her children, particularly to the son sharing her husband's male privilege. This is the demanding, dissatisfied Elizabeth Shelley sketched by a number of biographers. Another possibility lies in her accepting her assigned domestic role as the only one available for self-fulfillment. By making her relation as mother an "all in all" to counterbalance the inadequacies and attendant frustrations of her situation as wife, she demands a great deal of her children, albeit in a more positive way. Cameron appears to be imagining a family scenario of this second kind when he writes that "Mrs. Shelley, aware of the contrast between her capacities and her production, may have attempted to execute her own unfulfilled ambitions through her son" (*Young Shelley* 4). Certainly external pressures favored this option; in the years of Shelley's infancy and early childhood, 1792 to 1796, insistence on the mother's participatory function was, to judge by the number of conduct books published, at one of its highest points (St. Clair, *Godwins and Shelleys* 511).

There is not sufficient biographical evidence to say definitively whether in those early years Shelley experienced his mother as distant and unaffectionate or as deeply nurturing. But at the point in Shelley's adolescence when, through documents such as his letters and Harriet Grove's diary, we do begin to have direct evidence, the mother who emerges is very deeply involved in her children's lives. She is a confidante, even at times a co-conspirator in all sorts of schemes, besides being a tutelary presence, a source of encouragement and of admonishment. Such a strong identificatory and participatory maternal presence is by no means unproblematic, particularly when, as in the Shelley household, the mother's personal and thus sexual charisma is stronger than the father's *and* not directed toward the father. The sexual-sibling rivalry between father and child already fostered by the maternal ideology takes on an intensified acerbity, while interstices open in the barrier against fantasies of incest.

Before turning to later adolescent records, however, we must look carefully at whatever information is available about Shelley's infancy and childhood, beginning with the question of whether he was fed maternally or by a wet nurse. Obviously, if Elizabeth Shelley followed the exhortations of the medical literature about the importance of breast-feeding, she was his nurse. His being a first child, as well as a son and heir, in a comparatively late marriage also argues for that supposition, since advice books linked infant survival closely to maternal feeding. Judith Schneid Lewis, however, working from the evidence of aristocratic women's letters and diaries for the century between 1760 and 1860, concludes that maternal nursing was "far from universal," and adds: "The very short birth intervals that characterized our group indicate that the majority of women probably did not nurse their own children" (211). Lactation is by no means a dependable contraceptive, but on average, demographers judge, the interval between first and second births is eighteen months in nonlactating as compared to twenty-seven months for lactating mothers (Lewis 287). Elizabeth Shelley's second child, also Elizabeth, was born on May 10, 1794, twenty-one months after Shelley and so closer to the nonlactating than the lactating side of the average. Then, too, if Elizabeth Shelley had the active, "horsey" disposition ascribed to her as well as a strong mind of her own, she might well have put her infant son in the hands of a wet nurse in order to resume an independent life.

Two sentences in Hellen Shelley's letters to Jane Williams, written in 1856, make reference to Shelley's "old nurse," though whether she was a *wet* nurse is unclear. The context of Hellen Shelley's allusion is worth remarking, since her rambling memories are strung together associatively in ways that may have significance. The train of thought begins with her objection to accounts of Shelley's "discordant voice and stooping figure," moves on to her own recollection of his figure as "slight and beautiful," and then to hearsay descriptions: "As a child, I have heard that his skin was like snow, and bright ringlets covered his head. He was, I have heard, a beautiful boy." There follows immediately, within the same paragraph, a mention of his nurse:

> His old nurse lived, within the last two or three years, at Horsham. One of the curates there—a Mr. Du Barry—was a great admirer of my brother's poetry, and we were able, through him, to remind her of those years when she used to come regularly every Christmas to Field Place, to receive a substantial proof that she was not to be forgotten, though her nurse-child was gone from earth forever. (Hogg I, 28–29)

The juxtaposition suggests that the one from whom Hellen, born when Shelley was eleven, heard about his infant looks was not his own mother but his nurse. It seems reasonable also that these looks were the repeated—and ritual—subject of conversation each Boxing Day, the traditional feast for gift-giving to the servants. (The likelihood that Elizabeth Shelley, as "lady of the manor," was a participant in these talks is, by the way, another sign that the prohibition against mention of Shelley's name did not emanate from her.)

While allowance must be made for the sentimentality sugaring the entire passage, Hellen's use of the phrase "nurse-child" does suggest a closeness of relationship that involved breast-feeding. Also the nurse, old in 1853 or 1854, had cared for Shelley sixty-four years previously, when she would certainly have been a young and perhaps a lactating woman. The definite possibility therefore exists that Shelley was not maternally breast-fed, but the truly relevant point is that, whether he was or not, after the fact he felt most strongly that he should have been. His appalled reaction, discussed earlier, to Harriet Shelley's refusal to feed Ianthe suggests that he considered it enormously significant either that his mother nursed him herself, thus establishing him in his subjectivity—the nurse's soul entering the child—or that she, like Harriet, did not, and by this refusal made him all the more obsessed with an *ideal* of the maternal that would literally fulfill him: fill him full. At the same time the experience of actual nurturance—and admiration—from a surrogate mother would serve as one important element in the formation of that ideal. This is to say, Shelley's nostalgia for total maternal nurturance might well be greatest if he both experienced it from a surrogate mother, thus having an actual base for it in unconscious memory, and learned after the fact that he had not received it from his mother, thus finding the memory itself to be the sign of his lack. His vehemence over the breast-feeding of Ianthe seems to have been fueled by such doubled nostalgia.

The presence of a nurse also bears on Shelley's acquisition of language.

John Jeaffreson, deriding those Shelley idolators who fantasized an "aristocratic descent" for their poet, notes that they take as sign of this elegant class
Shelley's casualness about final g's. Jeaffreson labels this characteristic a "provincialism," not aristocratic negligence: "The Sussex peasantry seldom sound
the final g of words ending with that letter, and Sussex gentlemen are sometimes heard to say 'Good mornin' to one another. Shelley was sometimes
guilty of this provincialism. For instance, in *Laon and Cythna* (1817) and
again in *Arethusa* (1820) he makes *ruin* rhyme to *pursuing*" (I, 3).

This trace of Sussex on the adult Shelley's tongue survives from a childhood period in which, one gathers, he could speak the dialect fluently and
consistently. Hellen Shelley has at second hand an anecdote about a time
when Shelley as a little boy approached a Colonel Sergison in Horsham "and
asked, in Sussex language, to be hired as a gamekeeper's boy" (Hogg I, 28).
Since his nurse is described as living in Horsham in her old age and was likely
therefore to have had her roots in Sussex, his familiarity with this speech,
sufficient for him to enjoy showing it off, may have begun in his relationship
with her.

But his actual mother also had a formative part in his acquisition of language and perhaps in making linguistic facility his best way of receiving
praise—in other words, in making him a poet. Hellen Shelley describes her
mother as speaking often and admiringly not of Shelley's childhood looks but
of his intellectual precocity: "I have heard Bysshe's memory was singularly
retentive. Even as a child, Gray's lines on the Cat and the Goldfish were
repeated, word for word, after once reading; a fact I have frequently heard
from my mother" (Hogg I, 23) Probably coincidentally, but perhaps in response to this maternal praise, Shelley's "first recorded poem," dated by
Geoffrey Matthews and Kelvin Everest "probably about 1804" (*PS* I, 3), is
about "a Cat in distress." The language and versification of the poem warrant
no special attention, but a few lines bear interesting witness to Shelley's
Oedipal turn of mind: "Some a living require, / And others desire / An old
fellow out of the way" (I, 4). Timothy Shelley's long wait for the death of Sir
Bysshe may have prompted this thought, but the anger behind the schoolboy
gibe in the last stanza suggests that Shelley also had an elder whom he wanted
"out of the way":

> But this poor little Cat
> Only wanted a Rat
> To stuff out its own little maw,
> And 'twere as good
> Had some people such food
> To make them hold their jaw.
>   (*PS* I, 4)

If the story about Shelley's recital of "Ode on the Death of a Favorite Cat"
is literally true, Shelley's ability to repeat forty-two lines after a single reading
is indeed phenomenal, but the situation itself is interesting as well. While
Elizabeth Shelley may have employed a governess, just as earlier she may

have used a wet nurse, she was, as admiring auditor for this performance, also acting as a mother-educator. At six, Hellen Shelley tells us, Shelley was sent daily to learn Latin at a clergyman's house (Hogg I, 21)—that is, from Mr. Edwards, the elderly pastor in the neighboring village of Warnham—but he was otherwise educated at home until he went, at age ten, to Syon House. His sister Elizabeth, two years younger, was likely a co-pupil during his early years. Mary, the third surviving child, five years his junior, was not.

Like the Latin declamations which Hellen remembers Shelley performing at his father's bidding (Hogg I, 23), his special Latin lessons were a sign of his male privilege over female speakers of the mother tongue. Still, the bulk of his education until he was almost in his teens took place in the woman-centered, mother-dominated, female-inhabited enclosure of an upper-middle-class nursery/schoolroom with a younger sister as his only fellow pupil.[3] As Hellen's reminiscences suggest, it also took place within the "affective" family described by Stone and Trumbach as typical, though neither of their analyses fully takes into account the *negative* affect crackling along with the positive to create an electric family atmosphere.

In the environment of this womanly sphere, Shelley's gender and his seniority gave him dominance, but the nature of his "pranks" there suggests that he was an insecure, unappeasably vulnerable, and insidiously strong sibling rival, constantly striving in negative ways for attention that then focused negatively on him. For the mimetic Oedipal desirer strives not only to be— and so to erase—the father but to be and simultaneously to wipe out all other rivals as well.

A paradigmatic example of this kind of conduct surfaces in Hellen's recollection of a little drama enacted between the youngest Shelley child, John, who seems to have been about two, and Bysshe. The latter would therefore have been fifteen, but his actions in the scenario show characteristics of a much younger child:

> My younger brother, John, was a child in petticoats, when I remember Bysshe playing with him under the fir-trees on the lawn, pushing him gently down to let him rise and beg for a succession of such falls, rolling with laughing glee on the grass; then, as a sequel to this game, the little carriage was drawn through the garden walks at the rate a big boy could draw a little one, and in an unfortunate turn the carriage was upset, and the occupant tossed into the cabbages or strawberry-bed. Screams, of course, brought sympathetic aid, and, though the child was unhurt, the boy was rebuked; and when the former was brought down after dinner in the nurse's arms, "Bit" (Bysshe) was apostrophized as a culprit. His great delight was to teach his infant brother schoolboy words, and his first attempt at his knowledge of the devil, was an innocent "Debee!" (Hogg I, 23–24)

Frustrated desire for the rival's erasure builds up tension within an initially loving game until the temptation "accidentally" to throw him away, dump him out, gets too strong. But the rival, rescued, is stronger than ever and only deeper ensconced in the love he has usurped, while the desirer is cast further into darkness, is indeed made identical with it: "apostrophized as culprit." Yet if language defines him, the "culprit" can also use language to infiltrate the baby mind with concepts that make it share in deviltry.

Even if we allow for the fact that John, as Shelley's only *male* sibling, was a particular rival, the story told by Hellen suggests the sibling jealousy of a much younger child. It seems fair to suspect, then, that the birth of a sister when Shelley was twenty-one months old, the age most vulnerable of all to that passion, caused him much greater torment. For the weaned child, the spectacle of the newcomer contentedly nursing would serve as a particularly maddening exacerbation of that suffering.

Nathaniel Brown has taken note of the ubiquity of thirst in Shelley's work, "present wherever he seeks to formulate his love psychology, just as it consistently characterizes the many lovers of his work, notorious for their all-consuming thirsts which, if not slaked, annihilate them" (33). Among all the many examples one might cite on this theme, the poetic fragment "To thirst & find no fill" turns with special intensity on the trope of a weaned infant:

>   find no fill
> To thirst & find no fill—to ~~wail~~ & <wander>
>   short unsteady
> With <~~unn~~>   steps—to pause & ponder—
> To fell the blood run thro the veins, & tingle
> Where busy thought & blind sensation mingle;—
> To nurse the image of unfelt caresses
>   <dazed>
>   ~~dizzy fan~~ imagination just possesses
> Till ~~life is half created shadow~~
>   <and> ~~turning~~
> The half created shadow—~~then to tremble~~
>   ~~and, clasping air,~~
>   F~~<eel>~~ing
> ~~To find the form that dim then to gro<w>~~
>   then ~~to borrow~~
>   all the night
>   (*Bodleian MS.* III, 139)[4]

This fragment appears on the same page of a notebook as an early draft of "To Constantia [singing]," and P. M. S. Dawson, the notebook's editor, dates both to December 1817 (III, xvi). Ill health and financial difficulties had arisen together for Shelley at that time in one of their recurrent periods of crescendo. They may explain the angst this fragment struggles to express but not the trope of weaning as metaphoric vehicle for that angst. That may have surfaced in Shelley's consciousness with particular force at this time because of the situation of his son William.

On September 2, 1817, when William was twenty months old, Mary Shelley gave birth to Clara. She may have weaned William earlier, of course (for Mary, as impassioned daughter of Mary Wollstonecraft, there was no question of Harriet's stand against maternal breast-feeding), but William's recorded behavior after this event shows that he was experiencing or reexperiencing the hurt and angry sense of abandonment resulting from apparent withdrawal of his mother's total care and attention. His strategy in response, one typical enough, was to reject *her*. In late September Mary wrote to Shelley, who was in London to consult a physician about his own health: "You[r] babes are quite well but I have had some pain in perceiving or imagining that Willy has almost forgotten me—and seems to like Elise better—" (*Letters* I, 44).

Although Shelley's tubercular symptoms of this period were genuine,[5] they may well have been exacerbated by feelings mirroring those of his young son. Emily Sunstein drily remarks in describing this troubled time: "As before when she [Mary Godwin] gave birth, his [Shelley's] health precipitously declined" (144). So insistent were his demands for Mary's attention that she wrote on September 24 with brutal truth, lightly masked as concern: "My spirits however are much better than they were—and perhaps your absence is the cause—ah! my love you cannot guess how wretched it was to see your languor and encreasing illness" (*Letters* I, 41).

And while William turned a baby head away from his mother and toward the nurse Elise, Shelley in parallel fashion made this one of the times that he paid Claire Clairmont particularly amorous attention. Sunstein uses a schoolroom simile to describe the way in which Shelley and Claire excluded Mary— "Like children about a teacher, they commiserated over Mary's flaws and 'wise head' " (146)—but an image drawn from mother-child relationships would be equally appropriate.

"To Constantia" was written to and for Claire; according to the latter's testimony Shelley "wd. not let Mary see" it (*Bodleian MS.* III, xvii). The feelings described in it by the poetic persona as he hears "Constantia" sing have the character of those "oceanic" moments to which, in "On Life," Shelley says those persons who are "always children" will continue to have access: "Those who are subject to the state called reverie feel as if their nature were dissolved into the surrounding universe, or as if the surrounding universe were absorbed into their being" (*SPP* 477). The stanza sharing a notebook page (see figs. 5 and 6) with "To thirst & find no fill" begins, in its completed form: "I have no life Constantia but in thee; / Whilst, like the world-surrounding air, thy song / Flows on, and fills all things with melody" (*SPP* 102). In draft form, placed as they are side by side, the poems are Melanie Klein's "good breast" and "bad breast" textualized.[6]

Thus brought together, the evidence suggests that when he wrote "To thirst & find no fill," twenty-five-year-old Shelley was not simply observing and recording the experience of his twenty-month-old son; he was also reexperiencing emotions he had had at the same age and for a similar reason. And, as repeated incidents in Shelley's life show, his reactive strategy in the face of what he experienced as abandonment was, like William's, to become the abandoning one, while continuing to feel the violent hurt of being abandoned.[7]

Yet feelings toward both the usurper sibling and the betraying mother are truly ambivalent, fraught as they are with triangulated desire. Mikkel Borch-Jacobsen, working from the Girardian model, reminds us that mimesis is the

1a
1 To thirst & find no fill - written over > < > & find no fill - in pencil 1-2 to wait & <wander> With in
pencil 1 wait &] & d7 wall and W [wall] and L2 <wall> and O 3 fell slip for feel 6b a in <dazed> altered
from <1>] dim d7,W dizzy L1 [dizzy] L2 <?dazed> O ?c,?d,? d7,W omit 11 <?>altered from < > is consuming]
consuming extacies H,OH,d7,P,C consuming extacies W,L2 consuming exstasies O is now but thee] but in thee
H,OH,C,O 18a now possibly how 2s like] like cancelled for as H as OH,C,O 26b rocks] woods OH,C,O 2s summer]
summer's H,OH,C,O 2s where] when d7,P,W,L2 32a the] my H,OH,P,W,L2,C,O

10 I am come—dissolved in their   find no fill
11 <it to my My>   slumbers   To thirst & find no fill - to wait & <wander>
12 Thy voice   By   With <um>   steps — to pause & ponder —
13 My soul, to lost, dissolved in us<s>   short unsteady
14 Body & soul dissolved in liquid extacies   To fell the blood run thro the veins, & tingle
15 Slowly I am drunk up by   Where busy thought & blind sensation mingle:—
15a   dissolved in
16 I am dissolved in these consuming   thee   To nurse the image of unfelt caresses
18a   Constantia now   <dazed>
17 Now like   Till life the half-created Imagination just possesses
18 I have no life or rest or   but thee   The half created shadow <und> turning
19 I am not body or soul or ought but thee   <und> clasping air,
20 While that calm those divine   is misery   To find the form that dim then to borrow
                                                                                    all the night

21   Whilst thou like the Heaven dilating wind, thy song Sick
22a   world surrounding
22b   the Whilst like the world-surrounding wind, thy song
23   Flows on, with eclipsing and fills all things with melody.—
24a   Now is thy voice
24b   Now like a cloud it sweeps on a tempest swift & strong   rocks & waves
25a   In trance
25b   By in which, like one in dream upborne   Scud over hill & seas
26a   I tread nor earth nor sea over the earth seas & hills I pass
27   Rejoicing, like a now like new now it like a cloud of morn:
28   Now tis the breath of summer even night.
29b   starry
29a   Which, where the purple waters sleep,
30a   Round western glowing waters sleep,
30   Around the western odorous isles isles, with incense blossoms bright.
31a   Lope Wafts my dissolving feet
32   Lingering suspends my soul in its voluptuous flight.

Fig. 5. Transcription of Bodleian MS. Shelley e. 4, f. 34v. (*The Bodleian Shelley Manuscripts, Volume III.* Edited by P.M.S. Dawson. *Courtesy of Garland Publishing, Inc.*)

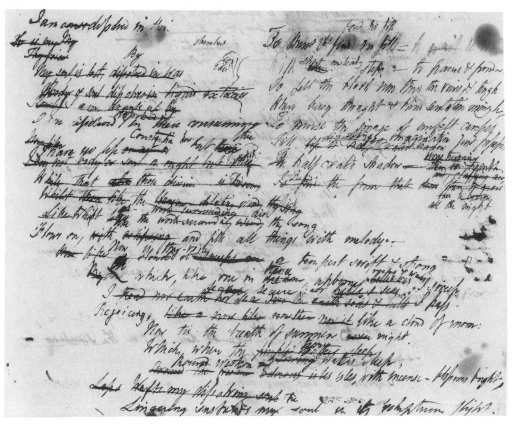

Fig. 6. "To thirst & find no fill." Draft page from one of Shelley's notebooks (Bodleian MS. Shelley e. 4, f. 34v. *Courtesy of the Bodleian Library, Oxford*)

salient aspect of mimetic desire. Strictly, the child does not desire the mother but rather desires to *be* her, desires her apparent autonomy. Thus, in Borch-Jacobsen's contribution to analysis of the "Fort/Da" game of Freud's little grandson, "when the child abandons his toys (what he 'has'), he is treating them the way his mother treats him. In this sense, by throwing his toys away he is not so much sacrificing the mother as himself: he himself is drawing away from himself by playing the mother's role" (33). Similarly, desire to be the mother and have what she has expresses itself as desire for "her" new baby; thus, as well as being in competition with the sibling for maternal attention, one is the mother's rival, wiping her out and taking her place as the one who will bestow attention.[8]

A reminiscence of Hellen's about one of the young Shelley's repeated fantasies suggests strongly that he availed himself of this appropriate mimetic strategy. The anecdote also provides evidence for the pervasive power of the maternal ideology within the Shelley nursery. Hellen's remarks come, in the same stream-of-consciousness fashion, just after her mention of the encouragement Shelley gave her through attention to and interest in her writing. Concerned suddenly that she has put her own possible talent too much forward, she deprecates her literary efforts, saying that she mentioned them only because "it will tend to show that my brother was full of pleasant attention to children, though his mind was so far above theirs." In the sentence that immediately follows, she describes his fantasy of adopting a child—a girl child[9]: "He had a wish to educate some child, and often talked seriously of purchasing a little girl for that purpose: a tumbler, who came to the back door to display her wonderful feats, attracted him, and thought she would be a good subject for the purpose, but all these wild fancies came to naught" (Hogg I, 27).

They "came to naught" in this early form, but the fantasy is one that Shelley repeatedly sought to implement throughout the rest of his life. Something of its aggressive and appropriative aspect surfaces in Hellen Shelley's language when she writes that he would take long walks with his little sisters during the school holidays "if he could steal away with us" (Hogg I, 24). A further, more elaborate instance occurred in the fall of 1814, when Shelley had extended daydreaming sessions with Mary Godwin and Claire Clairmont about a plan to kidnap two of his sisters, Elizabeth and Hellen, from their school in Hackney and carry them to the west of Ireland, where they would participate in a community that would include a reconciled Harriet Shelley as well as Peacock and Marianne de St. Croix, whom Peacock hoped to marry (M. Shelley, *Journals* I, 30). The fantasy enters into his relationships with Harriet Westbrook, Mary Godwin, Claire Clairmont, and Teresa Viviani, as it seems to have done in the bizarre "adoption" of the infant Elena in Naples in 1818.[10] An 1811 letter from Shelley to Joseph Merle offers a verbalization of it. Shelley is imagining himself as a Rousseauvian tutor in an educational experiment, but he changes Emile's gender: "I wish to find two young persons of not more than four or five years of age; and should prefer females, as they are usually more precocious than males. . . . I will withdraw from the world with my charge, and in some sequestered spot direct their education. They shall know nothing of men or manners until their minds shall have been sufficiently matured to enable me to ascertain . . . what the impressions of the world are upon the mind when it has been veiled from human prejudice" (quoted in Holmes 69). Merle's expostulations in response focused on the sexual and ignored the epistemological elements of the fantasy—and a number of the examples I have noted demonstrate that indeed an appropriative sexual desire for shaping the beloved and possessing her mind as well as her body enters into Shelley's pedagogic passion.[11] At the same time a certain naïve obliviousness to the sexual in Shelley's statement can be traced to his own identification with the feminine maternal. His very phrasing—"I will withdraw from the world with my charge, and in some sequestered spot direct their education"—echoes the language of those tales of mother-educators described in Chapter 2.

Given the psyche's penchant for the overdetermined, the adoption scenario reflects, however, not only the male tutor's identification with the mother as educator but also his transformation of the tutee into a daughter, thus screening the unthinkable fantasy of mother-son incest with the more socially acceptable, even covertly fostered, one of incest between father and daughter. It is possibly, then, another instance of the situation brilliantly analyzed by Sandra Gilbert in which the daughter functions for a man as "a miniaturized version of the mother whom patriarchal culture absolutely forbids him to desire" (373). Gilbert's analysis draws on the research published by Judith Herman and Lisa Hirschman in *Father-Daughter Incest,* whose findings throw light as well on Shelley's relationships with younger women in his many actings-out of the adoption fantasy. As I noted earlier when describing Shelley's psychological state after the birth of William, he made extraordinary emotional demands on women who in fact stood much in need of *his* attention and care. That is, like the actually incestuous fathers described in *Father-Daughter Incest,* Shelley transformed these young women into vessels for all his "infantile longings for nurturance and care" (Gilbert 373). But both actual father-daughter incest and Shelley's "screen" version of it are, respectively, only extreme and less extreme versions of an incestuous pattern institutionalized through the separation of spheres: women remain in the "coverture" of permanent daughterhood by virtue of their dependence on men's support, and men are permanently infantilized through their dependence on women's physical and emotional nurturance.[12] Signs of men's infantilization appear, as I have noted, very early in the literature on breast-feeding.

Other incidents besides the overturning of baby John suggest that along with assuaging his desire for possession of total maternal attention through his adoption fantasy, Shelley sought to gain that attention through "pranks." Although Hellen's emphasis is altogether on his kindness to the younger children and the fascination he brought to their games through the power of his imagination, her language conveys the sense of something dictatorial, overbearing, and frightening in the character of his games and stories.

To give a few examples: one of Shelley's delightfully terrifying themes was the Great Tortoise that, according to legend, lived in Warnham Pond; "any unwonted noise was accounted for by the presence of this great beast." Hellen's reminiscence moves Hogg to interpolate at this point his own associated memory of Shelley's many references to "the 'Great Old Snake' . . . which had inhabited the gardens at Field Place for several generations" (Hogg I, 22).

In another fantasy that filled the younger children with "pleasing dread," Shelley described a closed room in the Field Place garret as "the habitation of an Alchemist, old and grey, with a long beard." Hellen's story suggests that it was with a purpose of visiting him that Shelley made a hole in the hall ceiling, "a piece of mischief for which he was rebuked" (Hogg I, 22). Another "dangerous amusement" that also earned rebuke was a dabbling in alchemy itself. With his sisters dressed up "in strange costumes to personate spirits or fiends . . . [he] would take a fire-stove and fill it with some inflammable [sic] liquid and carry it flaming into the kitchen and to the back door." Hellen, with the others, was also a terrified subject of his experiments in electrical magnet-

ism, in which the children "were placed hand-in-hand round the nursery table
to be electrified" (Hogg I, 23). In different ways these boyhood fantasies all
argue for a profound and ambivalent involvement with a maternal presence
feared, admired, envied, and worshiped for its power.

Hogg's own comments on the "old Snake" suggest his awareness of its
association with the Mother Goddess. His first sentence about the Snake
makes it so ancient as to transcend time: "[It] had been known as the 'Old
Snake,' three hundred years ago." Immediately there follows a jauntily demys-
tifying sentence which suggests that legends like that of the Snake necessarily
perish and wither away in rational, historical time: "It was killed, accidentally,
through the carelessness of the gardener, in mowing the grass: killed by the
same fatal instrument with which the universal destroyer, Time, kills everything besides—by that two-handed engine, the scythe." The Miltonic allusion
"two-handed engine" casts heroic suggestiveness back over the bathetic mock
heroics that precede it and forward to the sentence that follows: "There is so
strong an affinity between serpents and all imaginative and demoniacal characters, that I cannot but regret to have entirely forgotten the legends of the 'Old
Snake' [that Shelley told]; narratives perfectly true, no doubt—not with the
commonplace truth of ordinary matters of fact, but with the far higher truth of
poetical verity and mythological necessity" (I, 22). So by the end of this
peculiar little aside, the possibly "matter-of-fact" story about the Snake's
death at the hands of a gardener takes on the "mythological necessity" of
confrontations with the Great Mother such as that of Apollo with the Python
at Delphi.

Hellen's biographical reminiscence of the attic necromancer corroborates—though it may also echo—Shelley's seemingly autobiographical passages, such as the one in "Alastor" (ll. 21–37) describing his long interest in
magic, alchemy, and all that knowledge that attempts to lay bare the sources of
life. Walter E. Peck, commenting on Shelley's interest in such knowledge,
makes the point that Shelley was not drawn to the practice of extensive, analytic
research but to experiments that produced sudden and spectacular metamorphoses. "Setting fire to a willow tree by the use of gunpowder and burning glass;
brewing strange, fiery liquids; invoking departed spirits; despatching fire-
balloons—only such essays in the field of science appealed to him" (23).

Another memory of Hellen's suggests the importance that the very word
"metamorphoses" had for Shelley. One gathers that she was writing on a topic
set by Shelley, its theme drawn from Monk Lewis's poems or some analogous
"tale of spirits, fiends, etc." She produced a poem of which she still recalled
one couplet: "There was an old woman, as I have heard say, / Who worked
metamorphoses every day." Her memory of those lines was still vivid, she
continues, because of the pleasure she took in her brother's praise: "Bysshe
expressed so much astonishment at my knowledge of the word *metamorphoses*" (Hogg I, 26). A line about "an old woman in her bony gown," from
another poem she wrote to one of his set topics, stayed with her for the same
reason.

Since Hellen's motive in writing was so clearly to earn the praise of her older brother, it seems very likely that she used the word "metamorphoses" because he so often had. Also her verse on a subject chosen by Shelley links the feminine with the power to change one form of life into another, and then, associatively, Hellen remembers another poem in which the feminine becomes the skeletal image of death. The associative pattern contains the same mixed emotions—awe at the female power to give birth, envy of that power and the desire to appropriate it, and fear that such appropriation will bring the punishment of castration/death—that Mary Shelley, with Percy as her primary model, made central to her characterization of Frankenstein.[13]

Symptomatic of such envy, according to Bruno Bettelheim, is pyromania. He writes, "I have often noticed the delight that boys take in setting fires and in playing with fire pumps, particularly boys in great doubt about their masculinity" (Bettelheim 167). His comment brings into juxtaposition Shelley's youthful pyromania and the subtitle Mary Shelley gave her novel: *The Modern Prometheus*. In large cultural terms the fascination the Promethean myth had for male Romantic poets, well outlined by Anne Mellor (70–80), may have its source not only in Faustian overreaching—"the desire to elevate human beings into living gods" (71)—but also in a fear of maternal power exacerbated by the gender politics discussed in Chapter 2.[14]

Within the microcosm of the Shelley home, Shelley's many "pranks" involving fire are alarming signals of divisions within him so great that setting Field Place afire seemed their only possible resolution. Or, to retreat from the dramatic metaphors favored by the unconscious and to use Cameron's more measured language, Shelley "grew up without a male ideal" (*Young Shelley* 5). Simply in terms of personality, Elizabeth Shelley's beauty, charisma, and forcefulness meant that she outshone her husband as the parent whose attention was most desired. And the maternal ideology of the period also underwrote her right, indeed her duty, to engage and focus that attention. But as the analyses of Slater, Rich, Chodorow, and Dinnerstein have all in their very different ways made clear, both sons and daughters suffer profound ambivalence toward the maternal when they are raised in a system of male power and denigration of the feminine, which nonetheless relegates child care entirely to women and *for that purpose only* gives women dominance within a confined domestic sphere.[15]

In Shelley's case, his fantasies both of adopting a girl child and of gaining power through the "magic" of alchemical knowledge point toward a desire for total maternal attention so strong that it engenders an antithetical desire for independence from the maternal altogether. The pranks in which this dichotomous desire expressed itself brought the negative attention of a reprimand, which served only to frustrate, and so strengthen, the need for attention of a different kind *and* the desire to be free of that need, the desire for desirelessness. Whether or not Richard Holmes is right in the opinion that Shelley was sent to Syon House as a final, most negative parental reaction to these high jinks (Holmes 4), the boy would almost surely have experienced his banishment as such a judgment—even though it was a banishment his actions had sought—and as a betrayal, particularly by his mother.

As I noted when describing the task of the mother-educator, little boys as well as their sisters were given their first teaching by their mothers, but according to the recollections of those present at his entrance into Syon House, Shelley appears to have been educated within a feminine circle longer than was customary for boys. Medwin, already at the school, traces the exceptionally severe hazing that Shelley received to the fact that he could not compete in boys' sports: "He was ignorant of pegtop or marbles, or leap-frog, or hop-scotch, much more of fives or cricket" (17). W. C. Gellibrand remembers him as being "like a girl in boy's clothes, fighting with open hands" (White I, 19–20). Inscribed, then, on "his spontaneous bodily habits" (Eagleton 23) was that mirroring of the feminine that was intended to serve as an *interior* core of "sensibility" ameliorating the rigors of autonomous individualism but was then, through the workings of an institutionalized misogyny, to be hidden under a rough and hardy masculine exterior. Shelley's body, as well as the shrill tones of his voice in moments of excitement or stress (Peacock III, 395), signified a subjectivity in which the aesthetic ideology had created not a fully satisfactory bourgeois citizen but a potential source of disruption. Years of ferocious hazing at Syon House and at Eton did not erase those signs, though such erasure was an important part of their purpose.

There is a suggestion also in Medwin's account that the schoolmasters as well as the boys mocked him as an effeminate exile from the maternal circle. With the help of Medwin's cribbing book, Shelley plagiarized a line of Ovid's beginning "Jam, jam . . ." for a Latin composition. According to Medwin, the schoolmaster, incensed not because he recognized the theft but because he thought the line a bad one, boxed Shelley's ears, saying, " '*Jam jam,*'—Pooh, pooh, boy! raspberry jam! Do you think you are at your mother's" (21). And, again according to Medwin, his mother's was indeed where he wafted himself in fantasy by doodling "rude drawings of pines and cedars, in memory of those on the lawn of his ancient home" (20). (As Medwin rightly notes in an aside, similar drawings appear in Shelley's notebooks throughout his life.) Medwin comments specifically as well on the depth of his feeling for his relatives, "and particularly for the females in his family. It was not without manifest joy that he received a letter from his mother and sisters" (18).

In "An Essay on Friendship" Shelley himself records a single memory drawn from the two years at Syon House. Hogg, who first reprinted the essay, states that Shelley wrote it "not long before his death," though without giving a rationale for that date (I, 30). The subject matter suggests that Shelley wrote it at around the same time that he translated the *Symposium* and also wrote "A Discourse on the Manners of the Ancient Greeks Relative to the Subject of Love" (August 1818). Either way, it was written after communication with or even recorded mention of his mother had ceased. A specific reference to her thus has significance in itself, but even more important is the illumination it casts on the nature of his relation to his mother at the time when he was sent away from home to school.

The fragment begins with musings in the first paragraph on the distinction between love and friendship, defining the latter feeling as "a profound and sentimental attachment to one of the same sex, wholly divested of the smallest alloy of sensual intermixture," with the conclusion that it "often precedes the former" (*CW* VII, 143). The meaning of "precedes" at this point appears to be that the feeling of friendship can lead to that of love. The next two sentences suggest, however that Shelley means "precedes" to refer to a particular time—and one time only—in the life span, one preceding the advent of heterosexual desire. He thereby makes even more vehement his disjunction of the close attachment of friends from the physical union of lovers, but the very words of negation make the potential sexuality of the relationship more rather than less a reality: "It is not right to say, merely, that it is exempt from the smallest alloy of sensuality. It rejects, with disdain, all thoughts but those of an elevated and imaginative character and the process by which the attachment between two persons of different sexes terminates in a sensual union has not yet begun." The last sentence in this paragraph takes as exemplum "an attachment of this kind" that Shelley had at school when he was around eleven or twelve.

The sentences describing the young friend have the character of an idealized self-portrait, consistent with Shelley's contention in "On Love" that "there is something within us which from the instant that we live and move thirsts after its likeness" (*SPP* 473) and in "A Discourse on the Manners of the Ancient Greeks" that love is "the universal thirst for a communion not merely of the senses, but of our whole nature, intellectual, imaginative, and sensitive" (Notopoulos 408). Physical union is not, by his earlier definition, in question here, but Shelley's description of the relationship focuses on shared feeling, indeed shared sorrow:

> The object of these sentiments was a boy of about my own age, of a character eminently generous, brave, and gentle; and the elements of human feeling seemed to have been, from his birth, genially compounded within him. . . . The tones of his voice were so soft and winning, that every word pierced into my heart; and their pathos was so deep, that in listening to him the tears ofter have involuntarily gushed from my eyes. Such was the being for whom I first experienced the sacred sentiments of friendship. (*CW* VII, 143)

Immediately there follow—as part of the same paragraph but as a kind of aside, since the last sentences of the paragraph return to his relationship with the unnamed boy—two sentences that allude to Shelley's mother: "I remember in my simplicity writing to my mother a long account of his admirable qualities and my own devoted attachment. I suppose she thought me out of my wits, for she returned no answer to my letter" (*CW* VII, 144).

"In my simplicity," writes Shelley. On the surface the phrase offers Shelley's admission that at the time of writing the essay, though not when he wrote his mother the letter, he was aware that such schoolboy friendships could be interpreted as having a sexual character. It posits his youthful unawareness both of the existence of homosexual relationships and of the homophobia rampant in his culture: thus his innocent surprise in his schooldays, though not at the time of writing the essay, that his mother's response is blank silence, denial. But the strong possibility exists that the writer of the essay is being *faux naïf* about the naïveté of his boyhood self, just as the boy was being *faux naïf* in writing the letter home.

As Louis Crompton has argued well in his analysis of Shelley's "Discourse on the Manners of the Ancient Greeks," the adult Shelley either shared or condoned the homophobia of his culture (294–98). But such attitudes are unconsciously registered, again through ideological agencies, long before adulthood. Therefore the schoolboy Shelley, even if he could not articulate his thoughts, even if he was indeed oblivious to the sexual mores operating in the school system itself,[16] would have had some sense that his "devoted attachment" would cause his mother alarm or at least concern.

The letter to Elizabeth Shelley, under this analysis, plays out the abandonment scenario so constantly repeated in Shelley's life. Full of hurt and a sense of betrayal over her abandoning him, he changes the situation into one in which he has abandoned her for another beloved of whom she cannot approve. Yet her initial action has put him into a situation where none but this unacceptable solace is available to him, and so any guilt attached is hers, not his. With him remains only the suffering sense of being the abandoned one.

But if the pattern of response seems through hindsight particularly Shelley's it was also shared by his peers, according to Thomas Moore's commentary in his memoir of Byron:

> One of the most striking results of the English system of education is, that while in no country are there so many instances of manly friendships early formed and steadily maintained, so in no other country, perhaps, are the feelings toward the parental home so early estranged, or, at the best, feebly cherished. Transplanted as boys are from the domestic circle, at a time of life when the affections are most inclined to cling, it is but natural that they should seek a substitute for ties of home in those boyish friendships which they form at school, and which, connected as they are with the scenes and events over which youth threw its charm, retain ever after the strongest hold upon their hearts. (I, 143)

As Crompton points out, however, when quoting from this passage in *Byron and Greek Love,* in writing it Moore is offering a rationale for the passionate relationships of Byron's schooldays that will in fact mask their homosexuality (Crompton 80). Moore's sentimental commentary and Elizabeth Shelley's blank silence both in their different ways exemplify the denial characteristic of parents and educators in their response to the actualities of boarding school life.

Shelley's extraordinary intelligence makes him in certain key ways atypical; still, he certainly qualifies as a person with the "steep gradient affect" that Stone considers a relatively new and widespread phenomenon by the end of the eighteenth century and ascribes (plausibly, to my mind) to "a series of changes in child rearing." Stone and I then part company completely, however, in our sense of what this personality was like and thus of what effect that child rearing had, since he concludes that it created among adults "a sense of trust rather than distrust" (268). His inference, then, is that this personality was empathetic, amiable, honest, and humane.

In my opinion the infant Shelley found himself in a social milieu that gave him not a full script but, commedia dell'arte fashion, a scenario. Changing Stone's social, interactive word "personality" to the more interior one of "subjectivity," I would venture that like other infant members of his historical and social cohort, Shelley acquired steep gradient affect through the socially orchestrated interaction between desire for the mother and its frustration by the incest taboo. All his strategies for overcoming the one to appease the other were to be expected—indeed *were* expected—and created, through the usual mechanisms of displacement, denial, projection, sublimation, and unconscious repetition, a subjectivity we can all recognize: unappeasable and therefore active, ambitious, competitive, flexible, inventive, appropriative, and violent; attuned to other subjectivities and thereby verbal, sentimental, manipulative, impassioned, engaged, and imaginative—a modern Promethean.[17]

A Mother-Son Alliance

If the experience of being sent away to boarding school estranged Shelley, like other boys of his class, from his parents and perhaps, to judge from his later memory, particularly from his mother, it by no means created a permanent rift. Late adolescence and early maturity are characteristically turbulent in any lifetime, fraught, among other things, with the stress of separation from family, including the mother. The turmoil of Shelley's life during that period—specifically between 1809 and 1814—exceeded the norm, but through most of its passionate events his mother figures as an ally, even a co-conspirator, not an adversary. One exception, involving Shelley's accusations of adultery against his mother, is not a true exception in that it too bears witness to an extraordinarily strong bond between mother and son.

Elizabeth Shelley figures, for instance, as a benevolent, even a presiding, presence in the events of 1809–10 surrounding Shelley's love for his cousin, Harriet Grove. The only earlier encounter between the cousins had been during the Easter vacation of 1804, when Shelley, on holiday from Syon House, stayed at Fern. There he was ringleader in a game of "carpenters" with two of Harriet's brothers, Charles and George, aged nine and ten, respectively, in which they cut down some of the young fir trees in Thomas Grove's park. Charles, remembering the incident nearly fifty years later, recalled, "My father often used to remind me of that circumstance" (*SHC* II, 477).

One takes it, then, that from the beginning Shelley had soured the attitude of the masculine authority in the Grove household. But the blood connection was on the Pilfold side, and Harriet Grove's diary of 1809–10 suggests that a romance between Bysshe and Harriet had the indulgent interest certainly of her aunt and probably of her mother, Charlotte. When Harriet's diary opens in January 1809, she is already corresponding not only with Bysshe but with "Aunt Shelley" (*SHC* II, 478–79). An exchange of letters could not long be a clandestine matter in an English country house,[18] and while the young people's cousinhood made such correspondence socially acceptable, it would also have demanded at least implicit indulgence from those elders scrutinizing the mail as it came and went. The fact that Elizabeth Shelley herself was writing to her sixteen-year-old niece suggests more: it signals an active fostering of the romance.[19] And although the tempo and mores of an upper-middle-class nineteenth-century woman's life made a wide correspondence customary, the time Elizabeth Shelley gave to writing so much younger a woman suggests as well that she took the role of mother-educator seriously. The correspondence thus offers retrospective evidence of Elizabeth Shelley's close involvement with her children.

Harriet and Shelley had their first significant opportunity to turn cousinly correspondence into personal relationship when the two families met in London in April 1809, but Mrs. Shelley was not a member of the group (*SHC* II, 516). In the year that followed, Harriet's diary records a steady, sometimes daily, stream of letters between her and Bysshe, as well as an ongoing correspondence with Shelley's mother and, beginning in August, an epistolary exchange with his sister Elizabeth also. In late March 1810, at the same time that plans were being made for a Grove visit to Field Place before another April meeting in London, Shelley sent Harriet and her sister Charlotte a copy of his newly published gothic novel, *Zastrozzi*.

The two days of the visit to Field Place, April 16 and 17, were ecstatically happy for Harriet, as is clear from her grumbling after the Groves moved on for a stay with the John Pilfolds at Cuckfield that they had left "the pleasentest party in the world for the most unpleasent" (*SHC* II, 576). But the entries for the Field Place days also contain several allusions to Harriet's puzzlement: "I can not tell what to make of it very strange"; "more perplexed than ever"; "I still know not what is meant" (*SHC* II, 575–76). Cameron speculates that Harriet's was a delicious surprise and bewilderment over the fact that the parents on both sides, plainly aware of the intense emotions of the two young people, were taking it, approvingly, that they were informally engaged (*SHC* II, 484).

Now, her perplexity could also be a sign of gathering family *dis*approval, but the dairy's record of events in London bears out Cameron's interpretation. Some sort of "understanding" would almost have had to exist for Harriet and Shelley to be allowed as much time alone together as they were when the two families regrouped. On April 26, for instance, after a walk together in the fields, the two joined their mamas for a shopping trip, then left their elders at a Mrs. Barton's. They forgot that they were expected to return, with the result that Elizabeth Shelley and Charlotte Grove were obliged to take a hackney coach—"a shocking dirty one"—back to their lodgings. There would have been good reason for both mothers to be annoyed, indeed furious, if the reason for the young people's general distraction had been unacceptable. Aunt Shelley's response, on the contrary, was a virtually conspiratorial mock reprimand: "Aunt S——says she shall send for a Chain & Chain us to her—" (II, 577). And on May 1–4, when Harriet was obliged to miss certain outings because she had allegedly hurt her foot, Bysshe was allowed to keep her company alone.

The Aunt Shelley of Harriet Grove's diary is a kindly older relative, perhaps even a confidante of at least some kind, since the letters between aunt and niece no doubt contained allusions to Bysshe as an interest they had in common; she is thus a fosterer of romance but not herself a romantic subject. Her son, however, shows a different sense of her. Mrs. Shelley's presence in London that spring is recorded once in Shelley's letters as well, and there she appears as a dashing, erotically interesting figure. The allusion comes in a series of letters to Edward Fergus Graham, a musician and music master of around twenty-three, who appears to have been a protégé of the Shelley family (*L* I, 5; *SHC* II, 623). On April 23, still clearly in high spirits after Harriet's recent Field Place visit, Shelley and his sister Elizabeth wrote from there to Graham to arrange a rendezvous with him; he was to meet them and their mother at Hellen and Mary's boarding school. The note uses gothic fantasy in the *Zastrozzi* style to transform the banal meeting into a demonic assignation. One paragraph, signed by Elizabeth but written in Shelley's hand, contains the sentence "Stalk along the road towards them [a line of elm trees]—& mind & keep yourself concealed as my mother brings a blood stained stiletto whic{h} she purposes to make you bathe in the life blood of her enemy" (*L* I, 10). While this is all high-spirited nonsense, Mrs. Shelley's part in the fantasy takes on added significance when one is aware that a year and a half later Shelley was to accuse his mother of an adulterous liaison with Graham. In *Zastrozzi* the lustful and violent character Mathilda gives Zastrozzi just the kind of assignment imagined as Mrs. Shelley's: he is to murder Julia, her successful rival for the love of the blameless Verezzi.

A letter to Graham in May 1810 contains a single sentence about Shelley's mother, worth noting only because of its presupposition that Graham will be interested in such a bulletin: Shelley writes that she had "a violent bilious fever" but is "now getting much better" (I, 12). A further message in August of the same year provides a piece of evidence in support of Cameron's theory that Timothy Shelley was treated by the other members of his family with a certain condescension (*The Young Shelley* 3, 5). In the letter, Shelley, his mother, and his sister Elizabeth became a "we" distinct from the father: "It is needless to say that should any business lead you to Sussex (you understand) we should always be happy to see you, I believe I may include my father. . . ." (*L* I, 14; the meaningful ellipsis is Shelley's).

A couple of months later Timothy Shelley, settling his son into Oxford, took him around to the bookseller Henry Slatter and boasted deprecatingly, "My son here has a literary turn; he is already an author, and do pray indulge him in his printing freaks" (*SHC* II, 605–6). But when in November Shelley published *Posthumous Fragments of Margaret Nicholson*, he mentions to Graham that he has sent a copy to his mother but "Of course to my Father Peg is a profound secret" (*L* I, 23). From the context it is clear that Graham has seen the text and has objected to lines in it that might be read as crossing over from the kind of sentimental poetry written by Charlotte Dacre into outright pornography: "Soft, my dearest angel, stay, / Oh! you suck my soul away; / Suck on, suck on, I glow! I glow!" (*PS* I, 121). Modern connotations of the word "suck" make it appear that Shelley had decidedly crossed that line, but its sentimental usage in his own time actually puts him precisely on the line. As the editors of *The Poems of Shelley* explain, this passage alludes to "the convention of lovers exchanging souls as they kiss, generally before dying (with possible equivocation over 'dying')," and they give among several parallel usages line 324 from Pope's "Eloisa to Abelard": "Suck my last breath, and catch my flying soul" (I, 121). The connection between sucking and soul is, then, the same as that expressed through the locution that the nurse's soul will enter the child; its "self-conscious fleshiness," in Jerome McGann's phrase (31), serves as witness to a possibly high-minded but certainly erotic—and aesthetic—intermingling of body and soul. In this particular instance, however, Shelley's strongest motivation for printing the lines was the commercial one that is also a complicating feature in the production of sentimental verse. He defends the lines as ones that will make the book "sell like wildfire" but says that the copy sent to his mother does not contain them (*L* I, 23).[20]

Unfortunately we have no record of Elizabeth Shelley's reaction to *Posthumous Fragments*. Even in a bowdlerized version, and even with pseudonymous authorship and a satiric title to camouflage treasonable poems such as the opening invective against the whole institution of monarchy, the very slim book contained material to concern a "liberal" but politically and religiously conventional parent. It may well be, however, that Elizabeth Shelley's attention was more focused on the four poems out of the six making up the book that, to one aware of the situation, clearly alluded to Shelley's pain over the dissolution of his relationship with Harriet Grove.

How Elizabeth Shelley herself felt about the breakup is unknown. The only extant account is Charles Grove's statement that there was a "continual correspondence" between the young people during the summer of 1810, "but she [Harriet] became uneasy at the tone of his [Shelley's] letters on speculative subjects, at first consulting my mother, and subsequently my father also on the subject. This led at last, though I cannot exactly tell how, to the dissolution of an engagement between Bysshe and my sister, which had previously been permitted, both by his father and mine" (*SHC* II, 488).

If Elizabeth Shelley *had* favored, even fostered, the match, as her latitude toward the pair in London seems to suggest, she may well have been disappointed at its end. She must also, one imagines, have been put on the somewhat embarrassed defensive by a coolness between her family and her sister's resulting, even if in small and temporary ways, from the rift. Some of the asperity of such feelings may lie in the response from her that Shelley records in a letter to Hogg from Field Place written on January 11, 1811: "My Moth fancies me in the High road to Pandemonium, she fancies I want to make a deistical coterie of all my little sisters" (*SHC* II, 701). Since the same letter describes Shelley's anguish on receiving the news that Harriet was engaged to

William Helyar and so "lost to me forever," this comment suggests that his mother's attitude was "Serves you right" rather than the deep concern shown by his sister Elizabeth. In Hellen's account the latter, fearing Shelley to be suicidal, "has frequently told me how narrowly she used to watch him and accompany him in his walks with his dog and gun" (Hogg I, 28).

Unrecorded also is Elizabeth Shelley's response to her son's expulsion from Oxford on March 25, 1811, for his refusal to answer questions put to him regarding his authorship, with Hogg, of *The Necessity of Atheism.* The letter that Shelley wrote to his father from London on March 28 describing what had occurred contains a message to his mother that seems designed to be hurtful in the distinction it draws between the two Elizabeths, mother and daughter: "Will you please present my affectionate duty to my mother, my love to Elizabeth." Still, the next sentence addresses itself equally positively to both: "I will not write today but shd. be happy to hear from them" (*L* I, 56).

And indeed, when Bysshe's enraged defensiveness and Timothy Shelley's blundering overreactions created a series of angry ultimatums, proposals, and counterproposals between father and son, badly mediated through William Whitton, the lawyer Timothy Shelley had engaged, Mrs. Shelley attempted to make peace. She intercepted a letter from Shelley that she thought would only make bad matters worse, sent him much-needed money, and asked him to come home (Ingpen I, 245). Shelley refused and returned the money, but a letter from Robert Parker, married to Timothy's older sister Hellen and thus a peacemaker on the Shelley side, shows that Shelley included his mother with his sister as allies. Parker writes: "Our conversation was long and not much gained by it—he expressed . . . a pretty strong desire to be reconciled to his family but an adherence to his own points, and of course very little bending to yours, but *an expression of affection towards his mother and sister.*" The emphasis given the final words was that of Timothy Shelley, who also added bitterly "never to me" (Ingpen I, 229).

Out of all the irate correspondence surrounding the weeks of Shelley's London exile in Poland Street, the letter that caused the strongest reaction made reference to Shelley's mother. On April 17 Shelley wrote to Whitton:

> As common report, & tolerably good authority informs me
> that part of Sir Bysshe Shelley's property is entailed upon me;
> I am willing by signature to resign all pretensions to such
> property, in case my father will divide it equally with my
> & My Mother
> sisters ∧ & allow me now 100£ per an: as an annuity which
> will only amount to 2000£: perhaps less. (*SHC* II, 752)

This proposal, as Whitton himself quickly pointed out, was not a legal possibility; as a minor Shelley could not make such an agreement. The fact that he would even conceive of it, however, so enraged Whitton that he replied to Shelley: "I am not a willing instrument by which insult may be offered to your father and I must therefore decline acting in any manner under the paper you have sent me" (*L* I, 63). He sent Timothy Shelley copies of the subsequent angry letters between himself and Shelley, but, in Ingpen's telling, "he withheld, on account of its 'indecency,' the letter containing the proposal to relinquish the entail" (I, 252). Timothy Shelley, even without the most damning evidence of his son's own words, wrote to Whitton: "I never felt such a shock in my Life, infinitely more than when I heard of his expulsion, for I could not then have thought it of so hidious [sic] a cast" (Ingpen I, 253).

Biographers comment in different ways on this incident as a shock to Timothy Shelley's sense of appropriate filial behavior but pass altogether over the *particular* way that Shelley had devised to challenge patriarchal order. Cameron sees the plan as the jaunty decision of someone "eighteen, republican, and Godwinian" (*Young Shelley* 84). White, somewhat similarly, judges that for Shelley the proposal "was merely a pleasant way of solving the present difficulties; it would give him all the income he wanted, would release him from all responsibility and property (no light consideration to a young Godwinian), and would leave him entirely free" (I, 129–30). Holmes judges it a genuine attack on Timothy Shelley but leaves unstated the gender issues being used as ammunition; he writes, "Shelley had instinctively struck at his father's most sensitive point: the ambition, inherited from grandfather to father, to secure the family name in the undivided and orderly inheritance from generation to generation of a solid body of English landed estates" (60).

As Cameron points out, however, in editing letters from this period for the second volume of *Shelley and His Circle,* Shelley was not "offering to give up the whole of the family estates but only 'that part of Sir Bysshe's property' which was entailed upon him, i.e., some £80,000 out of a total estate of some £200,000. He would still inherit the remaining £120,000" (*SHC* II, 752). In other words, Shelley scandalized Whitton and his father not so much because his Godwinian principles endangered a system of primogeniture but because his proposal pointed explicitly to the scandal, the stumbling block, of women's total dependence within patriarchy and made himself the heroic man who, by sharing his masculine privilege with women, would give them a measure of independence.

He had also—perhaps partly instinctively and partly through acute political awareness—chosen a historical moment when male paranoia over women's maintaining their "place" was at one of its high points. Although with the benefit of hindsight we now know that Napoleon, beginning to make plans for the invasion of Russia, was in 1811 shortly headed for catastrophe, he appeared at that time to be the conqueror of all Europe, with England as a frighteningly solitary exception. In *The Godwins and the Shelleys,* where William St. Clair juxtaposes twin graphs, one showing the price of government stocks and the other the number of women's conduct books published, 1811 appears as one of the low points for the price of stocks—less than £60—while just past the 1808 peak in the number of conduct books (511). As we saw in the fulminating tirades about feminine dress, two forces were taken to be the weakening factors making the country vulnerable to Napoleon, and therefore more horrible than Napoleon: loss of religious faith, with the moral order it imposed, and hope for the empowerment of women, with the political chaos it threatened. Shelley had managed within a month to exacerbate the fears surrounding both, but interestingly, Timothy Shelley found the latter the more "hidious."

Timothy was on his own terms right because within the politics of the family circle Shelley's proposal was certainly divisive. The way in which the phrase "& My Mother" is inserted in the letter to Whitton shows it to be an afterthought (*SHC* II, 752). By it Shelley changes a plan that could have brotherly concern for his sisters as its motive to one that baldly states the separation between men's and women's interests and allies itself with the latter. His strategy, which he was soon to repeat in another form by joking about his father's possible cuckoldry, is undoubtedly backed by the particular dynamics of the Shelley family. Ironically, though, it also reveals a debt to the ideas generated by the conduct books. Their purpose was to maintain social stability, but by dichotomizing masculine and feminine roles as strongly as they did and by defining women as, within the sphere of family life at least, the more admirable gender, they created a potential for imbalance that Shelley used to set Field Place rocking.

We have no way of telling whether Elizabeth Shelley shared her husband's response to Shelley's proposal. Reading back from Mary Shelley's much later comments about her mother-in-law's desire to provide a comfortable situation for herself in widowhood, one might judge that wry and ironic amusement characterized her reaction more than shock. In any case, it was relatives from her side of the family, her nephew John Grove and her brother Captain John Pilfold, who finally negotiated a peace between father and son. Shelley was to receive the £200 annual stipend that would give him the independence he wanted. Mid-May saw him reensconced at Field Place (*SHC* II, 783, 785).

The eighteen-year-old who returned to the family manor was, however, in a dangerously nasty frame of mind, if we can judge by the letters of the chaotic summer of 1811. With Cameron I hold that Shelley was virtually phobic about the possibility of being abandoned (*Young Shelley* 4), and within six months he had been cast off by Harriet Grove and her parents, particularly her father; expelled by the patriarchal institution of Oxford; and made to experience isolation and penury through the anger of his father and grandfather.

As Timothy Shelley's letters show, his irate feelings about his son's expulsion had their principal source not in religious outrage but in downright terror at the social stigma that might result. It was precisely the wrong response, first, because its self-centeredness did not give proper attention to his son's similar feelings of social humiliation (however much denied), and second, because its moral vacuity made Shelley feel himself all the more highly principled and altruistic in the stand he had taken. The venerable and impersonal institution of Oxford denied vengeance any access, but Timothy Shelley was more vulnerable. In retaliation for having himself been cast off, Shelley manipulated personalities and events so that his father would be the one left out of the family circle; to assuage the hurt of his rejection by Harriet Grove, he gave himself a companion in misery by at once arousing and dampening the brushfire emotions that his sister Elizabeth had aroused—sight unseen and so only through Shelley's own descriptions—in the susceptible Hogg. In both these intrigues Shelley assigned his mother a central role. They went on concurrently but must be treated seriatim for clarity's sake. A third plot—Shelley's relationship with Harriet Westbrook—cast the elder Elizabeth Shelley in a very different role and will be discussed later.

Shelley's first letter to Hogg on his return to Field Place, dated May 14, 1811, was addressed and franked, ironically, by Timothy Shelley. In having the postage paid this way, Shelley was availing himself of his father's postal privilege as a member of Parliament, as he customarily did. But the fact that he also left the letter open for his father to address and seal suggests to Cameron not that Timothy Shelley actually insisted on scrutinizing his son's mail but that Shelley, acting as if that might be his intention or his desire, "left it for Timothy to seal, daring him, as it were, also to read it" (*SHC* II, 789). The dare was all the cheekier in that Shelley's continued association and correspondence with Hogg had been a major source of contention during the previous weeks.

The reading would have been very unpleasant, not only for the obvious contempt expressed toward Timothy but for the contrast set up with Timothy on one side and his wife and her brother Captain Pilfold on the other. While discussing the religious hypocrisy that greeted *The Necessity of Atheism* with outrage, Shelley relays an anecdote told him by Captain Pilfold about "a relation"—in the context obviously his father—who in casual conversation admitted, "To tell you the truth *I* am an atheist." The captain, refusing further discussion, reportedly answered with a cool, "Are you indeed?" That Pilfold would relay the story suggests that he joined in the general dismissal of Timothy, but Shelley takes contempt further into outrage: "Is this irrational being really convinced <   > what we attained by the use of reason? <   > he is a disgrace to reason, & I am sorry that the cause [of atheism] has gained weakness by the accession of weakness" (*SHC* II, 785).[21]

Though weak, the last section of the letter suggests, Timothy Shelley is a domestic tyrant, ineffectual only because Shelley has as allies on his side Captain Pilfold and, significantly, Mrs Shelley: "—He ~~has~~ forbidden intercourse with my sister, but the Capt brought him to reason, he prevents it however as much as possible, which is very little . . My Mother is quite rational . . she says, 'I think prayer & thanksgiving is of no use. If a man is a good man, atheist or Xtian he will do very well in whatever future state awaits us.' This I call liberality." The letter concludes by saying, "I know you will excuse a longer letter as I am going to read to Eliza" (*SHC* II, 786; Shelley's ellipses), an example of what Cameron rather overbenevolently calls "teasing." Elizabeth, as Shelley says at the beginning of the letter, is recovering from scarlet fever, and so the words call up a vision of bedside intimacy most surely denied to Hogg.

Mrs. Shelley's words, taken as those of someone who is at least socially a Christian, *could* be placed on a continuum of hypocrisy somewhere near her husband's, but Shelley chooses to hear them as a rational contribution to religious speculation while his father's responses are maundering and hypocritical drivel. More important, though, in Shelley's mind his mother's words and accompanying attitude place her, like Captain Pilfold, actively on his side in the battle against his father.

Whether Mrs. Shelley saw herself as her son's partisan in this way is unclear. Shelley's allusions to moments of interaction with her suggest, however, that she was much troubled by his state of mind and was adopting a number of separate, perhaps even contradictory, strategies for calming him down. These attempts in themselves show a different frame of mind from the hurt and disgruntled antagonism into which Timothy Shelley had settled. We have as evidence, however, no outwardly and dispassionately observed acts but only Shelley's epistolary text of a "plot" that bears certain resemblances to that of *Hamlet,* with his mother cast as an ineffectual but loving Gertrude, Elizabeth as an overly docile Ophelia, Timothy as Polonius/Claudius, and Hogg/Shelley as Hamlet. His language, though, is much more sentimentally Della Cruscan than Shakespearean.

A letter to Hogg that Cameron dates as written on June 18 or 19 begins: "I wrote you on Sunday. . . . Reason have you to say that I was violent. . . . I was Mad! you know that very little sets my horrid spirits in motion; I drank a glass or two of wine at my Mothers instigation, then began raving . . She to quiet me gave me Pens Ink & Paper. I wrote to you" (*SHC* II, 810; Shelley's ellipses). The letter to which Shelley alludes, written with materials his mother had provided when that outlet seemed safer than the wine she had mistakenly imagined would calm him down, Cameron judges to be one written June 16, characterizing it, rather blandly, as a letter in which "Shelley is trying both to calm Hogg and to discourage him" (*SHC* II, 809). If so, Shelley is using an extraordinarily fiery medium for his purpose:

> A change, a great & important change has taken place in my sister. . . . [E]very look which was wont to be so expressive of openness now [is] enlisted in the service of prejudice. . . . [T]he experiment you recommend [of having Shelley plead for an interview on Hogg's behalf] has been tried within these few days repeatedly but without the slightest effect. Scorn, the most virulent, neglect & affected pity for my madness is all that I can obtain in reply. "You & yr mad friend Hogg! Those whom I have seen, who have seen me, have *some little excuse* for their folly"—This is all I could hear, nothing else she would say. (*SHC* II, 806: my ellipses)

The conclusion can be drawn that in Shelley's mind Elizabeth—like Ophelia acceding to Polonius's orders, like Harriet Grove obeying Thomas Grove's—has been influenced by her father's concern over her meeting with an atheist such as her brother, much less with Hogg. So in the Denmark of Field Place, Hamlet/Shelley broods disconsolate: "The ideas here rise in solitude, they pass thro' a mind as solitary; unheeded gloomy retrospection introduces them; anticipation even gloomier bids them depart to make way for others; these roll on, still, still will they urge their course, 'till Death closes all!" (*SHC* II, 807).

This is the state of mind to which Mrs. Shelley brought the therapeutic aids of "Pens Ink & Paper." In the same letter of June 18 or 19 Shelley makes a further mention of his mother: "I am a perfect hermite, not a being to speak with, I sometimes exchange a word with my Mother on the subject of the weather, upon which she is irresistibly eloquent" (*SHC* II, 810). Taken out of context, Elizabeth Shelley's notion of a conversational ploy might well seem evidence corroborating Houston's much later impression of her as totally devoid of imagination (100). Worth noting, however, in the light of past and future events as they played themselves out in this domestic drama, is the fact that Mrs. Shelley—and she alone, as Shelley describes matters—kept in communication with him, even if only on "safe" subjects like the weather. It is also clear that she listened to his rantings about Elizabeth's obduracy over Hogg, and in doing so at least implicitly allied herself with her son and his friend rather than with her daughter and husband.

Shortly, as external evidence proves, Mrs. Shelley's allegiance was to become explicit. In the June 16 letter to Hogg, Shelley made the brief comment "oh! that you were here!" (*SHC* II, 806), which Cameron dismisses, with textual corroboration, commenting that Shelley "clearly had no intention of inviting Hogg to Field Place" (*SHC* II, 809). Hogg, however, obviously chose to take the vague wish for fact because on June 23, Shelley wrote, "Come, then, my dear friend: happy, *most* happy, shall I be if you will share my little study" (*L* I, 113). And according to Cameron's dating, Hogg did indeed come on either June 28 or 29.

Evidence from later correspondence shows that Elizabeth refused to see him and that he got only a "peep" at her through the window at Warnham Church on Sunday, June 30 (*SHC* II, 851). There is also evidence that Timothy Shelley, though angered to learn of the visit later, was not aware of it at the time. But Mrs. Shelley, as a draft letter to her written by Hogg sometime between July 6 and July 18 proves, was apprised of it. Hogg's first sentence suggests that she may even have encouraged his suit. He writes, "As you were so obliging as to be interested in my health [substituted for "welfare"] I take the liberty of writing to you" (*SHC* II, 820). Moreover, Shelley was sure that Mrs. Shelley was not his father's informant and corroborates Hogg's belief that she might intercede with Elizabeth on his behalf. On July 22 Shelley wrote to Hogg from Wales:

> Your letter was sent to my Mother last post day, I am well assured that she will do nothing prejudicial to our interests, she is a good worthy woman, and altho she may in some cases resemble the fish & pheasant ladies honored with your animadversions of this morning, yet there is one altitude which they have attained to, to which I think *she* cannot soar. Intolerance. I have heard frequently from her since my arrival here; she is of opinion that my father could not by ordinary means have become acquainted with your visit to Horsham . . I regard the whole as a finesse to which I *had* supposed the Honble Members head piece unequal . . But the servants may . . No. they did not know your name.—I have heard from my sister since I came here, but her letter merely contains an account of a thunder storm, which demol-

ished a cottage of my father's . . I will not therefore send it to you. (*SHC* II, 851; Shelley's ellipses)

The allusion to "my sister" immediately after Shelley's dismissal of the servants as possible informants may be intended to point a suspicious finger at her. She, after all, must have known of Hogg's presence if she was to be entreated to see someone who had journeyed all the way from York in the hope of a meeting. Her concern about the patriarchal property also puts her in the father's camp. Shelley does not, however, question his mother's faithful silence.

Commenting on the draft of Hogg's letter to Mrs. Shelley, Cameron notes that "the manuscript throws new light both on Mrs. Shelley (always a somewhat enigmatic figure) and on the relations of Elizabeth, Hogg, and Shelley. It gives further weight, for instance, to Shelley's comments on his mother's tolerance" (*SHC* II, 824). It does indeed, and in other matters besides her willingness, as Cameron notes (*SHC* II, 829), to consider Hogg, a professed atheist if also a suitor from an acceptably squirearchical family, as a possible match for her daughter. Her "tolerance" for this romantic intrigue made her a participant, as her daughter refused to be, in a plot to get around her husband's explicit fiat. Also, since in the frequent letters exchanged between mother and son it is unlikely that Shelley modified his contemptuous language when referring to his father, she must at least passively have condoned his attitude.

The wording of yet another draft letter to Mrs. Shelley from Hogg, this one dated August 22, 1811 (*SHC* II, 873), shows that she had not answered the first one that Shelley had forwarded to her, as he assured Hogg, shortly after receiving it on July 21 (*SHC* II, 851). Her silence may mean that she was actually less "interested" for Hogg than Shelley believed—or said he believed. But it may also suggest that she had become in the interim since Hogg's visit *more* interested on behalf of another suitor, her nephew John Grove. From London Shelley wrote Hogg on August 15 with the "teasing" information "You have a rival," followed by the apparently mollifying words "Do not tremble for it is not one you have occasion to dread, if you fear merely those who are likely to be successful." Then, as salt on the wound: "His chances of success are equal to your own"—that is, nil (*SHC* II, 861).

The reason for Grove's sure failure lies in Elizabeth's total lack of interest, not in the attitude of her parents. Shelley, with another malicious dig in his emphasis on *he,* writes: "*He* has the opportunity of frequently seeing, & conversing with Elizabeth, yet his conversation is not such as is likely to produce an alteration in the resolve which she has taken not to encourage his addresses" (*SHC* II, 861). Grove's frequent visits certainly suggest paternal, and, more likely, common parental, approval. Indeed, if Mrs. Shelley had been as complaisant as her words and actions suggest about an engagement between Bysshe and Harriet Grove, and if the difficulties there had caused at least some degree of coolness between the family elders on both sides, as seems almost inevitable, she may have welcomed this opportunity to restore perfectly cordial relations with her sister and her sister's family. *And* it may have helped reestablish some harmony between the Shelley parents that they could agree on John Grove as a possible suitor, as they clearly had not agreed about Hogg. Nor had Hogg been the only source of marital discord during the weeks of May and June 1811 that Shelley spent at Field Place; there was also the trouble over Edward Graham.

Earlier letters from Shelley to Graham that make reference to Mrs. Shelley carry, as I have noted, the suggestion that as a couple they participated amusedly in Shelley's fantasies—while Timothy Shelley did not—and thus stood in some sort of relationship to each other. His letters also imply that, however it had come about that Graham enjoyed the patronage of the Shelley family, the Shelley parent more interested in his welfare was his mother.

According to Frederick Jones's tentative dating, it was on May 14—the same day that Shelley wrote and left unsealed his letter to Hogg about his return to Field Place—that he wrote a note to Graham as well. Briefly he mentions the terms of the settlement—"200£ per an[num], free agency &c"—and gloats over his allegiance with Captain Pilfold against his father: "—He [Timothy Shelley] looks rather blue today but the Capt[ain] keeps him in tol[erable] order." The rest of the short note describes an extraordinary incident: "We had this morning a letter addressed to my Father accusing him & my mother of [ge]tting drunk, & the latter of being [m]ore intimate with *you* than with my father himself. We all laughed heartily & thought it a good opportunity of making up. But he is as inveterate as ever" (*L* I, 85).

Before we turn to the substance of this anonymous message, we should consider the language used to describe its reception. "We *all* laughed" (my emphasis) suggests amusement around the family breakfast table, but the next sentence makes it clear that Timothy Shelley does not number among the "all" who thought the letter a happy excuse for restoring general harmony. The letter, then, creates another instance in which Timothy stands alone outside a feminine domestic circle that includes his son. But why should a message such as this one be the occasion for restoring peace? And why, given particularly the threatening nature of an anonymous letter so personal in its intent and allusions, should laughter be the general if not the universal response?

The reaction of all those in the room, including Timothy, becomes reasonable if they knew, or supposed, Shelley to be the author. Among Shelley biographers only Cameron gives it as his opinion that "most probably, Shelley himself wrote—in a spirit of semi-malevolent buffoonery—the accusing letter of May (a procedure in keeping with his penchant for pseudonymous letter writing), and that he either invented the story or elaborated it from some gossip he had picked up at Pilfold's" (*Young Shelley* 344). There is some further circumstantial evidence for this position that Cameron does not bring forward: Shelley would have had the opportunity to mail the letter secretly before his return from the Pilfolds, where he had stayed in the last stage of negotiations with his father. Also, when, on October 25, 1811, near the close of the series of events introduced by this anonymous letter, Timothy Shelley wrote to Whitton about "the perturbed state of P.B.'s mind," he stated: "I will not open a letter from him, and be cautious how I open any in other handwriting for fear he should endeavour to deceive" (Ingpen I, 347). Not paranoia—or not paranoia only—but simple experience could well have caused Timothy Shelley's caution about *all* handwriting.

Whether Shelley wrote the letter or not, he certainly took pleasure in entertaining its ideas and writing about them. Penned at the same time as the note to Graham, perhaps even as an enclosure with it (*L* I, 86), are sixty lines of doggerel tetrameter couplets; the elder Shelley's drinking habits get almost no space, except perhaps as unstated explanation for the blueness of "old Killjoy" 's ears. All attention is on the possible adultery between Graham and Mrs. Shelley, and for a number of lines this fantasy elides into one that involves the incestuous feelings of the son for his voluptuous mother.

The first twenty-eight lines concern themselves with the jealous fury of the deceived husband. The following four state that courting older women is not Graham's usual practice, but—the commentary goes on—there is reason to make an exception in this case:

> Since but once in an age is seen
> Of forty-eight a peerless queen
> Like Ninon famed, that girl of France
> Who at ninety-two could dance
> With such grace as did impart
> Improper flames to grandson's heart
> We fairly may acquit your soul—
> Though your life's pulses fiercely roll—
> Of having let one wild wish glow
> Of cornuting old Killjoy's brow.
>
> (*PS* 167)

Shelley's allusion is to Ninon de Lenclos, the French courtesan who lived to the legendary age of ninety. One does not find any anecdotes about a grandson, but one of the best-known stories about her pertains to a son of hers who fell desperately in love with her. Although different versions of the story circulate, Shelley would have had the opportunity to read one in the introduction to Ninon de Lenclos's *Memoirs* as translated from the French by Elizabeth Griffith in 1806. Or he might have shared the translator's source, a weekly newspaper, *The World,* a major outlet for "sentimental" publication (Longaker 29–44), which she quotes at length. The passage from *The World* reads as follows:

> It was in her fifty-sixth year, that the Chevalier de Villiers, a natural son, whom she had had by the Count de Gerze [Lord Jersey, of the Villiers family], arrived in Paris from the provinces, where he had been educated without any knowledge of his real parents. He saw his mother: he fell in love with her. The increase, the vehemence of his passion, gave the greatest disquiet to the affectionate matron. At length, when nothing but a discovery of the secret could put a stop to the impetuosity of his attempts, she took him into her bedchamber, and pointing to a clock, cried, Rash youth, look

there! at that hour, two-and-twenty years ago, I was delivered of you in this very bed! It is a certain fact, that the abashed, unfortunate young man flew into the garden, and fell upon his sword.

This catastrophe had like to have deprived the age of the most accomplished mistress that ever adorned the cytherean annals. It was above twenty years before the afflicted mother would listen to any addresses of a tender nature. At length, the polite Abbé de Gedoine pressed and obtained an assignation. He came, and found the enchanting Ninon reclining on a couch, like the GRANDMOTHER OF THE LOVES, in the most gallant dishabille. He asked her . . . why she had so long deferred the completion of his happiness? I must confess, replied she, it proceeded from a remain of vanity. I piqued myself upon having a lover at fourscore, and it was but yesterday that I was eighty complete.   (Griffith vii–viii; author's emphasis)

I too have quoted at length, first to show the contrast between the full, sentimental version of the story and Shelley's burlesque version of it and also to note a possible source of Shelley's shift to a *grand*son in the amusing, ultracytherean epithet "grandmother of the loves." Yet the exaggeration of Ninon's age, the greater distancing of the relationship, and the jocularity all help to serve as the censor's baffle before the unthinkable thought near which the allusion to Ninon has led him. I am not saying that Shelley was a young de Villiers consciously afflicted by a lustful passion for his mother. Still, the simile linking his forty-eight-year-old mother to the fifty-six-year-old Ninon is his, not mine. While its presence by no means justifies the thought that Shelley was tempted to actual incest with his mother, it does give very strong evidence that he shared the eroticization of the maternal so markedly present in this social milieu. He experienced maternity as sexual, or—to phrase the point another way—he found congenial the notion of the goddess of love as most centrally a *mother* of the loves.

The fantasy about Graham and his mother continued to amuse Shelley, for on June 7 he wrote another verse letter to Graham, this one forty lines long, on the same subject. Shelley had again just returned from a stay with the Pilfolds at Cuckfield, and this time, because his father was away in London, his mother and sister had joined him there. The poem opens by referring to a "penitential letter" that Graham has written, presumably to Bysshe, yet from the context the addressee appears to have been Timothy Shelley:

Dear dear dear dear dear Graeme!
When back from Cuckfield here I came
    I found your penitential letter,
But sackcloth cannot now prevail,
Nor even ashes aught avail,
For I can see there's no relenting.
Indeed I fear that all repenting
        Would act as but a temper-whetter,
For the more you repent, the more tears he demands,
The more you submit, the more he commands.
                              (*PS* 169)

The theme here seems related to that of another letter to Graham, to which Jones assigns a date sometime in June. There Shelley writes: "You may depend on it that I shall not suffer you to be involved in any crimination with my father,—I did not wish or desire you to accuse yourself to my father, nor when he speaks to me will I any longer suffer him to continue in that opinion & error" (*L* I, 112–13). In the context of the verse letters it sounds as if Graham responded seriously, and negatively, to the adultery story and thereby made Timothy Shelley all the more enraged because Graham's addressing the topic proved that the gossip was spreading.[22]

In the ensuing lines (11–28) the second verse letter expatiates on the theme of Timothy Shelley's sadistic pleasure in the penitent's misery. While not directly related to the "cornuting" of "old Killjoy," certain of them (ll. 21–28) warrant quotation because they show a very early stage in Timothy Shelley's transformation into the Jupiter of *Prometheus Unbound*. As in the case of Jupiter, though without the god's explicit sexual violence, the most specific instance of Timothy's tyranny lies in the coercion of women:

> But give him a prison, and give him a throne
> And give him a world to reign in alone,
> Full of death-groaning nations let it be crammed,
> And I wish no worse place for the souls of the damned,
> Or give him a daughter and give him a wife,
> I'll engage he'll torment 'em just out of their life,
> If so be't their peculiar wish lies this way
> With exactness our squire will their wishes obey.
>
> (*PS* 170)

Shelley's reading and writing of gothic fantasy had given him shrewd insight into the interactions of sadism and masochism in which, by the process Jung calls enantiadromia, the one turns into the other. If the women have a "peculiar wish" to suffer his domestic tyranny, the squire needs their contempt, particularly the sexual contempt of his wife's infidelity, to fuel his sadistic rage: "I think that our squire does mainly desire / That an horn on his dark frowning brow were implanted!" (ll. 33–34). As the reasoning of Shelley's broadside runs, however, the proof of his wife's independent power can finally become so galling that he has the urge to be rid of her altogether, thus breaking the cycle:

> I've hit it exactly, he'd get one directly,
> But the worst is that things will not come when they're wanted;—
> He wishes to drive from her own native hive
> The wife who so merrily laughs at each odd whim.
>
> (ll. 35–38)

It is very unlikely, though not impossible, that Shelley had by this time acquired knowledge of the ancient link in signification between bees and the Mother Goddess. His metaphor of Elizabeth Shelley as queen bee is apiarian, not mythological. By turning Field Place into a hive and making her its queen, he also by implication turns Timothy Shelley into a drone. Better yet, the fantasy played out through the metaphor helps quiet the fears aroused by the Poland Street exile: if the buzzing drone imagines that his fury effects the queen bee's departure, the truth is that she, her fertility still her own, flies off to found and mother a new hive, taking her cohorts with her, while the drone is deserted, he the one abandoned and left to impotent loneliness. Even without a specifically mythological context, the appearance of this trope within its familial, indeed matriarchal, context here suggests that when Shelley did find it later through the reading of ancient texts and monuments, themselves the products of nations of beekeepers, it would have jumped to his eye.

Comus at Field Place

No further allusion to this mock or semi–mock intrigue appears in the following months. Shelley, as we have seen, was on good terms with his mother through the rest of the summer and appears to have been so with Graham. True, during what was to become the real-life intrigue of Shelley's elopement with Harriet Westbrook, he stayed when in London with his Grove cousins and did not base himself at Graham's as he ordinarily had in the previous year or so. That change, however, actually suggests a continued connection between Graham and the Shelley family; Shelley had kept his relationship with Harriet Westbrook secret from all those at Field Place, including his mother, and he seems to have felt that Graham, if he got wind of the possible elopement, might alert the Shelleys.[23] Some evidence that that may have been the case comes in Shelley's letter from Edinburgh to his father, written on August 30, in which, as formerly, Graham is to serve as his agent. After two heavily ironic sentences calculated, though perhaps unconsciously so, to destroy his purpose ("I know of no one to whom I can apply with greater certainty of success when in distress than you"), Shelley continues with false jauntiness: "Be good enough to enclose me a D[raft] for 50£ [his quarterly allowance]. Mr. Graham will take care to forward your letter" (*L* I, 139).

The same letter shows that Shelley still hopes himself to be on good terms with his mother: "I hope Mother Sister & all are well. My love to them." Two further letters, written on September 27 and again on October 3, among several that Shelley sent his father in the following six weeks end with a similar message: "Love to Mother Sisters &c" (*L* I, 142, 143). These messages were not in fact being relayed, for Timothy Shelley was turning the letters over to Whitton unread. This strategy, while born of Timothy Shelley's own sense of hurt and betrayal,[24] was a course of action designed to activate Shelley's fear of abandonment to its highest pitch. And, as I noted earlier, Shelley's typical reaction in such an instance was to transform his situation of the one rejected into that of the avenging, but wounded and blameless, rejecter. The fantasies of murder that he ascribes to his father in the letter he wrote on October 15 have the sound of projections:

You have treated me *ill, vilely.* When I was expelled for atheism you wished
I had been killed in Spain. The desire of its consummation is very like the
crime, perhaps it is well for me that the laws of England punish murder, &
that *cowardice* shrinks from their animadversion. I shall take the first opportunity of seeing you—if *you* will not hear my name, *I* will pronounce it.
Think not that I am an insect whom injuries destroy—had I but money
enough I would meet you in London, & hollow in your ears Bysshe, Bysshe,
Bysshe—aye Bysshe till you're deaf. (*L* I, 149)

The next day, casting to one side the problem of his ability to undertake
the expense of such a trip, Shelley carried out his threat and returned to Field
Place to demand his allowance in person. He did not go there directly, however, but sought out his old ally, Captain Pilfold, at Cuckfield. And he wrote
the twenty-nine-year-old schoolteacher Elizabeth Hitchener, the "sister of his
soul" and the first of many surrogate mothers, asking her to meet him at the
Pilfolds' (*L* I, 149–50). According to Cameron's reckoning (*SHC* III, 21), he
arrived at Cuckfield on the morning of October 19, and on October 20 he
went over to Field Place for a confrontation—but now one that would include
his mother as well as his father. She, too, had become the enemy because of
gossip among the Pilfolds that she had yet another suitor in mind for her
daughter Elizabeth: Edward Graham.

Shelley's loving if brief messages to his mother in letters from the North
suggest, even prove, that he had received this story as new information. One
gathers that it was the subject of general discussion in a company that
included Elizabeth Hitchener, because Shelley, writing to Hitchener on October 28 after his return to York, states, "I *observed* that you were much
shocked at my mother's depravity" (*L* I, 163; my emphasis). Also, the tenor
of the rest of this October 28 letter, full of confidences about his elopement,
suggests that they did not have a private meeting at the Pilfolds' for talk
about such matters. "Depravity" seems a very strong word to describe match-
making between Elizabeth and Graham, even if one believed the proposed
fiancé "unsuitable," to use the euphemism masking class prejudice. (The
function of class, very much operative here, has numerous ironic twists,
since Shelley was in disgrace precisely for a misalliance with the daughter of
a wealthy but otherwise unacceptable tavern owner; and the father of Elizabeth Hitchener, the new sister of his soul, was a former smuggler and keeper
of a public house [*L* I, 97].) So it seems possible that Shelley, furious when
he heard the rumor of this projected engagement, connected it in his mind
with the earlier rumor that he himself may have concocted, and that he
certainly enjoyed spreading, of an affair between his mother and Graham
and made his connection public. That is, he accused his mother of using a
romance between her daughter and Graham as a cover for her own adulterous liaison with the same man.

Whether Shelley made this accusation openly at the Pilfolds' is unclear,
but a letter written to his mother from Cuckfield on October 22 gives solid
evidence that he raged furiously on the theme during the October 20 family
meeting at Field Place:

Dear Mother

I had expected before this, to have heard from you on a subject so important as that of my late communication. I now expect to hear from you, unless you desire the publicity of my sister's intended marriage with Graham. You tell me that you care not for the opinion of the world, this contempt for it's consideration is noble if accompanied by consciousness of rectitude; if the contrary, it is the last resort of unveiled misconduct, is the daringness of despaire not the calmness of fortitude.—You ask me if *I* suspect you. I do, my suspicions of your motives are strong & such as I insist upon shd. be either confirmed or refuted. I suspect your motives for *so violently* so *persecutingly* desiring to unite my sister Elisabeth to the music master Graham, I suspect that it was intended to shield *yourself* from that suspicion which at length has fallen on you. If it is unjust, prove it, I give you a fair opportunity, it depend on yourself to avail yourself of it. Write to me at [Mr. Westbrooks 23 Chapel St. Grosvenor Square *cancelled*]—

Your's Son

P B Shelley

(*L* I, 155)

The violence of Shelley's verbal onslaught can be judged from Timothy Shelley's October 25 letter to Whitton, in which he writes: "Had he [Shelley] stay'd in Sussex I would have sworn in Especial Constables around me. He frightened his mother and sister exceedingly, and now if they hear a Dog Bark they run up stairs" (*L* I, 165). Yet at the time Mrs. Shelley seems to have challenged him in turn, if in contradictory ways that suggest a certain bewilderment with the grounds of the argument. On the one hand, according to Shelley's reconstruction, she says that she defies social opinion; and on the other, by asking whether Shelley himself suspects her, she appears to be protesting her innocence. But innocence of what? Of favoring a match with Graham? The sneer in Shelley's allusion to "the music master" mirrors precisely the class prejudice that was casting him off because of a misalliance. Perhaps Mrs. Shelley's dismissal of social opinion was an attempt to make that point, while her claim of innocence was a response to the charge that she was using her daughter as a sexual cat's-paw.

In a comment on Shelley's October 22 letter to his mother, Neville Rogers shows the caution that has typified biographers' reactions to this bizarre episode: "Both the plan [to marry Elizabeth Shelley to Graham] and its alleged motives seem a trifle odd. Perhaps neither represented anything more than neurotic fantasy, symptomatic of the unhappiness of a home-loving boy brutally deprived of home and home affections" (21). That analysis leaves out of account the retaliatory pain that the "home-loving boy" inflicted on his mother, who had not decreed his banishment. Shelley's rage against her may have been fueled, it is true, by a growing feeling that she had joined ranks with his father, thus changing her status from co-conspirator to foe. He does not after the elopment mention letters from his mother such as the ones he had received in Wales. She appears to have accepted Timothy Shelley's dictum that the whole family put Shelley in Coventry, and that change of allegiance, despite Shelley's messages of love, still sent in order to gall his father, may have been filling him with the bitterness of rejection. The brief note to his sister, written at the same time as that to his mother, suggests something of the sort: "I write to inform you that my Mother has received a letter from me, on the subject of Graham's projected union with you.—My Mother may shew the letter to my Father—in this case do you speak truth" (*L* I, 156).

Even so, the particular form that Shelley's "neurotic fantasy" took, given the fantasies that he had been enjoying earlier in the summer, seems more than a trifle "odd." Why, when he had delighted in the thought of a union between Hogg and his sister did he now so object to her possession by Graham? Was the grossest class prejudice his reason? But how, then, had he earlier been so cheerful at the thought of a union, even if illicit, between Graham and his mother? No answer can match what I imagine to be the psychological complexity of the case, and any answer can be proffered only as some form of fiction, but even such a fiction seems preferable to an analysis that simply dismisses this incident as imponderable.

Shelley's "teasing" interest in Hogg's passion for his sister bears the character of displacement for his own incestuous feelings toward her, as Cameron notes (*Young Shelley* 16, 298). His fascination with the idea of an affair between Mrs. Shelley and Graham also bears overtones of an incestuous attachment to his mother. And in both, the two Elizabeths are closely associated, the mother made a fosterer of the first passion, the daughter brought in, virtually out of context, as a fellow sufferer of paternal tyranny in the second. He, so to speak, possesses both, but (if one remembers his adoption fantasies) he is both owner/mother and girl infant/beloved. Two-in-one and both one with him (for homoeroticism is also present in each intrigue); both his as long as the fantasy was his, but only as fantasy, and displaced fantasy at that. But then the news of a plan made for his sister during his absence, one in which his own fantasy had no part, brought to the fore that element of aggression present in all identification. The mother was making the baby sister hers in a way that emphasized the separate existence of both women, and he lashed out wildly in protest.

Freudian analytical tools, such as the concept of displacement, while relevant, function ahistorically and need to be balanced with Shelley's own context for these fantasies, the Della Cruscan mode of experiencing sentiment as relayed to him through the works of Charlotte Dacre (Reiman, "Introduction" x–xi). As McGann notes, and his point bears on Eagleton's discussion of the aesthetic as "the ultimate binding force of the bourgeois social order" (20), sentimental poetry of the type that Shelley admired and imitated made love central to human experience. Moreover, "true love had to involve a total intensity of the total person—mind, heart, and (here was the sticking point) body." Yet love, if true, is by virtue of its intensity completely pure and guarantees its freedom from lust by being purely imaginative—by being, then, that "sex in the head" which to D. H. Lawrence is lust at its most depraved

(McGann 31, 46). The kinds of exchanges fostered by this literary form thus replicate the "mirroring" or "live entering" at the heart of subjectivity itself and celebrate impressionability as the essentially poetic.

The separation between entertaining a fantasy and acting it out leads to a further paradox: as shown in the newspaper exchange of impassioned verse between Della Crusca (Robert Merry) and Anna Matilda (Hannah Cowley) which brought the Della Cruscans to prominence, a grounding in crass reality—such as say, any actual acquaintance with the beloved—bore no relevance to the honesty of one's passion (Longaker 34–35). On the contrary, it guaranteed good faith. So, while as post-Freudians we tend to read Shelley's fantasies about his mother's adulterous liaison with Graham and his sister's union with Hogg as exposés of his own incestuous and homoerotic feelings, he may well have considered them proof of his admirable intensity. His mother, by contrast, manifested depravity if the gossip about her were true because she was sullying pure emotion with the sordid business of actual sexual relations.

As one who shared Shelley's historical milieu, and in all likelihood shared this sentimenal "women's" reading as well, Mrs. Shelley may have been able to discount its violence, at least to some extent, as part of the rhetoric of true feeling. Also, if alarmed, angered, and hurt by her son's verbal accusations, neither she nor her daughter saw the written version of them, which, like Shelley's other letters, Timothy Shelley forwarded unopened to Whitton. Shelley's words could thus more easily fade from memory than they would have had they been given inky permanence. When in May 1813 the Duke of Norfolk and the Groves were working to bring about a reconciliation between father and son, Shelley's mother and sisters were in at least indirect, and perhaps direct, communication with him and with Harriet over the exciting possibility. The tone of Shelley's full apology to his father, written on May 13, attests to the strength of his own desire for such a reconciliation: "I once more presume to address you, to state my Sincere desire of being consider'd as worthy of a Restoration to the intercourse with yourself & my Family which I have forfeited by my Follies" (*L* I, 366–67). Three days later Harriet confided to an Irish friend, Catherine Nugent, that "Mr. Shelley's family are very eager to be reconciled to him, and I should not in the least wonder if my next letter was not sent from his Paternal roof, as we expect to be there in a week or two" (*L* I, 367).

Unfortunately—disastrously as far as both the short- and long-term effects on Harriet's own life were concerned—Timothy Shelley turned to Whitton and perhaps to his father, Sir Bysshe, for advice on how to react to his son's overture (*SHC* III, 188–89, 447) and so demanded that Shelley "publickly disavow" his atheistic views (*SHC* III, 188). Such terms were impossible and negotiations were closed. Another letter from Harriet Shelley to Nugent describes all communication as broken off, at least officially, but unofficially Shelley's mother and sisters were in touch and trying to arrange at least to see him: "It seems that so long as he lives, Bysshe must never hope to see or hear anything of his family. This is certainly an unpleasant circumstance, particularly as his mother wishes to see him, and has a great affection for him" (*L* I, 372).

Shelley now entered into one of the very troubled periods of his life, plagued by mental instability, actual as well as psychosomatic ill health, dangerously high debts, and a collapsing marriage (White I, 332; Holmes 218; Crook and Guiton 84). Interestingly, this downward spiral becomes noticeable after the birth of his first child, Ianthe, on June 23, 1813, and is thus another example of the way in which Shelley's periods of special crisis correlate with the births of his children (Sunstein 144). During these months we have again Harriet's testimony that his mother, as in the period before his elopement and his subsequent accusations against her, was in a conspiratorially close relation with him, even if from a distance: "The post has just brought me a letter from Mr. Shelley's sister, who says that her father is doing all in his power to prevent his being arrested . . . [paper torn] keeps everything a secret, but Mrs. Shelley tells her son everything she hears" (*L* I, 377). And a Captain Kennedy, whose regiment was stationed at Horsham in 1814 and who occasionally visited Field Place, reports: "At this time I had not seen Shelley, but the servants, especially the old butler, Laker, had spoken of him to me. He seemed to have won the hearts of the whole household. Mrs. Shelley often spoke of her son; her heart yearned after him with all the fondness of a mother's love" (Hogg II, 152).

Kennedy's account—filled with a saccharine reverence, as one can see in the quoted passage, and on that account unreliable—is nonetheless our principal source of information about the last visit Shelley had with his mother and his two older sisters in early June 1814. Shelley was staying at Bracknell, at the home of Mrs. Boinville. She was another mother surrogate, Elizabeth Hitchener having been jettisoned, with whom Shelley had a relationship at once filial and implicitly erotic while at the same time engaging in a "brotherly" erotic dalliance with her daughter, Cornelia Turner. (White, commenting on Shelley's ardent admiration for Mrs. Boinville, adds: "It is easy to guess that if any of Shelley's letters to Mrs. Boinville could be found they would in some respects resemble the letters to Elizabeth Hitchener" [I, 306].)

Harriet, again pregnant, was in Bath with the baby Ianthe, and, presumably, with the carriage whose purchase was largely responsible for Shelley's indebtedness, when Mrs. Shelley found the opportunity for a visit with her son. According to Kennedy, "It was during the absence of his father and the three youngest children that the natural desire of the mother to see her son induced her to propose that he should pay her a short visit" (Hogg II, 152). In a gesture that testified to his filial devotion, or to his desire to impress his mother with that devotion, or both, carriageless Shelley walked the forty miles from Bracknell "until within a very few miles of Field Place, when a farmer gave him a seat in his travelling cart. . . . The poor fellow arrived at Field Place exceedingly fatigued" (Hogg II, 152).

The "short visit," according to Kennedy's account, lasted for at least two nights, perhaps longer, and so Shelley had many hours of recuperative attention from his mother and sisters. Certain elements of Kennedy's story suggest a madcap, raffish quality to some of the incidents of the visit, like that characterizing Hogg's secret visit in 1811, with Mrs. Shelley again a participant:

As it was not desirable that Bysshe's presence in the country should be known, we arranged that on walking out he should wear my scarlet uniform, and that I should assume his outer garments. So he donned the soldier's dress and sallied forth. His head was so remarkably small, that though mine be not large, the cap came down over his eyes, the peak resting on his nose, and it had to be stuffed before it would fit him. . . . He certainly looked like anything but a soldier.

The metamorphosis was very amusing; he enjoyed it much, and made himself perfectly at home in his unwonted garb. We gave him the name of Captain Jones, under which name we used to talk of him after his departure; but, with all our care, Bysshe's visit could not be kept a secret.   (Hogg II, 153)

As another way of strengthening the bonds created through past shared experience, Shelley seems to have availed himself of the sentimental power of music. Kennedy writes: "In music he seemed to delight, as a medium of association: the tunes which had been favorites in boyhood charmed him. There was one, which he played several times on the piano with one hand, that seemed to absorb him; it was an exceedingly simple air, which, I understand, his earliest love was wont to play for him" (Hogg II, 154). The associations called up by these musical interludes may have been more complex than the *ingénu* Kennedy realized, since the spectral presence of Graham, the music master, would be one of those invoked. But as phantasms from a shared period of intense past emotion, the *nature* of that emotion no longer relevant, Graham along with Harriet Grove could, however paradoxically, help reaffirm Shelley's preeminence in that circle of "his" women.

But Shelley alone in that circle could, at least at that moment, be aware of a further irony: his sentimental attitudinizing over a past love served to mask his immediate and obsessive passion for Mary Godwin. *His* recollection of that visit to Field Place, written to Hogg on October 4, 1814, as part of an explanation of his elopement, centers totally around her image:

I recollect that one day I undertook to walk from Bracknell to my father's (40 miles). A train of visionary events arranged themselves in my imagination until ideas almost acquired the intensity of sensations. Already I had met the female [Mary Godwin] who was destined to be mine, already had she replied to my exulting recognition, already were the difficulties surmounted that opposed an entire union. I had even proceeded so far as to compose a letter to Harriet on the subject of my passion for another. Thus was my walk beguiled, at the conclusion of which I was hardly sensible of fatigue.   (*L* I, 402)

He had *not,* then, been so dreadfully fatigued; but let that pass. In this account one must make another, more important adjustment to counteract Shelley's manipulation of the truth. Jones's insertion of the name "Mary Godwin" confuses Shelley's meaning, though he is more faithful than Shelley to the facts. The import of the passage I have quoted, as of the whole paragraph in which it appears, is that the image of an ideal woman *as yet unmet* obsessed him. In the next paragraph he writes: "In the month of June I came to London. . . . Here I met his [Godwin's] daughter Mary" (*L* I, 402), with the implication that he only then encountered the woman who fulfilled that ideal. But in fact he had met Mary Godwin on May 5 (Sunstein 70). The visit to Field Place occurred during the ten days between the latter part of May and June 8 when Shelley was absent from London and so from the Godwin ménage, where he was a constant visitor (White I, 668–69). We can be virtually certain, then, that the fantasies of female perfection that occupied his long walk had not a little to do with the actual young woman he had recently met.

Once implemented, his vague but impassioned plans for leaving Harriet were to close the doors of Field Place against him for the rest of his life. That this was Mrs. Shelley's response to her son's elopement with Mary Godwin offers good evidence of how deeply she herself was imbued with the domestic ideology of the time. In clandestine but effective and important ways she had maintained or at least recovered relations with him when he was expelled from Oxford for refusing to answer allegations of atheism; when he eloped and made an "unsuitable" marriage; when he accused her, perhaps unfairly and certainly in a hurtful and humiliating way, of adultery. The bond that could endure such stresses had to be very strong. Only the fourth serious blow snapped it: his desertion of his wife, mother of one child and pregnant with another.

In the summer of 1811 Shelley had concealed his relationship with Harriet Westbrook from his mother as well as his father, even though she was a confidante in other intrigues. His secrecy suggests that he knew that Elizabeth Shelley, like Timothy, would not approve of the match. Still, part of the reconciliation Mrs. Shelley desired clearly involved Harriet's reception at Field Place. She was prepared, then, to honor the marriage, and her later reactions suggest that she at last joined her husband in ostracizing Shelley only after his desertion of Harriet. When Sir Bysshe died on January 5, 1815, less than five months after Shelley's last clandestine visit, Whitton asked that Shelley's solicitor prevent Shelley's using the occasion to go to Field Place, on the grounds that his presence would be "most painful to Mrs. S." (Ingpen II, 449). Defying that request, Shelley went to the house on January 12 for the reading of Sir Bysshe's will, but he was denied entrance. He sat in the front doorway, reading Mary Godwin's copy of *Comus*.

Shelley had chosen his text carefully. The occasion for the writing of *Comus,* or *A Masque Presented at Ludlow Castle,* was the celebration of the Earl of Bridgewater's accession to the presidency of the Council of Wales (June 26, 1631) and to the Lord Lieutenancy of Wales (July 8, 1631) and so matches this moment of Sir Timothy's rise to knighthood. Also the dramatic action of *Comus* centers around the return of three siblings, a sister and two brothers, "to attend their father's state, / And new-entrusted sceptre" (ll. 35–36). They, then, were doing what Shelley had been forbidden to do. But besides presenting himself as a dutiful child, a celebrant, despite rebuff, of his father's elevation in status, Shelley at the doorstep acts out the part of Comus, Dionysian lord of misrule, and the object in his hand (Mary Godwin's book) serves as signifier for the deed that has banished him. The gesture was not entirely lost. A Dr. Blocksome, who emerged with the message that Shelley's father, now Sir Timothy, was very angry with him, took in the title of the book and the name of its owner (Ingpen II, 450). But Shelley had not the pleasure of further reactions. From his mother came only a silence that, as far as we can tell, continued during the remaining seven and a half years of his life.

Since Shelley's relationship with Mary Godwin caused the final breach between mother and son, Mary was probably right in thinking Lady Shelley her most particular enemy—with the consequences mentioned at the beginning of this chapter. Yet the two women had much in common in that both drained to its dregs the experience of mothering Shelley. Because Mary Godwin was only sixteen at the time of their elopement, and because of the seemingly tutelary nature of the couple's intellectual life together, with Mary in the role of tutee, we tend not to notice the extent to which she had to cope with Shelley as her eldest and most demanding child. The period after Clara's birth, discussed earlier, provides only one of many examples of how this necessity worked itself out in their daily lives. Her finding it possible—even "natural"—to do so is another manifestation of the way in which the ideal of "the bourgeois family" shaped her life, as Anne Mellor's *Mary Shelley* has shown, and of her own psychosexual training in what Sandra Gilbert calls "daughteronomy" through her intense girlhood devotion to Godwin. Also, as daughter of Mary Wollstonecraft—whom Shelley, as Emily Sunstein writes, "adored" (20), and I think that the literal truth—Mary Godwin, while Shelley's lover and another "sister of his soul" and adoptive pet, bore the charisma of the Mother Goddess. Thus, however sentimental its form, the monument with which Lady Jane Shelley enshrined their relationship is true to its inner dynamic (see fig. 7). Combining the iconographic themes of the Pietà and the lament for Adonis, the ever-young and ever-maternal figure of Mary grieves over the dead body of Shelley, the son/lover whose death is the meaning of her life.

In the intensity of its emotions—positive and negative—its overt sexual intimacy, its range of shared experience, and its significance for the Victorian reception of Shelley's poetry, the relationship with Mary Shelley has a deserved importance in his life. But as far as significance goes, the relationship that Mary Godwin displaced was not so much with Harriet Westbrook as with Elizabeth Shelley *mère*. Spanning almost three-quarters of Shelley's life and filled with formative incident, recorded and unrecorded, the connection with the maternal was of imponderable but immense depth. The strength, perhaps even fascination, of Elizabeth Shelley's own personality took on ever greater power through the mystique of motherhood current at the time of Shelley's birth. Moreover, maternity carried a specifically erotic ambience later expunged from it, with the result that (to express the point mythically) the Mother Goddess, ever a survivor, then made her presence felt with particular force, and Shelley's family background led him to feel it with peculiar intensity and to describe it with extraordinary frequency.

Sometimes she is the overt subject of a poem, as in *Adonais* or as the

Fig. 7. Monument to Percy Bysshe Shelley and Mary Shelley at the Christchurch Priory, Dorset, by Henry Weekes. (*Courtesy of the Bettmann Archive*)

figure of Asia in *Prometheus Unbound.* Cythna is avatar of the "foam-born" in *Laon and Cythna;* in the "Ode to Liberty" the Goddess is "written" iconographically over the prayer that Liberty may lead forth Wisdom "as the morning star / Beckons the Sun from the Eoan wave" ([*SPP*] XVIII. 257–58). Indeed, though the word may be inelegant, one can only say that she is scrawled iconographically across all of Shelley's work. Multiple examples can give only a notion of her pervasiveness, and it would be impossible to draw up an exhaustive list. Also, though her signs are everywhere, they have different, at times contradictory, at time multivalent meanings; each demands its own reading. In "To a Skylark" her unseen or scarcely seen planet in the daylight sky ([*SPP*] ll. 21–25) seems to signify a beneficent, inspirational presence resembling the "Power" of "The Hymn to Intellectual Beauty" that "Floats though unseen amongst us" ([*SPP*] ll. 1,2), while in "The Triumph of Life" a series of juxtaposed images carries the suggestion that the guidance seemingly offered by the Goddess's "star" is in fact delusory (ll. 412–31). The Goddess's moon-boat carries Asia back to Prometheus (II. iv. 156–57), but the horned moon also impassively watches the expiration of the Poet in "Alastor" (ll. 645–55).

In humdrum reality Field Place was not Bryant's "hive of Venus," and Elizabeth Shelley, characterized by her son himself as having the "fish & pheasant" qualities of a county gentlewoman, was not an avatar of Aphrodite. But as evidenced by a number of instances already discussed, Shelley habitually lived texts and textualized life. One observes that occurring when he transformed a garret into an alchemist's cell, made a boarding school visit into a gothic assignation, superimposed Elsinore on Field Place, or carried a book that turned Field Place into Ludlow Castle.[25]

My examples all take on a reductively comic character because the biographical and therefore down-to-earth nature of my own text makes the Don Quixote fantasist's imaginings bathetic. Shelley, as we have seen, can at times enjoy this reductive humor himself, but more typically—more Romantically— his imagination focuses rather on the gigantic paradigms that rise up in dramatic shadow representations of puny human events. His eyes are on those "masterful images," as Yeats calls them when describing this dichotomy, not on "the foul rag and bone shop of the heart." Just as the dreary bickerings of the O'Neill family take on tragic grandeur and significance when enacted as *Long Day's Journey into Night,*[26] so in *Prometheus Unbound,* upon the veil or scrim of the Aeschylean sublime, the conflicts, alliances, and strategies of Field Place are writ large and also written anew, rewritten: mother and son again in alliance against the father. Mother and son united in the spirit of Dionysian Comus.

NOTES

1. Medwin offers additional evidence of Shelley's prowess at field sports: "I well remember one day in the winter of 1809, when we were out together, his killing at three successive shots, three snipes, to my great astonishment and envy" (68).

2. *The Private Stable,* a guide for American horse owners written at the end of the nineteenth century, estimates the total upkeep of a single horse for one year to be $3,229–$7,216 in the city, $1,619–$2,591 in the country (Garland 22). In 1900 the U.S. dollar equaled roughly the value of 1.5 milligrams of fine gold, as compared with the pound's value when England went on the gold standard in 1816 of 7.3 grams in fine gold. The fact that the dollar in 1792 had almost the same value as in 1900 (1,603.8 milligrams of fine gold in 1792 as opposed to 1,504.656 milligrams in 1900) aids in making a computation back to a point before 1816 (Pick and Sédillot 100, 431). The 1900 American dollar would therefore be worth approximately £4.8 in English 1792 currency, and the cost of keeping a horse would have ranged from a low of £335 to a high of more than £1500. Patricia Branca judges £300 to be "the maximum income level of most middle-income families in the nineteenth century" (40). This finding is corroborated by William St. Clair's computation of annual incomes in Britain in 1801 ("Impact of Byron's Writings" 4–5).

3. While some biographers have noted the female-centeredness of Shelley's formative years, they have not considered the stress placed on maternal influence within Shelley's social class or analyzed with any depth the nature of Shelley's experience in that feminine circle. Cameron considers the fact that Shelley was "not in the normal atmosphere of association with other boys" to be "one unusual factor" about his early environment (5) but does not discuss the nature of that environment further or speculate on its possible effects. Medwin (17) and White (I, 19) mention it only as explanation for the effeminate mannerisms that made Shelley a scapegoat at boarding school (see p. 102).

4. In transcribing Shelley's notebook pages, Dawson uses <angle brackets> to signify an uncertain reading (*Bodleian MS.* III, xxiv).

5. Betty T. Bennett, editor of Mary Shelley's *Letters,* in a note on Shelley's cremation cites Arthur Norman's "Shelley's Heart" to explain the fact that Shelley's heart did not burn. Norman thinks it "very probably that Shelley suffered from a progressively calcifying heart" (*Letters* I, 256). Joseph Perloff, Streisand/American Heart Association Professor of Medicine and Pediatrics at the UCLA School of Medicine, has further suggested that this calcification was "chronic tuberculous calcific pericarditis," caused by a tuberculosis bacillus that went into remission in the lungs but then attacked the heart (personal correspondence).

6. Klein in "The Psychogenesis of Manic-Depressive States" writes that "in the earliest phase the persecuting and the good objects (breasts) are kept wide apart in the child's mind. When, along with the introjection of the whole and real object [the mother], they come closer together, the ego has over and over again recourse to that mechanism—so important for the development of the relations to objects—namely, a splitting of its imagos into loved and hated, that is to say, into good and dangerous ones" (143).

7. I am helped in seeing this particular repetitive pattern in Shelley's relationships by R. D. Laing's description of a similar sequence of events in a patient who came for treatment because he "felt destroyed by a woman" and connected her behavior, as he had that of other women previously, with the way his mother had acted when he was three. Laing, through analysis and with "collateral evidence from parents and others," reconstructed a prototypical childhood sequence constantly reenacted in adult life:

Prototypical sequence

1. He is with the woman he loves (his nanny).
2. His mother returns, sends nanny away
3. and then sends him away to boarding school,
4. while his father does not intervene.
5. Mother vacillates between him and affairs with men.
6. He runs away from boarding school and is returned by the police.

Repeating scenario as an adult

1. He falls in love with A.
2. He leaves A for B,
3. And breaks up with B.
4. C does not intervene.
5. He and B vacillate between each other and affairs with others.
6. He tries to escape but can't. (10)

Laing notes that the sequences differ principally because "in the latter *he tried to do what was done to him. He leaves A. B does not take him away. He drives B away.* In making B leave him, he seems to be in control. But he experiences each repeat of the scenario as though he is the victim of B, and finally of the scenario, for which his mother is held responsible. B took him away from A, then deserted him, then forced him into the wilderness. I [Laing] looked on like his father" (9–10; author's emphasis).

We do not have the kind of evidence Laing was working from that might make it possible to reconstruct Shelley's "prototypical sequence"; but the "repeating scenario" shows interesting parallels with a similar pattern in Shelley's relationships, particularly with the women he loved but also with members of his family: that is, his are the acts of betrayal, yet he feels himself the one betrayed.

8. May E. Romm, in "The Unconscious Need to Be an Only Child," describes as a typical strategy on the child's part "accepting a sibling as one's own child and in this way removing it from the parents" (332).

9. White, in discussing Shelley's lifelong obsession with the adoption of a girl child, traces the idea to Shelley's childhood fascination with Robert Paltock's adventure story *Peter Wilkins* (I, 25, 29: II, 422). There the king of the Glumms adopts two of the children whom his daughter Youwarkee has borne to Peter (211), but this event receives only passing mention. A fantasy like that of "The Abandoned Infant," recounted in Chapter 2, is much closer to Shelley's daydream.

10. Emily Sunstein offers a review of the evidence and gossip surrounding the documented fact that, without Mary's knowledge, Shelley illegally registered as his own a girl infant baptized as Elena Adelaide Shelley, giving her birth date as December 27, 1818, and her mother's name as Maria Padurin (White II, 547). Perhaps "Padurin" was a clerical error, for the baptismal certificate names Mary Godwin as mother (White II, 548). White (II, 72–83; 546–50), Cameron in *Shelley: The Golden Years* (64–73), and Holmes (465–74) extensively discuss the incident and come to very different conclusions: White believes that Elena was a foundling adopted by Shelley because in his loneliness after his daughter Clara's death and Mary's subsequent depression the old fantasy of adopting a girl child took a particularly strong hold on him (II, 78–79); Cameron believes it impossible to make "even a reasonable guess as to the identity of either the father or the mother of the child" (72); Holmes is convinced that Elena was Shelley's child by the servant Elise (471). Another theory, that Elena was Shelley's child by Claire Clairmont, has been judged untenable because Claire's method of marking her journal shows that she was having a menstrual period at the time when conception would have to have occurred (Kessel 1180–83). Sunstein takes it as "sensible" to "believe Shelley, who told Thomas Medwin and Byron that he took charge of the child to help a young married English lady who had fallen in love with his poetry, and whom he met again at Naples" (Sunstein 434; Medwin 204–10). My own sensible side turns skeptical, however, when I read Medwin's melodramatic tale. Since I am not undertaking a full biography of Shelley, I refrain from taking a position about the perplexing incident but feel that I can fairly use it as evidence of Shelley's repeated urge to adopt a girl child.

11. Merle's purported repudiation of the sexual element in Shelley's fantasy gives him the opportunity to entertain it further: "The idea of a youth of twenty shutting himself from the world with two females until an age when, without religious instruction, they would have no other guarantee for their chastity than the reason of a man who would then be in the summer of his life, with all his passions in full vigour, was more than absurd—it was horrible" (quoted in Holmes 69).

12. Anne Mellor's comment on Shelley's "unresolved Oedipal desire to possess the mother" (*Mary Shelley* 73–74) is relevant here. She suggests that Shelley's "persistent desire to be the sexual partner of every woman he admired" can be traced to "a fundamental inability to separate his ego from his mother's and to function normally without the unquestioning emotional and sexual support of a devoted woman" (74). More generally, Adrienne Rich has described men's infantilization as "one of the most insidious patterns between the sexes" (213). The *double* incest pattern created through the separation of spheres has received beautifully succinct formulation from Stacey Vallas: "A husband mediates between the home and public institutions, providing

financial resources as well as social status—and a name—just as his wife's father once did for her; a wife in turn maintains the home, attends to the care of bodies, cooks, cleans, sews, nurtures as her husband's mother once did for him" (149).

13. Mellor (*Mary Shelley* 72), citing particularly William Veeder's coverage of this theme in *Mary Shelley and "Frankenstein"* (47–80), gives a bibliographic footnote on other scholarly treatments of it as well (235).

14. Leon Waldoff and William Ulmer do not comment explicitly on the significance of Shelley's youthful pyromania, but, on the basis of Freud's comment with regard to the Promethean legend that "the shape and movements of a flame suggest a phallus in activity" (Freud XXII, 190), they both note the appropriateness of contention over fire in the conflict between Jupiter and Prometheus (Waldoff 81; Ulmer 82).

15. Philip Slater's explication for Greek misogyny takes as crucial the first six years of a Greek boy's life, in which he was sequestered in the women's quarters with his mother. The low social status and confined way of life accorded women in Greek society created strong ambivalence in mothers toward their sons: on the one hand, resentment at the husband's superiority could take its revenge on the boy child left in the mother's care (28–29); on the other, the woman's sexual frustration as a result of marriage to an "indifferent and largely absented husband" meant that "some of the mother's sexual longing was turned upon her son" (31). Both expressions of ambivalent feeling, in Slater's analysis, created fear of maternal power in Greek men, a fear that then served to perpetuate the injustice toward women that initiated the latter's angry feelings, and so around in generational circles.

While highly problematic as historical analysis, Slater's reconstruction of Athens serves as a relevant commentary on the institution of motherhood created by the "feminine mystique" of the 1950s—and by extension on the same institution produced by the maternal ideology of the late eighteenth century. Rich, while regretting Slater's failure to see the source of the difficulty in patriarchal dominance, considers him "refreshingly aware that [the mother's] relationship to her son occurs in a social context, the *reductio-ad-matrem* which gives no other opportunity for action, makes motherhood the definition of womanhood, and child-care (in the middle classes) a full-time, exclusively female occupation" (123). And though Rich gives more sympathetic attention than Slater does to the emotions experienced by a domestically confined woman, she also finds that the constriction shared by mothers and children leads to ambivalence in the sons, to a belief that "a woman is nothing so much as an emotional climate made to soothe and reassure, or an emotional whirlwind bent on their destruction" (276).

Dorothy Dinnerstein points out that "woman's limited opportunity to develop her own self does in fact often make her batten on, and sabotage, the autonomy of others." But the central theme of her book is that infants' initial experience of dependence on the female parent given sole responsibility for their care creates "another, deeper-lying truth: that the threat to autonomy which can come from a woman is felt on a less rational, more helpless level, experienced as more primitively dangerous, than any such threat from a man" (112).

16. Jeremy Bentham, in a passage quoted by Crompton, dared to state openly that boarding schools fostered homosexuality by having the boys share beds. Comparing English education with that of ancient Greece Bentham writes: "On the present plan [boys] are often forced together under circumstances still more favorable to it [i.e., homosexuality] by the custom of lying together in feather beds, implements of indulgence and incentives to the venereal appetite with which the ancients were unacquainted." Crompton adds: "At Eton it was the custom for masters to lock boys into

dormitories at eight o'clock and to leave them unattended" (79). It therefore stretches credulity to suppose that Shelley never at least witnessed or had knowledge of homoerotic incidents during his boarding school years.

17. This analysis applies to the effect of the taboo against mother-son incest for a male subject; the scenario is very different for a female, given, in Sandra Gilbert's phrasing, "the prescription for father-daughter incest that lies at the heart of female psychosexual development in patriarchal society" (377).

18. Mary Favret observes: "In [Jane] Austen's major novels, and in the novels of her successors, we find an increasing emphasis on the letter as an object of scrutiny . . . rather than a frame or medium of expression" (214). Many eyes could scan the addresses of letters placed in readiness for the post and the handwriting of those that came into the house. Letters also were publicly received—surely not without family comment.

19. The romance may have seemed particularly appropriate in the Grove family because its members "ran to" marriages between cousins. Harriet Grove's aunt Elizabeth Grove—her father's elder sister—married a cousin, William Chafin Grove (*SHC* II, 495); and Harriet's brother William married a cousin, Frances Grove (*SHC* II, 499), though after the break with Shelley.

20. In " 'My Brain is Feminine': Byron and the Poetry of Deception" McGann lists Shelley as one of those influenced by Dacre, and indeed, as his important study suggests, a careful assessment of that influence is needed for a better understanding of Shelley's poetry. Shelley's debt to Dacre's gothic novel *Zafloya* in writing *Zastrozzi* has long been recognized, but the influence of her *Hours of Solitude* (1805) on Shelley's early poetry has not received the attention it deserves.

21. Editorial procedure in *SHC* is to use arrow brackets < > as sign that "words are missing due to physical damage to the paper—an ink blot, a hole caused by tearing open the seal" (*SHC* I, xxxvi).

22. Matthews and Everest project a somewhat different scenario leading up to the second verse letter to Graham. In their reading Graham "had evidently played up with a letter of mock-penitence to the scandal . . . and this poem follows up the joke" (*PS* I, 169).

23. As White suggests, to tell Graham "would bring interference from Field Place if Graham proved loyal to his benefactor, or unpleasant consequences for Graham if he proved loyal to Shelley" (I, 152).

24. I am following Cameron's analysis of Timothy Shelley's actions: "Shelley, it is clear, had not realized how bitterly his father had resented his actions, how keenly he felt the disgrace of his son's elopement with the daughter of a tavern keeper (as Timothy saw it), and especially how deeply he had been hurt by the loss of his son's confidence" (*SHC* III, 14).

25. This characteristic in Shelley shows him to be a fully typical Romantic reader, according to Robert Darnton's analysis. Darnton writes that "Rousseau taught his readers to 'digest' books so thoroughly that literature became absorbed in life," and asserts that the "peculiar species of reader" so created "arose in the eighteenth century and . . . began to die out in the age of Madame Bovary" (*Great Cat Massacre* 251). Von Mücke's work, in turn, takes up with more specificity than Eagleton's the "pedagogical function" of "aesthetic transparency": "the formation of the subject, the internalization of a mode of authority" (10, 48).

24. I am indebted to Robert Latham for this parallel to Shelley's vision to be found in Eugene O'Neill's mythic imagination.

II

Re-Membering the Mother

For to us who stand on the boundary line between the different forms of existence, the Hellenic prototype retains this immeasurable value, that all these transitions and struggles are imprinted upon it in a classically instructive form.

Friedrich Nietzsche, The Birth of Tragedy

I wish there were somewhere
actual we could stand
handing the power-glasses back and forth
looking at the earth, the wildwood
where the split began

Adrienne Rich, "Waking in the Dark"

Back of the Muses, so the old teaching goes, is Mnemosyne, Mother of the Muses. Freud, too, teaches that the Art has something to do with restoring, re-membering, the Mother. Poetry itself may then be the Mother of those who have destroyed their mothers. But no. The image that Freud projects of dismembering and remembering is the image of his own creative process in Psychoanalysis which he reads into all the Arts. Mnemosyne, the Mother-Memory of Poetry, is our made-up life, the matrix of fictions. Poetry is the Mother of those who have created their own mothers.

Robert Duncan, "The H.D. Book"

4

Seeing Through Mirrors
(*Prometheus Unbound,* Act I)

The terms on which Shelley objected to the resolution of Aeschylus' lost drama *Prometheus Lyomenos,* or *Prometheus Unbound*[1]—which I will give its Greek title in order to avoid confusion with Shelley's play—center the dramatic conflict in the same standoff between two masculine superpowers as that which constitutes virtually the whole action of *Prometheus Bound:* "I was averse from a catastrophe so feeble as that of reconciling the Champion with the Oppressor of mankind" (*SPP* 133). Act one of *Prometheus Unbound,* in recalling and reinscribing that situation, understandably maintains an Aeschylean character: Prometheus helped to bring Zeus/Jupiter to power, but the latter objected to Prometheus' befriending the human race and in punishment pinioned him to a cliff face. Prometheus, however, even if helpless, has the weapon of his foreknowledge. He knows that if Jupiter has sexual relations with Thetis, the son born of their union will overthrow his father. So, as an immortal, he need only endure his agony *while keeping his knowledge secret,* and eventually, inevitably, Zeus will fall from power. In the opinion of Aeschylus, that fate must not overcome the Supreme Father. The power of Zeus, its initial insecurity manifest through the very violence of his treatment of Prometheus, must be stabilized and perpetuated. Prometheus must, therefore, tell the secret before Zeus has sexual relations with Thetis—a revelation that will make finally and eternally impregnable the rule that Prometheus himself so violently and gallantly opposed throughout the action of *Prometheus Bound.* This is the reconciliation suggested by the extant fragments of *Prometheus Lyomenos,* which Shelley considered a catastrophe in two senses of the word.

A masculine narrative focus on the plot such as the one that I have just outlined takes special note of only one female character, Thetis, and assigns her the function of being the pawn of male combatants; elements even in Aeschylus' rendering of the story, however, suggest that the struggle between male powers masks an underlying drama in which the Mother Goddess acts as Prometheus' ally in contesting patriarchal power. In his dramatization Shelley

137

highlights and emphasizes this aspect of the legend as the statement quoted from his preface does not. The first act of his play, functioning in part as a reprise of *Prometheus Bound,* is strongly Aeschylean in structure and tone (Rogers, *Shelley at Work* 151). Interchanges between Prometheus and the feminine presences of Earth, the Furies, and the two Oceanides who are the sorrowful witnesses to his suffering dominate this act. The very gender of the protagonist undergoes metamorphosis in act two when Asia becomes central to the dramatic action, and that action has as its underlying mythos the legend of Venus, the Mother Goddess, and her beloved, Adonis. In act three Shelley uses traces of an ancient, mother-centered ritual as substructure to a new plot for world history.

Before turning to Shelley's revision of Aeschylus, however, we must look briefly at the changes Aeschylus made in the Promethean legend as he in turn had it from Hesiod. In Hesiod's creation story, initial Chaos is quickly given form through the female power of "wide-bosomed Earth, the ever-sure foundation of all." Earth bears "starry Heaven [Ouranos], equal to herself, to cover her on every side," and the couple produce a great many very powerful children. But their father hates them and hides them away in Earth as soon as they are born. Earth, conspiring with Kronos, "youngest and most terrible of her children," who more than returns his father's hatred, provides the jagged sickle with which Kronos cuts off the phallus of Heaven, separating the primal pair (Hesiod 87, 89, 93).

The offspring, to whom Ouranos gives the reproachful name of Titans, or "Strainers," come forth from Earth's interior and multiply, with Kronos as their leader. He and his sister Titan Rhea also produce many children, all of whom wily Kronos swallows because the primal parents have foretold his downfall in turn at the hands of one of his sons. Rhea at last saves the youngest one, Zeus, substituting a stone in his place. She has Zeus secretly raised in Crete until he comes to the fullness of his powers. At that point, in a second circle of conspiracy Earth reenters the story; she beguiles Kronos into disgorging all of his offspring—and the stone. They take sides with Zeus and overthrow Kronos (113, 117).

A third cycle is about to begin. Metis, "the wisest among gods and mortal men," was Zeus' first wife, and she too would eventually have borne a son to displace him: "But when she was about to bring forth the goddess bright-eyed Athene, Zeus craftily deceived her with cunning words and put her in his own belly" (143). As Marcel Detienne and Jean-Pierre Vernant point out, this appropriative act ensures his absolute and unending power: "By swallowing her Zeus locks upon her the bond which is to hold her forever imprisoned. He encloses her forever within himself so that, being part of his own substance, she will give him the constant knowledge of the chances that the future holds which will enable him to control the shifting and uncertain course of events" (112).

In Hesiod, then, there is no question of *anyone's* having secret foreknowledge that gives power over Zeus, and the conflict between him and Prometheus has a completely different character from that dramatized by Aeschylus. Hesiod's Prometheus, son of the Titan Japetus and of a daughter of Ocean named Clymene, is a rather bumbling trickster. His first attempt to outwit Zeus on humans' behalf leads Zeus to deny them fire. Defiantly Prometheus steals it back, and in reprisal Zeus binds him, drives a shaft through his middle, and sends an eagle daily to eat his liver. From this torture Prometheus is finally, and rather anticlimactically, delivered by Heracles, but "not without the will of Olympian Zeus," who simple allows Heracles this feat as a way of showing off his favorite's strength (117–19).

In Aeschylus' *Prometheus Bound,* Prometheus is not the son of Japetus and Clymene. His mother is the goddess Themis, whom Prometheus identifies with Earth: "My mother Themis, who is also called Earth / (she's one, only one, always the same form / though she has many names)" (ll. 311–13). As Nikolaus Wecklein notes succinctly, "His father is nowhere mentioned" (7). The link to Clymene survives only in that Aeschylus has the Oceanides serve as chorus. They are compassionate witnesses to the Promethean agon, and as specifically feminine presences they also draw attention to a central feminine involvement in the struggle between Zeus and Prometheus. It was on his mother's advice about the superiority of craft over brute force—advice that the other Titans rejected—that Prometheus, allied with his mother, went over to the cause of Zeus. Their aid enabled Zeus to hurl Kronos and his Titan allies into Tartarus.

Prometheus' subsequent quarrel with Zeus arose over the latter's intention to destroy the human race as a failed experiment and create a new one; in defiance of Zeus' plan, Prometheus worked to improve on the poor, botched product, not only by stealing fire for humans but by leading them into a consciousness that gave them control over the environment that had previously engulfed them. That is, he dowered them with the arts and sciences (ll. 630–738). In a reprisal that seems the overreaction of a young and insecure ruler, Zeus has Prometheus fastened to a rock somewhere on the outer boundary of the world, in "the uttermost parts of Scythia," but this decree provides only the play's setting (ll. 1–123). Its *action* turns on Prometheus' continued alliance with his mother, through the possession of her secret, and the power he thereby holds over a vulnerable Zeus. In other words, Prometheus has the power to decide whether universal history will continue in the older, established pattern—with Father Gods functioning through a power first given and later withdrawn through the greater power of Mother Goddesses—or under a new system that puts power permanently in the hands of a Father God.

Aeschylus could point to the historical records as rationale for his denouement: a Father God has historically and virtually universally remained in power, thereby also maintaining a masculine dominance that rules in and with his name. But besides, as one who, in Jane Harrison's phrase, is "all for the Father" (*Themis* 386), Aeschylus is convinced that Zeus' rule *must* and *should* be so established and wants his audience's joyful acceptance of the same outcome. Surprisingly, then, he complicates that acceptance not only by stressing Zeus' tyrannical misuse of power in his violent treatment of Prometheus (ll. 108–11) but also by focusing as much as he does and in the way that he does upon Zeus' rapacity toward Io.

In imagining a long dialogue between Prometheus and Io, Aeschylus makes another total departure from Hesiod, although Zeus' treatment of Io shows an appropriative violence reminiscent of the swallowing of Metis in Hesiod's account. Furthermore, in phrasing Io's description of her sufferings, Aeschylus puts all the emphasis on Zeus' sexual violence and downplays Hera's part in the story. Zeus in his lust for the virgin Io first haunts her dreams in ways that terrify her, then through oracles forces her father, Inachus, to cast her out of doors or lose his own life and the lives of all the other family members (ll. 942–90). This is not the traditional version of the story as Shelley would have found it recorded in, say, Lemprière's *Classical Dictionary*. There Io is simply a priestess of Hera at Argos. Zeus becomes enamored of her, as was his wont, and Io suffers more from being the object used by both royal partners in a deadly mutual game than from Zeus' particular ferocity. When Zeus tries to hide Io by changing her into a heifer, Hera, aware of the deceit, makes her restoration to human form impossible by acquiring her from Zeus and setting hundred-eyed Argus to guard her. Zeus counters by sending Hermes to kill Argus; Hera's riposte is the gadfly that drives crazed Io forth to wander the earth (Lemprière 367).

Ignoring Hera, Aeschylus elides Io's metamorphosis into a heifer, her constant surveillance by Argus, and the torment of the gadfly into a unity that makes the lustfulness of Zeus appear sole cause of her misery (ll. 1000–1018). Moreover, Io's pitiful story serves as turning point for this segment of the Promethean drama: Prometheus, more enraged by the sufferings that Zeus has caused Io than by those inflicted on himself, is led to talk more openly and more recklessly than he has before about his secret knowledge (ll. 1393–1425). All-hearing and all-seeing Zeus instantly sends Hermes to threaten Prometheus with far worse tortures unless he reveals that secret: first confinement, cliff and all, in the depths of Tartarus, and after that the torment of the eagle. Prometheus stands fast, the Oceanides refuse to abandon him, and the play ends with the thunder peals that hurl them all down to Tartarus (ll. 1550–1670).

As D. J. Conacher comments, this extreme view of Zeus' cruelty creates "a state of affairs ripe for the kind of reversal of perspective observable elsewhere in Aeschylean trilogies," giving as his examples the *Oresteia* and the *Danaid* (60). Conacher focuses only on the concept of reversal itself, but in fact each of the three important examples he cites takes up different aspects of a similar problem: an initial act of male violence arouses in female protagonists, and in the masculine figures taking their side, the desire for vengeance. Moreover, cross-references among the plays underscore this singleness of theme. Also, though the dating of both *The Suppliants* and *Prometheus Bound* is fraught with problems, recent combination of knowledge and surmise suggests that all three trilogies were written in the last decade of Aeschylus' life (Lloyd-Jones vii; Garvie 1–28). Possibly, then, all might be read as an extended meditation on Aeschylus' understanding of "the woman question."

Only the first play, *The Suppliants,* survives of the *Danaid* trilogy, but Prometheus himself in *Prometheus Bound* gives us what may be a plot summary of the whole when he foretells Io's destiny and his own eventual release (ll. 1280–1333). At a critical juncture in *Prometheus Bound,* then—a play performed late in Aeschylus' life and so in the years just preceding his death in 456 B.C.—Aeschylus makes an intertextual allusion back to the *Danaid* trilogy that had won first prize in the dramatic competition held about a decade before.

Prometheus tells Io that her maddened and terrifying journey will finally and peacefully end in Egypt, where Zeus will restore her, "stroking you / with a hand you no longer fear" (ll. 1286–87). As a result she will bring forth a son, Epaphus ("touch-born"). Five generations later, fifty maidens, her descendants through him, will return to Io's native Argos, fleeing there for refuge from marriage with fifty Egyptian cousins, who follow in enraged pursuit. The Egyptians will take them by force, but the "brides"—with one exception—having armed themselves with daggers, will kill their rapist husbands before morning. Only one, Hypermestra, having fallen in love with the man who desires her, will refrain. From their line of descendants will come Heracles, who will free Prometheus. Concluding his story, Prometheus alludes again to Themis: "This was prophesied by the Titan Themis, my mother / born in archaic time" (ll. 1334–35).

The allusion to oracular Themis creates a link with Aeschylus' *Eumenides.* That play opens at the inner shrine of the Temple of Apollo in Delphi, where Orestes is about to seek sanctuary from the Erinyes, the Fates of the old order pursuing him in vengeance for the murder of his mother, Clytemnestra. The Pythia, priestess of Apollo and speaker of his oracles, gives a brief history of the shrine, stressing the peacefulness of its transfer from a feminine to a masculine power:

> First among the gods in this prayer I honor
> the first prophet, Earth; and after her Themis,
> she was the second to take her seat
> in this place of prophecy, as tradition tells; and third
> in succession, with the consent of Themis, and with no violence done to any,
> another Titaness, a child of Earth, took her seat here,
> Phoebe. And she gave it as a birthday gift
> to Phoebus; and he bears a name taken from hers.
>
> (ll. 1–8)

As I shall discuss further when considering more particularly the significance of the Delphic oracle in relation to Shelley's *Prometheus Unbound,* Aeschylus' narrative of a peaceful, indeed loving, transfer of power at Delphi explicitly denies other, more violent versions of the story. And the strategy seen here in miniature also characterizes the sweeping scenarios of the trilogies. In each Aeschylus gives full and sympathetic dramatic expression to characters that are either feminine or (like Prometheus) allied to a feminine order. They are wronged, supplanted, or brutalized by a usurping, tyrannical, masculine force in ways that make peaceful solution of the gender conflict seem impossible.

The love that makes Hypermestra spare her Egyptian captor puts order and fertility in the place of rape, murder, and insterility; Phoebe gives the Delphic oracle to Apollo as a present; the conclusion of the goddess Athena that the mother only bears the father's seed and that matricide therefore does not require vengeance calms the violent Erinyes and allows their transformation into the beneficent Eumenides; Prometheus' own prophecy of the gentle touch with which Zeus will bring Io to her apotheosis foreshadows a peaceful reconciliation between Zeus and himself as well. Time and again Aeschylus thus dramatizes a shift whereby masculine prerogatives are finally established and maintained by loving allegiance from a co-opted feminine power. At the same time, this reconciliation becomes possible because male power, expressed earlier through rapacity in various forms, changes to the friendly persuasion of a seductive gentleness.

The hypothesized denouement of the conflict between Zeus and Prometheus exemplifies this typical Aeschylean "turn." Several manuscripts of *Prometheus Bound* list Earth (i.e., Themis) and Heracles among the cast of characters (Aeschylus, *Prometheus Bound* 102–3). Since they do not appear in this play, the scholarly assumption historically has been that they must have appeared in *Prometheus Lyomenos*. (Shelley's own cast of characters reflects this thinking.) We know also from the quotations of *Prometheus Lyomenos* that appear in the writings of Arrian and Cicero that the Chorus of that play was no longer the Oceanides but the Titans, whom Zeus had now freed and who might therefore bear witness to a change in policy on Zeus' part. The lines quoted by Cicero make it clear also that Prometheus' tortures are breaking his spirit (*Prometheus Bound* 103–6). Working from this evidence as well as from the context of other Aeschylean resolutions, R. P. Winnington-Ingram speculates that "right-counselling Themis" may be instrumental in reconciling Prometheus to Zeus. Alluding to the old pattern whereby a stronger son eventually overthrows the father, Winnington-Ingram asks: "Was it she who brought Prometheus to see that a more forcible son of Zeus might be worse not better for that [human] race? We are reduced to mere speculation" (187). Wecklein also hypothesizes that "the part of mediator was taken, it would seem, by Gaea, the mother of the Titans" (11).

Winnington-Ingram writes of the standoff in *Prometheus Bound* in words that could apply equally well to all these conflicts: "The situation *must* have been resolved" (177; author's emphasis). Implied through his emphasis is the historical point mentioned earlier—males have retained dominance—and a moral position as well: it was necessary to human culture that they do so. Although Jane Harrison, following Johann Bachofen, called attention to an Olympian takeover from an earlier mother-centered religion and culture, she too sees the transition involving a transfer of power from feminine to masculine as one "modern psychology and anthropology know to be a necessary development" (*Themis* 393). Aeschylus plots that it is also an accepted and acceptable development. Shelley, in challenging that plot, raises the question of whether it had, indeed, a necessary, much less an acceptable, resolution.

Let us go back now to the point at which this chapter started. Shelley's objection to a reconciliation between Zeus and Prometheus and his determination to imagine a different denouement necessitates a return to the Aeschylean moment of crisis: the Father God in power but that power not permanently established. Imagine, then, the almost unimaginable: What if Prometheus had *not* been persuaded by his mother to make Zeus impregnable by warning him against sexual relations with Thetis? What if, in a situation paralleling the one that Shelley maneuvered for at Field Place, mother and son remained in alliance against the tyranny of the father?

In the second act of *Prometheus Unbound,* Asia, recounting the protagonist's importance to human history, says: "He gave man speech, and speech created thought" (II.iv.73). Prometheus' situation as the drama opens, the situation he has been in for three thousand years—which is to say the time span that nineteenth-century scientists believed separated their present from the earliest beginnings of civilization (*SPP* 136)—makes a bloody spectacle of what the price of that gift was, and is, since the figure of Prometheus fuses phylogenetic and ontogenetic human experience. "We are ourselves . . . depositories of the evidence of the subject which we consider," Shelley writes about "the science of mind" (*Shelley's Prose* 185). As such a depository, Prometheus is also a gigantic icon, spread-eagled there on a precipice of the "Indian Caucasus," a manifest embodiment of the process by which we enter the symbolic order, by which we speak. In act two the audience will have the opportunity to survey what was gained thereby; act one fixes our attention on its cost.

The description of the setting, then, is itself an image to which we should apply Shelley's statement from the play's preface: "The imagery which I have employed will be found in many instances to have been drawn from the operations of the human mind, or from those external actions by which they are expressed" (*SPP* 133). If as gloss on that statement we remember Shelley's thought that "we ought to consider *the mind of man and the universe as the great whole,* on which to exercise our speculations" (*Shelley's Prose* 186; my emphasis), we better understand the imaginative scope of his drama. "External actions" that function as images for the operations of the mind should be understood to include geographical loci—countries of the mind—as well as the events occurring in them.

Aided by the slipperiness of signifiers, Shelley has chosen to move the action of the play's opening scenes from Aeschylus' setting for *Prometheus Lyomenos,* the Caucasus Mountains that lie between the Black and Caspian seas (*Prometheus Bound* 104), to the Caucasus Indicus, the Hindu Kush, which Shelley's scholarly sources led him to believe circle "the cradle of the race" in the Vale of Kashmir. (These mountains are also the setting for the final events of "Alastor," where they bar the Poet's attempt to return to the

Vale [*SPP* 74]). We learn as the play progresses that in that valley is Asia,
Prometheus' beloved, separated from him through the millennia.

In other words, Prometheus' situation depicts synchronically the process
of achieving separate, speaking consciousness as, according to Freudian
theory, it is diachronically experienced by human subjects throughout history.
Bringer of language and thus both bestower and epitomizer of human consciousness, he is thereby perpetrator and victim of the "murder" (Kristeva,
Revolution 75) that is its price. His body serves as inscription of the sacrifice
that has been made: castration.

Not only his body but his very name manifests it. "Prometheus" is translated from the Greek to mean "forethought" or "forethinker." Closely associated for the Greeks with the idea of cunning, the word "forethought" matches
his characterization by Hesiod as a lovable, wily trickster. But turn to the
Indo-European sources of his legend and his name, and one discovers that
both hark back to the Aryan nations' first fire instrument, a boring stick
rotated in the hole of a wooden plate. Through metaphor the stick becomes
the phallus kindling the fire of life in the womb. So in the Vedic hymns,
written in a language more ancient than Sanskrit, the nineteenth-century
comparative mythologist Adalbert Kuhn can trace stages of the signifier
matha. Its first signified, "a boring stick," changes through metaphor to "penis"; the original signifier for boring stick having been thus displaced,
paramantha becomes its replacement, though as Heymann Steinthal, discussing Kuhn's findings, points out, "with only a shade of difference in the meaning" (370; see also Wecklein 2).

These scholarly findings postdate Shelley by more than half a century, and
so he may not have been conscious of the association of the name Prometheus
with the penis. At the same time, he had no less metaphoric a turn of mind
than those ancient Indo-Europeans. Also the Greek legend with which he was
working gives a hint of this meaning in the image of Jupiter's vulture that eats
away Prometheus' liver each day, while the organ grows back each night. In
Prometheus' opening address to Jupiter he alludes to this torment, but Shelley
makes two extremely significant changes in the legend. The vulture or eagle
takes sputum from Jupiter's lips—"polluting from thy lips / His beak in poison
not his own" (I.i.34–35)—and with it poisons not Prometheus' liver but his
heart. The poison, as we will learn when we meet Jupiter himself in act three,
is that of venereal disease, and other tortures described just previously—the
piercing cold, the gnawing chains—also have associations with venereal disease in Shelley's poetry. Nora Crook and Derek Guiton in their study of
Shelley's obsession with venereal disease note these associations and describe
the change from liver to heart as "a shift away from the organs of digestion to
those of generation" (Crook and Guiton 188)—as, then, a displacement even
more transparent than that of the Vedic hymns.

Poisoned by fluid drawn from the lips of Jupiter, Prometheus, in this
aspect of his sacrificial victimization, is as blameless as Beatrice Cenci, diseased by her syphilitic father's rape. And I take it that Shelley does indeed
consider patriarchal rule as one that forges a chain whose links of rape,

prostitution, venereal disease, and loathsome death entwine us all. At the same time, he establishes from the very opening of *Prometheus Unbound* a strange camaraderie, almost an identification between Prometheus and Jupiter, reminding us that in the symbolic order established in the Name-of-the-Father, the sacrificial, castrated son will in time himself rule as father. (How to change that system without in the process sacrificing male dominance is in a very real sense the problem addressed by Shelley's play, as it was in a different way by Aeschylus'.)

Prometheus' opening monologue addresses Jupiter in words that join their two pairs of eyes into a single constancy of power:

> Monarch of Gods and Dæmons, and all Spirits
> But One, who throng those bright and rolling Worlds
> Which Thou and I alone of living things
> Behold with sleepless eyes!
>
> (I.i.1–4)

Despite Prometheus' degrading and tormented position, my statement that he and Jove share power seems verified by Prometheus' claim that "One," whom critics have generally agreed is Prometheus himself (*V* 341), is not under Jove's rule. That critical judgment is sustained by the exclamation a few lines later: "O Mighty God! / Almighty, had I deigned to share the shame/ Of thine ill tyranny" (I.i.17–19). Arthur Wormhoudt, however, in his psychoanalytic reading of the play, identifies the "One" as Demogorgon, whom he characterizes as "primarily a pre-oedipal figure" (89). His argument takes its rationale from later events in the play in which Demogorgon is the agent of Jupiter's downfall precisely because he has never been under the latter's power. The best answer, as I see it, is that the unconquered "One" is both Prometheus and Demogorgon, or Prometheus/Demogorgon. Allegorizing, as the psychodramatic material virtually demands, we can provisionally think of Demogorgon as that hidden but still vital aspect of Prometheus that holds potential for social change. Further consideration of what that potential makes of his function in the drama is better placed in the discussion of act two.

For a few lines after the close association between Prometheus and Jupiter created by the linked pronouns "Thou and I," the connection between them breaks, as Prometheus describes the alienation ("fear and self contempt and barren hope" [I.i.8]) made universal by Jupiter's reign. But in the lines "Whilst me, who am thy foe, eyeless in hate, / Hast thou made reign and triumph to thy scorn, / O'er mine own misery" (I.i.9–11), the grammatical ambiguity involving two possible modifiers for the adjectival phrase "eyeless in hate" again underscores some strange fusion of the two. Does the phrase refer to "me" in the same line or forward to "thou" in the line following? And, of course, the words also call up the description of the aged Lear on the heath raging at the elements: he "tears his white hair, / Which the impetuous blasts, with eyeless rage, / Catch in their fury" (III.i.7–9).

In Shakespeare's lines "eyeless" modifies the rage of "the impetuous blasts," but they in turn serve as metaphoric projection for the wild but impotent rage of the shattered king. Thus Shelley binds into the single word allusions to four dramas: *Oedipus the King, Oedipus at Colonus, King Lear,* and *Samson Agonistes,* all of which turn upon the theme of symbolic castration, and three of which deal specifically with the conflict between male parents and their offspring. Each also dramatizes sudden cataclysmic shifts in power, foreshadowing the action of *Prometheus Unbound.* Most strikingly, the phrase in its grammatical ambiguity sets up the endless circle of temporary impotence and temporary power that serves as the permanent substructure of patriarchal rule: the son submits, perhaps unwillingly and angrily at first but then with resignation. In time he denies the very existence of his incestuous desire, driving it into the unconscious; he undergoes this temporary and symbolic castration with the understanding that in time the father, through enfeeblement and then death, will resign his place and the son succeed to it, in turn symbolically castrating his son, and so on. Fathers and sons are both, then, for certain periods of life "eyeless," and so the phrase applies appropriately to both Prometheus and Jupiter. At once static and cyclic, this standoff produces the violent human history for which Shelley is determined to imagine an end.

The first action of the play, and so the first step toward fulfilling this ambition, occurs at line 58 when what appears to be the beginning of a new thought occurs to the protagonist and opens up a possibility for change. Groping toward it, Prometheus tries to remember the violent interaction between himself and Jupiter that initiated all his own and the world's woe but finds that he cannot: "The Curse / Once breathed on thee I would recall" (I.i.58–59). That "recall" has the specific meaning of "remember" is clear from the context, although, of course, it also looks forward to a revocation of the curse already somewhat prepared for by the fact that Prometheus, while as convinced as ever of Jupiter's evil, is able to think of him with sorrowful pity rather than with the hatred that repeats and reinforces that of its object.

Voices from all four elements—mountains; springs; the air; and whirlwinds, associated with volcanoes' "flaming fountains"—as well as from Earth herself answer, but Prometheus hears them as sound, not language: "I hear a sound of voices—not the voice / Which I gave forth" (I.i.112–13). There follows quite a lengthy discussion between Prometheus and Earth, whom he addresses as "Mother," on precisely how he is to "recall" that moment. In the scholarly nattering over this interchange, E. B. Hungerford has expressed an impatience with the whole passage that is, one senses, shared by others. Shelley, he writes, although "capable of dealing with subtle complexities [here] attempts the unnecessary," and "the action is bogged down in the question whether Prometheus can or cannot understand what is said to him by his mother" (188–89).

But Shelley pauses over this difficulty because through the discussion around it we learn of the traumatic and thunderous moment that established subjectivity and speech. As we heard in the narratives of both Lacan and Stern, the "infans" reaching this point substitutes speech for an unmediated experience that is thereafter lost, unheard. Earth recounts, briefly, a story that adumbrates that later psychoanalytic formulation. When Prometheus, her infant, is born to her, the two experience an affect attunement mirrored by the structure of her verse sentence:

> Joy ran, as blood within a living frame,
> When thou didst from her bosom, like a cloud
> Of glory, arise, a spirit of keen joy!
>
> (I.i.156–58)

The two "joys" answer each other across the three lines, bringing before the eye the sympathy the words present to the mind. The phrase "a spirit of keen joy," by sharing its appositiveness with both the maternal "Joy" of line 156 and the infant "thou" of line 157, further reinforces her point.

Prometheus' potential seems limitless, giving heart to the "pining sons" who have succumbed to Jupiter's rule. This force, heard in Prometheus' voice, made Jupiter fear for his power "until his thunder chained thee here" (I.i.162). Her words both foreshadow and contradict Prometheus's statement roughly two hundred lines later: "I gave all / He has, and in return he chains me here" (I.i.381–82). Involved in Earth's flashback is an aspect of the plot inherited from Aeschylus that will be discussed in a later chapter. Considered within the purely psychoanalytic formulation that is my gloss here, Prometheus must be split into two separate aspects: he represents the human potential and the human institutions that make speech possible, and he enacts the process by which each individual achieves speech. In his first aspect Prometheus gives power to Jupiter as a prerequisite for his gift of language to the human race. Jupiter is the necessary "third term," the bar between the mother-infant dyad of the speechless semiotic. His power must be acknowledged, even established, in order that the leap to the symbolic may occur: for Prometheus in his second aspect to become the achiever of speech who then suffers the consequences of the gift.

In violent metaphors drawn from upheavals of the entire planet, Earth then describes the psychic events surrounding that accession to subjectivity, Prometheus' thetic moment, the occurrence that created his situation at the opening of the play. In earthquate and tempest, "new fire / From earthquake-rifted mountains of bright snow / Shook its portentous hair beneath Heaven's frown" (I.i.166–68). That is to say, in a cataclysm some volcanic potential is banished, disappears, and the unified joy and delight of "the beginning" changes to desire, expressing itself as lust, exploitation, and injustice. Such, I take it, are the psychological events and their social consequences behind Earth's images, but her emphasis is particularly and specifically on the blight laid upon sexual relations. The color blue, which Shelley associates in a number of other contexts with venereal disease and prostitution—and also, significantly, with Timothy Shelley (see pp. 116–17)—appears in this passage, as do references to plague and contagion: "Blue thistles bloomed in cities; foodless toads / Within voluptuous chambers panting crawled" (I.i.170–71). And while Earth's allusions in the lines that follow call up the mourning of Demeter for Persephone, they suggest also, in images that will have a significant reprise in act three, a historically repeated antagonism between mothers and fathers, the bereft and the powerful: "for my wan breast was dry / With grief; and the thin air, my breath, was stained / With the contagion of a mother's hate / Breathed on her child's destroyer" (I.i.176–79). Memory of this volcanic moment in which the subject acquired meaning descends to the unconscious along with its lost "being" and so is not available to Prometheus: thus his need to have the curse repeated.

Before turning to the curse itself, however, we should pause for a moment to note a point that will later have considerable significance. Prometheus has not lost all memory, all traces, of the period before Jupiter's thunder chained him to the precipice. He is able, though dimly, to catch glimpses of the beautiful valley in which he was once united with Asia, and that creative memory maintains the link to natural beauty, keeping it in existence. Addressing the sounds coming to him from the elements he says:

> Know ye not me,
> The Titan, he who made his agony
> The barrier to your else all-conquering foe?
> O rock-embosomed lawns and snow-fed streams
> Now seen athwart frore vapors deep below,
> Through whose o'er-shadowing woods I wandered once
> With Asia, drinking life from her loved eyes;
> Why scorns the spirit which informs ye, now
> To commune with me?
>
> (I.i.117–25)

Also, as Earl Wasserman points out (266), while we, the auditors, must hear both Prometheus and Earth as speaking the same language, we are to understand that their languages are different, although Prometheus can understand Earth's. (The convention, then, is much like that of old-style Hollywood movies in which English spoken with a German accent conveys the information that the characters are speaking in German.) Wasserman notes, too, without further analysis, that Earth's speech "works strangely" on Prometheus, who says, "I feel / Faint, like one mingled in entwining love, / Yet 'tis not pleasure" (I.i.147–49).

This "mingling" recalls the state of "reverie" described in "On Life," experienced by children and later by those "who in this respect are always children," "as if their nature were dissolved into the surrounding universe, or as if the surrounding universe were absorbed into their being" (*SPP* 477). The suggestion is that this bizarre, nonverbal dialogue with Earth casts Prometheus into that stage of an infant's life before words become arbitrary signifiers for concepts but when they are "signs" of presence and are introjected as such. Prometheus is thus experiencing—in the terms of Kristevan discourse— "the semiotization of the symbolic" that characterizes artistic production (*Revolution* 79) and that comes as the shadowy possibility of an answer to his plight just as he is reviewing the nature and history of the plight itself. Significant also is the fact that Prometheus does not see Mother Earth; he only hears tones he at once does and does not understand as emanating from one "moving near" him who loves him (I.136–37). His situation, then, replicates that of earliest infancy, and the ambivalence of his reaction registers the shifting psychic situation between immersion within that state and separation from it that Kaja Silverman describes in *The Acoustic Mirror* (73). Poised within this ambivalence, he cannot yet summon the will to change. Nonetheless, his initial mirroring of Jupiter has experienced a deflection through the power of this acoustic mirror's sound.

To progress further, he must "recall" the words of his curse to Jupiter, and Earth's voice guides him toward that end. She says:

> Ere Babylon was dust,
> The Magus Zoroaster, my dead child,
> Met his own image walking in the garden.
> The apparition, sole of men, he saw.
> For know, there are two worlds of life and death:
> One that which thou beholdest, but the other
> Is underneath the grave, where do inhabit
> The shadows of all things that think and live
> Till death unite them, and they part no more.
> (I.i.191–99)

From this realm "underneath the grave" she proposes any number of possible "phantoms," though her first suggestions are the most closely linked: "Thine own ghost, or the ghost of Jupiter" (I.i.211). Prometheus' quick choice is that the "Phantasm of Jupiter" appear to intone for him what he himself had once spoken to Jupiter.

While critics have legitimately found Zoroastrian, Platonic, Neoplatonic, and Paracelsan sources for these "two worlds of life and death" in existence simultaneously until death fuses them, these hermetic traditions do not explain what is occurring in this spirit raising as well as does Jung's identification of a world "beyond the grave" with the unconscious (VII, 186). Considered this way, Shelley's strategy in having the Phantasm that arises from Prometheus' unconscious take the form of Jupiter to repeat Prometheus' words is a dramatic enactment of an identification between them already made through certain phrases, as we have seen. It also re-presents what Lacan's theory tells us of the third and finally formative stage in the acquisition of subjectivity.

Lacan states that subjectivity occurs in "the space of the Other," and we have seen that in the pre-mirror and mirror stages of the infant's maturation, that Other, creating the primary unconscious, is the m(Other). As the infant enters the symbolic, however, in the series of dramatic events described earlier, a different, masculine Other rises, overshadowing—though not eliminating—the m(Other): "It is in the space of the Other that he [the subject] sees himself and the point from which he looks at himself is also in that space" (*Four Fundamental Concepts* 144). Shelley's thought that the nurse's soul enters the child seems a very rough parallel to the elaborate Lacanian discourse on the mirrored nature of subjectivity, but it does make possible the conceptualizations that went into imagining the Phantasm of Jupiter. For other souls besides the nurse's enter the child, above all the soul that is the "ego ideal" of a society intent on possessing autonomy, authority, and ever-widening power. So as the mythic representative of the human achievement of speech, Prometheus must also suffer the unconscious impress of the dominant social attitudes within which that achievement occurs. To distinguish among them, choosing between harmful and beneficent reflections, he must bring them into consciousness.

So understood, the appearance of the shade of Jupiter and its repetition of Prometheus' words resembles an intensely packed and clarifying session in analysis. Prometheus must "recall" first that he cursed Jupiter and then realize that in doing so he locked the two of them into an immutable relation of mutual loathing in a very Jupiter-like way, and invoked on them both a similar punishment. Prometheus' words "Rain then thy plagues upon me here, / Ghastly disease and frenzying fear" (I.i.266–67), dare Jupiter to mete out these tortures, but their imperative mood makes them also something of an order. Moreover, the nature of the punishments (the body's invasion by disease, the psyche's invasion by fear, with allusions to venereal disease) are, as Crook and Guiton point out, "the very plagues that Jupiter had inflicted on him" (188–89):

> I curse thee! let a sufferer's curse
> Clasp thee, his torturer, like remorse,
> Till thine Infinity shall be
> A robe of envenomed agony;
> And thine Omnipotence a crown of pain
> To cling like burning gold round thy dissolving brain
>   (I.i.286–91)

Shelley sets before us what Lacan has analyzed as the correlation between narcissism and aggressiveness. The fact that in the process of coming to subjectivity we grow through a series of mirrorings that become hidden away in the unconscious means that from its inception the *moi* is alienated. As Anthony Wilden explains, "It is the strength of the alienated *moi* . . . which would therefore account for the paranoid structures of identification with the aggressor, persecution mania, erotomania, doubling, jealousy, and so forth, all related to the subject's internal rivalry with himself" (173). René Girard's reminders about the mimetic nature of desire come at the situation from a slightly different but not oppositional angle. "Being"—self-fulfilled being not subject to desire (Lacan's "phallus")—Girard takes as the supreme human desire; mimetic rivalry involves not desire for something another has but desire for the "being" that such possession seems to confer: "The subject thus looks to that other person to inform him of what he should desire in order to acquire that being" (*Violence and the Sacred* 146).[2]

What, though, would Prometheus have been looking to Jupiter for? Are we to take it that he has been tainted by a desire for Jupiter's power? Not in any simple way; but Prometheus' language in describing Jupiter and the words of his curse suggest that Jupiter's fullness of being comes in his apparent control over the fearsome permeability by which we are "informed" by others. "O thou / Who fillest with thy soul this world of woe" (I.i.282–83), says Prometheus. Shelley's metaphor, as we have seen, for this malevolent capacity to possess through aggressive infiltration is venereal disease, and so Prometheus' body becomes a microcosm of the "world of woe" filled with Jupiter's soul. But Prometheus' curse, with its allusion to the invasive robe of Nessus, shows his own soul's possession by the desire to act in the same way. A "repeat in biography," to modify Ezra Pound's phrase, appears in Shelley's desire to enter the porches of his father's ears, deafening him with the repetition of "Bysshe, Bysshe, Bysshe" (*L* I, 149).

Hegel's dialectic of master and slave as it is used by Lacan to describe the intersubjective conflict of the *moi* also parallels the eons-long interaction between Prometheus and Jupiter. Lacan points out, as one of the possibilities that Hegel did not consider in his argument, that the slave, knowing his own mortality, is assured of his master's also and waits, meanwhile renouncing all pleasure, for that end. But in doing so "he is in the anticipated moment of the master's death, from which moment he will begin to live, but in the meantime he identifies himself with the master as dead, and as a result of this he is himself already dead" (*Écrits* 100). Literal death is not in question between these two immortals, but the situation is essentially the same: the process of identification means that the punishment Prometheus imagines so fervently for Jupiter is the one he himself also endures. (At whatever risk of the bathetic, let me point out that "A Cat in distress" shows Shelley already moving toward this idea when he punningly contrasts the desire of some for "a living" with that of others for the death of "An old fellow" and adds, "And which is the best / I leave to be guessed / For I cannot pretend to say" [*PS* I, 4].)

This is the "bind," the static identification that Prometheus escapes from when, having heard his words, he repents them, adding, "I wish no living thing to suffer pain" (I.i.305). Without question, then, this is a dramatically significant moment, but it is by no means the resolution of the problem, as commentators used to suggest (e.g., Baker 98). Indeed, it creates no outward change in Prometheus' situation at all, and a repetition of the torture inflicted by Jupiter is about to commence. The only movement forward is that Prometheus, having reviewed the events leading to his present anguish and analyzed his response to them, concludes that an attitude of enraged defiance compounds the evil it had hoped to destroy. He must abandon that strategy.

Just at this point Mercury as Jupiter's messenger comes to parlay for a truce, virtually a reprise of the culminating action in Aeschylus' *Prometheus Bound*. There Mercury alludes to some secret that Prometheus has and suggests that the sharing of it will considerably alleviate his sufferings, which will otherwise be intensified (ll. 1447–1640). Like the protagonist of *Prometheus Bound*—but not that of *Prometheus Lyomenos*—Shelley's Prometheus stands firm. Interestingly, in Arthur Wormhoudt's Freudian reading of the play the response sought by Mercury and finally elected by Aeschylus' protagonist is indeed more adult and reasonable than that chosen by Shelley's protagonist: "Shelley's Prometheus seems to be considerably less master of himself than Aeschylus', for the latter at least knows when to submit" (89). Wormhoudt's comment points up how closely the conclusion of the Aeschylean narrative parallels those of Freud and of Lacan. The son's murderous rage against the father for barring access to the mother must, for the sake of psychological health, be swallowed, forgotten. Indeed, the son must identify with the father's power and wait for the time when it will be his. For this denouement, even in a fiction, Shelley shows the contempt he expressed in the preface to *Prometheus Unbound* at the feebleness of Aeschylus' resolution. *His* Prometheus, then, must reject that answer precisely because to accede is to admit that there is no other possibility: "Submission, thou dost know, I cannot try: / For what submission but that fatal word, / The death-seal of mankind's captivity—" (I.i.395–97).

His words suggest that, even chained as he is on this precipice and helpless in the face of untold human misery inflicted in and by Jupiter's name, Prometheus does save humankind from a "death-seal." This claim harks back to his earlier words to Earth about his being "the barrier to your else all-conquering foe" (I.i.119). If he, the language giver, allies himself completely with an abstract, legalizing, and arbitrary language encoding and perpetuating rule by the father, there may continue to be a verbalizing race on earth, but it will not be the *human* race. Prometheus, then, is the link to what Eagleton designates as the "aesthetic," which is essential to the creation of bonds among bourgeois individuals (23) and which I have linked further to the infant-mother bond. Reestablishment of Prometheus' relationship to his mother—the major focus of the first act up to the entrance of Mercury in that Prometheus and Earth are the only characters in extended dialogue—has thus a crucial connection with his giving humankind a speech that fosters community. But there rises now a threat to that possibility for reunion: the advent of the torturing Furies.

In using the Furies as agents of Prometheus' torture, Shelley makes a foray out of *Prometheus Bound* into the *Oresteia,* thereby conflating Prometheus with the mother-slayer Orestes in a way that bewildered Medwin. In Medwin's opinion, their attributes were different from those needed, inasmuch as "Jove knew that Prometheus was beyond their power. His conscience must have been at rest, he had nothing to unsay or wish undone" (213).

Medwin is working from the fairly common theory, mentioned earlier, that Prometheus, having "unsaid" his curse, has in effect resolved the action of the play almost from the moment it starts. To such interpreters the long scene involving Prometheus' torture has little dramatic purpose except to underline, if that is needed, the vengefulness of Jupiter. But when Prometheus renounces the hate-filled defiance that has characterized him, his change in attitude does not change the ontogenetic or phylogenetic situation. His relinquishing of the desire to control the process by which psyche and soma mirror an Other does not free him from the effects of that process. Quite the contrary.

Through these tortures, administered by those who avenge the mother, we assess in more detail the physical, psychological, historical, political, and religious effects of the Name-of-the-Father. The Furies hammer away at the point that the gifts with which Prometheus endowed mankind—beginning with language, the means toward "clear knowledge"—have also been the source of incalculable misery. Prometheus' visions of Jesus' crucifixion and of the failed French Revolution demonstrate in repetitive fashion what has happened and what will continue to happen in the system Prometheus has established. The teachings of Jesus and the hopes that created the Revolution are analogous to Prometheus' gifts in that, while meant to bring liberation, they actually lead to greater oppression. They also have this effect *because* of Prometheus' prior gift of speech, linked as that is to a Promethean split subjectivity made violent by its unappeasable longing. Lacanian and Girardian language resonates through the Furies' jibes:

> Dost thou boast the clear knowledge thou waken'dst for man?
> Then was kindled within him a thirst which outran
> Those perishing waters; a thirst of fierce fever,
> Hope, love, doubt, desire—which consume him forever.
>
> (I.i.542–45)

The Furies are the appropriate torturers for another reason. Just as the phantasm of Jupiter demonstrates the presence within subjectivity of a hated and (consciously) rejected father, so the Furies' vengefulness mirrors the infant aggression, anger, and violence against the mother, as recorded and analyzed in the writings of Melanie Klein.[3] It makes psychological sense that the effort to call up and exorcise that aspect of oneself formed through one's old struggle with the father draws in its train anger against the mother for her traitorous (and/or ineffectual) part in that battle. As Klein's work testifies, infant desire for a relationship so perfect that it transcends the concept of relationship (since that predicates duality) runs berserk when frustrated into sheer destructiveness, denial of all relationship, cutting of all bonds. The pathos of an infant's sense of abandonment verbalized in "To thirst & find no fill" is inseparable from a desire for revenge. A verbal echo within act one hints at that ambivalent feeling. The intermingled joy between Earth and Prometheus that was compared to "blood within a living frame" (I.i.156) changes to the internalized Furies, described as "dread thought beneath thy brain / And foul desire round thine astonished heart / And blood within thy labyrinthine veins / Crawling like agony" (I.i.488–91).

Critics have found the last taunt from one of the Furies dull and anticlimactic (*V* 398) because of its balanced phrasing and abstract vocabulary: "The good want power, but to weep barren tears. / . . . The wise want love, and those who love want wisdom" (I.i.625, 627). Yet Yeats turned to this passage in devising his own description of historical and psychological chaos: "The best lack all conviction, while the worst / Are full of passionate intensity" ("The Second Coming" ll. 7–8). Also, the first line and a half of the Fury's speech contains so violent an image that decorum virtually demands a subsequent retreat into abstraction: "In each human heart terror survives / The ravin it has gorged" (I.i.618–19). Here is another instance where the ambiguous reference of a pronoun—does "it" refer to "heart" or to "terror"?—elides both referents in an astute psychological analysis. The human heart, cannibalizing (in fantasy) the m(Other) that it desires to possess, destroys her. But since that m(Other) has in fact been introjected, the cannibal heart has eaten itself. Meanwhile, the heart, having projected the terror of its own violence upon the m(Other), introjects terror, experiencing it as self-hatred. Thus in two ways one eats one's heart out.

All the gothic rantings of Shelley's adolescent fiction come to controlled expression in these grim lines, but the means whereby Prometheus breaks in upon the cycle of projection and introjection that creates the Furies are too pat to be entirely credible. With a reprise of the strategy that freed him from identification with Jupiter, Prometheus transforms terror into pity. His response to the Fury—"Thy words are like a cloud of winged snakes / And yet, I pity those they torture not" (I.i.632–33)—states that in *his* heart pity has overcome terror, and at that the Furies evaporate into thin air. Since the Furies *are* the internalized terror, their disappearance when replaced by pity makes logical and psychological sense; but can terror so easily be dismissed? Relinquishing patriarchal power through the institutions that "act upon . . . consciousness" (*SPP* 135) is one thing. Admitting one's own vulnerability to inscription from countless sources, beginning with the maternal imago, is quite another.

Such real-life challenges aside, the genre in which Shelley is working at this point in the play may also help explain his difficulty in presenting interior conflict. As Stuart Curran has pointed out (*Poetic Form and British Romanticism* 198), the term "lyrical drama" which Shelley uses to designate the genre of *Prometheus Unbound* (*SPP* 132) was the classification current at the time for "any serious dramatic effort containing music, from opera to choral drama," and as such the work has the generic fluidity of a mixed form. Much of act one parallels the Aeschylean tragic model, but with the entrance of Mercury and the Furies, the drama begins to take on many of the characteristics of the opera-related masque. The language grows brisker, and at times flatter; stage business proliferates; characters tend to be representational rather than individual. By the time the Furies make their huddled departure, the transition to masque is complete. A chorus of Spirits appears, called up in traditional fashion by the leader of the revels (Mother Earth in this instance); its lively tetrameters serve as frame for a number of individual lyric solos. The transition is not abrupt, however, because, as critics have noted, there are metrical parallels between these Spirits' songs of hope and the Furies' litanies of despair (*V* 404). Also, the subject matter of both—history's long record of human suffering—is much the same, though differently interpreted.

These Spirits, who characterize themselves as "Gentle guides and guardians" (I.i.673) of humankind, function as agencies within human thought but are not precisely the thoughts themselves. Those thoughts, at first an "atmosphere" (I.i.676), become, slipping through metaphoric metamorphoses, a watery deep: "We make there, our liquid lair, / Voyaging cloudlike and unpent / Through the boundless element—" (I.i.687–89). Making the associative transferences demanded by this language, Hogle intuits the presence here of "a Lucretian 'floating,' the movement of a Venus (or a love) producing relationships" (179–80). Now, Eagleton uses remarkably similar language when describing the Enlightenment's concept of how the "aesthetic" creates ties that bind humans together: "Within the dense welter of our material life, with its amorphous flux, certain objects stand out in a sort of perfection dimly akin to reason, and these are known as the beautiful. . . . Because these are objects which we can agree to be beautiful, not by arguing and analysing but just by looking and seeing, a spontaneous consensus is brought to birth within our creaturely life" (17).

The first among such intrinsically and universally satisfying "objects" that Shelley describes is the human ability to band together and, if need be, die together to achieve liberty, the theme of the first Spirit's song. Another such beautiful object is the spectacle of a human accepting death in another's place; the second Spirit comforts Prometheus with the description of a moment during a violent naval engagement when a castaway "gave an enemy / His plank—then plunged aside to die" (I.i.721–22).

The third Spirit appears not from a scene of violent conflict, as did the first two, but from a quiet room where a philosophical thinker has fallen asleep beside the book that has been his food for thought: "I sate beside a sage's bed / And the lamp was burning red / Near the book where he had fed" (I.i.723–25). Shelley's line reworks the cliché I have just used—food for thought—to renew it and refurbish its sensuality. The dramatic adjective "red," associated as it is with the erotic, hints at a sexual as well as a gustatory joy in the exercise of the mind, an eroticism underlined by the lines that follow: "When a Dream with plumes of flame / To his pillow hovering came" (I.i.726–27). Archibald Strong's suggestion is that the allusion here is to that "passion for learning which Plato had called the intellectual Eros and considered akin to sexual passion" (*V* 406).

Two such references to fire in a drama about Prometheus prepare us for the connection that follows between this thinker's dream and the gift of Prometheus, the forethinker. The "Dream with plumes of flame" is "the same / Which had kindled long ago / Pity, eloquence and woe" (I.i.728–30). In William Hildebrand's paraphrase, "The Dream is the Promethean fire-gift that, *ab origine,* revealed to man his fallen condition. Here as elsewhere in the drama (Cf. I.i.542–45 and II.iv.33–105) Shelley conceives the Promethean myth as involving the birth of self-consciousness, as a rupture in the primordial symbiotic relationship of man with nature" ("Spirit Songs" 93–94). The lines, then, recall the central problem of the play, the recognition that speech, while creating thought, places the alienation of symbol between human beings and all that they experience.

Thus far I agree with Hildebrand's gloss, but his interpretation of what the sage's dream accomplishes seems too negative. He writes that the sage's "waking, active search for wisdom makes it possible for him to suffer (while passive, asleep) the Dream which, as long as it lasts, is joyful but which will inevitably lead to grief" (94). This interpretation rests, presumably, on the Spirit's concluding lines, which say that he must ride the dream back "ere morrow, / Or the sage will wake in sorrow" (I.i.735–36). We can surely take it, however, that this is a responsible spirit who, indeed, *will* ride the dream back. In that case, the sage, on waking, will still have the insight given him by the dream.

The language of the play keeps circling back to the originary moment, to the acquisition of subjectivity, though Shelley's purpose is not simply to mourn an inevitable fall but to recompose the earlier script, to find what went wrong and revise it, making the world new. He has, moreover, a model. There was a time—Earth has alluded to it earlier in the play (I.i.156–62), and Asia describes it at length later within the lines cited by Hildebrand (II.iv.59–99)— in which symbolic understanding illuminated without rupturing the natural rhythms of human life: "And the world awhile below / Wore the shade its lustre made" sings the third Spirit (I.i.731–32). That period, Asia's later descriptions suggest, occurred in ancient Greece.

If the Spirit does return on the wings of the dream, then, the sage will not "wake in sorrow" but, on the contrary, will awake to write a book of his own. That book may in turn feed others the ideas that will create the longed-for change. True, this is still insubstantial dream food, and in that sense the sage still partakes in the woe of human creation. But if his dream does become a book which in turn feeds a poet, then there has been progress toward the answer to the play's great question.

Putting together all these considerations, I would like to propose a possible candidate from the German idealist school of philosophy for the sage and for the book that he wrote. The thinking of these philosophers was, like that informing the songs of the two previous Spirits, very much "in the air" and had, like the others, a formative effect on Shelley's subjectivity. Its most eminent exponent was Immanuel Kant, but there is some question about how much of Kant's own work Shelley had read in 1819. My candidate, rather, is an interpreter of Kant, particularly of Kantian aesthetics, Friedrich Schiller; his book, the work collected as *On the Aesthetic Education of Man*.[4]

Writing at the very time of the French Revolution, Schiller was as convinced as Shelley was to be that aesthetic interests are inseparable from political concerns. Indeed, he fuses the two and holds "the spirit of philosophical inquiry" to be "expressly challenged by present circumstances to concern itself with that most perfect of all works to be achieved as the art of man: the construction of true political freedom" (7). Art and freedom (or art/freedom) together form the single answer to a human dialectic between two opposing impulses or instincts, the sensuous and the formal. The first, the sensuous, "proceeds from the physical existence of man, or his sensuous nature. Its business is to set him within the limits of time, and to turn him into matter." The formal instinct "proceeds from the absolute existence of man, or from his rational nature, and is intent on giving him freedom . . . to affirm his Person among all his changes of Condition." Within a few sentences Schiller notes that the formal instinct "gives laws, laws for every judgment where it is a question of knowledge, laws for every will where it is a question of action" (79, 81).

Schiller's vocabulary is different from either Shelley's or Lacan's, and his presuppositions differ as well. In such circumstances close analogies can be misleading, but it does seem to me legitimate to say that the authors of *On Aesthetic Education, Prometheus Unbound,* and *Écrits* are all considering the same problem: a split between a preconscious being that experiences itself as mirroring and mirrored by its environment and a conscious subject functioning within human culture but obliged to suffer all experience at a "symbolic" remove. For Lacan the dilemma is unanswerable; his psychoanalytic function is to describe it so that his disciples, analysands, or readers may come to terms with it.[5] The formulation of Shelley's response is in process throughout the rest of this book. Schiller sees not a hopeless dilemma but a dialectic mediated by a third instinct, that of play.

Play, linking pleasure in natural function with pleasure in intellectual analysis, is at once erotic and intellectual while also being noncoercive, disinterested. One of the reasons why Schiller qualifies so well as "the sage" in the third Spirit's lyric is that Schiller's love for philosophical learning, besides having in itself the erotic component noted by Strong as present in engaged scholarly activity, also creates a theory about the significance of Eros to all forms of human creativity, including the sciences and the arts. Then, too, just as—according to common interpretation—the third Spirit links the sage's dream to Greek myth, so Schiller finds in ancient Greece the best and fullest expression of this instinct of play, an expression now lost but recapturable: "For, to mince matters no longer, man only plays when he is in the fullest sense of the word a human being, and he is only fully a human being when he plays. . . . [This proposition] was long ago alive and operative in the art and in the feeling of the Greeks, the most distinguished exponents of both; only they transferred to Olympus what was meant to be realized on earth" (107–9).

Schiller's source of disappointment with the Greeks is that they gave up the attempt to synthesize natural drives and rational symbolic analysis in their own somas/psyches, projecting that synthesis instead on the images of the gods: "[The Greeks] freed those ever-contented beings from the bonds inseparable from every purpose, every duty, every care, and made idleness and indifferency the enviable portion of divinity—merely a more human name for the freest, most sublime state of being" (109).

Desire, once aroused, is unappeasable; the will, set in motion, is unstoppable. So the two circle endlessly and hopelessly. In Schiller's view the resolution found by the Greeks, though incompletely formulated and thus imperfectly realized, is through will to leap imaginatively past desire to its appeasement. Will to be there, and one is. (Medwin makes the comment that "Shelley believed, with Schiller, that mankind had only to will, and that [sic] there should be no evil" [213].) One is rapt, in Schiller's example, in aesthetic contemplation of the maternal *Juno Ludovici*[6]:

> The whole figure reposes and dwells in itself, a creation completely self-contained, and, as if existing beyond space, neither yielding nor resisting; here is no force to contend with force, no frailty where temporality might break in. Irresistibly moved and drawn by those former qualities, kept at a distance by these latter, we find ourselves at one and the same time in a state of utter repose and supreme agitation, and there results that wondrous

stirring of the heart for which mind has no concept nor speech any name. (109)

Academic discourse now does have a name—*jouissance*—for the state Schiller describes. That state also resembles the "general glow of delight" by which Darwin characterizes aesthetic pleasure, the desire we feel in the presence of a beautiful object, "to embrace it with our arms, and to salute it with our lips, as we did in our early infancy the bosom of our mother" (*Zoonomia* I, 146). So, if the sage in the third Spirit's lyric is a Schiller-like philosopher, his dream tells him that the secret of perfected human life, of artistic achievement, of philosophical insight is to be a "love-adept"—that is, one capable of desire-free, endless *jouissance,* a quality that involves return to the experience of being-with-the-mother. And the human capacity to achieve such pleasure—not, in Eagleton's phrase, "by arguing and analyzing but just by looking and seeing" (17—is itself a source of bonding that underlies satisfaction in particular objects or acts.

The situation described by the third Spirit is reversed in the message brought by the fourth; the indoor night scene with a sleeping sage and a watching Spirit changes to a sunlit day in the outdoors, the Spirit sleeping, a poet contemplative. Shelley's introduction to *Prometheus Unbound,* while placing poets—along with philosophers, painters, sculptors, and musicians— among those lofty minds that are subjected all the same to the internal influences current in their societies, is preceded by a sentence that nonetheless gives poets hierarchical precedence: "A Poet, is the combined product of such internal powers as modify the nature of others, and of such external influences as excite and sustain these powers; he is not one, but both—" (*SPP* 135). So by implication poets, while undergoing "subjection" to external influence as others do, have more power than others to be themselves the molders of their societies. A similar hierarchicalism occurs in the ordering of the Spirits' songs. What the sage perceives as an intellectual concept, albeit a concept about the mind-body connection, the poet experiences as a lived reality and reproduces in art that will subject others (beneficently) to its influence.

For the close analysis demanded by the fourth Spirit's song, we need the full text:

> On a Poet's lips I slept
> Dreaming like a love-adept
> In the sound his breathing kept;
> Nor seeks nor finds he mortal blisses
> But feeds on the aerial kisses
> Of shapes that haunt thought's wildernesses.
> He will watch from dawn to gloom
> The lake-reflected sun illume
> The yellow bees i' the ivy-bloom
> Nor heed nor see, what things they be;
> But from these create he can
> Forms more real than living man,
> Nurslings of immortality!—

One of these awakened me
And I sped to succour thee.

(I.i.737–51)

The striking word "love-adept" makes eroticism an important component of the Spirit's solace. An ambiguity in the meaning of the word "like"—"in the same way as" or "along with"—offers the possibility, confirmed in the poem's fourth line, that both the Spirit and the poet on whose lips he sleeps are love-adepts. Hildebrand notes that "the lips are the organ of love and of the Word. They are peculiarly the poet's organ, and for Shelley they are 'the seat of the imagination' " (95). Appropriately, Hildebrand's reference is to a comment made in Shelley's description of a Juno in "Notes and Sculptures in Rome and Florence" (*CW* VI, 327). For connection is the great work of the imagination, and the lips function, after the umbilical cord is severed, as the very first organ of connection, literally the point of contact between the infant and the source of its life. The specific mention of lips, of feeding, and of the rhythmic sound of common breathing in the song's first three lines create an affect of montage. Our focus on the poet's lips on which the Spirit is sleeping while (as we shall hear shortly) the poet contemplates a natural scene becomes overlaid with images of a suckling infant as well as of a skillful lover. Having aroused these possibilities, the Spirit straightway denies their relevance, in the process re-inforcing their presence in metaphoric language that links physical pleasures (gustatory, visual, sexual) to the play of the imagination (hide-and-seek, tag) with its received impressions: "Nor seeks nor finds he mortal blisses / But feeds on the aerial kisses / Of shapes that haunt thought's wildernesses" (I.i.740–42).

Never unmindful of the fact that to the conscious subject all experience is mediated by consciousness and so is symbolic, Shelley suggests here that the love-adept poet can through the imagination make a connection of some kind, an aerial kiss, with unmediated experience. "But feeds on the aerial kisses / Of shapes" also carries the possible meaning that the poet is feeding on the sight of the shapes kissing one another. This ambiguity prepares the way for the lyric's three central lines (six lines lead up to them, six follow as commentary and conclusion), where we learn what the poet as participant/voyeur is feeding on: "He will watch from dawn to gloom / The lake-reflected sun illume / The yellow bees i' the ivy-bloom."

"Lake-reflected sun" is one of those many reflexive images in Shelley's work that, it is generally agreed, show his fascination with narcissism, although opinions differ widely on the moral significance of that interest.[7] It is also typically Shelleyan in its Platonism, though it revises Plato in a significant way. Shelley's poet becomes associated, through the image of the "lake-reflected sun," with that Platonic enlightened one in the *Republic* who, climbing painfully out of the cave of common opinion and into the light outside, is able, after further accustoming himself to the light, to look upon the sun "and not mere reflections of him [the sun] in the water" (255). In Shelley's poem, however, the poet appears not to strive for some final, sun-identified transcendence of the human mind's limitations. Instead he rests, lake-identified, at

Plato's second-to-last stage, with reflected sun his source of illumination. Metaphorically his situation predicates subjectivity as created by a positive form of narcissism or mirroring which cancels the division between subject and object. It does so not by appropriation of all that is not one into a sun-identified subjectivity but by a dual, lake-identified recognition: first, each subjectivity is formed through introjection of the "not-me," and second, each subjectivity is also an object to other subjects.[8]

After this epistemological prelude, there follows the metonymic heart of the rune: "yellow bees i' the ivy-bloom." Again there is mirroring; each bee is a little yellow sun reflection. These are also, as others have noted, Platonic bees (*V* 406). In a passage from the *Ion* that was among the portions of that work that Shelley later translated, Socrates compares the souls of poets to bees "wandering over the gardens and the meadows and the honey-flowing fountains of the Muses" and returning "laden with the sweetness of melody; and arrayed as they are in the plumes of rapid imagination" (*CW* VII, 238).

As the bees feed, their furry bodies transfer pollen from the male stamens of the flower to the female pistil, a process that does not involve literal genital intercourse in human terms but that Erasmus Darwin in *The Botanic Garden* anthropomorphizes constantly into a variety of erotic positions and modes of intercourse matching those known to the most learned and supple of love-adepts (II, passim). Ironically, the bees, while such important participants in this erotic activity, are neuter females, as Shelley knew ([*SPP*] *Queen Mab* IX.53; [*SPP*] "Witch of Atlas" LXVIII.5). At the same time, the fertile—and sexual—queen bee is historically a transsexual. The ancients, as James Frazer notes in *The Golden Bough,* "mistook the Queen bee for a male, and hence spoke of King bees" (II, 136). Shelley would have seen an allusion to king bees in Virgil's *Georgics,* which he had been reading only the summer before in Bagni di Lucca when he was finishing his "modern eclogue" "Rosalind and Helen" (M. Shelley, *Journal* I, 223).

This ancient misattribution of bees' sexuality gets mention in Frazer's work because bees—"King bees"—are associated with the worship of the many-breasted Diana of Ephesus, a Mother Goddess whose heredity lies with "Asiatic goddesses of love and fertility" (I, 37). Shelley would have found an allusion to the goddess in Drummond's *Academical Questions* (268) and would have learned from Pausanias' *Description of Greece,* which he ordered along with the *Georgics,* as it happens, from Hookham in August 1817 (*L* I, 549), that the goddess was worshiped at Ephesus by a cortege of male priests called "Essenes [King Bees]," who during their year in office had to live celibate and practice special rites of cleansing (Pausanias I, 390). Erotic but, during the period of their priesthood, nongenital, they are represented as bees on the statues of Diana of Ephesus. In his Roman sightseeing Shelley could have come upon such representations of the goddess in several museums: the Vatican, the Lateran, and the Palazzo dei Conservatori on the Capitol (Frazer I, 38). But also in a comment about Pausanias' Essenes based on sources familiar to Shelley (Pindar, Callimachus), Frazer notes that "the Delphic priestess was called 'a bee' . . . and the title was given especially to the priestesses of Demeter" (Pausanias IV, 223). Mirrored by bee servitors of both sexes, the divine mother, metonymically represented by the bee—nonsexual yet pullulating with life; self-fertilizing; source of all creativity, including the honey of verse—might well be food for an entire day's poetic contemplation.

Equally labyrinthine in its significance is the ivy-bloom, Shelley's particular choice for the bees' forage. Like the bees, the plant merges and unifies dual sexual characteristics, since it is bisexual. That in plants is not unusual, but the ivy's duality-in-unity is particularly striking. As Shelley knew (see "Adonais," l. 292), the ivy is sacred to Dionysus, and Walter Otto describes its growth cycle as "suggesting the two-fold nature of Dionysus": "First it puts out the so-called shade-seeking shoots, the scandent tendrils with the well-known lobed leaves. Later, however, a second kind of shoot appears which grows upright and turns toward the light. The leaves are formed completely differently, and now the plant produces flowers and berries" (154). This doubleness mirrors not only Dionysus' being "the twice-born," as Otto suggests, but also the god's dual sexual nature. A phallic deity, Dionysus is also female-identified: women are his principal followers, and he bears such epithets as "Gynnis (the womanish), Arsenothelys (the man-womanly), Dyalos (the hybrid), Pseudanor (the man without true virility)" (Hillman, *Myth of Analysis* 259).

Ivy also binds together the figures of Dionysus and Prometheus. Using classical sources such as Theophrastus and Pliny, with which Shelley was familiar (*L* I, 344; II, 7), Frazer discusses at length the parallels between the Greeks and the Agnihotri, or fire-priests, of India in the kinds of wood used by ritual precept for the drill and the flat board in which it whirls in the making of fire, for "they draw out the analogy between the process of fire-making and the intercourse of the sexes in minute detail":

> Like the ancient Indians, the Greeks seem to have preferred that one of two fire-sticks should be made from a parasitic or creeping plant. They recommended that the borer of the fire-drill should be made of laurel and the board of ivy. . . . When we consider the analogy of the Indian preference for a borer made from a parasite, and remember how deeply rooted in the primitive mind is the comparison of the friction of the fire-sticks to the union of the sexes, we shall hardly doubt that the Greeks originally chose the ivy or wild vine for a fire-stick from motives of the sort which led the Hindoos to select the wood of a parasitic fig-tree for the same purpose. But while the Hindoos regarded the parasite as male and the tree to which it clung as female, the Greeks of Theophrastus's time seem to have inverted this conception, since they recommended that the board, which plays the part of the female in the fire-drill, should be made of ivy or another creeper, whereas the borer, which necessarily represents the male, was to be fashioned out of laurel. This would imply that the ivy was a female and the laurel a male. Yet in Greek, on the contrary, the word for ivy is masculine, and the plant was identified mythologically with the male god Dionysus; whereas the word for laurel is feminine and the tree was identified with a nymph. Hence we may conjecture that at first the Greeks, like the Hindoos, regarded the clinging creeper as the male and the tree which it embraced as the female,

and that of old, therefore, they made the borer of the fire-drill out of ivy and
the board out of laurel.   (II, 251–52)

Like the bees, ivy—and the deity with which it is identified—is a highly
charged erotic symbol but also an ambiguous, bisexual one. The poet, brood-
ing over these mystic "signatures," comes to a vision of life not as it is but as it
might be, in which the old, suffering Promethean human race will have a new
birth. His answer involves mirroed bisexualities, an erotic, fruitful, and
creative—but nongenital—merging of bee and bloom. Functioning both as
metaphor for an unnamed process and as metonymic displacement of that
unspoken because unspeakable interaction, it is a fantasy of return to the
narcissistic, presubjective stage in the construction of subjectivity as a positive
(and so nonregressive) answer to the evils created by the jostling of subjectivities in the post-subjective genital state inaugurated by the problematic
Promethean gift of language.

The fourth Spirit, startled into wakefulness by the astonishing results of
the poet's long meditation, speeds to Prometheus' side with the riddling words
that offer hope: "And I sped to succour thee" (I.i.751). Before taking up the
way in which this "succour" serves as instigator to the events in act two,
however, I would like to pause and look back over act one, with Herbert
Marcuse's *Eros and Civilization* in hand as hermeneutic guide.

I have no evidence that Marcuse read *Prometheus Unbound,* but so precise
a connection is unnecessary. Marcuse, like Shelley, was deeply influenced by
German idealist philosophy. Both men had a strong desire to witness radical
change in social institutions—Shelley, in Marx's opinion, would have been a
Marxist,[9] and Marcuse was, in a broad use of the term, a Marxist—but both
Shelley and Marcuse also were middle-class intellectuals writing during periods of hegemonic conservatism. Finally, both had psychological investigation
as one of their central interests and considered it possible to fuse the subjectivity and interiority of psychology with the communal aims of revolutionary
activism (Robinson 147–244). Not surprisingly, then, Marcuse's *Eros and
Civilization* is a useful commentary on *Prometheus Unbound,* stating in abstract discourse what Shelley embodies in the dense materiality of poetic
language and dramatic action.

Part one of *Eros and Civilization,* like act one of *Prometheus Unbound,*
reviews the construction of individual subjectivities (the ontogenetic) and the
historical organization and maintenance of social institutions (the phylogenetic). Both works also (though my terms here are Marcuse's Freudian
ones) see the acquisition of subjectivity and establishment of culture as
brought about through submission to the "reality principle" and denial of the
"pleasure principle"; in the family this is experienced as submission to the
dominance of the father and in the state as subordination to male-headed
institutions. Part two of *Eros and Civilization,* like acts two and three of
Prometheus Unbound, considers the possible role of fantasy in overturning
this order through the triumph of the pleasure principle.

Marcuse's first section draws heavily on Freud's psychological and social thinking for descriptions of the grim sacrifice of instinctual satisfactions necessary for the establishment of culture. He takes issue, however, with Freud's pessimistic assertion that such sacrifice is inevitable. In part two, where Freudian thinking is inapplicable because Freud would consider the project itself inadmissible, Marcuse turns to the re-visioning of myth, specifically the myths of Orpheus, Narcissus, and Prometheus; to the aesthetic theories of Kant and Schiller; and to the psychoanalytic ideas of Sándor Ferenczi and Géza Róheim.

Like Freud (as well as Lévi-Strauss and Lacan for that matter), Marcuse takes the establishment of the incest taboo as prerequisite to the establishment of culture and the maintenance of subjectivity:

> In the primal horde, the image of the desired woman, the mistress-wife of the father, was Eros and Thanatos in immediate, natural union. She was the aim of the sex instincts, and she was the mother in whom the son once had that integral peace which is the absence of all need and desire—the Nirvana before birth. Perhaps the taboo on incest was the first great protection against the death instinct: the taboo on Nirvana, on the regressive impulse for peace which stood in the way of progress, of Life itself. Mother and wife were separated, and the fatal identity of Eros and Thanatos was thus dissolved. . . . Tenderness is created out of abstinence—abstinence first enforced by the primal father. Once created, it becomes the psychical basis not only for the family but also for the establishment of lasting group relations. (76)

This passage is uncharacteristic of the book as a whole, however, in the attention it gives to incest. In general Marcuse's focus is not so much on the mother-infant relationship per se as on the inhibition of infant sexuality, its repression through guilt, and its sublimation into work. The sequence he outlines is not specifically the infant's desire for the mother blocked by the incest taboo and repressed through submission to the father. Rather Marcuse describes a transmutation from infant erotic experience of the pleasure principle to adult desexualization through the sublimation demanded by the reality principle (12). Nonetheless, at a number of points Marcuse implicitly links the pleasure principle with the mother's preeminence during infancy and the reality principle with the father's assumption of dominance. Marcuse charts the movement from one principle to the other:

from:	*to:*
immediate satisfaction	delayed satisfaction
pleasure	restraint of pleasure
joy (play)	toil (work)
receptiveness	productiveness
absence of repression	security

Guilt forces the change from pleasure to the restraint of pleasure. In Marcuse's reading of Freud, this guilt has two sources, which again operate

ontogenetically and phylogenetically: anxiety over feelings of aggression toward the father and remorse at "the crime against the pleasure principle"
(68), by which Marcuse seems to imply that betrayal of the mother is involved
as well. Guilt marks the inception of culture phylogenetically, of subjectivity
ontogenetically, and guilt links its every stage, accumulating in complex modern technological societies to the point of explosion, the point to which we
have come in advanced industrial capitalism. The result is alienation from and
desexualization of a body that is only an instrument of alienated labor:
"[Man's] work and its products have assumed a form and power independent
of him as an individual" (105). As image of this state Marcuse uses Freud's
interpretation of the Prometheus myth as "centered upon the connection
between curbing of sexual passion and civilized work" (81).

In the *Enneads* Plotinus makes a connection not unlike Freud's between
the figure of Prometheus and the misery of work but suggests that humans are
not inevitably or permanently bound in this way: "The maker is bound because he is somehow in contact with that which has been made, and a bond of
this kind is eternal; and his freeing by Herakles means that he has power even
to free himself" (IV.3.14). Marcuse does not cite Plotinus, and the two would
have very different notions of what Prometheus' eventual freedom would be
like. Still, like Plotinus, Marcuse turns to a power truly never lost to humans
as the one that will bring release. This power, much resembling Eagleton's
"aesthetics," is "phantasy" (imagination) which "retains the structure and the
tendencies of the psyche prior to its organization by the reality, prior to its
becoming an 'individual' set off against other individuals" (142).

Marcuse's thought appears to be that *without losing the subjectivity acquired historically and individually,* humans can permit a return of the repressed pleasure principle: "Art is perhaps the most visible 'return of the
repressed,' not only on the individual but also on the generic-historical level.
The artistic imagination shapes the 'unconscious memory' of the liberation
that failed, of the promise that was betrayed" (144). Infiltrating all culture,
this "regression" would reactivate all the erotogenic zones desexualized by the
repressive genitality of the reality principle. And "while eroticizing previously
tabooed zones, times, and relations" (202), the released libido would eroticize
work. Yet, Marcuse insists, "this 'cultural' trend in the libido seems to be
genitofugal, that is to say, *away* from genital supremacy toward the eroticization of the entire organism" (208).

Interestingly, however, while the infant's first bond with its mother is
time and again Marcuse's implicit model for the renewed and eroticized
body, he explicitly denies the centrality and even the significance of the
Oedipal struggle:

> But if human happiness depends on the fulfillment of childhood wishes,
> civilization, according to Freud, depends on the suppression of the strongest
> of all childhood wishes: the Oedipus wish. Does the realization of happiness
> in a free civilization still necessitate this suppression? Or would the transfor-
> mation of the libido also engulf the Oedipus situation? In the context of our
> hypothesis, such speculations are insignificant; the Oedipus complex, al-

though the primary source and model of neurotic conflicts, is certainly not the central cause of the discontents in civilization, and not the central obstacle for their removal. The Oedipus complex "passes" even under the rule of a repressive reality principle. Freud advances two general interpretations of the "passing of the Oedipus complex": it "becomes extinguished by its lack of success"; or it "must come to an end because the time has come for its dissolution, just as the milk-teeth fall out when the permanent ones begin to press forward." The passing of the complex appears as a "natural" event in both cases. (203–4)[10]

Marcuse is using the ontogenetic-phylogenetic parallel to argue that since the Oedipus complex is resolved, the "complex" unknotted, in the mature subject, so regression to a presubjective condition will not occur among the inhabitants of a mature civilization. At another point in the argument he does briefly consider again the psychoanalytic contention that "return of the repressed" will break down subjectivity, but he does so in negatives that conjure up some more positive prophecy of his own without actually describing it or establishing a clear rationale for his argument:

> The impulse to re-establish the lost Narcissistic-maternal unity is interpreted as a "threat," namely, the threat of "maternal engulfment" by the overpowering womb. The hostile father is exonerated and reappears as savior who, in punishing the incest wish, protects the ego from its annihilation in the mother. The question does not arise whether the Narcissistic-maternal attitude toward reality cannot "return" in less primordial, less devouring forms under the power of the mature ego and in a mature civilization. (230)

In summary, the answer that Marcuse brings to succor the Promethean agony of Western civilization has certain ideas in common with those expressed in the fourth Spirit's lyric. Both focus on the liberatory effect of erotic fantasy as it informs works of art; both see these fantasies as reproductive aesthetically but as "perverse"—that is, not genitally reproductive—physically; both also link this erotic-aesthetic play to a positive narcissism in which twin dualities-as-unities mirror each other. The point of difference comes in Marcuse's sidestepping of incestuous fantasies in this erotic dance. In contrast, while veils of displacement admittedly obscure its clear outline, through them I discern the presence of incestuous, nongenital, polymorphous eroticism in the fourth Spirit's helpful song.

The fifth and sixth Spirits bring no further answer but re-echo the theme of present misery, particularly the miseries of political tyranny and sexual frustration, and of future hope. When they have left, the culminating effect on Prometheus is a narcissistic yearning toward a remembered relationship with Asia:

> and thou art far,
> Asia! who when my being overflowed
> Wert like a golden chalice to bright wine
> Which else had sunk into the thirsty dust.
> (I.i.808–11)

Read, as on one level they simply have to be, as an allusion to genital heterosexual intercourse, the lines are a startlingly crude expression of a phallocentrism that makes women the passive vessels for male autoerotic ejaculation. This unpleasant possibility may lie behind Reiman and Powers' impulse to offer an interpretive, disembodying footnote: "The simile suggests that Asia is in some sense the creation of Prometheus—that the human conception of the Ideal or Intellectual Beauty comes from the overflow of man's spiritual imagination" (*SPP* 159). And some rationale for this reading appears in Panthea's final words in act one, which describe Asia's presence as one that would fade if it "were mingled not" with Prometheus (*SPP* 159).

There is another possibility. Prometheus' words echo a striking image used by Socrates in the *Symposium*. Shelley had translated that dialogue, titling it *The Banquet,* during July 1818, and actually alludes to a passage in it through the sixth Spirit's link between love and desolation (I.i.778–79). His work on the *Symposium* is of special importance, given Reiman's conjecture that it radically altered Shelley's theories about the nature of love (*SHC* VI, 642).

As the banquet is about to begin, Agathon asks Socrates to sit beside him "so that by the mere touch of one so wise as you are, I may enjoy the fruit of your meditations." Socrates, in Shelley's translation, replies: "It would be well, Agathon, if wisdom were of such a nature as that when we touched each other, it would overflow of its own accord . . . like the water in the two chalices, which will flow through a flock of wool from the fuller into the emptier, until both are equal" (*CW* VII, 168).

The situations are not entirely parallel, but the echoes in the words "overflow" and "chalice" call attention to a similarity in theme: both passages describe a virtual fusion of two subjectivities. The lines in *Prometheus Unbound,* however, convey this fusion in the image of a chalice filled with "bright wine" to illustrate Prometheus' "being" as it is saved from dissolution—that is to say, to illustrate the process by which every human being comes to subjectivity. Margaret Mahler, searching for an image to describe the process in which an infant's interactions with her or his mother call forth a particularized and specific but also bonded and imprinted identity, uses precisely the same metaphor: "There exist[s] . . . primitive somatic identification of flowing-over mechanisms or, should we say, assimilatory kind of mechanisms which involve cathecting the apparatus of touch, smell, taste, and temperature, and also . . . the kinesthetic sense and that of a deep sensibility" (quoted in Lichtenstein 205). The mother's sense of or feeling for the infant's identity flows over the chalice of her own, creating the chalice of the infant's while the infant's response fills the mother's sense of her self as in turn relational and responding. Created thereby, one can see, is the foundation for all other experience of the "aesthetic."

The process imaged in these ways harks back to the circling "Joy" of Earth's first speech. At the same time, the link created by Prometheus between his very sense of being shaped as an identity and his erotic relation with Asia blurs the line between infant and adult interchanges of "sensibility," as it does between the dramatic figures Asia and Earth. It serves, then, as a further sign of that "regressiveness" in Shelley, noted earlier, that led him to seek full mothering for himself from women also caring for the infants produced by his adult, and very active, sexuality. True, in their *excess* Shelley's demands suggest regression—a regression "programmed" by the maternal ideology's infantilization of men as well as by the circumstances of his own family life—but the identification created by Shelley's chalice image between the interactions of mother and infant and those of adult lovers also expresses a concept of women's function strongly and generally operative in his own society as it still is in ours. Thus, in Heinz Lichtenstein's discussion "the maternal" functions not as a separate, conscious individual interacting with another but as an unconscious that makes, shapes, spills over into that of the infant: "The way in which the mother is touching, holding, warming the child, the way in which some senses are stimulated, while others are not, forms a kind of 'stimulus cast' *of the mother's unconscious,* just as a blind and deaf person may, by the sense of touch, 'cast' the form and the personality of another person in his mind" (206; my emphasis). So, while forming subjectivity, the mother is not— or not importantly—herself a conscious subject. Similarly, by changing the two Platonic chalices into a single Promethean chalice, Shelley maintains full, bounded subjectivity as a male prerogative.

In "A Defence of Poetry" Shelley compares "drama of the highest order" to a "prismatic and many-sided mirror," its concern not "censure or hatred" but rather the teaching of "self-knowledge and self-respect": "Neither the eye nor the mind can see itself, unless reflected on that which it resembles" (*SPP* 491). His poetic practice is consistent with his critical analysis; Shelley structures act one of *Prometheus Unbound* as a series of mirrorings, initiated and then overseen by Mother Earth, that guide the protagonist into ever-deeper levels of self-knowledge.

Hearing his own words spoken by the Phantasm of Jupiter, Prometheus can see his participation in the violence that underlies the cruelty and injustice of society. The Furies force mind and eye to see the interior ravages created by blind anger, guilt, and repressed desire. They admit, however, that though they overrun most of the psyche's space, they cannot totally obscure "the soul which burns within" (I.i.485). For most of the act, reflections of this "soul" are metaphoric rather than dramatic mirrors: the poet's vision by the "lake-reflected sun" and the comparison between Asia and a "golden chalice" holding the "bright wine" of Prometheus' being. Its specifically dramatic mirroring comes only in the last lines of act one, when Panthea reminds the depressed and nearly despairing Prometheus of her faithfulness in standing by him. Prometheus, in responding, notices *her* love: "I said all hope was vain but love—thou lovest" (I.i.824). His ability to recognize it serves as reflection of his own still inviolate capacity to love. But also, as he had said earlier to the Furies, "I grow like what I contemplate" (I.i.450). Thus, reflecting on and reflecting her love, as once he had reflected Earth's joy, his own grows stronger. The "external action" by which this interior change becomes expressed is the warmth that begins to transform the valley of Asia's exile.

NOTES

1. Controversy surrounds not only the dating but also the authorship of *Prometheus Bound*. Mark Griffith outlines the central issues in the introduction to his edition of the play:

> A number of scholars . . . have concluded, from the structure and the style (and, in a few cases, the conception) of the play, that it is not the work of Aeschylus at all, or that it was left unfinished by him, and completed by a member of his family (e.g. his son, Euphorion, himself a tragedian of note). Of these critics, some argue that *Prom.* was composed as part of a trilogy (with *P. Lyomenos* and *P. Pyrphoros*) by the unknown dramatist; others, especially those who find the figure of Zeus in *Prom.* incompatible with Aeschylean theology, that *Prom.* was written as a separate play, perhaps directed in some sense against the Aeschylean *P. Lyomenos* (itself also a monodrama). On this view, the author of *Prom.* presents a daring challenge to Aeschylus' more conventionally pious view of Zeus, and leaves us with a most disturbing picture of unresolved divine conflict. (32–33)

D. J. Conacher discusses the terms of the controversy in more detail (141–74), his commentary a distillation of the views pro and con put forth, respectively, in C. J. Herington, *The Author of "Prometheus Bound,"* and Mark Griffith, *The Authenticity of "Prometheus Bound."* Conacher himself concludes that "belief in the Aeschylean authorship of *Prometheus Bound* should not, in the present state of the evidence, be abandoned" but admits that "real difficulties lie in the way of its certain and unqualified acceptance" (173).

As one outside the field, I must number myself among the even simpler faithful, as my commentary on the trilogy makes clear. For purposes of my argument, in any case, the matter need not be settled; *Shelley* believed the plays to be a trilogy and their author to be Aeschylus. It is interesting, though, that a central argument brought forward against this position is the very one that set Shelley to writing his own version: the anomalous relationship between the action of *Prometheus Bound* and that of *Prometheus Lyomenos*.

2. For further and much fuller discussion of the ideas sketched here within a more explicitly political context, including a brilliant juxtaposition of Girard's "mimetic desire" with speculations about anthropomorphic projections that Shelley would have found in Hume, see Jerrold Hogle (87–95). Also, William Ulmer's analysis of the mirroring between Prometheus and Jupiter (81–83, 86–88, 101–2), excellent in itself, provides useful bibliographic summaries of relevant earlier scholarship on this point.

3. See, for instance, "Early Stages of the Oedipus Conflict" (1928), "Infantile Anxiety Situations Reflected in a Work of Art and in the Creative Impulse" (1929), and "The Importance of Symbol Formation in the Development of the Ego" (1930), all in *Selected Melanie Klein* (69–111).

4. In January 1812 Shelley ordered the works of Kant in a Latin translation from Hookham (*L* I, 350). Hogg, a few months later, saw a Latin edition of Kant in Shelley's lodgings but described it as unread (II, 27). Later references to Kant do not occur in Shelley's letters until 1821 (*Letters* II, 350 and 363). There is no such specific documentation for tracking Shelley's knowledge of Schiller's work, but we do know that he considered such knowledge essential. Writing to a woman about the importance of learning languages, he notes that her imperfect knowledge of the modern European languages "conceal[s] from your intimacy such names as Ariosto, Tasso, Petrarch, and Macchiavelli; or Goëthe[*sic*], Schiller, Wieland, etc." (*L* II, 278). Schiller is thus on the very short list of German authors specifically mentioned.

5. Something autocratic and peremptory in the tone of Lacan's pronouncements lends itself to this interpretation of his theoretical position. Kaja Silverman describes it as a theory "whose very rigors seduce" (*The Subject of Semiotics* 192). Paul Smith, by contrast, finds in the Lacanian theory of the "split subject" precisely a release from the neo-Marxist concept of an interpellated, ideologically inscribed subject: "The imaginary—what I would call the plane of the subject's *self*-cerning—operates to construe for the 'subject' the sense of plenitude or lack-of-lack which is a necessity for the ego and its functioning" (76). To my mind this is a creative misreading of Lacanian doctrine, which has, nonetheless, considerable pragmatic value, but Smith in his determination to "dis-cern" the subject gives insufficient attention to human vulnerability through the mirroring that produces subjectivity.

6. In a note on Schiller's choice of *Juno Ludovici,* Elizabeth Williamson and L. A. Willoughby, the editors of Schiller's *Aesthetic Education,* suggest that he fixed on that particular statue as illustration "no doubt under the recent influence of Goethe, who had come under the spell of the colossal bust during his Roman sojourn, and taken great pains to install a cast of this, his Roman 'sweetheart,' as he called her, in his rooms" (254). Goethe's erotic pleasure (inevitably an incestuous pleasure, given the character of the goddess) is a strong component in Schiller's aesthetic theorizing as well. By coincidence, the statue may be that of an actual mother, identified by the editors as "the head of a statue commissioned by the Emperor Claudius in honour of his mother, Antonia Augusta" (254–55).

7. Cf., on the positive side, William Keach on reflexive imagery in Shelley's work (79–116); on the negative, Barbara Schapiro (1–32).

8. My language here draws on Reuben Fine's analysis of the positive narcissism he considers optimal for infant development. While based on identification with the mother, it frees the infant for further mirroring on its own. Fine writes: "When the infant has all its major needs satisfied, it moves out to seek other stimuli. . . . In order to facilitate this love affair with the world (which as will be seen is the origin of healthy narcissism), the mother must be 'in tune' with the infant. . . . This capacity is based in large measure on the mother's ability to differentiate her child's needs from her own and maintain an appropriate level of stimulation and need satisfaction for her infant" (73–74). Fine therefore distinguishes (and here he is summarizing recent research on this topic, including Stern's) between two types of narcissism: "healthy narcissism, deriving from the disengagement with a loving mother and the clinging, anxiety-laden, reassurance-seeking narcissism, deriving from overattachment to or disengagement from a hostile unloving mother" (76).

9. Without giving a source (which may well have been Eleanor Marx's memory), Edward Aveling and Eleanor Marx quote Marx as saying: "The real difference between Byron and Shelley is this: those who understand and love them rejoice that Byron died at thirty-six, because if he had lived he would have become a reactionary *bourgeois;* they grieve that Shelley died at twenty-nine, because he was essentially a revolutionist and he would always have been one of the advanced guard of socialism" (16).

10. By so historicizing the Oedipal, Marcuse simply posits that the kind of regression that Freudian theory warns against will not occur: "Imagination envisions the reconciliation of the individual with the whole, of desire with realization, of happiness with reason. While this harmony has been removed into utopia by the established reality principle, phantasy insists that it must and can become real, that behind the illusion lies *knowledge*" (143; author's emphasis). The strategy by which he avoids the specifically incestuous component of the "phantasy" looks, however, very much like a continuation of the repression he thinks can be eliminated.

5

The Source of Desire Seeks the End of Desire (*Prometheus Unbound,* Act II)

The Gaze of Soul-Making (Scene i)

Although the centrality of Mother Earth's interactions with Prometheus in the first act of *Prometheus Unbound* has received little comment, critics have always noted that feminine presences function as the protagonists of act two in an obvious, if theatrically anomalous, way. In its five scenes Asia, joined by Panthea, hears of two dreams Panthea has had that in some way prefigure an end to Prometheus' sufferings (sc. i). Guided and instructed by mysterious voices connected with the second dream, the two sisters journey through a forest (sc. ii) to a cave (sc. iii). There Asia holds with a power named Demogorgon a colloquy that in some obscure way effects the freeing of Prometheus and the downfall of Jupiter (sc. iv). The last scene describes Asia's apotheosis as the chariot of "the Spirit of the Hour" whirls her and Panthea to the reunion with Prometheus that the sisters' journey has made possible.

What we are given is clearly not so much a plot as a series of significatory acts, in themselves dreamlike, that we can best read by sharing the author's consciousness in the way described by Tilottama Rajan: "Communication proceeds only when the internalizing and personalizing of knowledge described by the German word for recollection, '*Erinnerung,*' occurs through an identification of author and reader" (324). Under this rubric, my reading of act two mirrors the salvific action being dramatized.

The setting for the first act of *Prometheus Unbound* was an Aeschylean given, even though Shelley could displace its geographic position to the Indian Caucasus and also add his own vivid details drawn from Alpine scenes, particularly from the "crawling glaciers" (I.i.31) of Mont Blanc. In writing act two, he had to draw on the resources of his own fantasy for the props of his scene, "a lovely Vale in the Indian Caucasus" (*SPP* 160). This involved revisiting a textual site in which his youthful imagination reveled during his impassioned reading and rereading of *The Missionary: An Indian Tale* by Sydney Owenson. There "the vale of Cashmere" (sic) is the dwelling place of the Brahmin priestess Luxima.

During the emotionally intense summer of 1811 just preceding Shelley's elopement with Harriet Westbrook, Owenson's creation became so real to him that he had daydreams in which Luxima stepped through her textual veil into embodied life: "Luxima the Indian is an Angel. What a pity that we cannot incorporate these creations of Fancy; the very thought of them thrills the soul," he wrote to Hogg (*L* I, 107), and in another letter to Hogg written the next day, he rephrases the same thought: "Luxima the Indian Priestess, were it possible to embody such a character, is *perfect*" (*L* I, 112; author's emphasis). From the period of Shelley's late teens, then, the visionary Luxima in faraway Kashmir serves as the paradoxical and at times frustrating medium for fantasies of a perfected body possessed and enjoyed as one's own.[1] She reappears now as Asia.

In the collage of fantasy's juxtapositions, other textual elements are present in the scene as well. Asia's vale has none of the subtropical lushness of Luxima's, and the "innumerable rills" and "foaming torrents" conjured up by Owenson (136) have been transformed into a dark and quiet lake. This scenery is more Alpine than Indian; the introductory image of a woman in reverie beside a lake calls up associations with Rousseau's Julie—another textual fabrication Shelley experienced as real (*L* I, 486)—as well as with Shelley's opening lines of "Rosalind and Helen," in which Helen comes upon Rosalind by the shores of Lake Como (*CW* II, 7).

In the scene setting that is a necessary function of Asia's opening lines, she draws vivid attention to the morning star. The conjunction of the star, a woman, and a body of water in turn evokes a scene from another poem Shelley had only recently completed, *Laon and Cythna*. In its first canto the narrator meets "a Woman, beautiful as morning" (I.xvi.136 [*CW* I, 261]), beside a sea. That woman's devotion to human liberty, and a life expressing it that bears certain resemblances to Mary Wollstonecraft's, takes its inception from a vision of the morning star, which she describes as "like an eye which seemed to smile on me" (I.xli.361 [*CW* I, 268]).[2]

Such associative and evocative image clusters create a drifting atmosphere of reverie around the solitary female figure of Asia, an effect reinforced by the fact that reverie is also the theme of her first lines: the sweet sadness, the "idle tears," the pain and pleasure mingled in the recapture of an attenuated memory, a trace. In this mood emotion takes precedence over its source; also the mind's passage along linked associations gives similitude precedence over its attendant recognition of difference. "Like" is linked to "like" in similes that encircle an undefined center in a process of transference that has received Hogle's brilliant analysis. Thus Spring, indentified only after six emotion-filled lines in which it has been addressed as "thou," becomes obscured once more among the phrases that supposedly describe it:

                                    As suddenly
          Thou comest as the memory of a dream
          Which now is sad because it hath been sweet;
          Like genius, or like joy which riseth up
          As from the earth, clothing with golden clouds
          The desert of our life. . . .

                                    (II.i.7–12)

The conjunctive pronoun "which," from its position in the verse sentence, should refer to "dream," but the meaning involved demands that its referent be "memory," while "it," further removed from "dream" than "which," nevertheless serves as "dream" 's pronominal substitute. A similar confusion arises over whether the two phrases "like genius" and "like joy" might refer to "memory" or to "dream." The realization that the similes actually point back to "thou" comes just as "joy" changes into a strangely inverse metaphor for dew, and, through evaporation, wafts us into clouds.

While the New Critics judged slippages of this kind to be literarily immoral, Shelley is using them to create reverie, the state that they describe. And, unlike the modernists as well as those in the critical school influenced by them, Shelley does not insist on the clear, clean line, believing on the contrary that the mergings and dissolution of reverie serve as legitimate, even privileged loci of moral intuitions (see Hogle 15–16). In "On Life," for instance, Shelley describes states of reverie as those "which precede or accompany or follow an unusually intense and vivid apprehension of life" (*SPP* 477). Gaston Bachelard, who gives Shelley particular mention in *The Poetics of Reverie* (13), likewise believes that this state creates new possibilities for being-in-the-world: "Poetic reverie is a cosmic reverie. It is an opening to a beautiful world, to beautiful worlds. It gives the I a non-I which belongs to the I: my non-I. It is this 'my non-I' which enchants the I of the dreamer and which poets can help us share. For my 'I-dreamer' it is this '*my non-I*' which lets me live my secret of being in the world" (13). Later Bachelard formulates more clearly the precise nature of this "non-I," describing it as the core of his thesis: "*Reverie is under the sign of the anima.* When the reverie is truly profound, the being who comes to dream within us is our *anima*" (62; author's emphasis). Putting aside objections that this process may be different for women with only the waspish comment that "it has been repeated often enough that feminism ruins femininity," he reiterates his point: "In a pure reverie which returns the dreamer to his tranquil solitude, every human being, man or woman, finds repose in the *anima* of the depths, by descending, ever descending 'the slope of reverie.' A descent without fall. In those indeterminate depths reigns the repose of the feminine" (63).

So, as act two opens, we witness a dramatic character given the name Asia, a female figure experiencing reverie who is at the same time the vehicle for the reverie that will create a new world. In that context the ambiguous and shifting connections of Asia's opening lines are not an example of Shelley's falling prey to the slippage in language of which he himself is aware. Rather, they show him consciously using the ambiguities characteristic of words as signs in order to reproduce linguistically the oceanic experience of those in reverie who "feel as if their nature were dissolved into the surrounding universe, or as if the surrounding universe were absorbed into their being" (*SPP* 477).

Relevant here is Hildebrand's suggestion that Prometheus does not actually disappear from the action of act two: "If we ask what Prometheus does from the end of Act I until his release, the answer would be that he dreams" ("Naming Day" 195). I would modify that statement only to say that Prometheus is experiencing the waking dream of reverie. In that state, as in the instances of reverie described by Bachelard, Prometheus' subjectivity becomes assimilated into his anima, and indeed Hildebrand uses the word "anima" to describe Asia's function in the drama. The term, however, is itself an example of a reification that, carelessly used, leads to "an education of error" (*SPP* 477). What precisely does Hildebrand mean when he describes Asia as Prometheus' "anima," with Panthea and Ione as "modifications of her"? What is actually happening when she and other agents in act two have an "intersubjective meeting of presences" ("Naming Day" 197)? Or when, in Ross Woodman's phrasing, Prometheus withdraws "from his own limited maleness" and permits "the unknown female to assume control" (227)?

James Hillman, who describes Jung's concept of anima as "a portmanteau idea packed thick with other notions," begins his unpacking with this "basic definition" by Jung: "The anima can be defined as the image or archetype or deposit of all the experiences of man with woman" ("Anima" 99; Jung 13, 58).[3] Since the primary experience of woman (in two senses of the term "primary") is with the mother or mother surrogate, one would expect that relationship to figure largely in the "deposit," but in fact Jung often takes pains to separate the mother image from the anima. As Hillman points out: "Jung associates a host of feminine forms with anima; but one in particular he generally keeps outside its confines. This is the mother. 'The most striking feature about the anima-type is that the maternal element is lacking' " ("Anima" 120; Jung 10, 75).

Erich Neumann makes a similarly strong differentiation between the two but at the same time suggests an initial connection or fusion. Describing the outcome of the fight with the dragon, which serves as his mythic paradigm for a young male's separation from the mother, he writes:

> The transformation which the male undergoes in the course of the dragon fight includes a change in his relation to the female, symbolically expressed in the liberation of the captive from the dragon's power. In other words, the feminine image extricates itself from the grip of the Terrible Mother, a process known in analytical psychology as the crystallization of the anima from the mother archetype. (198)

His further comments show, however, that this "crystallization" is a process which he himself sees as optimal but which does not necessarily occur. Moreover, his summary sentence—"What the hero kills is only the terrible side of the female, and this he does in order to set free the fruitful and joyous side with which she joins herself to him" (199)—completely excludes the mother only if we take all interactions with her as "terrible" and none "fruitful" or "joyous." Such concern with separating the mother from all the rest of the "deposit" that makes up anima reflects the cultural strength of the mother-son incest taboo more than it describes the actuality of this distinction.

Certainly the experience of the mother cannot be separated out from those elements contributing to the formation of Asia. In his learned account of Shelley's sources for Asia, Stuart Curran points out that most genealogies of the Titans name Asia not as Prometheus' wife but as his mother (*Annus Mirabilis* 45) and notes as well the associative links between the triple Mother Goddess of antiquity and Asia, Panthea, and Ione (47–51). Curran goes on to say that these three, considered as sources of comfort to Prometheus in his sufferings, serve in ironic contrast to the three Furies, who "according to Jacob Bryant's euhemerist reduction . . . were originally priestesses on Mount Caucasus" (51). Curran's shift to the "euhemerist reduction" distracts attention from the thought that the Furies are another—in this case horrific—manifestation of the triple goddess, the "mothers" of fate, life, and death. By contrasting the two sets of tripartite female figures, Shelley does not disconnect "all the experiences of man with woman" from the experience of the mother, as a Jungian analyst would advise him to do, but he does make careful division between the Terrible and the Good Mother.

As we have seen earlier, Prometheus vanquishes the manifestations of the Terrible Mother by refusing to mirror the vindictive and despairing emotions of which they are themselves projections. Without that mirror, according to the stage directions, the Furies "vanish" (I.i.634). Mirroring is at least as important a part of act two as it is of act one. If, as Hildebrand suggests, act two is a representation of Prometheus' dream/reverie, then its incidents all mirror the Promethean subjectivity that, having turned from the Furies, now reflects the Oceanides.

The metaphor contained in the signifier "mirror" used to describe this process is misleading, however, in that it creates the image of a subjectivity that projects itself on another, seeing that other in its own image. The exact reverse is also often the case, as it was in Prometheus' identification with Jupiter and is in this instance, since the dramatis persona named Prometheus is not visibly present in act two. This presence/absence is best explained through the reinterpretation and critique of Freud's theories of identification made by Girard and Borch-Jacobsen as well as by Daniel Stern.

In Borch-Jacobsen's words: "We do not love because we identify, we identify because we love. Mimesis is articulated on—and grounded in—sexuality" (15). Applied to the action of this drama, this theory suggests that Prometheus does not desire Asia as an object, nor does he even desire to be with Asia; he desires to *be* Asia.

Borch-Jacobsen makes it clear that he is simply extrapolating from Freud's own analysis of identification; he quotes from *The Interpretation of Dreams:* "Identification is not simple imitation but *assimilation* [*Aneignung* = appropriation] on the basis of a similar aetiological pretension; it expresses a re-semblance [*gleichwie* = just as] and is derived from a common element [*Gemeinsames*] which remains in the unconscious" (Borch-Jacobsen 14; *Interpretation,* in *Standard Edition* IV, 150). Asia's association with the mother, taken in conjunction with the mother's function in the formation of subjectivity itself, tells us what this "common element" is. The mother's gaze is experienced by the infant not simply as one that watches her or him but also as one *with which* the infant sees himself or herself.

Daniel Stern, as I noted earlier, uses the concept of affect attunement to consider the identification between infant and care giver, describing it as a "process that occurs between parents and infants which allows an infant to perceive *how* he is perceived" and noting that this process is thought to be "essential in the acquisition of a sense of self" ("Affect Attunement" 249). Stern's emphasis, unlike that of Freudian theory and of Borch-Jacobsen, tends to be on the positive nature of these interactions, particularly on the fact that when they function as they should, the infant subjectivity acquires a steadily growing sense of self-regulation and of capacity to control the amount of stimulation received from the other. Averting the gaze is one of the first and most important of the infant's strategies for this regulation (*First Relationship* 117). Even so, Stern records enough evidence of failed interactions between infants and their mothers to call attention to the potential for unease and disequilibrium through the interactions with an Other that produce subjectivity (*Interpersonal World* 205–20). The power of the mother can be feared on the one hand for its potential invasiveness and desired (i.e., imitated) on the other through acts of appropriation that block true interaction (Stern, *First Relationship,* 122–28).

Ellie Ragland-Sullivan, working from more pessimistic Lacanian premises, describes sources of tension similar to those mentioned by Stern in the emergence of subjectivity: "Prior to speech and the birth of subjectivity the *moi* has become characterized by conflict and tension because it depends on specular recognition from another for its own existence and perpetuation" (46). A corollary given much less attention within all the theories, psychoanalytic and behavioral, but brilliantly analyzed in Kaja Silverman's "Fragments of a Fashionable Discourse" is that a male strategy for the resolution of this conflict lies in the disavowal of dependence on the mother's gaze, which is expressed through appropriation of the gaze as a male prerogative (142–43).

We shall return shortly in another context to the function of the gaze. Its significance at this juncture turns upon the nature of appropriation. The gaze triggers in the infant the mimetic identification expressive of desire, and desire, impelling one as it does to put oneself in another's place, can annihilate, or "kill," the other (Borch-Jacobsen 13).

These signifiers again are metaphoric and so express a dissimilarity as well as a similarity between actual murder—though that possibility is always there—and the appropriativeness of the mimetic subject. Even as metaphors they cast a gloom over the lyricism of Bachelard's description of reverie as that which "gives the I a non-I which belongs to the I: my non-I" (13). Asia, along with Ione and Panthea, as Prometheus' non-I—as *his* non-I—is not a subjectivity in the same way that he is. The three figures are dramatis personae for those aspects of Prometheus' subjectivity formed through experiences of the feminine—principally from those that were positive experiences, though, as we shall see, hints of "conflict and tension" persist there as well. The Jungian terminology that Woodman uses when he writes that the "action" of *Prometheus Unbound* can be summed up in the phrase "the gradual constellation of the androgyne" (230) therefore seems to me appropriate, though not a matter for celebration.[4] Were I to agree that Woodman's phrase encompasses the *whole* meaning of Asia's journey, I would myself step no further. But my interest turns on other suggestions raised by the figure of Asia, other possibilities having to do not with a safely bounded masculine individuality perfecting itself through encapsulating an "eternal feminine" (Woodman 227), but with a permeable subjectivity that problematizes stable notions of gender altogether.

One other aspect of the setting created by Asia's opening speech needs comment before we turn to the dramatic action itself; the morning star is reflected intermittently through drifting mist in the dark waters of the lake:

> The point of one white star is quivering still
> Deep in the orange light of widening morn
> Beyond the purple mountains; through a chasm
> Of wind-divided mist the darker lake
> Reflects it—now it wanes—it gleams again
> As the waves fade
>
> (II.i.17–22)

As the dawn grows brighter, the star fades from sight, but its physical image is repeated in the simile Asia uses within a very few lines to describe Panthea's eyes: "Those eyes which burn through smiles that fade in tears / Like stars half quenched in mists of silver dew" (II.i.28–29).

In Sumerian, Greek, and Roman mythologies, Venus as both morning and evening star—"the star of Death / And Birth," as Shelley describes it in "Epipsychidion" (ll. 379–80)—is sacred to the Great Mother goddess: Ishtar, Astarte, Venus. Her power manifests itself in the star's dual gender: the Babylonians described the morning star as the "male Venus" and the evening star as the "female Venus"; or both morning and evening stars might be given masculine names—Lucifer, Phosphorus, Hesperus—yet be associated with Venus; or the star might be linked to the union between Astarte and her lover Adonis (Langdon 24). Significant in the interpretation of "Adonais," this last association is a meaningful foreshadowing also of the action in *Prometheus Unbound*. In certain rituals, as James Frazer describes them, the rising of the morning star marked the approach of Venus to recall her son/lover to life (V, 258; VI, 34–35).[5] The romance tradition also gives a starry context to the reunion of lovers. The word "desire," which enters English through Old French romance literature, has its origins in the Latin prepositional phrase *de sidere,* "from the stars." To desire meant originally "to await what the stars will bring" (*Barnhart Dictionary* 269).

The same metonymic shifts contained in the lines from *Prometheus Unbound*—from star to a mirrored image to a pair of gazing eyes—occur at other significant points in Shelley's work, sometimes with negative, sometimes with positive meaning. The Poet in "Alastor" looks up from a "silent well" to see "two starry eyes, hung in the gloom of thought" (ll. 484, 490) which offer him a delusory promise of confirmed subjectivity. A somewhat similar image in *Laon and Cythna* conveys a fulfilled promise of dualities resolved into a unified consciousness; when Laon and Cythna are reunited after a long separation and are about to make love, Cythna's eyes are compared to "twin phantoms of one star that lies / O'er a dim well" (VI.xxxiii.293–94 [*CW* I, 337]). This particular passage thus shows links between images and attendant ideas related to maternal power which appear elsewhere in Shelley's work but here have a particularly compressed form: from Venus the planet (star); to the Great Mother Venus; to the mirrored star as gaze; to the gaze, linked with the smile, as guarantor of subjectivity; to the mother's gaze specifically as that of a benign Divine Assistant—at least when, as in this instance, the gaze serves to construct and not to annihilate the sense of being-in-the-world.[6]

Panthea's opening words to Asia begin a discussion of dreams that forms the central action of this scene. In part perhaps because of the subject matter but also through the images evoked by her words, the speech gives evidence of how well the Kristevan concept of the semiotic serves as a theoretical gloss on the function of the Oceanides—Asia, Panthea, and Ione—within the Promethean subjectivity. Panthea describes an earlier time, a once-upon-a-time "erewhile" (II.i.43), in which hers was the erotic but nongenital experience of a body at ease in its sense of fusion with a female body as well as with the surrounding material world. In that state she slept

> Under the glaucous caverns of old Ocean,
> Within dim bowers of green and purple moss;
> Our young Ione's soft and milky arms
> Locked then as now behind my dark moist hair
> While my shut eyes and cheek were pressed within
> The folded depth of her life-breathing bosom. . . .
>   (II.i.44–49)

There, in the "semiotic chora," her experience-of-body (properly given the feminine name Ione because it involves introjection of the mother's body) is inscribed with the "letters" that are "the effects of touch, sound, the gaze, images, and so forth as they intermingle with sensory response" (Ragland-Sullivan 20). In that "erewhile" her experience was passive; but now, although Panthea retains a connection with the "chora" in that Ione's "soft and milky arms" still hold her, she has an active mediating role between the semiotic and the symbolic. She is the wordless "breath" associating these memory traces with a verbal signification that catches yet fails to catch them, since it "dissolves" them into their symbolic representatives in language:

I am made the wind
Which fails beneath the music that I bear
Of thy most wordless converse; since dissolved
Into the sense with which love talks, my rest
Was troubled and yet sweet.

(II.i.50–54)

Transmitted to Asia as repository and inscriber, Panthea's description of the ways in which the introjected tripartite experience-of-the-feminine functions both "erewhile" and at present in the Promethean subjectivity serves only as context for her actual topic, the fact that she also was in a state of reverie brought on by two "dreams." In response Asia asks, "Lift up thine eyes / And let me read thy dream" (II.i.55–56). In so using the word "read," Shelley adumbrates the Lacanian dictum that "the unconscious functions like a language." At the same time, the simile "*like* a language" contains difference as well as sameness, as will become clear within a few lines; Asia, through the intersubjectivity of the gaze, can become so "sutured" to Panthea that she will have the experience of the dream itself, unmediated by the re-presentation of language. Yet Panthea—surprisingly, since she has just mourned the mediated nature of language—insists on giving a verbal account of the one dream she remembers: the transfiguration of Prometheus' "pale, wound-worn limbs" into a glorified body.[7]

Modeled on the New Testament accounts of Jesus' transfigured appearance to three of his disciples shortly before his Crucifixion (Matt. 17:1–8), this vision seems also to have a similar purpose: to offer a prophetic foretaste of ultimate victory that will serve as inspiriting comfort through an intermediate period of trial. The genders and situations of the two participants call up as well the appearance of Jesus after the Resurrection to Mary Magdalene (John 20:11–18). But a sexual aura explicitly denied in the gospel story—though present, admittedly, precisely through the injunction "Do not touch me"— suffuses all the language describing the communion of spirit between Prometheus and Panthea. Thus, in addition to its explicitly Christian allusions, the passages hints at a Dionysian presence and "sees" Panthea as a member of the enraptured Dionysian worshipers, the *thiasos*.[8]

The passage is rather long, but since the interaction it describes needs detailed comment, I quote it in full:

Then two dreams came. One I remember not.
But in the other, his pale, wound-worn limbs
Fell from Prometheus, and the azure night
Grew radiant with the glory of that form
Which lives unchanged within, and his voice fell
Like music which makes giddy the dim brain
Faint with intoxication of keen joy:
"Sister of her whose footsteps pave the world
With loveliness—more fair than aught but her
Whose shadow thou art—lift thine eyes on me!"
I lifted them—the overpowering light

Of that immortal shape was shadowed o'er
By love; which, from his soft and flowing limbs
And passion-parted lips, and keen faint eyes
Steam'd forth like vaporous fire; an atmosphere
Which wrapt me in its all-dissolving power
As the warm ether of the morning sun
Wraps ere it drinks some cloud of wandering dew.
I saw not—heard not—moved not—only felt
His presence flow and mingle through my blood
Till it became his life and his grew mine
And I was thus absorbed—until it past
And like the vapours when the sun sinks down,
Gathering again in drops upon the pines
And tremulous as they, in the deep night
My being was condensed, and as the rays
Of thought were slowly gathered, I could hear
His voice, whose accents lingered ere they died
Like footsteps of far melody. Thy name,
Among the many sounds alone I heard
Of what might be articulate; though still
I listened through the night when sound was none.
                    (II.i.61–92)

More than half a century ago Carl Grabo noted briefly that in these lines Shelley "employed the technic of mesmerism of which he had some knowledge" (53). Newman Ivey White found that idea "very destructive indeed" when he took exception to Grabo's emphasis on mesmerist theories for the interpretation of "The Witch of Atlas." White objected that Grabo's attribution to Shelley of a knowledge of mesmerism had only Medwin's discussion of that subject for its scholarly evidence, and Medwin states flatly that "Shelley had never previously heard of Mesmerism, and I shewed him a treatise I composed" (270). Since Medwin arrived in Pisa in late October 1820, nearly two months after "The Witch of Atlas" was completed, Grabo's interpretive use of mesmerism—so the argument runs—is simply misleading. This passage from *Prometheus Unbound,* written in the early spring of 1819, would of course be equally outside such consideration (White II, 598).

Richard Holmes also accepts Medwin's account as factual and gives little attention to the topic of mesmerism, despite the thematic importance to his biography of Shelley's "lifelong exploration of psychic and parapsychic phenomena" (65). Crook and Guiton's careful tracking of Shelley's medical history offers evidence to support a counterargument to White's. Since, however, they give mesmerism no specific discussion, and since the topic is of such importance to an understanding of Shelley's thought about the formative, informative, and transformative aesthetic in relation to subjectivity, I must pause to make the point that, to my mind, Grabo was right and White's dismissal of his interpretation was misleading.

In the first place, there are enough queries about Medwin's memory and his record keeping to leave his statement at least open to question, especially since, disciple-like, he took pleasure in stressing Shelley's dependence on himself. Or perhaps when Medwin states that Shelley "had never previously heard of Mesmerism," he meant that Shelley had not heard specifically of Franz Anton Mesmer (though that seems unlikely). In any case, given the multitudinous ways in which mesmerist theories had infiltrated the whole cultural milieu, and given Shelley's obsessive concerns with precisely the areas of speculation most affected by these theories, Medwin's statement is simply not credible. Robert Darnton's fine study *Mesmerism and the End of the Enlightenment in France* focuses on France in the 1780s, but his description both of Mesmer's antecedents and of the wide-ranging postrevolutionary effects of his ideas, particularly on utopian and apocalyptic visionaries, suggests clearly enough the potential for intellectual kinship with Shelley. Darnton notes:

> Mesmer's opponents spotted his scientific ancestry almost immediately. They showed that, far from revealing any new discoveries or ideas, his system descended directly from those of Paracelsus, J. B. van Helmont, Robert Fludd, and William Maxwell, who presented health as a state of harmony between the individual microcosm and the celestial macrocosm, involving fluids, human magnets, and occult influences of all sorts. . . . Von Humboldt thought the moon might exert a magnetic force, and Galvani was experimenting with "animal electricity" in Italy at the same time that Mesmer used animal magnetism to cure hundreds of persons in France. Meanwhile, the Abbé Nollet and Bertholon and others had discovered miraculous powers in the universal electric fluid. (14)

When Shelley, during his days of banishment to Poland Street in the spring of 1811, considered the possibility of surgery as a career and attended the medical lectures of John Abernethy, he was hearing expounded the theory that a "sympathy" exists between the whole body and its parts, and that through and among all bodies there flows a "subtile substance of a quickly powerfully mobile nature" which "appears to be the life of the world." Commenting on Abernethy's theories, Crook and Guiton add that the doctor took no stand on disputed points about whether the fluid "should be called electricity, magnetism, or 'calorie,' " but he posited a fluid whose conduit was the nervous system, "the means whereby one part of the body sympathised with another." They add: "Abernethy was not being original—he was using a keyword of his age. 'Sympathy,' which of course is originally a medical term, was the point at which Romantic medicine touched on physics, chemistry, philanthropy and literature; 'sympathy' related man to nature and man to man" (Crook and Guiton 70).

Although they do not take up the connection between "sympathy" and hypnotically induced somnambulism, for that is not the focus of their study, the link certainly exists, especially in the concept of a fluid. In laying out the basic principles of "animal magnetism," with Anton Mesmer as his acknowledged source, Joseph Deleuze writes: "We suppose that a substance emanates from him who magnetizes, and is conveyed to the person magnetized, in the direction given it by the will. This substance, which sustains life in us, we call the magnetic fluid. The nature of this fluid is unknown: even its existence has not been demonstrated, but everything occurs as if it did exist" (21), a pragmatic "as if" which puts his thinking very close to Abernethy's.

In describing the nature of the relationship between the magnetizer and the patient, Deleuze uses the word "rapport," which his American translator renders as "in communication" (31), but the word "sympathy" would be even more appropriate, particularly in the medical sense described by Crook and Guiton. To this "rapport" we must also add the perception of an "influence," with both the celestial and the fluid connotations of that word. Deleuze writes: "That is to say, we mean by the word *communication,* a peculiar and induced condition, which causes the magnetizer to exert an influence upon the patient, there being between them a communication of the vital principle" (31). Among the effects that this influence could produce, one of the most dramatic was that of "magnetic somnambulism," to be distinguished from somnambulism per se, or sleepwalking. (Deleuze expresses the need for a "more appropriate" term [68], but "hypnotism" was not introduced into the language until 1842 [*OED* VII, 568].)[9]

In sum, while it may be possible to quibble over Grabo's use of the term "mesmerism" in his interpretation of Panthea's dream, on the gounds that Shelley may not have heard or read of Mesmer, Shelley had from numerous sources both read and heard about theories of what might be called more generally animal magnetism and of the influence that one subjectivity can exert on another so as to produce a condition now described as hypnotic. What happens in the lines under discussion is that Prometheus hypnotizes Panthea.

There emanates from Prometheus' body the fluid metonymically ascribed to his "soft and flowing limbs" (II.i.73). The "vaporous fire" (II.i.75) issuing from those limbs as well as from his "passion-parted lips, and keen faint eyes" (II.i.74) renders Panthea at once unconscious and united to the consciousness of her magnetizer:

> I saw not—heard not—moved not—only felt
> His presence flow and mingle through my blood
> Till it became his life and his grew mine
> And I was thus absorbed—
>
> (II.i.79–82)

Typical also of the hypnotic experience is the fact that although Panthea has a sense of being absorbed into a single shared subjectivity, she also maintains awareness of duality-in-unity; she is hypnotized but not psychotic.

In *Things Hidden since the Foundation of the World,* Jean-Michel Oughourlian, in a dialogue with René Girard, remarks that "the subject under hypnosis never loses sight of the difference between himself and the hypnotizer, the god who is possessing him. So there is a fundamental structural difference between psychosis, on the one hand, and possession and hypnosis, on the other" (317). The contrast made by Oughourlian is between a hypnotic state or religious trance and the situation of a psychotic. All involve the subject's being moved in on, as it were, by an Other; but while in the first two cases the psychic room is shared, in the last it is not, becoming wholly the space of the Other.

In *Dire Mastery* François Roustang, presenting a theory about psychosis, ascribes the condition to a family structure in which "the mother—or father— speaks in place of and in the name of the child in order to explain it to herself or himself (that is, to establish that it has neither place nor name); the mother has no need to hear the child speak in order to know what it thinks, for it thinks only what she has implanted in it so that the child will think it. . . . The result is that the psychotic does not experience thoughts as her or his own but as an alien, and therefore often terrifying discourse registered but not initiated by a consciousness emptied of subjectivity and inhabited by others(s)" (134). The roots of psychosis, according to Roustang's argument, can thus be traced back to the infant's primary identification with her or his caretaker, and the condition actually differs from the normal process of identification only in the space created to maintain duality through the presence of the Freudian "third term," discussed in Chapter 1.

As I noted there, the third term is best conceptualized not as another person but as the caretaker's own sense of an autonomous existence, separate from the infant's. In this regard, the acquisition of subjectivity can be as well illuminated by Girard's theory of mimetic desire as by the interaction of the Freudian three terms: the needy and unformed potential subjectivity of the infant identifies with the caretaker as one fulfilled, that is to say as one whose needs are fulfilled elsewhere. The primary caretaker (and this would be true for either gender) is as much a Girardian model/obstacle for the infant—and in just the same ways and for just the same reasons—as the beloved (of either gender) is for the admirer (of either gender), or, in a psychoanalytic context, as the analyst is for the analysand.

Thus, while the mimetic relationship between nursling and caretaker is for the infant a source of frustration and aggression as well as of joyful union, the caretaker *must* appear to have her or his needs already met elsewhere—that is, must appear grandly and heartbreakingly autonomous—for there to be the third term that prevents psychotic possession. Indeed, this is *the* third term, stripped of Oedipal myth or the culture's preconceptions about gender. The nurturer who, from the infant's point of view, does not seem self-sufficient but leans in upon the infant with anaclitic[10] yearning threatens that psychic space needed for the acquisition of an individuated subjectivity, just as the hypnotizer must, as Oughourlian points out, maintain a certain psychic distance from the hypnotized. The threat of psychosis in both cases is held off only through the establishment and maintenance of a difference (or third term) along with an identification so total that it involves some sharing, often unconscious, of psychic "space." If the infant's introjection of the caretaker's very being (Ragland-Sullivan 34) is one of the most dramatic examples of mimetic desire; if hypnosis is the "caricature of mimetic desire—at once its simplest and strongest manifestation"; if the psychoanalytic process of transference can be compared to "the fluid of the magnetizers, from Mesmer and Puysegar to the charlatans of the present" (Girard, *Things Hidden* 327, 328), then in all three situations the seductive but spurious autonomy of the caretaker/hypnotist/analyst both lures the infant/somnambulist/analysand into a state of identification and prevents that identification from being total.

After this long detour the reference to "the fluid of the magnetizers" leads us back to the effect on the magnetized Panthea of the "vaporous fire" emanating from Prometheus. That the energy flows from him to her is surprising, given their particular situation and the normal practice of magnetism. Prometheus is the one with "pale, wound-worn limbs" (II.i.62), desperately in need of healing, while Panthea in act one has served not only as the witness of his sufferings but as a source of comfort and support. Yet in this scene he is the magnetizer/healer and she the magnetized/patient whose experience of the body (Ione) feels the restorative effects of his power. When Panthea returns to consciousness after her trance, Ione greets her by saying:

> when just now
> We kissed, I felt within thy parted lips
> The sweet air that sustained me; and the warmth
> Of the life-blood for loss of which I faint
> Quivered between our intertwining arms.
> (II.i.102–6)

Why is there this peculiar reversal?[11]

An answer consistent with Hildebrand's argument that act two occurs within Prometheus' dreaming mind is that what Panthea relates as her dream experience is actually a form of self-hypnosis. Freed from his destructive miming of Jupiter, Prometheus can now call on the inner powers of his "soul" to continue the healing process. Even so, would those powers not logically be visualized as a female magnetizer in this enactment of such an interior process? The events that occur next in the drama, along with those projected events that Shelley sketched in but then canceled, show why a female magnetist, even if a dramatically logical choice, is not a psychological possibility: Shelley needs the reversal he makes in order to stave off the potential for psychosis produced by the maternal gaze.

Panthea's dream of Prometheus' transfiguration displays proleptically the conclusion of the process that constitutes the unseen Promethean action of act two dramatized through the interactions of Asia, Panthea, and Demogorgon. In Marcuse's Freudian terminology one could say that Prometheus is reaching back to the oceanic state of primary narcissism in which "the libidinal cathexis of the ego (one's own body) may become the source and reservoir for a new libidinal cathexis of the objective world—transforming this world into a new mode of being" (169). In effecting "organic interpenetration," Prometheus in Eagleton's terms is functioning as an agent of the "aesthetic" (15).

Shelley's post-Paracelsan and pre-Freudian conception is of a mysterious fluid of "vaporous fire" which reestablishes not only a lost sympathy among the disjoined aspects of the psychosomatic whole, the body/mind, but also that early state in which human nature is "dissolved into the surrounding universe" or "the surrounding universe [is] . . . absorbed into [its] being" (*SPP* 477). Without commenting on the "magnetic" nature of the image, Ulmer (19) calls attention to a passage in *A Defence of Poetry* that makes a further connection between hypnotism, poetry, and social reform. Shelley describes poems as "sacred links of that chain . . . which descending through the minds of many men is attached to those great minds [the poets], whence as from a magnet the invisible effluence is sent forth, which at once connects, animates and sustains the life of all" (*SPP* 493).

For this sympathetic transformation to occur, Prometheus and Asia must be brought into connection, a process made possible through the instrumentality of Panthea. Deleuze notes: "The magnetic fluid may not only act directly upon the person whom we wish to magnetize, but it may also be conveyed to him by an intermediate body, which we have charged with this fluid, to which we have given a determinate action" (22). Panthea, thrown into somnambulism by the influence of Prometheus, bears that influence to Asia and delivers it when she is once again placed by Asia in a state of trance.

Yet Panthea is a peculiarly recalcitrant medium. She shows her reluctance first by changing her immediate experience into the mediated symbolic expression of language, which represents but also takes the place of its referent. Impatient, Asia makes this point: "Thou speakest, but thy words / Are as the air: I feel them not. . . . oh, lift / Thine eyes, that I may read his written soul!" (II.i.108–10).[12]

At this point in Shelley's autograph fair copy of the drama a long passage is transcribed but then deleted; the next two leaves of the notebook have been torn out and may have contained more canceled material (*Bodleian Shelley Manuscripts IX,* 269–71). As the dramatist, Shelley has the task of presenting the transfer of energy from the medium, Panthea, to the final recipient, Asia, and must do so on stage, as it were. Feeling his way into the situation, Shelley appears to experience the frightening aspects of "magnetism": the possibility for the takeover of one subjectivity by another. A hair's-breadth line lies between this power as a participatory one of psychic and physical healing and an aggressive one of psychic annihilation. The transmitted vision of Prometheus' "keen faint eyes" which "steam'd forth like vaporous fire" (II.i.74–75) has in these rejected lines the terrifying second effect both on Asia and, by a doubling back of the mirroring, on Panthea also. This is the passage as transcribed from the *Bodleian* manuscript:

> Asia
>   Thou speakest, but thy words
>   ~~Lift up thine~~
> Are as the air. I feel them not . . . . oh lift
>   soul.
> Thine eyes that I may read his written ~~spirit~~
> ~~Lift up thine eyes Panthea~~ — —they pierce — they burn!
>   Panthea
> Alas I am consumed—I melt away

```
The fire is in my heart—
            Asia
                Thine eyes burn!—
Hide them within thine hair
            Panthea
                O quench thy lips
I sink I perish
            Asia
                Shelter me now—they burn
It is his spirit in thier orbs . . my life
Is ebbing fast—I cannot speak—
            Panthea
                    Rest, rest!
Sleep death annihilation pain! aught else
```

                                (*IX*, 269)

Lawrence Zillman, who conjectures that this passage may have been deleted "because of its unfortunately melodramatic tone," passes along, though without positive endorsement, Charles Locock's thought that it is the "germ" of the "Life of Life" lyric at II.v.48–71 (*SPU* 114). This possibility is suggested also by Tilottama Rajan, who reads the draft as showing Asia in "ecstatic communion with the burning image of Prometheus in Panthea's eyes" (326). Without question there are parallel ideas to be found between this dialogue and lines of the lyric such as "In those looks where whoso gazes / Faints, entangled in their mazes" (II.v.52–53), but a stronger link, one involving both idea and affect, joins this canceled passage to Thetis' cries when she is raped by Jupiter:

> Insufferable might!
> God! spare me! I sustain not the quick flames,
> The penetrating presence; all my being,
> Like him whom the Numidian seps did thaw
> Into a dew with poison, is dissolved,
> Sinking through its foundations.
>
> (III.i.37–42)

What appears to have happened is that Shelley, intent on dramatizing a positive moment in the sympathetic identification that will build his new world, has stumbled into the violently aggressive and annihilating features also present in identification, which turn on the ambivalent nature of the gaze. Shelley can—and does—simply cancel the passage, replacing it with a more harmonious one, but his temporary difficulty—his "stumbling block," in Girard's terminology—betrays the crack in the engendered nature of his concept of full subjectivity that threatens his utopian foundation.

Returning to Asia's request that Panthea raise her eyes, Shelley allows some small part of this ambivalence to remain in Panthea's agnostic and ego-bound response: "I lift them, though they droop beneath the load / Of that they would express—what canst thou see / But thine own fairest shadow imaged there?" (II.i.111–13). Hildebrand comments that Panthea's words express "the residuum of the Jupiterean consciousness in Prometheus and Asia against which Asia must struggle" ("Naming Day" 198–99). I agree that the conviction that separate subjectivities must be closed to one another because all supposed knowledge of the Other can be explained as projection of the self—Panthea's meaning, as it seems—is Jupiterean. But also the recognition that subjectivity is shared must maneuver past a Jupiterean impulse to enter appropriatively into another if it is to reach a Dionysian joy in shared life.

At last Asia's gaze and Panthea's meet. The assonance and repetitions in Asia's words open Panthea's subjectivity mesmerically and return us to the process by which subjectivity is woven in the first place. The infant introjects the non-I through its eyes and also introjects the non-I as "eyes" and as "I." So Ragland-Sullivan makes the comment that "existentialist philosophers demonstrated that the *regard* is always 'out there.' Lacan connects it to dreams and shows that it is also always 'in here': the gaze of the Other (A)" (44). Lacan's own language is even more dramatic: "What determines me, at the most profound level, in the visible, is the gaze that is outside. It is through the gaze that I enter light and it is from the gaze that I receive its effects" (*Four Fundamental Concepts* 106). Commenting on this passage in "Fragments of a Fashionable Discourse," Silverman notes that it is "most classically the mother" who provides the "visual mediation" that builds toward the self-recognition of a subjectivity (142–43). Or to describe the process in yet another way, infinite but undefined potential takes the shape of a coherent subjectivity when eyes meet the gaze of an Other's eyes and, united to the gaze, see what it sees. Laying bare that process, Asia's words reaffirm Panthea's subjectivity but also open it up to the sharing that created it. Her words bear as well on the statement in "On Life" that "each [human life] is at once the centre and the circumference; the point to which all things are referred, and the line in which all things are contained" (*SPP* 476):

> Thine eyes are like the deep blue, boundless Heaven
> Contracted to two circles underneath
> Their long, fine lashes—dark, far, measureless,—
> Orb within orb, and line through line inwoven.—
> (II.i.114–17)

At one with Panthea, Asia can at last experience Panthea's vision of the renewed Prometheus:

>   'tis He, arrayed
> In the soft light of his own smiles which spread
> Like radiance from the cloud-surrounded moon.
> Prometheus, it is thou—depart not yet!
> Say not those smiles that we shall meet again
> Within that bright pavilion which their beams
> Shall build o'er the waste world?
>   (II.i.120–26)

The mood evoked is one of ethereal sensibility, and critics, respecting that, have restrained any snickers over the fact that Prometheus is wearing *only* his smiles. O. W. Firkins, for instance, notes simply as "remarkable" Shelley's "way of conceiving beauty as a highly rarefied but physical emanation hanging around or suffusing the object from which it springs like an aerial vestment or a lucid atmosphere" (*V* 428). Remarkable, I would say in this instance, to the point of being risible. Moreover, the "soft" and thus seemingly textured smiles of line 121 become in the audacious—or foolhardy—pun of line 125 "beams" that shall build a "bright pavilion . . . o'er the waste world."

Like certain metaphysical poets, Shelley, here attempting to fuse physical description with psychological insight, pushes language so far that it teeters on or falls into the bathetic. But however outlandish the tropes, they are true at least to their psychological function. That is to say, the facial expression of a smile, met and returned by an infant subjectivity, does serve as the "costume" of that subjectivity, in which it acts and interacts. And these intersubjective actions in turn form the stage on which human life takes place. Smiles therefore do both clothe and build psyche, as the writers of advice books to mothers well knew. Lydia Maria Child writes, "If he [the infant] looks up in the midst of his play, a smile should always be ready for him; that he may feel protected and happy in the atmosphere of love" (3).

As tends to be the common strategy in conduct books, the emphasis in this passage is positive; even so, one senses in it a demand for constant, consistent, and *totally selfless* watchfulness that might well fill an actual and necessarily imperfect mother with anxiety. More explicitly terrifying is the adjuration in *On the Management and Education of Children,* where a discourse on the importance of outdoor play for children is at the same time filled with warnings to the overseeing mother on the dangers she must guard against, "for a Moment, if your Eye be off from him, may cost him his Life" (Hill 61).

In the watched and potentially appropriated child the power of the maternal gaze creates anxiety also, but for a different reason, and this anxiety remains full-blown in the adult psyche. The passage of dialogue between Panthea and Asia that Shelley canceled shows that he was well aware of the negative, appropriative, and intrusive potential of the gaze. The idea of such ambivalent power when associated with the mother—and then, by extension, with women in general—becomes intolerable.

Shelley's project is to replace Jupiterean solipsism and its attendant paranoia with a Dionysian awareness that subjectivity, like the universe as a whole, is participatory, mingled, *shared*. In the contemporary discourses both of science and of child rearing that would have been familiar to Shelley, the efficacy of the gaze offered substantiation for the concept of *inter*subjectivity as the human reality. But other philosophical and sociological givens of the period created imperative reasons for a control of the gaze that undercut the very intersubjectivity Shelley was attempting to portray. One is the Humean view of subjectivity encapsulated in Shelley's statement that "nothing exists but as it is perceived." Since this predicates an isolated subjectivity whose experience is reduced to perception, "I" *as an Other's perception* has no separate existence. I must therefore perceive the Other, but the Other cannot—comfortably—be conceived of as perceiving me.

The second barrier to a doctrine of true intersubjectivity lay in the terms of the Lockean social-sexual contract. Its denial of full subjectivity to women makes the woman's gaze that of a nonsubject, makes it therefore an abyss of nonbeing (see Bachelard's "indeterminate depths" where "reigns the repose of the feminine" [63]). Also, its identification of women with vulnerability engenders and makes negative the very quality—acceptance of such vulnerability—that is demanded if subjects are to share being. Through both these theories, then, the experience of intersubjectivity carries the threat of dissolution. As a way of warding off this perceived danger, Shelley establishes Prometheus' gaze, not Panthea's or Asia's, as the one that will re-create the world. *His* must be the position of the healing magnetizer, and he, not Asia, must have charge of the gaze's shocking power.

While this negative view of Shelley's strategy must be kept in mind, one can find a much more positive rationale for Prometheus' control of the gaze. Again, Prometheus must be considered as both creator of a new human subjectivity and as its prime exemplum. As we saw occurring at the end of act one, his sense of a foundation in Panthea's enduring love begins that creative process. And the "beams" that make up its foundation are maternal beams of love establishing the infant subjectivity as one in which both mother and infant have joy. (So, for example, Shelley's nurse gave him joy in his body with her exclamations over his skin, his hair; his mother joy in his mind by proud acknowledgment of his intelligence, his powers of memory, his verbal skill.) The mirroring subject receiving these loving images of self—or, to change the metaphor, these wholesome influences—becomes in turn throughout life a potential source or transmitter of healing joy. Panthea's first dream comes as a sign that Prometheus has regained contact with the "fluid" of this influence; healing thereby flows into and also emanates from his body. One line of Asia's encapsulates this to-and-fro of influence, with Panthea as the point of connection. Seeing Prometheus, Asia names him: "Prometheus, it is thou" (II.i.123). As instrument and providential overseer of his renewing life, she reconfirms a being who in turn beams a promise of renewal upon her.

The Caverns of Thought (Scenes i and ii)

Although the break between the textual analysis of the last section and that of this one comes within a single speech made by Asia to Panthea, it has a rationale in that a shift occurs between a description of the first of Panthea's "two dreams" to a dialogue that reconstructs the second. Then, too, the first dream, while prophesying Prometheus' future liberation, also recalls by implicit contrast the sufferings that we have witnessed in act one. The second dream points forward much more specifically to the action of act two, culminating in the meeting with Demogorgon, while also taking us back into a more remote past, some "fair seed-time" before Prometheus' tortures began. Finally, the faculty of sight dominates the account of the first dream, while in the second, visual images take on a kaleidoscopic indeterminacy, and sound comes to the fore, though mingled as well with touch and smell.[13]

After Asia has identified Prometheus and reaffirmed his destiny, the vision of him that she sees, with Panthea's eyes as screen, changes to what in a cinematic presentation would be a dissolve, and another figure is superimposed:

Asia

What shape is that between us? Its rude hair
Roughens the wind that lifts it; its regard
Is wild and quick, yet 'tis a thing of air
For through its grey robe gleams the golden dew
Whose stars the noon has quench'd not.

Dream

                                              Follow, follow!

Panthea

It is mine other dream.

Asia

                                        It disappears.

Panthea

It passes now into my mind.

                                       (II.i.127–33)

This "shape" remains undesignated and therefore can take on different identities according to the interpretive bent of each analyst (*V* 429). And indeed it numbers among the many Shelleyan images that the conciliatory wisdom of G. M. Matthews would characterize as "overdetermined" (193). That granted, I see the figure primarily as Demogorgon. Like the Demogorgon whom we shall encounter before long, it is strangely formless. Its "regard" makes us aware that it is alive—"a living Spirit" like Demogorgon (II.iv.7)—and yet " 'tis a thing of air," just as Demogorgon has "neither limb / Nor form—nor outline" (II.iv.5–6). Also, if this shape is Demogorgon, the second dream, like the first but with more specificity, is a proleptic summary of the play's dramatic action. Over the vision of the apotheosized Prometheus falls the shadow of Demogorgon: the way to the one lies through the other, and that way involves achievement of a new Promethean dawn by the recovery of an earlier one. The words "the golden dew / Whose stars the noon has quench'd not" echo the lines with which Asia greeted Panthea, describing the latter's eyes as burning "through smiles that fade in tears / Like stars half quenched in mists of silver dew" (II.i.29–30). The silver dew over starry—and so implicitly golden—eyes now as in a palimpsest becomes the "golden dew" of Prometheus' eyes, still holding their promise through the "noon" of Jupiterean power. So this dew is of the future; but since it serves as metaphor for the potential in an earlier Promethean dawn, it is also of the past.

If the speaker in the dream is the mighty and portentous Demogorgon, his single line "Follow, follow!" seems rather ineffectual. It might serve as the refrain in a children's game, or as the much-repeated chorus sung excitedly by the chorale in a baroque oratorio. Indeed, it is to be repeated, as a critic has sourly noted, twenty times in the space of seventy lines and three times rhymed thumpingly with "hollow" (*V* 429). How could Shelley risk placing so much emphasis on so banal an injunction?

Banal but also mystifying, since the injunction demands an object: *What* are Asia and Panthea to follow? For more than forty lines, through repeated adjurations to "follow," we wait for an answer. Then, since the "Echoes" describe themselves as receding (II.i.174), we can be sure that they indeed are what is to be followed. Before that, when the word seems to function as the imperative of an intransitive verb, "follow" takes on the meaning related to the noun "follower"; understood that way, the adjuration is "Put yourself in the state of mind of one willing to be led, to be a follower."

Frederick Pottle's analysis of Asia's dramatic function underwrites that last interpretation of the word's meaning. Perhaps the theory that all the dramatic action of *Prometheus Unbound* occurs in act one has so many adherents, Pottle speculates, because "significant action, critics seem to feel, needs to be embodied in language like that of the First Act, language that testifies to resistance, language that asserts difficulty" (136). In act two, the language changes to that of "a stream of sound," and the difficulty to be presented is only the negative one (hard to present dramatically) of letting oneself be led: "Asia's difficulty in these scenes is to overcome the scruples that would keep her from surrendering herself to a duty which is disquietingly pleasant" (137).

Although Pottle does not comment on the many repetitions of "follow," those serve as an added piece of evidence in favor of his argument, since an easily obeyed command would not need such continued reinforcement. Indeed, disquiet more than pleasure seems to me the emotion experienced in giving one's will over to an unknown agency that is leading one to an unknown destination. The "struggle," and the different language with which it is enacted, parallels that of an analysand who stretches quietly on a couch with no clear indicators of where the drift of association may terminate.

After an interchange that once again lays emphasis on the way in which subjectivities can be shared without being totally merged—Asia's "seeing" of Panthea's dream serves to recall it into Panthea's consciousness—Panthea articulates it:

> Methought
> As we sate here the flower-infolding buds
> Burst on yon lightning-blasted almond tree,
> When swift from the white Scythian wilderness
> A wind swept forth wrinkling the Earth with frost . . .
> I looked, and all the blossoms were blown down;
> But on each leaf was stamped—as the blue bells
> Of Hyacinth tell Apollo's written grief—
> *O follow, follow!*
>
>   (II.i.133–41)

Earl Wasserman's analysis of this passage contrasts the "brilliant serenity" of the first dream with the "powerfully, nervously energetic" character of the second. Still, his own very helpful exegesis of the symbolism of the almond tree suggests that the *theme* of both dreams is similar. As Wasserman notes (309), Shelley would have read in Pliny that the almond tree is spring's first herald, since it buds in winter, blossoms in January, and bears fruit in March. The tree's impetuosity serves as metaphoric base for the Hebrew pun in which the same word (*sheqed*) means both "almond" and "hasten." Jeremiah takes advantage of this pun in describing God's promise to bring his prophet's words to speedy fulfillment: "And I said, I see a rod of an almond tree. Then said the Lord to me, Thou hast well seen: for I will hasten to perform it" (Jer. 1:11–12).

Shelley makes the "lightning-blasted almond tree" the dream's displacement for the "wound-worn" body of Prometheus, blasted by Jupiter's lightning bolts but now suddenly and prophetically shining with new life. But besides pointing forward, the dream, with its description of the wind "wrinkling the Earth with frost," also recalls that earlier moment, described by Earth in act one, when she and Prometheus were united, before the devastation wrought by Jupiter's "thunder." Like the "golden dew / Whose stars the noon has quench'd not," this sudden bloom, despite its reenactment of that early loss, gives hope for renewal. The lines immediately following suggest that a reinvigorated language, a language like that of "the infancy of society," will both produce and reflect the promised change.

My evidence for this interpretation is the strikingly beautiful comparison between the almond flowers "stamped" with the words "*O follow, follow!*" and the bluebells marked with the "Ai" of "Apollo's written grief" over the death of Hyacinth. So positive a reading demands further discussion, however, since Susan Brisman interprets both this allusion to writing and the line it echoes, in which Asia hopes to read Prometheus' "written soul" in Panthea's lifted eyes (II.i.109–10), as possibly reflecting "a resurgence of Shelley's skepticism in the face of a speech too burdened with the power of presence to sustain itself" (79). Her argument is that through these allusions to writing, Shelley's attempt to manifest the fusion between word and thought actually reminds us that words are abritrary, dead signs, the opposite of the experiential reality they necessarily betray.

True, the more passionate Shelley's affirmations about the veracity of language, the more vivid the awareness called up in their train of the falsehood involved in substituting signs for their referents in experience. But at the same time, with the "multistability" between figure and ground that transforms vase into profile (Behrendt 2), Shelley subscribes to Rousseau's belief in language as the full, adequate, and laden medium of presence. The shift involves changing one's point of attention from language as a present actuality to language at its originary moment.

Not surprisingly, Rousseau's theory about the origin of language attends much more to the affect-laden content given expression in words than to the signifying system itself. Even his sense of an inadequacy between signifier and

signified bases itself not on the representational and therefore alienated nature of the verbal sign but on the diminution and eventual falsehood of the
emotions expressing themselves through the use of signs.

Rousseau posits a preverbal society of self-sufficient families perpetuating
themselves by inbreeding—that is, by copulation between brothers and sisters. (He sets the boundaries of his discussion safely far from the abjection of
incest between parents and children.) A manipulative footnote concedes that
he may have startled his readers with this bland dismissal of the incest taboo,
and goes on to recognize the necessity of the taboo, which he defines as of
"human ordination," because the profound intimacy of domestic life has,
when eroticized, such potential for vice. Yet in the text itself Rousseau makes
the assumption that these early incestuous unions so lacked interest that there
was in them nothing "to loosen the tongue, nothing to provoke accents of
ardent passion often enough to conventionalize them" (*Origin of Language*
46). These "accents of passion" he imagines as having had their origin in
meetings between unrelated members of the two sexes at watering places
where "girls would come to seek water for the household, young men to water
their herds" (44). And the suggestion is that these "accents," even when
conventionalized into verbal signs, were adequate to the feelings they expressed until competitiveness forced humans into an emotional isolation
which made the communicative function of language a constant lie (46).

Rousseau's tale about the origin of language in the harsher climates of the
north also posits an expressive and physical basis for speech, but the physicality in need of expression arose not from erotic passion but from shared
danger and hardship. Thus the first words among the northerners were not
"*love me*" (aimez-moi), but "*help me*" (aidez-moi). And here, too, competitiveness in the fight for survival vitiates the original mutuality presumed by
the use of conventional signs (47–48; author's emphasis). It is worth noting
here for future relevance to my argument that Rousseau's repression of the
passionate feelings of infancy toward the mother makes it necessary for him to
create an elaborate—and unlikely—historical myth. But if interpreted ontogenetically and not phylogenetically, his theory becomes a parable describing
the process of language acquisition as viewed by developmental research. The
infant's desire for and physical dependence on the caretaker—*aimez-moi* and
aidez-moi—meeting with an affective response create the mutuality that
makes possible the shared significatory system of language.

Whether or not Shelley was familiar with Rousseau's *On the Origins of
Language*—and with Brisman (57) I think it very likely that he was, given his
interest in the topic and his admiration for the author—the same attitude
about expression as the source of language and about an original adequacy
between expression and its sign gives the phrase "Apollo's written grief" its
rhetorical power. Apollo's "Ai" even carries both the originary emotions
described by Rousseau: desire and need. Moreover, the mention of Hyacinth's death, and the use of the word "Scythian" to describe the blossom-
shattering wind, serve as possible allusions to the greedy, competitive, and
divisive emotions that in Rousseau's analysis lead to the decay of language.

That is to say, the jealousy of Zephyrus, Apollo's rival for the love of Hyacinth, fanned the breeze that made Apollo's discus swerve and kill his beloved, while "Scythian" gives what could have been a purely climatic statement associations with human rapacity and tyranny. It recalls Lear's allusion to "the barbarous Scythian / Or he that makes his generation messes / To gorge his appetite" (I.i.116–18) and the description of Tamburlaine as "that sturdie Scythian thief" (*Tamburlaine* pt.1, I.i.36). Finally, both the almond blossoms, even when torn from the tree, and Hyacinth's flower imprinted with the lament over his death are images of an eventual rebirth, a new beginning. Yearly at Apollo's temple in Amyklai, where, according to tradition, Hyacinth was buried, there took place a festival. As in the rites for Adonis, its first days were given over to grief, but it concluded with a joyous celebration (Pausanias I, 164).

These themes are all reinforced by the pictorial images in the parallel dream that, by a process of free association, returns to Asia's mind as she listens to Panthea: "Your words / Fill, pause by pause my own forgotten sleep / With shapes" (II.i.141–43). Brought together in the scene she remembers are references to diurnal, seasonal, and phylogenetic infancy: the dawn, the spring, and the pastoral form of life. In the lines that follow all three endure mutability and eventual death. The morning clouds vanish, and the grasses wither, while a comparison between the sighing of the pine boughs and "the farewell of ghosts" (II.i.156–58) recalls the passing of human generations. Yet the paradoxical message of each is that a return to those origins—"*O follow, follow, follow me!*" (II.i.160)—holds the secret of renewed life.

Generalizing from such passages as these, Daniel J. Hughes writes that "Shelley, in his most ambitious poem, can be seen as cleansing the ontological situation, restoring our sense of the potential, turning, through a series of verbal strategies, the actual back upon itself" (108). I agree but would underline the significance of human infancy to that "sense of potential." No infants appear in Asia's dream, but the infant state is implicit in the other images of newly formed life filled with vulnerable potential. They serve as metaphors for the period in which the predawn of infancy merges into the dawn of "thought" through the acquisition of language. "Echoes" from that time dominate the remainder of this scene and the one that follows.

Shelley's deliberate choice of the word "echoes" or "echo" in place of "voices" or "voice" used in the draft and fair copy versions (*SPU* 118, 120; Shelley, *Prometheus Unbound Notebooks* 281–83) to describe those whom Lilian Steichen has called the "ministers" of Demogorgon (48; *V* 431) is a dismayingly unscientific use of the term for a Newton among the poets, since, as Grabo notes, "these are not echoes [but] rather spirit voices" (57). Although any explanation involves guesswork, I take it that Shelley wanted the concept of repetition associated with the word "echo," which is already present in the many reiterations of the rhyming word "follow." These echoes do not repeat words we hear spoken in the immediate dialogue, save in the first instance (II.i.162), when the Echo takes up Asia's closing words, "Follow, follow." They must, then, be repeating words spoken or heard before or

elsewhere which they serve to recall. To call them echoes conjures up a
"before" that remains mysteriously uncharacterized.

Also the echoes are elusive. The chirographic stability granted in the
letters stamped upon the almond blossoms has already changed by Asia's next
speech. There the words "*Follow, O follow*" (II.i.153) are "written" once
more, but on clouds, and they (clouds and words) vanish; they appear as
blazing letters on "each herb," but these letters become "a withering fire"
(II.i.155). Now they become sounds only, and the echoes insist on submission
to the temporal mutability of speech: "Echoes we—listen! / We cannot stay /
As dew-stars glisten / Then fade away" (II.i.166–69). Walter Ong's interpretation of the same message is:

> Sound exists only when it is going out of existence: in uttering the word
> "existence," by the time I get to the "tence," the "exis" is gone and has to
> be gone. A spoken word, even when it refers to a statically modeled
> "thing," is itself never a thing or even a "sign" ("sign" refers primarily to
> something seen and thus, however subtly, reduces the aural to the visual
> and the static). No real word can be present all at once as the letters in a
> written "word" are. The real word, the spoken word, is always an event,
> whatever its codified associations with concepts, thought of as immobile
> objectifications. In this sense, the spoken word is an action, an ongoing
> part of ongoing existence. (20–21)

Ong's ironic quotation marks around the written "word" bracket off static
visual language from the real, because such language gives a factitious and
delusory sense of escape from time; spoken words, by contrast, are real
through their immersion in temporality. So his very positive conclusion to this
paragraph of analysis suggests; but the opening ideas of the same paragraph
open up questions about the *spoken* word's reality as well. "Word" in this
instance too is something of a misnomer, since it gives the illusion of singleness and coherence to what is actually a continuum of sounds, broken by
pauses of varying lengths, impossible to circumscribe as a whole or an entity,
and irretrievable even while it is being uttered.

In the Echoes' statement "We cannot stay," the pronoun "we," referring
as it does to the echoes both as sounds and as (presumed) entities, draws a
close parallel between the temporal and thus evanescent nature of spoken
language and the mutability of subjectivity itself. As it does in Ong's analysis
of language, the mutable nature of the subject has strong positive as well as
negative aspects: only as "an ongoing part of ongoing existence" does subjectivity function at all; yet as such an ongoing part it constantly "fades
away."

By juxtaposing the Echoes' self-description with Ong's commentary on the
difference between the written and the spoken word, I do not intend to
contradict my earlier positive reading of "Apollo's written grief." Or, better
said, the contradiction may arise unavoidably from unresolved oppositions in
Shelley's own thought. As another instance, in *A Defence of Poetry* the same
paradoxical difficulty arises when Shelley contrasts poetry with the subjectiv-

ity that creates it. He repeats the thought extrapolated from Sir William Drummond's epistemology that "all things exist as they are perceived: at least in relation to the percipient," and in a complicated misreading he brings Milton's authority forward as witness to this Humean concept: " 'The mind is its own place, and of itself can make a heaven of hell, a hell of heaven.' " With exactly the same language that Milton uses to describe Satan's permanent state of damnation, Shelley dismisses the possibility that any permanence exists and then adds, "But poetry defeats the curse that binds us to be subjected to the accident of surrounding impressions" (*SPP* 505). Shelley writes as a proto-modernist when he so states his faith in the stability of an artwork produced by a cursedly unstable subjectivity and at the same time as a proto-postmodernist when he demonstrates the instability even of art through his misreading of Milton.

In the present scene Shelley adopts another strategy, turning his attention from the possibility of an immortal product that will arrest "the vanishing apparitions which haunt the interlunations of life" (*SPP* 505) and thinking instead in positive rather than negative terms about the evanescence of both language and subjectivity. That is, the Echoes are asking Asia and Panthea to give over that sense of language's spatiality that also structures a belief in a constant, formed, and enduring consciousness—"a being within our being," as Shelley writes in *A Defence* (*SPP* 505)—and immerse themselves in a temporal experience of language and subjectivity as process. The Echoes' self-description—"We cannot stay / As dew-stars glisten / Then fade away— / Child of Ocean! (II.i.167–70)—also allows a reading in which the culminating apostrophe to Asia includes a command that with and like them she "fade away."

Such an interpretation of their task adds a further dimension to Pottle's statement that "Asia's difficulty in these scenes is to overcome the scruples that would keep her from surrendering herself to a duty which is disquietingly pleasant" (137). His emphasis in describing this duty is on Asia's abnegation of physical control over her body's movements. I would take such loss as symptomatic of a deeper surrender of the organizing consciousness to an influx of powerful sensory perceptions.

Asia's duty seems precisely the task and the achievement ascribed to poets as they struggle to create that which "purges from our inward sight the film of familiarity which obscures from us the wonder of our being" (*SPP* 505). The fact that two female characters perform it here may in part be Shelley's way of distancing his masculine persona from the vulnerability of thus losing control over the ego's boundaries. Also, by an associative projection the renewed experience that will transform a language grown false becomes one with a feminine presence encountered in an earlier introduction to "the wonder of our being."

In their next song the Echoes describe the route to be taken as one that follows the sound of their voices "through the caverns hollow / Where the forest spreadeth" (II.i.175–76)—that is, through the cavern of the mouth, which serves as instrument for making sound; the cavern of the ear, which is the sound's auditory medium; and the cavern of the skull, where signals from the organs of sense become sensory perceptions.

My basis for this reading of the lines, apart from Shelley's statement in the preface to *Prometheus Unbound* that the imagery of the drama is "drawn from the operations of the human mind, or from those external actions by which they are expressed" (*SPP* 133), is the striking metaphor in Drummond's *Academical Questions* that makes the ear a "cavern." But the caverns in which sounds are either made or heard demand another in which they are actually registered, since, as Drummond points out, it is necessary to distinguish between the ear's physical reception of a sound and the mind's recording of it, though "when we are asked, how the mind becomes percipient of the existence of sound by means of the ear, we find it impossible to answer" (122).[14]

Wary of possible reification, particularly in light of Matthews's comment about the "overdetermined" nature of the imagery in *Prometheus Unbound,* I am confident nonetheless that a proper understanding of our location at this point puts us within a perceiving mind described metonymically as a landscape. In "Mont Blanc" that landscape was a river flowing through a mountain gorge; here it is a forest towered over by huge caves. In other words, it is a scene very like the one surrounding Shelley as he wrote in the Baths of Caracalla, "among the flowery glades, and thickets of odoriferous blossoming trees which are extended in ever winding labyrinths upon its immense platforms and dizzy arches suspended in the air" (*SPP* 133). While writing, however, Shelley was presumably seated up on one of the platforms; the Echoes' song leads down into the labyrinth so thick with vegetation that noontide there is "darkness deep":

> As the song floats, thou pursue
> Where the wild bee never flew,
> Through the noontide darkness deep,
> By the odour breathing sleep
> Of faint night flowers, and the waves
> At the fountain-lighted caves,
> While our music, wild and sweet,
> Mocks thy gently-falling feet,
>   Child of Ocean!
>   (II.i.179–87)

Shelley's substitution of "wild bee" for what in the draft version was "night bird" (*SPU* 118), offers somewhat Bloomian evidence that Shelley sees the "intellectual philosophy," with Drummond as its explicator, as one that makes available to him concepts that Shakespeare lacked. When changed thus, the line alludes very explicitly to Ariel's "where the bee sucks, there suck I," but suggests farther and more daring flights. Also the lines mock, in the sense of that word to which I return later (i.e., keep time with or imitate in another form), the prosodic beat of Ariel's song. How much Ariel was in Shelley's consciousness as he wrote shows in a repetition of the word "aerial"; one draft version of "Mocks thy gently-falling feet" reads "Echoes thine aerial feet" only twelve lines after a previous use of the word (*SPU* 120).

I pause over this very simple example of intertextuality only for the evidence it gives regarding Shelley's sense of his purpose and method in writing *Prometheus Unbound*. Like Shakespeare, he wants, through the construction of what is admittedly an "insubstantial pageant," to lay bare the evils of society and to offer the vision of a better one. But although Ariel, as Prospero's agent, uses his sleights to lead characters into self-betrayal of their mendacity or brutality, his magic does not explore those hidden areas of the psyche from which arise both the motivations for such acts and the human bonds that may forestall them. So *this* Ariel song will take up where the other left off.

If, as Asia is soon to say, "speech created thought" (II.iv.71), then this entire exploration of the nature of human subjectivity can be considered an inquiry into the nature of language. The next lines of the Echoes' song bring forward that theme, although they offer an exemplification rather than an analysis of the way in which language works: "By the odour breathing sleep / Of faint night flowers, and the waves / At the fountain-lighted caves" (II.i.182–84).

Paraphrased just for conceptual meaning the lines say: "Follow the sound of our voices past night-blooming flowers, difficult to see because of this deep shade and also because they are now closed up, it being noon. You can, though, smell the perfume they give off. You will also pass the fountain sources of streams which, reflecting the little light there is, cast prismatic shimmerings up on the cavern walls overarching your way." The grammatical construction of these phrases, however, including the character of their parts of speech, gives this informational aspect of their function a place totally secondary to their auditory effect. For instance, every significant word, including "faint," in the phrases governed by the prepositions "by" and "of" is a possible noun, although some take on adjectival function in context—once we know the context. So as we set out, spatially oriented through the presence of "by," we first meet "odour," then "breathing," then "sleep." Each elicits response from different senses: the olfactory (and possibly the closely related gustatory), the auditory, and the proprioceptive. But since within the phrase "odour" and "breathing" modify "sleep," they take on the functions of adjective and participle to create a grammatical and linear disorientation accompanied by a tripling of their synesthetic physicality. This slight rational disorientation highlights the nonarbitrary, affective, kinesthetic, and presence-laden attributes of language.

The link between prelinguistic communication and the transmodal perception so important in infancy also makes language more than a purely arbitrary system of signs. Again, lines in the Echoes' song illustrate the nature of that perception without abstract comment on it: "While our music, wild and sweet, / Mocks thy gently-falling feet, / Child of Ocean!" (II.i.185–87). In *On the Origin of Language* Rousseau states that "at first, there was no music but

melody and no other melody than the varied sounds of speech" (51).
Phylogenetically unverifiable, his thought is at least borne out ontogenetically
by those observing the interactions between infants and their mothers. Anne
Fernald's research has shown, for instance, that "the intonations of motherese, characterized by exaggerated pitch level and range, slow rhythm and
tempo, and relatively smooth and simple pitch contours, appear to be attractive to infants" ("Perceptual and Affective Salience" 9).[15] Speech, then, according to both the Kristevan and the developmental narratives, is first experienced as melody.

The auditory experience of hearing is also a visual experience, since the
speaking lips move, and, as Daniel Stern shows, infants do indeed note these
audio-visual correspondences (*Interpersonal World* 50). But Lawrence Marks
points out the close connection as well between touch and hearing: "Both
modalities are excited by mechanical energy, that is, by changes in patterns of
pressure at the receptors, and both show phenomenological as well as psychophysical similarities" (182). Such relatedness makes them well suited to the
fostering of the "affect attunement" between mother and child described by
Stern. The mother's sense of participation in the infant's experience expresses
itself not through a total imitation or mirroring (which can easily become
mocking in the negative sense of that word, and which, moreover, gives
evidence only that the mother has noted an action and not that she shares an
emotion) but as a repetition of the child's response in another modality. And,
as was discussed in Chapter 1, this use of the infant's early and extraordinary
capacity to perceive transmodally functions as an important step toward language and at the same time fills language during the process of its acquisition
both with powerful affective content and with the traces of these fused experiences across all sensory modes. Wittgenstein appears to refer to some process
of this kind, when, as a comment on the possibility that "every familiar
word . . . actually carries an atmosphere with it in our minds, a 'corona' of
lightly indicated uses" (181e), he suggests: "Now, I say nothing about the
causes of this phenomenon. They *might* be associations from my childhood"
(216e). Paradoxically, the aspect of language that seems to Wittgenstein most
idiosyncratically bound up with the separateness of each individual psyche
may offer insight into a psychic permeability, an interpersonal relatedness at
the heart of subjectivity and language.[16]

Wittgenstein's speculation becomes transformed into factual description
when considered from Bakhtin's very different view of the nature of subjectivity. In "The Spatial Form of the Hero" Bakhtin describes the growth of
subjectivity in terms that bear some resemblance to Lacan's "mirroring," but
with the crucial difference that, like Stern, Bakhtin predicates an interaction
between two (or more) subjectivities—even if one is frailer and more incipi-
ent than the other—rather than the delusory introjection by an as yet unformed subject of an Other that shapes it. Bakhtin writes:

> The plastic value of my outer body has been as it were sculpted for me by
> the manifold acts of other people in relation to me, acts performed intermit-

tently throughout my life: acts of concern for me, acts of love, acts that recognize my value. In fact as soon as a human being begins to experience himself from within, he at once meets with acts of love and recognition that come from the outside—from his mother, from others who are close to him. The child receives all initial determinations of himself and of his body from his mother's lips and from the lips of those who are close to him. It is from their lips, in the emotional-volitional tones of their love, that the child hears and begins to acknowledge *his own proper name* and the names of all the features pertaining to his body and to his inner states and experiences. . . . The child begins to see himself for the first time through his mother's eyes, and begins to speak about himself in his mother's emotional-volitional tones—he caresses himself, as it were, with his first uttered self-expression. (Art and Answerability 49–50; author's emphasis)

The Echoes' description of what will happen during Asia's journey with Panthea should, then, allay any fears the travelers might have, calling up as it does the situation of a mother playing with her child, the movements of the one "mocked" by the participatory rhythmic sounds of the other. Indeed, the draft version uses the word "answers," which suggests my positive and "interpersonal" interpretation of "mocks" (*SPU* 120). Both in the connection made among speech, song, and rhythmic movement and in the disorientation of strict linear meaning in order to highlight the affective power of language, the Echoes' song exemplifies the "true" language that Shelley hopes will vanquish the false Jupiterean language repudiated by Prometheus in act one. And this redemptive language can best be understood through analysis of infant experience.

Moreover, while the correspondences between language, music, and rhythmic movement are implied in the lines just discussed, they become explicit in the Echoes' pun at the conclusion of the next brief song: "In a world unknown / Sleeps a voice unspoken; / By thy step alone / Can its rest be broken, / Child of Ocean!" (II.i.190–94). The Echoes encourage Asia to follow because her presence alone has the power to release a potential energy so far dormant and hidden from others' knowledge. Their words also associate that untapped potential with language now holding a "rest"—an interval of silence—albeit a very long interval. Her "step" becomes the conductor's baton that prompts its renewed sound.

Thus, while I agree with Daniel Hughes's thesis that the action of *Prometheus Unbound* turns on the "cleansing" of the actual through the retrieval of potentiality (108), we have very different interpretations of what that potentiality involves. He writes that Shelley "*is* concerned with reform in the poem, but the reform is more metaphysical then political and more ontological than social" (122; author's emphasis). In fact, the constant emphasis in the drama on the nature of language fuses the political, the social, and the ontological into seamless unity. And since the ontological involves the mystery of subjective being, one can on those terms restore "metaphysical," making unity fourfold. By following the Echoes, Asia is told, she will open up a form of language now lost and in doing so create a new humanity living in a new world.

The mention of a "voice unspoken" calls up through the association of contraries the opening of the Gospel of John, a hymn in praise of Jesus, the spoken Word of God through whom the world is created. As such a subtext, the gospel underlines the theme of Creation, but it also serves to emphasize the routing of a previous order in the establishment of this new one. In act one Prometheus refuses to name Jesus because (although Prometheus absolves Jesus of blame for what occurred) his Word has been used to justify the institutions of despotic power in both their religious and their secular form (I.i.603–15). That power as represented in Shelley's drama by Jupiter has banished another potential Word at the same time that Prometheus was pinioned on the Caucasus. The story told in act one by Mother Earth about the conflict hints at this in the mention of a volcanic presence driven underground but still active: "and new fire / From earthquake-rifted mountains of bright snow / Shook its portentous hair beneath Heaven's frown" (I.i.166–68).

The last song of the Echoes and the conclusion of this scene recall the same moment. Repeating their earlier mention of "caverns" (II.i.175, 178) and the allusion to woods so deep that the dews of morning remain even at noontide, they describe the rest of the journey through a landscape that suddenly roughens:

> O follow, follow!
>   Through the caverns hollow,
> As the song floats thou pursue,
> By the woodland noontide dew,
> By the forests, lakes and fountains,
> Through the many-folded mountains,
> To the rents and gulphs and chasms
> Where the Earth reposed from spasms
> On the day when He and thou
> Parted—to commingle now,
>   Child of Ocean!
>   (II.i.196–206)

In Earth's account of the cataclysm, her emphasis was on her own parting from Prometheus ("for my wan breast was dry / With grief" [I.i.176–77]). Here Earth's spasms at the separation fuse with and mirror the feelings of desperate alienation experienced by Asia and Prometheus—another piece of textual evidence for the close link between Asia and Mother Earth. At least Prometheus seems to be the referent for "He," given Earth's earlier version of the story. Yet the immediacy of "now" and the allusion in the Echoes' previous song to "the voice unspoken" which is Asia's present goal suggest that "He" may be—or may also be—the now silent possessor of that voice. An earlier draft of these lines gives the owner of the voice a name and makes the "He" whom Asia is about to meet much more unambiguously Demogorgon: "Hunt the babbling of the fountains / To their cradles in the mountains / Where on Demogorgons throne / A veiled darkness sits Alone" (*SPU* 120). If that draft, palimpsest-fashion, is seen as a shadowy presence below the final version, the effect is one of virtual identification, with Asia parted from and about to commingle with them both.

By canceling these lines, Shelley eliminated the phrase "cradles in the mountains" that makes the metaphorical connection, so dear to the Romantics, between the source of a stream and infancy. In its place, however, he puts a much stronger allusion to life's source when he uses language that evokes the violence of a human birth to describe the earthquakes that produced this landscape. The effect is to make us as fully—even uncomfortably—aware as it is possible to be of a metaphoric and a metonymic relation between Asia's journey into these "rents and gulphs and chasms" and the exploration of yet another fleshly cavern, the interior of the mother's body, an unknown but once familiar "world."

The "forest" setting of act two, scene two, its formal structure, and its allusive complexity make this part of the play both a commentary on the pastoral and an example of the genre. In August 1818 Shelley had given himself what amounted to a graduate seminar in the pastoral, reading Theocritus, Virgil's *Georgics,* Horace, and Spenser's *Shepheardes Calender,* while he finished *Rosalind and Helen.* That venture, as Shelley himself seems to have realized, was not particularly successful (White I, 533), and stubbornly in *Prometheus Unbound* he returned to the challenge of what in *Rosalind and Helen* he had attempted but not achieved. In the semichoruses of the Spirits that make up the greater portion of act two, scene two, using the urbane, mediated, and in Paul Alpers's phrase "self-reflexive" (244) tradition of pastoral poets, Shelley interiorizes landscape, transmuting it into text, into multiple texts juxtaposed and superimposed.

Matthews takes us at an elegantly brisk pace through the forest filled with the throbbing song of nightingales that is described in these semichoruses. He reads the packed literary allusions as a brief summary of "successive schools of poetry," with special mention given to "Spenser (in echoes of the opening canto of the *Faerie Queene*); Shakespeare (the opening of *Twelfth Night*); Milton (the opening of the 'Nightingale' sonnet); probably Gray, whose 'Progress of Poesy' had adopted the same idea of successive schools of poetry; perhaps the 'frail form' of Shelley himself (the anemone)" (207).

The works cited by Matthews are all, indeed, by a succession of poets and exhibit a variety of different verse forms, but, like the model for this scene— Virgil's *Sixth Eclogue,* as Wasserman has noted (310)—they are all versions of pastoral or have reference to the tradition of pastoral. Moreover, the allusions tend to cluster around the myth most closely identified with that tradition, the story of Venus and Adonis. Matthews associates the lines "The path through which that lovely twain / Have past, by cedar, pine and yew, / And each dark tree that ever grew" (II.ii.1–3) with stanzas near the opening of Spenser's *Faerie Queene* that catalogue the trees in the grove where Una and the Red Cross Knight take shelter (bk. I, canto 1, st. 8–9). But an at least equally apt referent is Spenser's description in book three of the Garden of Adonis (canto 6, st. 34). Indeed, the second seems the more important connection, since it forms a link in turn with Gray's "Progress of Poesy." The "progress" of the title refers punningly both to the advancement of poetry "from Greece to Italy, and from Italy to England" (*Poetical Works of Gray and Collins* 49) and to the imaging of that advance as Aphrodite's procession in state. Her progress culminates in a union/reunion with Shakespeare-as-Adonis: "To Him the mighty Mother did unveil / Her aweful face" (ll. 86–87).

In sum, all the poets on Matthews's list wrote noteworthy pastorals, and within the pastoral tradition versions of the Venus and Adonis story reappear constantly as laments for a beloved youth, himself an exquisite lyricist, struck down by early death but still alive within the landscape that he loved and in the poems his mourning comrades sing for him. David Halperin in *Before Pastoral* gives special attention to this theme. His research on it leads him to the conclusion that, while Theocritus may be credited with the invention of a literary mode named "bucolic" by him and his contemporaries, "all the components of pastoral poetry can be found long before Theocritus" (115). Among these "components" are a number of ancient laments in Sumerian literature for the shepherd-god Dumuzi: "The original identity of Dumuzi is much disputed, but it is generally agreed that he was a divine figure associated in some way with the pastoral economy, that he died or was killed, and that he was the subject of ritual mourning which continued into historical times and of which traces still persist today" (112).

Explicit knowledge of Sumerian culture was not available to Shelley. Even without such scholarly background, however, he could—and did—find the theme Halperin describes in the classical pastoral poetry to which he gave his close attention. What is more, the poems expressing that theme so fascinated Shelley that he chose to translate them: Bion's elegy to Adonis, Moschus' elegy on the death of Bion, the love mourning of Gallus in Virgil's *Tenth Eclogue,* and a passage from Virgil's *Fourth Georgic* that includes the lines: "He went in wonder through the path immortal / Of his great Mother, and her humid reign" (*CW* IV, 284–89). And of course this particular "component" of pastoral was shortly to be the theme of "Adonais."

The poetic allusions in the first two semichoruses, then, are not so much to "successive schools of poetry" as to a single poetic tradition, the pastoral, and more specifically to a strong theme in that tradition: the boar's tusk of sexuality that kills the mother's son/lover, the shepherd/poet, also produces those poetic forms that shape into landscaped text what would otherwise be endless and speechless vegetation. The shepherd's brother poets, bound in the same service, pipe his songs as part of their own in a process epitomized by the poetic echoes of the semichoruses. So breath, image of the ephemeral human, is the medium that ensures immortality, as with the nightingales described in "Semichorus II" of this scene, when one "Sick with sweet love, droops dying away / On its mate's music-panting bosom—/Another from the swinging blossom, / Watching to catch the languid close / Of the last strain, then lifts on high / The wings of the weak melody" (II.ii.28–33). It is worth noting briefly at the same time that in Shelley's topos the *singing* nightingales are male; the mate's bosom pants in response to his music, but she, like the surrounding woods, is mute.

I will consider in the next section the particular appropriateness of the pastoral as accompaniment to the Oceanides on this journey but turn now to the significance of other allusions. The song of the nightingales in this thick forest of texts creates a link between the wafted passage of the "destined" Asia and Panthea and the final journey of the aged Oedipus, who finds himself at his foreordained resting place, the grove outside Athens sacred to the Eumenides. As critics have noted (Locock 610; Wilson 44–45), these "noonday" nightingales echo those in *Oedipus at Colonus* who sing within the dark recesses of the goddesses' "maternal land." In both passages also the birds are associated with Dionysian ivy:

> In the god's untrodden vale
> Where leaves and berries throng,
> And wine-dark ivy climbs the bough,
> The sweet, sojourning nightingale
> Murmurs all day long.
>
> (ll. 671–75)

The close connection in Shelley's mind between the action of *Oedipus Tyrannus* and *Oedipus at Colonus* reveals itself in a footnote drafted originally for the preface to *The Cenci* but eventually quoted in Mary Shelley's note to *Prometheus Unbound*. Shelley, commenting on line 67 of *Oedipus Tyrannus*— "Coming to many ways in the wanderings of careful thought"—moves quickly away from the actual context, Oedipus' attempt to unravel the mystery of the plague, to consider what the line foreshadows:

> If the words ὁδοὺς and πλάνοις had not been used, the line might have been explained in a metaphorical, instead of an absolute sense, as we say "ways and means," and wanderings for error and confusion; but they meant literally paths or roads, such as we tread with our feet; and wanderings such as a man makes when he loses himself in a desert, or roams from city to city, as Oedipus, the speaker of this verse was destined to wander, blind and asking charity. What a picture does this line suggest of the mind as a wilderness of intricate paths, wide as the universe, which is here made its symbol, a world within a world, which he, who seeks some knowledge with respect to what he ought to do, searches throughout, as he would search the external universe for some valued thing which was hidden from him upon its surface. (Shelley, *Poetical Works* II, 137)

The phrase "a world within a world" is yet another way of expressing Shelley's dictum that "nothing exists but as it is perceived"; it is the inner world of perceptions bound up with the thoughts, reflections, memories, and emotions they create that can be described. The "outer" world *means* only in terms of the inner and thus is its "symbol" or complement.

Allusions to the Oedipal story, sprinkled as they are at key points throughout the action of *Prometheus Unbound,* suggest that the two dramas enact a similar interior journey. Act one of *Prometheus Unbound*—where, as we have seen, the phrase "eyeless in hate" (I.i.9) has ambiguous reference to both Jupiter and Prometheus—like one part of the Oedipus cycle describes the tragic conflict with the father produced by the mirroring nature of desire. All male relationships involve a struggle for power, in which language is a false and tyrannical instrument given its fullest expression in a curse.

This is the pattern for human interaction that Prometheus rejects in act one by withdrawing his curse on Zeus, and act two explores another basis for social ordering, for which again the Oedipus cycle offers a model: reestablishment of an ancient connection with the mother. Just as Asia and Panthea are borne by "the storm of sound" to Demogorgon's cave, so Oedipus, "driven / By an insistent voice that come from God" (ll. 1541–42), makes his own way—unguided despite his blindness—deep into the Eumenides' grove. And, dying there, he, like the Dionysian Adonis and the dead young shepherd of the pastoral tradition, lives again in the fertility of the land and its related artistic riches.[17]

The two Oceanides, we are told, have the sense of a goal toward which they move with what they imagine to be "their own swift wings and feet" (II.ii.55). In fact, however, "from the breathing Earth behind / There steams a plume-uplifting wind / Which drives them on their path" (II.ii.52–54). In back of them, impelling them and surrounding them, is the Mother. All the sounds they hear are ventriloquisms of her breath. So while Earth, like Prometheus, does not appear on stage during act two, the actions of those who do—Asia, Panthea, and Demogorgon—serve as outward representations of some continuing inner interaction between mother and son. We are, then, in a state of reverie in which the mind reviews different instances of the pastoral myth about an erotic relation between the Mother Goddess of Love and the shepherd-poet and broods on the meaning of that legend. Doing so it moves— or is moved—toward the answer to questions as yet unframed.

Ritual Descent (Scenes iii and iv)

The critical opinion that placed the entire dramatic action of *Prometheus Unbound* in act one, seeing it as centered on the moment at which Prometheus repents his curse against Jupiter, has given place over the past two decades to an interpretation that makes the turning point of the play occur at Asia's meeting with Demogorgon. In Curran's words, "the center of *Prometheus Unbound* occurs in Demogorgon's chthonic realm where Asia confronts the ultimate force of the drama's universe" (*Annus Mirabilis* 38). Yet a conviction that the center occurs there does not in itself carry knowledge of what occurs at that center, and Demogorgon's own dark shapelessness can have a contagious effect on the scholarly prose of those struggling, as I am here, to limn his outlines.

Matthews's account, at once learned and clear, manages to resist the cave's vapors. According to his reading of the images and allusions of act two, what occurs is that the watery Oceanides, Asia and Panthea, pour into Demogorgon's "molten magma, the obscure and terrible volcanic agent hidden in the depths of the earth" (215). The result, predictable according to the volcanic theory of Shelley's time, is "a violent eruption, accompanied by the classic symptoms: earthquakes; mephitic vapors; the familiar pine-tree cloud" (216). The common metaphorical connection between such volcanic upheaval and social revolution makes this "external action" the depiction of a widespread popular uprising against autocratic rulers, with δῆμος-γοργώ [people-terror] a fitting name for the power thus unleashed (222).

While fully convincing, Matthews's interpretation, as he himself was the first to acknowledge, leaves a number of questions unanswered. Most significant among them are: "What is the relation of Demogorgon to Prometheus?" and "What is the purport on a social level of Asia's part in the drama?" (228). All the same, his reading cuts a preliminary route, carving out a series of handgrips and footholds for successive scholarly descents.

Grateful for them, Wasserman adds others: the volcanic imagery of act two makes it possible for Shelley to fuse Boccaccio's description of Demogorgon as the first of all the gods, who dwells below Mount Taenarus or Aetna, with Virgil's account in the sixth book of the *Aeneid* of the volcanic region through which the Sibyl guides Aeneas to Anchises in the underworld (156–57). Curran, acknowledging the importance of Wasserman's intertextual reading, adds to it the significant point that Aeneas' descent serves as the only extensive account of the ancient initiatory mystery rituals (*Annus Mirabilis* 53). He draws out the allusions to Eastern, Middle Eastern, and Greek cults embedded in the text of *Prometheus Unbound,* while focusing mainly on Zoroastrian conceptions as those that influence "the structure, machinery, and ideas of *Prometheus Unbound*" and "reinforce the ethical problems and antitheses at the drama's core" (85).

There is no need to rehearse the details of Curran's readily available and enormously helpful scholarly findings. Still obscure, however, is Shelley's motive for employing this cumbersome machinery. Curran rejects the notion that "Shelley's learned fusion of occidental and oriental mythic structures in *Prometheus Unbound*" spirals, like Peacock's, around pleasure in knowledge for its own sake (95) or betrays, like John Newton's, the quirkiness of an idiosyncratic crank (90). Behind Shelley's syncretism, he suggests, is the desire to construct a humanist ethic (87). Precisely how the esoteric lore and the ethical purpose join, however, evades final articulation. And Matthews's questions remain unanswered.

Just at the point where Curran begins to build his own argument on the foundations laid by Wasserman, he provides a link between syncretism and a revolutionary humanist ethic: "Descending into the cave of the great Demiurge is the ritual process of the Orphic and Mithraic mysteries, preserved in altered form for Shelley's time in the initiation rites of Masonry" (53). A later footnote alludes to the fact that French Masonic rituals were designed to achieve a oneness with the " 'Soul of the World' and . . . the German Illuminati, the subject of Hogg's *Memoirs of Prince Alexy Haimatoff,* patterned their rites after the Mithraic models" (217). Perhaps Curran judges Shelley's own fascination with the Illuminati to have been only a youthful enthusiasm, for he makes no mention of it. I would like to consider the very

real possibility that Shelley's interest in Masonic rituals of various kinds continued for a number of years, influenced his thinking about other possible forms
of "brotherhood," and had considerable imaginative effect on his dramatization of Asia's descent into the cave of Demogorgon and her colloquy there
with that mysterious power. I am not thereby trying to suggest that Shelley
himself was an initiated Mason. My point, rather, is that Shelley, like the
Masons, is using symbols drawn syncretically from Eastern, Middle Eastern,
Greek, and Christian sources in order to give ritual substance to a transfigur-
ing vision that makes possible a renewed humanity—and that he is doing so
aware of the Masonic precedent.

From Oxford on March 2, 1811, Shelley wrote his first letter to Leigh
Hunt, congratulating him for having been acquitted of the government's accusation of libel for material printed in *The Examiner* and inviting his interest in
a "scheme of mutual safety and mutual identification for men of public spirit
and principle." He proposes the founding of a "methodical society" and adds:

> It has been for want of societies of this nature that corruption has attained
> the height at which we now behold it, nor can any of us bear in mind the very
> great influence, which some years since was gained by *Illuminism* without
> considering that a society of equal extent might establish *rational liberty* on
> as firm a basis as that which would have supported the visionary schemes of
> a completely-equalized community.   (*L* I, 54; author's emphasis)

Shelley's mention of Illuminism refers to a secret society, the Illuminati of
Bavaria, founded in 1776 by Adam Weishaupt. Though not Masonic in origin,
the society used Masonic rituals and by the 1780s was inextricably involved
with Masonic lodges in Austria (Chailley 64). The source of Shelley's knowledge about Weishaupt's doings was, paradoxically, a four-volume fulmination
against them by Abbé Barruel in *Memoirs Illustrating the History of Jacobinism,* published in 1797 (*L* I, 264).

Writing as an impassioned believer in monarchy, hierarchy, and property,
Barruel lays responsibility for the destructive French Revolution that endangered all three at the door of Freemasonry and identifies that movement with
doctrines secretly promulgated by Weishaupt's order—doctrines that in turn
show the effect of "Jacobin" influences such as Voltaire, Rousseau, and Con-
dorcet: "What Jean Jaques teaches his Sophisters, the modern Spartacus
[Weishaupt] infuses into his Illuminized legions, *The fruits belong to all, the
land to none*" (III, 273; author's emphasis). While Shelley decries the secrecy
of the Illuminists and their hierarchicalism, he takes Barruel's revelations
about their activities and their motivations to be true, simply giving them a
strongly positive rather than a negative interpretation. His own "Proposals for
an Association" are based on "the discoveries in the sciences of politics and
morals, which preceded and occasioned the revolutions of America and
France. . . . The names of Paine and Lafayette will outlive the poetic aristocracy of an expatriated Jesuit [Weishaupt]" (*CW* V, 263).

Printed in 1812, "Proposals for an Association" goes back seven years
before the writing of *Prometheus Unbound,* by which time Weishaupt's secret

order could conceivably have become simply a youthful memory for Shelley. But in fact his reading of Barruel continued. In Switzerland during the hectic summer of 1814 and again in the equally hectic autumn, he read the *Memoirs* with Mary and Claire; and Mary sets the title of the book down in her reading list for 1815 (*Journal* I, 19, 34, 90). While in Switzerland Shelley began a "romance," to be titled *The Assassins,* which describes "an ancient brotherhood" whose opinions "considerably resembled those of the sect afterwards known by the name of the Gnostics. They esteemed the human understanding to be the paramount rule of human conduct; they maintained that the obscurest religious truth required for its complete elucidation no more than the strenuous application of the energies of the mind" (*CW* VI, 155), a version of "Gnostic" doctrine that shows the same fusion of esoteric mysticism and rationalist humanism that Barruel attributes to the Illuminati.

Meanwhile, in 1813 Hogg published the *Memoirs of Prince Alexy Haimatoff,* which one might flatteringly describe as a picaresque novel. Its penultimate incidents take place in Germany, where Alexy goes through the preliminary stages of initiation into a secret society but is banished to England when he refuses to swear absolute obedience to the council of Eleutheri, whatever their command (100–129). Hogg terminated the initiation in this fashion, very possibly, because after imagining for Alexy a night's vigil sitting beside a corpse and holding a skull, he could think up no further trials and no enlightenments, Barruel's account being too general for his purposes. Shelley, in reviewing the book, gives that segment of it special notice as "the sketch of a profounder project" and regrets that it "is introduced and concluded with unintelligible abruptness" (*CW* VI, 181).

Although Barruel's work remained in Shelley's library, there are no further references to it after 1815, and a Shelley as yet unembarked on "Alastor" is different from the Shelley at work on *Prometheus Unbound.* Still, between 1815 and 1818 Shelley's association with a small brotherhood continued a lived as well as a literary connection between esoteric knowledge, radical politics, and fraternal bonding. Shelley, Peacock, Hogg, and Hunt were the "Athenians" (in Walter Sidney Scott's locution) who made up the group, with John Frank Newton as a presence on its periphery through his continued friendship with Hogg. Writing to Peacock in April 1819, Hogg, bedridden with rheumatism and so perhaps exaggeratedly elegiac, gives a sense nonetheless of how significant the interaction was. He contrasts his "now lifeless life" with "that winter at Bishopsgate [1815], which was a mere Atticism"—"mere" used, appropriately, with its Latinate meaning of "undiluted"—and concludes, "When I think of these the most splendid hours of my existence . . . I trust that I shall find a road, which will lead me back to these good things and that some God will be to me a giver of them" (Scott 55–56).

Like the secret language in which the Eleutheri train Alexy Haimatoff, Greek served as the group's private means of discourse. True, knowledge of Greek was open in a way that initiation into the Eleutheran signs was not, but it had the cachet of *special* knowledge. When describing to Hogg the bust of Isis to be placed over his study door, Hunt wrote that already inscribed there was a line from Davenant, "To study quiet Nature's pleasant law," and adds: "You, who have perhaps only Greek friends, will say that the inscription should have been in Greek; but I who have friends that *love* Greek, I may say, *without knowing it . . .* ought not to make them sensible that they do not know it" (51; author's emphasis). The insiders-outsiders dichotomy created by Hunt suggests that the knowledge of Greek functioned as a special sign of brotherhood.

Moreover, the kinds of works shared among members of the group tended to be more arcane than those read by the few Greek scholars among educated, upper- and upper-middle-class men of the time, since Latin, not Greek, was the classical language emphasized in public schools and in the universities. The "Athenians" pored over the better-known works such as those by Plato, Aristotle, the dramatists, and Herodotus, but read besides in more recondite authors such as Nonnus, Pausanias, Porphyrius, and Strabo (Scott 36). And enthusiasm for such reading took on for them a certain cultic significance. So it is in the language of religious conversion (mocking that language but also echoing it) that Hogg writes to Shelley: "When you did not esteem the Classics ('pace vestra,' let me use so impious an expression that once there was a time when you preferred the Ghost seers of Germany to the Philosophers of Greece.) I was anxious that you should see your error, but not very anxious for I knew that such an error could not be lasting" (42).

By admiring all things Greek, this circle was, of course, swimming in what had been the cultural mainstream for over a generation, but they were also disporting in quieter (though still fairly crowded) bywaters where knowledge of the "mysteries"—Egyptian, Mithraic, Greek, and Gnostic—lent itself to a variety of countercultural purposes. A presiding spirit there was Thomas Taylor, whom Coleridge described as "the English Pagan" (*Collected Letters* 260). Anticlerical and anti-Christian but not in other ways a social revolutionary,[18] Taylor seems to have hoped to restore the worship of the old gods, and among this group of much younger men Taylor's ideas are echoed or mentioned. Hunt writes (with Huntian insouciance) of the hope that someday the unregenerate "will be struck with a Panic Terror, and that a voice will be heard along the water saying, 'The Great God Pan is alive again,'—upon which the villagers will leave off starving and singing profane hymns, and fall to dancing again" (Scott 44).

Hunt's light allusion to the political, social, and economic as well as the religious consequences of the Great God Pan's resurgence takes on genuine significance with the context of *Prometheus Unbound* because of the important link between Pan and Demogorgon. When Peacock, in a long footnote to canto six of *Rhododaphne,* explains the significance of Demogorgon, this relation to Pan is one of the first things mentioned: "Mythological writers in general afford but little information concerning this terrible Divinity. He is incidentally mentioned in several places by Natalie Comes, who says, in treating of Pan, that Pronapides, in his Protocosmus, makes Pan and the three sister Fates the offspring of Demogorgon." And like Pan, Demogorgon is associatively connected to the pastoral: "This awful Power was so sacred among the Arcadians, that it was held impious to pronounce his name" (VII, 94).[19] Peacock does not mention Lucan's *Pharsalia* in this footnote, a puzzling omission because the context in which Demogorgon's name is used in *Rhododaphne* is best explained by Lucan's epic. Since that context in turns bears upon Demogorgon's significance in *Prometheus Unbound, Rhododaphne* demands a little excursus.

The poem opens in a "hypæthric fane" (VII, 9), the Temple of Love at Thespia, which Peacock had read of in Pausanias (IX.xxvii.1–4). Its Arcadian protagonist, Anthemion, comes there to offer prayers for the health of his beloved, Calliroë, languishing in proto-Victorian fashion from an obscure malady. He has the misfortune, however, to fall into conversation, and from there into an embrace, with a mysterious and very beautiful lady named Rhododaphne. He tears himself away, true in his heart to Calliroë, and returns home to find the latter in blooming health. But alas, when he kisses her with lips last touched by Rhododaphne, his beloved drops lifeless at his feet.

Wandering Byronically "Where giant Pelion's piny steep / Oe'rlooks the wide Ægean deep" (VII, 52), Anthemion is captured by pirates who shortly afterward seize a helpless maiden as another victim. But soon, singing (in terms that owe a great deal to both Ovid and Nonnus) of how the god Dionysus overwhelmed his pirate captors, she stands revealed as Rhododaphne, a Thessalian witch. Through her spell the sailors are shipwrecked, while she and Anthemion are brought safely to shore on her own Thracian coast.

There Anthemion turns in passionate expostulation against her treachery to Calliroë (forgetting his own), to which Rhododaphne responds:

> The Genii of the earth, and sea,
> And air, and fire, my mandates hear.
> Even the dread power, thy Ladon's fear,
> Arcadian Dæmogorgon, knows
> My voice: the ivy or the rose,
> Though torn and trampled on the plain,
> May rise, unite, and bloom again,
> If on his aid I call: thy heart
> Alone resists and mocks my art.
> (VII, 67–8)

The context in which this allusion to Demogorgon appears, as well as the relationship described between that power and Rhododaphne, makes it clear that her literary ancestor, however different in outward aspect, is Erictho, most powerful of the Thessalian witches, whom Pompey's son Sextus visits in book six of *Pharsalia* in order to learn the outcome of the impending battle. This incident must be added to the ritual descents in search of illuminating knowledge that were discussed earlier, for Erictho's abode is a cave not far from "the sightless caverns of Pluto" (Lucan VI. 698), and corpses are her sustenance. Her prophetic medium is the corpse of a soldier, whom she wrests temporarily from the power of Pluto with these words:

> And on you, worst of the world's Rulers, I shall launch the sun's light,
> bursting open your den; and the sudden light shall blast you. Do ye obey
> me? Or must I appeal to Him, at the sound of whose name the earth ever
> quakes and trembles. He looks on the Gorgon's head unveiled; He lashes
> the cowering Fury with her own scourge; He dwells in Tartarus beneath your
> view. (VI. 742–49)

The important parallel between Rhododaphne and Erictho is that both
Thessalian witches can lay claim to the services of this terrifying male presence, while at the same time, as the passage in Lucan makes clear, the sexual
politics involved are very complex because Demogorgon in turn controls the
strongest sources of feminine power.

While I have added a few more examples to Curran's extensive review of
the elements fused into Shelley's "syncretic quest" (*Annus Mirabilis* 67), what
I am at this point more concerned to show is, first, that the syncretism turns
upon an initiatory ritual "descent" and "rebirth" and, second, that its significations, drawn like those of the Freemasons from a number of different myths
and cultic practices, have the human, not the divine, as their central mystery.[20]

Whether Shelley had very specific initiatory rites in mind when describing
the descent of Asia and Panthea is hard to tell. He begins, at least, with a
practice common to many: the blindfolding of the initiate, who is then led
along a circuitous path to the chamber of revelation, where the blindfold is
removed. Barruel describes such a process as the preliminary stage in the
Illuminati's "lesser mysteries" (III, 161). A catechetical dialogue is a customary feature as well (Barruel III, 158–60), but Shelley reverses the usual order
of things by making the initiate, Asia, the interrogator, while the initiator,
Demogorgon, acts as respondent. All the same, since Demogorgon tells her,
"I spoke but as ye speak" (II.iv.113), there is a real sense in which the answers
are hers. Also the catechetical form itself serves, as it does in initiation rituals,
as the outward sign for a gradually developing illumination through dialogue,
the specific roles within the dialogue being subservient to the mystery that is
revealed.

A third important element in those sections of the Illuminists' rituals
known to Barruel is a recapitulation of world history (III, 173–86). What
seems to be involved there is an imaginative reenactment of what has occurred not only in one's own past but in all human experience. Gradually this
builds up the conviction that although "*we were once possessed of liberty, and
we lost it,*" through the enlargement of understanding it is possible "*to find it
again and never to lose it more*" (III, 179; author's emphasis). This enlightened understanding is made possible by "the secret schools of Philosophy."
The ritual declamation goes on to make the point (to Barruel's horror) that
"these schools *shall one day retrieve the fall of human nature,* AND PRINCES AND
NATIONS SHALL DISAPPEAR FROM THE FACE OF THE EARTH, *and that without any
violence.* Human nature shall form one great family, and the earth shall become the habitation of the man of reason" (III, 186–87; author's emphasis).

Although I have skipped details in the discourses "recorded" by Barruel, I
have touched on all the major ritual occurrences that he describes, and these

in fact make up the essential elements in the transformative ritual that Asia undergoes in the cave of Demogorgon. One further point of connection, discussed by Robert Hartley (528–29), is that the symbol of the uroboros has a prominent place on one of the altarlike tables used for the initiatory ritual (Barruel IV, 349–50).

Barruel includes a section on "the greater mysteries" but prefaces it with the statement that "by the great importance which the sect places in the last mysteries of Illuminism, and by the many precautions which it has taken to conceal them from the public view, I am compelled to begin this chapter with candidly declaring, that every attempt to discover the original text of this part of the Code has been fruitless" (III, 237). The promised revelations, therefore, end in an experience of anticlimax much resembling the response that generations of critics have registered to the dialogue between Demogorgon and Asia. Arthur Clutton-Brock's is one of the more acid comments: "Something happens in the middle of the play; but Shelley cannot tell us what it is, because he does not know" (*V* 451). Curran, while more circumspect, implies something of the sort when he notes that "Demogorgon is even more tight lipped than oracles are wont to be" (*Annus Mirabilis* 38).

If my supposition that Shelley had initiatory rituals—both those of the ancient mysteries and their syncretic revisions in Masonic rites—as his models for scenes three and four of act two, then it could indeed be lack of knowledge that forced him into Demogorgon's laconicisms. Final revelation of the Masonic rituals had eluded even the assiduous Barruel, and the actual ritual events of the ancient mysteries went to the grave with their initiates. What we do know—the ritual display of "holy things" at the Eleusinian mysteries, for instance (Burkert, *Ancient Mystery Cults* 5)—has the portentousness but also the elusive lack of meaning heard in Demogorgon's statement that "the deep truth is imageless" (II.iv.116).[21] We might then judge that while "something" does occur in act two, scene four, in that Asia comes to some sort of enlightenment and Prometheus is (thereby?) delivered from his bondage, we readers, like a congregation separated from the altar of mystery by the high rood screen, have only the bells of a cryptic dialogue to signal for us that something of great significance has occurred. In my opinion, however, this does not fully describe what the scene accomplishes. My point, involving as it does a comparison between the ancient and the Masonic mysteries on the one hand and the practice of psychoanalysis on the other, necessitates a detour from Demogorgon's cave to the consulting rooms in which Freud met his patients.

Describing her experiences as one such analysand, the poet H.D. refers often to details about the room's furnishings. Mentioned so often that it becomes a leitmotif in her account is a "semicircle of priceless little *objets d'art*" on Freud's desk (8), an arrangement "now I come to think of it, almost like a high altar, in the Holy of Holies" (68). As her story nears its close, she repeats and thereby underscores that thought: "There were the immemorial Gods ranged in their semicircle on the Professor's table, that stood, as I have said, like the high altar in the Holy of Holies. There were those Gods, each the carved symbol of an idea or a deathless dream, that some people read: Goods" (93).

These "Gods," once icons within living systems of belief, are now to some mere objets d'art, "Goods." But between these two readings of them lies a humanist rendition of their function as a ritual semicircle overseeing explorations in self-knowledge. These presences also serve to draw the parallel between the Freemasons' use of syncretic lore to reveal the nature of the human and the psychoanalytic interaction with the unconscious through "the speaking cure." Shelley surrounds the scene in the cave of Demogorgon with the trappings of ritual initiation because those are the only signifiers he has for an as yet nonexistent institution: the psychoanalytic session.

H.D. recalls Freud's saying after such a session, *"Today, we have tunneled very deep"* (92). In commenting on his words, she herself associates psychoanalytic practice and Masonic ritual; she writes that the knowledge gained from this tunneling came from "those realms from which the *illuminati* received their—'credentials' seems a strange word as I write it, but it 'wrote itself' " (92). Since H.D.'s analytic sessions occurred in Vienna, where Weishaupt's Illuminati had a period of considerable power (Chailley 62),[22] the term "credentials" may have arisen of itself because, while a somewhat odd way of describing an initiate's enlightenment, it is an excellent term for the sign of status conferred on one of Weishaupt's band.

This triune analogue for the scene in Demogorgon's cave—mystery ritual, Masonic initiatory rite, and psychoanalytic practice—allows a different reading of its seemingly anticlimactic nature. As in the dialogic discourse of psychoanalysis and in the procedures of an initiation rite, what occurs is not so much informative as performative.

Shoshana Felman's brilliant and lucid discussion of the performative nature of psychotherapy centers on Lacan's comments about the work of Melanie Klein. In outlining Klein's account of the play therapy involving toy trains through which she effected the cure of a virtually speechless four-year-old boy named Dick, Lacan deplores the reductiveness of her interpretive approach: "She sticks symbolism into him, little Dick, with the utmost brutality, that Melanie Klein! She begins right away by hitting him with the major interpretations. She throws him into a brutal verbalization of the Oedipus myth, almost as revolting to us to as any reader whatever—*You are a little train, you want to fuck your mother"* (Felman 107–8; Lacan's emphasis).

Yet, despite this "brutality," Klein's strategy has a virtually immediate effect, and its pragmatic efficacy captures Lacan's admiration. Felman comments:

> What then has Melanie Klein in effect done? Nothing other than to provide verbalization. She has symbolized an effective relation, the relation of being, named with another. . . . The child verbalizes a first call—a spoken call. He asks for his nurse, with whom he had entered and whose departure he had taken as though nothing were the matter. For the first time, he produces a reaction of appeal, of call . . . which henceforth entails an answer. (113)

Prior to the child's call for the comforting presence of his nurse, he must come to a sense of himself as one who needs to call because he is a separate subjectivity. This recognition is instilled through Klein's "speech act": "And how does Klein's speech act produce the call in Dick? By calling him ('Dick— little train'), by naming him within the constellation of a symbolic structure, by thus performatively constituting him, through her discourse, as a subject" (118). Similarly, for an adult subjectivity muted through neurotic conflict, the psychoanalytic process involves a renaming and calling forth of a subject who can call (i.e., conceive of and function within relationships) in a way not possible before:

> Each time the analyst speaks, interprets in the analytic situation, he gives something asked of him. What he gives, however, is not a superior under- standing, but a reply. The reply addresses not so much what the patient says (or means), but his call. Being fundamentally a reply to the subject's ques- tion, to the force of his address, the interpretive gift is not constative (cogni- tive) but performative: the gift is not so much a gift of truth, of understand- ing or of meaning: it is, essentially, a gift of language. (119)

I shall take up shortly the relevance of this way of understanding analytic praxis to the dialogue between Asia and Demogorgon but must first consider as well Felman's explanation of the necessarily dialogic nature of the analytic speech act. Felman points out that for Lacan the originality of Freud's discov- ery was not the existence of the unconscious, "intuited before him by the poets," but the fact that *"the unconscious speaks"* (57; author's emphasis). It speaks or signifies, as is now common knowledge, through dreams, slips of the tongue or pen, jokes, and physical symptoms. A common understanding of the psychoanalytic process is that the analyst, the expert, reads these signs and interprets them for the analysand (21). That notion greatly oversimplifies, as Felman notes:

> Lacan's view is more radical than that. For the activity of reading is not just the analyst's, it is also the analysand's: interpretation is what takes place *on both sides* of the analytic situation. The unconscious, in Lacan's eyes, is not simply the object of psychoanalytic investigation, but its subject. The uncon- scious, in other words, is not simply *that which must be read* but also, and perhaps primarily, *that which reads*. (21–22; author's emphasis)

What occurs, then, is not that the integrated, self-aware psychiatrist, free to stroll at will through the familiar streets of her or his own unconscious, maps the analysand's unconscious to allow similar strolling without terrors. On the contrary, the discourse of the analysand speaks to and about the unconscious of the analyst as well, opening it up, but only as the gap, the place of difference, splitting, cleft, where no one strolls: "The unconscious . . . is the radical castration of the mastery of consciousness, which turns out to be forever incomplete, illusory, and self-deceptive" (Felman 57). At one point in H.D.'s analysis, Freud compares his discovery to striking oil (*Tribute* 83). This "oil" was his realization that his own unconscious was reading—but at the same time being read by—the discourse of the hysteric Other who was his patient (Felman 23).

Since the significance of Demogorgon and the dramatic function of his dialogue with Asia have baffled generations of critics, one can only agree with Felman that while poets—Shelley among them—most certainly intuited the existence of the unconscious, they did not fully understand the way it functions because they did not grasp its ontology in the split within consciousness that makes possible the speaking subject. In other words, had Shelley's tunneling hit on the Freudian gusher, the fuction of Demogorgon would be less puzzling. Still, if Shelley by no means articulates this process in the figure of Demogorgon, his mythic figuration adumbrates Freud's metaphysical analysis.[23] Or, to put the idea another way, Shelley in his own tunneling came upon a symbol, the jagged half of an idea yet to be fully articulated. Like the figure of Elpenor in Ezra Pound's *Cantos,* the unnameable Demogorgon had "a name to come."

As the one who cannot be named (*V* 314) and so the antithesis of the Name-of-the-Father, Demogorgon demonstrates the same paradox present in the very term "unconscious"; he is *named* as the presence who cannot be named, just as the unconscious, as that which cannot be known, names itself—speaks—to the consciousness. Also, in Earth's account of the moment when the castrating power of Jupiter pinioned Prometheus and separated him from the object of his desire, she mentions the simultaneous appearance of a "new fire" beneath the "earthquake-rifted mountains of bright snow" (I.i.165–66), which, though thus buried, continues to defy Jupiter. The volcanic terminology, when transposed into psychoanalytic discourse, describes the moment at which the unconscious appears in a psyche split yet driven by the incestuous desire it must consciously repress.

So, then, in this consulting room Asia, the "forbidden" memory of the primary relationship to the mother, comes into the presence of the unconscious created by repression of desire for the mother and by simultaneous entry into speech. The image for this described by Matthews, that of seawater pouring in upon lava, is by no means an overly dramatic "objective correlative" for such a cataclysmic event. Matthews, who discusses Demogorgon's volcanic energy as a metaphor for revolutionary power, writes of the volcano as an "archetypal image," but in context a deprecatory irony surrounds his use of that Jungian term. Because his analysis does not take up the intertwining of social and psychological forces, he does not consider the link between revolutionary energy and repressed desire. That Shelley made such a connection, however, seems to me borne out by the repeated juxtapositions of the volcanic with the moment in which Earth and Prometheus were separated.

The situation in Demogorgon's cave is fraught with sexual energy, emotional urgency, and intellectual activity, just as a psychoanalytic session might be at some critical moment of the interpretive task, and yet, as again might be true of such a session, the occasion appears anything but violent. Asia comes to read and be read by the unconscious. Writes Lacan: "The Other is, therefore, the locus in which is constituted the I who speaks to him who hears, that which is said by the one being already the reply" (*Écrits* 141). His words serve as gloss to a puzzling exchange: to Asia, very near the end of their colloquy, Demogorgon says, "I spoke but as ye speak" (II.iv.112). Shortly thereafter Asia rephrases his thought: "So much I asked before, and my heart gave / The response thou hast given; and of such truths / Each to itself must be the oracle" (II.iv.121–23). But she clearly does not mean thereby that the dialogue is useless, for she goes on to ask the last, crucial question.

Before considering that question, however, I must place questioner and respondent in still another context: that of a supplicant before an oracle, specifically the oracle at Delphi. A detailed analysis of Delphi as the site of Demogorgon's cave belongs properly to the next chapter, for at this point we have no textual evidence for thus identifying it; still, certain aspects of the sanctum sanctorum at Delphi make premature mention of it necessary here.

At the very beginning of act two, scene three, Panthea's scene-setting lines liken Demogorgon's "mighty portal" to both a volcanic crater and an oracular fissure: "Like a volcano's meteor-breathing chasm, / Whence the oracular vapour is hurled up" (II.iii.3–4). Her following lines, stressing as they do the seeming untrustworthiness of oracular language as a "voice which is contagion to the world" (II.iii.10), tend to minimize the allusion to an oracle. Consider, however, this passage from Varro's *On the Latin Language,* in which, discussing the word "umbilicus," he argues that the *umbilicus* stone at Delphi—contrary to widespread popular belief—is *not* the center of the world:

> The *umbilicus,* they say, was so called from our *umbilicus* "navel," because this is the middle place of the lands, as the navel is with us. But both these are false statements: this place is not the middle of the lands, nor is the navel the middle point of a man. But in this fashion is indicated the so-called "counter-earth of Pythagoras," so that the line which is midway in sky and earth should be drawn below the navel through that by which the distinction is made whether a human being is male or female, where human life starts— and the like is true in the case of the universe. . . . Besides, if the ball of the earth has any center, or *umbilicus,* it is not Delphi that is the centre; and the centre of the earth at Delphi—not really the centre, but so called—is something in a temple building at one side, something that looks like a treasure-house, which the Greeks call the ὀμφαλος [*omphalos*], which they say is the tomb of the Python. (VII.17)

Putting Varro's negatives to one side—that is to say, accepting the ancient belief that the stone called the *omphalos* at Delphi *did* mark the center of the earth—and remembering yet again that the imagery of *Prometheus Unbound* is "drawn from the operations of the human mind" (*SPP* 133), we can say that Asia and Panthea have arrived at the center of the experiential human, a center at once umbilical and genital, presided over by the unseen presence of a great sacred snake. If we keep in mind Shelley's equation of "life" and the "world" with "the wonder of our being" (*SPP* 474–75), then this passage from Drummond's *Essay on a Punic Inscription,* quoted by Hartley, makes the uroboros an emblem of that "wonder":

Plutarch, concerning Isis and Osiris, tells us that the people of the Thebais acknowledged no mortal god, but only *Cneph,* who is unborn and immortal. From Eusebius we learn, that the serpent was the type of the *Agatho-daemon* among the Phoenicians, and that the *Agatho-daemon* was the *Cneph* of the Egyptians, and was also represented by a serpent in the form of a circle. All this may be easily admitted, for the Egyptians had many Gods, and more symbols. It is more to my purpose to observe, that *Cneph* was the representative of spiritual nature. It was therefore said, that *Cneph* was incapable of birth or of death. It was thence, that Proclus considered the serpent, which represented him, as the type of the soul of the world; and thence it was that the Egyptians called him *the Demiourgos.* (Drummond 78; quoted in Hartley 537)

So, what Lacan has described as the central issue in psychoanalytic theory and practice—"the realization of the truth of the subject" (Felman 58–59)—is what is at stake in the descent to Demogorgon's cave. Asia's thirty-two-line "aria" on the sublime panorama surrounding her and Panthea before they are blindfolded and led down to their destined meeting with "a Voice unspoken" has just that, the truth of the subject, as its theme.[24]

Traditionally these lines have not been read in the way that I suggest but rather as an admission on Shelley's part of some creative Spirit or Power which shadows itself forth in the physical universe:

> How glorious art thou, Earth! and if thou be
> The shadow of some Spirit lovelier still,
> Though evil stain its work and it should be
> Like its creation, weak yet beautiful,
> I could fall down and worship that and thee.—
>   (II.iii.12–16)

I am given pause, I admit, by the fact that even C. E. Pulos, who gives such emphasis to the parallels between Drummond's form of skepticism and Shelley's philosophical principles, reads these lines Platonically: "While Shelley . . . generally conceives of Beauty as a feeling arising from an unknown cause or power, he sometimes—particularly after 1818—expresses some sceptical form of faith in its objective and independent existence" (*The Deep Truth* 83–84); Pulos goes on to find the conditional verb forms as the only "scepticism" in these particular lines. Yet by a similar consensus the simile at the conclusion of Asia's speech in which the towering drifts of snow are compared to the thoughts "in Heaven-defying minds" (II.iii.39) serves as one of the best examples of figures "drawn from the operations of the human mind" that Shelley discusses in the preface to *Prometheus Unbound* (*SPP* 133).

Perhaps, since Shelley makes the point in "On Life" that he does not consider it possible that the mind is self-created (*SPP* 478), we can compromise between Shelley the Platonist and Shelley the relativist. Human experience, for which "nothing exists but as it is perceived," finds the image of itself in its perceptions but finds as well the sense of mystery involved in recognizing that "mind cannot create, it can only perceive" (*SPP* 478). There is, then, as in "Mont Blanc," with which this passage has themes and even poetic techniques in common, a recognition that "Power" may transcend the human, but an even greater interest in the human mind whose perceptions at once are and are not images of its potency.

The presence of rhyme in this passage will help me explain my meaning. In doing so I draw on Keach's dazzling exposition of the significance of rhyme in "Mont Blanc." Noting that in "Mont Blanc," as in "Lycidas," only three lines end with words that are not rhymed and that the presence of this rhyme is masked through enjambement, Keach continues:

> There is no precedent for Shelley's crossing of extended blank verse enjambement with irregular rhyme in a poem which raises such fundamental questions about the mind's powers and limitations. . . . The cognitive play between or among rhyme words shows Shelley taking advantage of the way in which the very arbitrariness of linguistic signs he speaks of in the *Defence* can produce an expressive coincidence and thus a resource for a mind contending, ultimately, with its own and nature's blankness. (195–96)

In shaping Asia's lines, Shelley can work from his own precedent in "Mont Blanc," though not, of course, in exactly the same pattern. Only four of Asia's thirty-two lines have no responding rhyme or half-rhyme. The first, "Magnificent," is set apart in any case as a virtual statement of the theme: "Fit throne for such a Power! Magnificent!" (II.iii.11). The six lines that follow, rhyming *a b a b a b*, set up a tripartite correspondence among Earth, the "Spirit" it shadows, and the mind envisioning relation between the other two. This harmonious potential culminates in the last line of the sestet, where all three elements appear together": "*I* could fall down and worship *that* [the Spirit] and *thee* [the Earth]" (II.iii.16; my emphasis).

Rhymes and half-rhymes—sometimes even quadrupled, as in mist/mist/vast/mass or howl/snow/round/now—continue from this point on but in no logical sequence and often many lines apart, as if the word must grope after its correspondent syllables. Finally, as "expressive coincidence" to the weakness dramatically placed in the phrase "weak yet beautiful" (II.iii.15), there are three lines besides the first for which there is no rhyme at all: "rolling on," "mountains," and "truth." So three rhyme patterns, each figuring forth a philosophical possibility, occur in these lines. The first seven set up a system of heavenly correspondences. Those that follow allow for the possibility that the human subject, though groping, uncertain, and liable to sudden descents, can, through its limited perceptions, find means of shoring itself up against alienation. And then there are the clefts, the abysses within consciousness that make it aware of its weakness, its separation from any answers.

The words "weak" and "weakness" appear at crucial points in the song chanted by the Spirits as Asia and Panthea, blindfolded and thus physically helpless, move down to the cave. The song's theme, a virtual truism in mystical traditions worldwide, is the delusory nature of life's seeming oppositions; those mentioned in the first stanza—Death/Life, appearance/reality—are also, so to speak, traditional. The particulars given in the next stanza, however, are more unusual: "As the fawn draws the hound, / As the lightning the vapour, / As a weak moth the taper" (II.iii.65–67). Besides the mutual attraction that brings these opposites into unity, the lines describe strange reversals of strength and weakness. The fawn ("stag" in an earlier version, a revision that proves "weakness" the quality Shelley wanted to emphasize [*SPU* 132]), weak in itself, has power over the hound; ephemeral water vapor, drawn up from the earth by the sun, is thereby made powerfully electric (Grabo, *A Newton Among the Poets* 129); the evanescent, flickering taper is stronger than the moth drawn to it. In the concluding stanza, the Spirits draw the moral: "Resist not the weakness" (II.iii.93). Indeed, nonresistance to weakness has become so crucial that it alone (though in ways not yet expressed) will bring about the denouement:

> Resist not the weakness—
> Such strength is in meekness—
> That the Eternal, the Immortal,
> Must unloose through life's portal
> The snake-like Doom coiled underneath his throne
> By that alone!
>
> (II.iii.93–98)

For the moment, however, the connection between weakness and "the snake-like Doom" is enigmatic, and attention takes another focus when Asia faces Demogorgon.

Demogorgon initiates the dialogue with Asia, though in doing so he presupposes on her part a need or desire for knowledge. He places her in the position of questioner, not that of the one being questioned: "Ask what thou wouldst know" (II.iv.7). When she, with spunky practicality, replies, "What canst thou tell?" (II.iv.8), he pushes up the ante. Since he will tell "all things thou dar'st demand" (II.iv.8), the challenge rests with her to address herself to the significant and useful question, not with him to provide universally valid wisdom. As in an initiation ritual, then, the enlightenment proceeds not so much from the mysteries revealed as from the disposition of the one desiring to be illumined. Or again, in a psychoanalytic session, the analyst in replying to the "call" of the analysand for knowledge gives only the opportunity for illumination about "the place where his [the analysand's] *ego* is . . . to know through whom and for whom the subject poses *his question*" (Lacan, *Écrits* 89; author's emphasis).

I follow the wisdom of J. A. Cousins, who decades ago noted that Asia's three following questions have as their topic "not the general realm of nature, but the special realm of human nature, the psychological world in which the drama-poem moves" (*V* 457). Shelley gives this signification to "world" in the opening sentence of "On Life": "Life, and the world, or whatever we call that which we are and feel, is an astonishing thing" (*SPP* 474). Understandably so, since if "nothing exists but as it is perceived" (*SPP* 476), knowledge of "the world" *and* of "that which we are and feel" (the two being one and the same) involves the attempt to call forth words to express the "thoughts and feelings [that] arise, with or without our will" (*SPP* 475). So Asia's question "Who made the living world?" (II.iv.9) is addressing ontologically "the truth of the subject."

Demogorgon's reply is "God" (II.iv.9). His later statement that "the deep truth is imageless" (II.iv.116) contains the admission that this signifier reveals only the inadequacy of signification, or—in the phrasing Shelley uses in "On Life"—"the dark abyss of—how little we know" (*SPP* 478). Still, his words also convey another Shelleyan conviction: "It is infinitely improbable that the cause of mind, that is, of existence, is similar to mind" (*SPP* 478). Yet if words cannot "penetrate the mystery of our being," Shelley muses in "On Life," "rightly used they may make evident our ignorance to ourselves, and this is much" (*SPP* 475–76). And the place in which both Shelley, the questioner in "On Life," and Asia, the fictive subjectivity addressing Demogorgon, choose to probe through language for this secondary sort of answer is in the experience of reverie, with its link to some previous, half-forgotten time in childhood. Asia's second question is filled with echoes from her opening soliloquy and, like those lines, with discussion of "our sensations as children" (*SPP* 477):

> Who made that sense which, when the winds of Spring
> In rarest visitation, or the voice
> Of one beloved heard in youth alone,
> Fills the faint eyes with falling tears, which dim
> The radiant looks of unbewailing flowers,
> And leaves this peopled earth a solitude
> When it returns no more?
>
> (II.iv.12–18)

An ungrammatical question: it circles a blank center, in that the pronominal conjunction "which" never meets its appropriate verb. Meanwhile, the adverbial clause governed by "when" has the double subject "winds" and "voice" and two verbs, "fills" and "leaves." In consequence, both "that sense" with the meaning of "vague impression," and the senses (i.e., sensations) of touch, smell, and hearing empty into these two contrasting verbs. So, while ungrammatical, the verse sentence functions performatively to signify a fused yet unverbalized experience of sensation/feeling/thought: "the truth of the subject." "Or" creates a metaphoric connection between the plural "winds of Spring" and the singular "voice" of a beloved "heard in youth alone" that rules the singular form of the two contrasting verbs "fills" and "leaves." The missing verb stands in for an unverbalizable question at the heart of subjectivity which then cannot call forth its answer, while the words that *are* there designate a subjectivity formed and maintained through the maternal breath that is experienced simultaneously as fulfilling presence and mourned absence. A textual mirror for the subjectivity being described, then, is the notebook page that contains both the fragment "To search & find no fill" and the draft of "To Constantia Singing," with its lines "Whilst, like the world-surrounding air, thy song / Flows on, and fills all things with melody" (*SPP* ll. 13–14).

Subjectivity, a boon in that it makes "that sense" of presence possible, makes it inevitably as well a sense of loss. Also, while subjectivity gives one a place upon "this peopled earth," that separate place of the perceiving subject poses the constant threat of something like solitary confinement. Demogorgon's positive answer, "Merciful God" (II.iv.18), places emphasis on subjectivity as a necessary condition not to mingled feeling per se but to knowing that one is feeling—that is, to human experience. Nevertheless, the last two lines of Asia's question point toward the one that follows, a definition of the essential human experience as one of embittered and violent alienation:

> And who made terror, madness, crime, remorse,
> Which from the links of the great chain of things
> To every thought within the mind of man
> Sway and drag heavily—and each one reels
> Under the load towards the pit of death;
> Abandoned hope, and love that turns to hate;
> And self-contempt, bitterer to drink than blood;
> Pain whose unheeded and familiar speech
> Is howling and keen shrieks, day after day;
> And Hell, or the sharp fear of Hell?
>
> (II.iv.19–28)

While the question's opening words suggest an external cause for the appearance of these violent human emotions, the question as a whole fixes its attention "within the mind of man." And while Oedipus is not mentioned by name as this prototypical human, the situation described in each particular fits that of Oedipus near the conclusion of *Oedipus the King:* horribly aware of his responsibility for actions which he was nonetheless predestined to commit, in his circling thought he can only reenact, reinscribe his crime.

Three times in answer to Asia's previous questions Demogorgon's response has been, with slight but positive variations, "God." His next three responses make no mention of God but repeat the statement "He reigns." His later characterization of Jove (the one who, by Asia's own account, has for some time reigned [II.iv.49]) as "the supreme of living things" (II.iv.113) convinces me that Demogorgon's parallelism is aimed at making a contrast and not an identification between God, who created the human subject, and Jove, an aspect of the human subject that historically has dominated the human psyche. Jove is "the supreme of living things" in the "living world" of "thought, passion, reason, will / Imagination" (II.iv.10–11). An important part of Asia's quest for the answer to how that tyranny became established involves her recapitulation of that world's macrocosmic and microcosmic history. As I mentioned earlier, such historical panoramas form a customary part of initiation rituals; Lacan makes them central as well to the psychoanalytic project: "Analysis can have for its goal only the advent of a true speech and the realization by the subject of his history in his relation to a future" (*Écrits* 88).

Asia's account explains at last the circumstances under which Prometheus entrusted Jupiter with the power he still wields. The hominids of the first age ("earth's primal spirits" [II.iv.35]) lived and died as peacefully as the vegetable and animal forms surrounding them, but their human potential for conscious existence—"the birthright of their being"—was denied them. Asia breaks the qualities making up this conscious subjectivity into a series of attributes, each linked to the next: "knowledge, power, / The skill which wields the elements, the thought / Which pierces this dim Universe like light, / Self-empire and the majesty of love" (II.iv.39–42). Ideally, knowledge grants the power, first of those skills needed to control the external environment; then of the capacity to understand and control the forces creating that environment and those operating within the psyche; and, as culmination, of a harmonious inner freedom that makes it possible to love another. This seems to have been the line of logic adopted by Prometheus, the forethinker, in giving dominance to Jupiter, knowledge-as-power, with what turns out to be the supremely ironic proviso "Let man be free" (II.iv.45).[25]

Instant alienation is the effect of his rule on Jupiter himself; an enslavement worse than their previous "semivital" existence falls upon his subjects. Prometheus, as custodian and epitome of the potential within human consciousness—as the human imagination—has mitigated human misery with countless products born of human learning and artistic creativity, but these serve only as panaceas. Asia concludes with the Oedipal question "but who rains down / Evil, the immedicable plague"? (II.iv.100–101).

As Asia, the analysand/initiate/supplicant, importunes for answer, her questions betray the obsessions she seeks to cure. Knowledge becomes so totally identified with dominating power—"Who is his master? Is he too a slave?" (II.iv.109)—that she becomes Jupiter-like in her conviction that to discover this overlord would be the means of regaining control over human life. Such a purpose, like Prometheus' curse, is entangled in the moral evil it attempts to undo.

Asia's flailing questions at last move Demogorgon to remind her (for this is but a Platonic recollection of something she already knows) that she, one with Prometheus as she describes his ambitions for mankind, has like him been so seduced by the equation of knowledge with control that she continues to take the source of the problem to be its solution. "Resist not the weakness." A Faustian, Jupiter-identified, Promethean consciousness believes that it can control, measure, and possess both itself and all it surveys; it should consider rather its inadequacy and incapacity to conceive, much less to verbalize, the mystery of life, beginning with the mystery that consciousness itself carries within it the void or abysm of the unconscious. Rest in that; let its meaning play over you; let yourself love the fractured, incomplete nature of human subjectivity. Begin, then, where the original Promethean concept of the human ended, with "the majesty of love," but as something to which one is subject, not as something that one will possess. Give up the very notion that one can achieve "self-empire" (a hopeless task in the face of vast self-ignorance) and that knowledge, power, thought serve as vehicles for control.

In short, withdraw your allegiance to rule by a Jupiterean, masculine insistence on knowledge as power (an allegiance shown despite yourself by the very framing of your questions), and align yourself, as I, Demogorgon, am aligned, with "a different voice," with Love, the Mother Goddess.

Taking this in, Asia is able to call Prometheus into his new life as "the Sun of this rejoicing world" (II.iv.127), the world that is human subjectivity. The sun image harks back to Panthea's dream vision and so to the transfiguration/resurrection of Jesus, thus underlining the homonym "son." In act one Prometheus makes the point that Jesus, considered as Son of the Father and founder of a patriarchal, hierarchical religion, served only to intensify the tyranny he sought to end (I.i.546–555). Humanly, though, Jesus is unfathered son of a woman, himself father to no one. Similarly, if as Son, not as Father, Prometheus is restored, his sonship must claim alliance with the mother, not the father, so that the rule of Jupiter may be overcome—a point that will receive much fuller attention in the next chapter. Understood politically and psychologically in this fashion, the concluding lines of the Spirits' "entrance song" take on such extraordinary significance that they bear repeating:

> Resist not the weakness—
> Such strength is in meekness—
> That the Eternal, the Immortal,
> Must unloose through life's portal
> The snake-like Doom coiled underneath his throne
> By that alone!
>
> (II.iii.93–98)

Consistently in Shelley's poetic iconography (and, for that matter in the political iconography of the period, extending back at least to the American Revolution) the snake serves as a sign for liberty (Hartley 529–30). But as the uroboros, the world-serpent with its tail in its mouth, the snake is also emblem of the power residing not so much in the mother per se as in the mother-infant relationship. Demogorgon *is* that relationship, the snake his totem, the womb experience his "place."[26] Reentering that place, the commonplace, for that matter, for initiation rituals of all kinds, Asia makes possible Prometheus' rebirth. Serpent/Demogorgon/Prometheus—in a reversal of those many initiatory rites in which the mother's son is reborn as father's son as well as in a mirrorlike reversal of the sexual act, an orgasmic birthing—is called forth "through life's portal" as mother's son, not father's son, a guiltless because Laius-free Oedipus.

Prometheus/Adonis and the Mother Goddess (Scene v)

Still unaddressed, however, is Matthews's question about "the purport on a social level of Asia's part in the drama" (228). Rephrasing it, we can ask why, if the transformation achieved through this ritual death and rebirth is that of

Prometheus, does Asia have the role not only of the initiate/analysand but also of the one whom we are shortly to *see* transfigured?

Part of the answer may lie in the psychological practicalities involved. The fantasy of descent into a cave or enclosed underground space in search of esoteric enlightenment is a much-repeated and critically much noted "return of the repressed" in Shelley's works. In his early "gothics," where one finds the motif constantly, the desirous male who forces his way into the maternal cave meets there the terrifying destiny that the story's Oedipal fantasist seems to find inevitable. In *St. Irvyne,* for instance, the protagonist, Wolfstein, agrees to meet the mysteriously powerful Ginotti in the vaults of the castle of St. Irvyne. (As it happens, Wolfstein's childhood and youth were passed in St. Irvyne with his mother and two sisters.) There Ginotti will pass on to him the secret of the elixir of eternal youth. At the tryst, Ginotti's first question is, "Wolfstein, dost thou deny my Creator?" When Wolfstein replies, "Never, never," the devil himself appears before them. Wolfstein dies blackened and convulsed by lightning bolts, and Ginotti becomes a gigantic skeleton, yet still alive, locked in an eternal gaze from his "eyeless sockets" upon a vision of pure evil (*CW* V, 199).

Similarly, in *The Wandering Jew,* when Victorio obeys a witch's invitation to "follow me to the mansions of rest" and rushes after her "into the mountain's side"—with "side," as Shelley again uses it in the dedication to *Laon and Cythna* (1. 77), a euphemism for womb—he asks her for a charm to turn Rosa's love from Paolo, the Wandering Jew, to himself. Her incantation summons Satan into the cave instead, and again he has an annihilating "basiliskine eye" (*PS* I, 80). Much subtler in the telling but similar in the content of the fantasy is "Alastor." The Poet, who pursues his dream of love into the "slant and winding depths" of a "cavern" (ll. 363–64), meets extinction there; "his last sight" is the seeming gaze from the twin points of light that mark the "mighty horn" (1. 647) of the setting moon.

In short, an imaginative fiction that makes possession of the mother's "secret" its quite straightforward aim calls up the attendant guardian/owner of that secret who enacts the castration the guilty desirer fears and expects (Klein 96–97). If, however, the desirer reifies the memory traces of relationship with the mother into a feminine presence and with her as cover makes his way to the fantasized source of his desire, then he is relieved of guilt and fear; the responsibility lies with "her."[27]

It seems possible that Mary Shelley's shrewd analysis of Shelley's youthful fantasies through her depiction of Victor Frankenstein clarified Shelley's understanding of the dangers attending the intrusive masculine troubler of "Mother Nature" and so led him toward a new imaginative strategy. But if Shelley's careful reading of *Frankenstein, or The Modern Prometheus* before he and Mary Shelley left England in March 1818 perhaps gave this negative rationale for a shifting of genders in the scenario of descent, other reading during this period may also have provided a positive impetus. The classical texts that engaged Shelley's attention at this time lend themselves to a revision of the ancient myth, with its associated ritual, in which the goddess/ mother/lover descends to the underworld to retrieve the lost son/fructifier and restore a dessicated world through his resurgent power. More than that, the works that he was reading in combination could well have sparked an intuitive flash linking Prometheus to such fertility figures as Daphnis and Adonis, and to the related figure of Dionysus.[28]

Such a connection occurred to William Berg when he juxtaposed classical texts that were also, as it happens, important parts of Shelley's reading and even of his translation between 1816 and 1818. The thought that produced Berg's scholarly essay in 1965 could well have been one that occurred to Shelley in 1818 as he began his re-vision of the Aeschylean Prometheus. The classical sources Berg offers as evidence for the link between Daphnis and Adonis were important to Shelley as well: Bion's "Lament for Adonis," Theocritus' *Idyll* (15, ll. 112–21), in which the presiding ministrant chants the ritual dirge for Adonis, and Lucian's *De Dea Syria* (6). Berg goes on to mention the cultic affiliation with other figures, such as the Thracian Dionysus and Osiris, concluding this part of his argument with the comment that "Vergil's genius has managed to combine the aforementioned elements from older traditions, both literary and religious, into one great shepherd-poet who presides over the bucolic world in its entirety" (14).

Certain intertextual signs, through which Berg shows a connection between this transferential vegetation deity, with his many names and many functions, and the Aeschylean Prometheus apply to Shelley's protagonist as well. Berg links the lament of Daphnis at the beginning of Virgil's *Fifth Eclogue,* in which he calls on trees and rivers "to witness the mourning of the Nymphs and the complaint of his mother to gods and stars," to the first speech Aeschylus gives to Prometheus (ll. 134–42) having him call on "sky, winds, rivers, waves, earth 'the mother of all' (his own mother) and sun to witness his suffering at the hands of the gods" (Berg 15). Shelley's Prometheus similarly invokes Earth, Heaven, and Sea as witnesses of his agony (I.i.25–30). Berg's second large area of comparison (16–17) is between Daphnis' "aretology" (*Eclogue* 5.29–34, 43–44) and the account Aeschylus has Prometheus make of his gifts to the human race (ll. 630–738), one that appears also in Shelley's play, though transferred to Asia's lips (II.iv.43–99).

Berg concludes: "The conception of Daphnis as a devoted *benefactor* of the bucolic world is a reflection, in my opinion, of the Aeschylean view of Prometheus as bringer of civilization. . . . Vergil had drawn upon the Athenian tragedy in order to construct the figure and to formulate the praises of his bucolic hero" (20; author's emphasis). My argument reverses that process: the delineation of Prometheus in *Prometheus Unbound* reflects the ways in which Shelley's imagination is steeped in the central myth and ritual of the bucolic tradition, that of the death and rebirth of Adonis.[29]

The very personality of Prometheus, in Shelley's depiction of him, exhibits the characteristics that David Halperin, summarizing the findings of Thorkild Jacobsen, sees as common to these shepherd heroes, beginning with the ancient Sumerian figure of Dumuzi, beloved of the goddess Inanna, and continuing through the millennia into the pastoral poetry so familiar to Shelley: "intransitiveness," "ethical neutrality," "youthfulness," "belovedness," "defenselessness and suffering," and "attractiveness to women" (Jacobsen, *Toward the Image of Tammuz* 74–101; cited in Halperin, "Forebears of Daphnis" 194). "Intransitiveness" describes the quality in Dumuzi that identifies his presence with his power. Or, one might express the idea by saying that his is a power of presence, not of action. "In all we know of Dumuzi from hymns, laments, myth, and ritual, there is no instance in which the god acts, orders, or demands; he merely is or is not" (Jacobsen, *Treasures* 10, and also *Toward the Image of Tammuz* 28–29 and 73–74). Commenting on this quality within a pastoral context, Halperin notes that scholars in like fashion "have often remarked the essential passivity of Theocritus' Daphnis—he is less a personality or a force than he is the genius of the landscape, an embodiment of natural plenitude" ("Forebears of Daphnis" 195). A similar passivity marks the personality of Prometheus, in sharp contrast with the characterization of Jupiter. Jacobsen's words about other Mesopotamian deities who, unlike Dumuzi, conduct an active, even intrusive, rule—"they lend help in war, or they destroy in anger their own cities" (*Toward the Image of Tammuz* 76)—could also describe a Jupiterean will that it is Prometheus' task to relinquish. This process begins in act one, when Prometheus withdraws his energizing assent from his curse against Jupiter, and continues through the ritual mediation of Asia in act two as she learns the significance of "Resist not the weakness." In acts three and four it is the reunited presences of Prometheus and Asia, not their actions, that radiate the harmony that thereby surrounds them.

Jacobsen links the "intransitiveness" of Dumuzi-like figures such as Tammuz with their "ethical neutrality" and that in turn with "youthfulness." This aspect of the power in Tammuz as "being rather than doing, as having no responsibilities, innocently self-centered, yet pleasing and attractive, is very finely expressed in its symbolization as a young boy, a youth, a symbol shared by all the aspects of Tammuz" (*Toward the Image of Tammuz* 76).

While these qualities do not seem particularly applicable to the Aeschylean Prometheus whom we first meet in act one, locked in an eons-long conflict with a Jupiter he has come in a certain way to resemble, there are suggestions of Prometheus' "youthfulness" even there. Mother Earth's recollections of his infancy and Prometheus' yearning for the time of his union with Asia, as well as Asia's own nostalgic language at the opening of act two, all suggest that the "real" Prometheus, eclipsed and frozen under Jupiter's tyranny, does indeed resemble the playful, innocently self-centered, youthful Tammuz of Jacobsen's description. Proof comes when Prometheus, restored to his full being, describes to Asia, Panthea, and Ione the idyllic life that will now be theirs. He is not an organizing, bustling, provident deity. On the contrary: "We will sit and talk of time and change / As the world ebbs and flows, ourselves unchanged" (III.iii.23–24).

Not his active power or moral grandeur, then, but this youthful attractiveness, this pleasure in being in and for himself, makes Dumuzi/Tammuz lovable and beloved. Jacobsen speculates that Dumuzi's name may mean "the true son" or "the good child," and sees his belovedness as related to his child-likeness and to a quality of "defenselessness and suffering, which invite feelings of pity and compassion allied to those of love" (*Toward the Image of Tammuz* 322, 91), particularly from the groups of women who search after him, surround him, and minister to him:

> The attitude of mother and sister as they search for the dead god is through-out one of pure maternal instinct, as if they were searching for a small child who had become lost. . . . In fact, the very nature of the love for him insists on his helplessness; he is the more loved for his helplessness and weakness. Thus in an almost complete reversal of the normal roles of god and wor-shiper it is the god who is powerless. He clings to the mother and sister. . . . In part, this closeness and intimacy in the response traces . . . to the general closeness and intimacy of emotional experience in the woman's world, the home, which is the inner horizon of the cult.   (96–98)

In precisely this way, Prometheus' Earth Mother and his companions Ione and Panthea yearn after and console him during his long sufferings; Asia and Panthea, in whom attributes of mother, lover, and sister blend kaleidoscopically, just as they do in the searching women of the ancient myths, are Mother Earth's agents of his release; and his Elysium is a return to domestic intimacy with three devoted women.

Jacobsen's language as he describes the characteristics of the ancient cult suggests as well those sociological and biographical factors that would have drawn Shelley to the myth of the Mother Goddess's retrieval of her son/lover. The home, "inner horizon of the cult," is also, in the ideology of the maternal, established as the locus for creating those interpersonal bonds of sympathy through and under the mother's watchful eye that will offset selfish, entrepreneurial individualism. Shelley's lifelong need for constant mothering, for being "the more loved for his helplessness and weakness," produced by the combination of strong ideology and his own very strong mother, finds its answer in this tale of the Mother Goddess's loving power. At the same time this power, operative within "the general closeness and intimacy of emotional experience in the woman's world," calls up the need for defenses such as appropriative identification on the one hand and dispersal through a household of sisters on the other.

The fusion of Adonis with Prometheus creates an important change in the "status" of the Adonis figure, one that reflects the same desire to appropriate rather than interact with maternal power. Berg describes Daphnis as reflecting "the dying and rising divinities popular among the Greeks, like Adonis, the Thracian Dionysus, and Osiris, not to mention such heroes as Heracles, the Dioscuri, and Romulus, who found their way after death to the company of the gods" (13–14). The slippage from "divinities" to "heroes" who later participate in "the company of the gods" reflects a certain fluidity in the myths themselves, but a fluidity contained within and by a fairly consistent plot line: Dumuzi, Tammuz, and Adonis begin their existence as human males and take on the divine numen through their relationship to the goddess. Shelley's poem, on the contrary, establishes a male deity, Prometheus, whose resemblance to the "human" shepherds of the pastoral tradition is only gradually revealed. Meanwhile, given masculine dominance, Asia's status as a goddess becomes reduced in Shelley's version of the myth to that of consort. She is celebrated in the ritual not as herself a source of divine power but as the male deity's first, most blessed disciple and reflection of his numinosity.

The political change effected when the Daphnis-like Prometheus is a god in his own right can best be seen in Asia's apotheosis. As the bride anticipating her union with the bridegroom, she bears considerable resemblance to Inanna ritually adorned for her marriage to Dumuzi. Indeed, Panthea's description explicitly identifies her for the first time as the Great Mother—Aphrodite/Venus/Astarte. In footnoting this passage, Reiman and Powers judge that "by naming her Asia, Shelley frees his creation from the specific limitations associated with the myths of Aphrodite/Venus" (*SPP* 178). What those "limitations" are is unclear—perhaps Aphrodite's association with lascivious and fickle passion? But in fact, through this strategic renaming, Shelley limits the power of the Mother Goddess. As Asia, not Astarte, she takes on the "intransitive" character of the Daphnis figure in that she emanates a fructifying, harmonizing power—but one that reflects her relation to (in this case) a god, not one she wields in her own right. While verbally bedecked in Aphrodite's splendor, she could not appropriately speak the words given to Inanna in one of the ancient hymns:

> Then shall I caress my lord, a sweet fate I shall decree for him,
> I shall caress Shulgi, the faithful shepherd, a sweet fate I shall decree for him,
> I shall caress his loins, the shepherdship of all the lands,
> I shall decree as his fate.
>
> (quoted in Kramer, *Sacred Marriage* 64)[30]

While necessarily unaware of the most ancient sources, Shelley wrote act two of *Prometheus Unbound* as a re-vision of a topos central throughout the long history of pastoral: the descent of the Mother Goddess to rescue her lost beloved. So, appropriately, the act begins with a vision of the morning star, whose appearance signified for the peoples of ancient Egypt and of Babylon the descent of the Mother Goddess into the underworld to retrieve her lover (Frazer VI.iii.34–35).

In Shelley's psychological transposition of the myth, Asia is the foundation or "chalice" (I.i.810) of the Promethean subjectivity, the "soul" imbibed through loving relationship, and thus the source of desire—but a desire in eclipse that must search for its object. Revelation of that object comes in the secret precincts of Demogorgon's cave, when the power of the memory of the maternal relation unveils it: Prometheus can recognize that the rejoicing world of which he is the sun/son, the world that is "whatever we call that which we are and feel" (*SPP* 474), has its source in that primary relationship. He thereby puts the experience of sympathy, connectedness, shared love ("affect attunement") at the center of human subjectivity not as a lost memory or absence or vacancy but as a lived fact; he re-members the mother.

The last scene of the second act, Asia's progress to a Prometheus freed through this new understanding, serves, as would any royal progress, as epiphanic gesture revealing an inward power already received. As would also be fitting in any such progress, the story which now serves as cause for celebration and was once the cause of grief is again rehearsed, this time by Panthea. In language filled with allusions to Aphrodite's birth from the sea, Panthea describes Asia as that love which once filled the Promethean "living world." She gives no explanation for the change that ensued, saying only that it occurred when "grief cast / Eclipse upon the soul from which it came" (II.v.30–31). An ambiguity about the referent for "it" creates a small discord in this joyous paean. The metaphor carried by the word "eclipse" suggests that "it" refers to "love, like the atmosphere / Of the sun's fire" (II.v.26–27) emanating from Asia, but the noun closest to "it" is "soul"; was the Promethean "soul" the source of grief?

A late revision recorded in the Bodleian fair copy, creates the ambiguity. There the lines read:

> till ~~Earth~~
> grief cast
> Eclipse upon the soul from which it came:
> (*Bodleian MS.* IX, 367)

Since Earth is gendered throughout the play, "it" can refer only to the "light of love," but Earth is made in some way responsible for the eclipse. The revision eliminates that disturbing possibility, leaving only a question about whether Prometheus indeed imbibed grief from his nurse's soul.

Furthermore, the two concluding arias of the scene, exquisite as they are, leave one wondering whether Prometheus as a still desirous subject can truly be a subject filled full of love. The first, the lyric beginning "Life of Life" (II.v.47), is sung by an unidentified "Voice," according to the final stage directions. The fair copy has Asia call Panthea the singer, in her capacity once more as linking breath between Asia and Prometheus:

> *Asia*
>
> spoke
> You ~~say~~ said that Spirits ~~speak~~, but it was thee
> Sweet sister, for even now thy curved lips
> Tremble as if the sound were dying there
> Not dead
>
> *Panthea*
>
>   was   spoke
> Alas it ~~is~~ Prometheus ~~speaks~~
>   and I know
> Within me, ~~if I spoke~~, & ~~even now it~~ it must be so
> I mixed my own weak nature with his love
> And
>
> (*Bodleian MS. IX*, 375)

Again revision smooths away some of the difficulty, but Panthea's canceled "Alas" has numerous echoes in the lyric's ever more plangent expression of desire for an unattainable beauty. The fourth and culminating stanza addresses Asia metaphorically and metonymically as her planet, "Lamp of Earth" (II.v.66), and describes the effect of her presence: "the souls of whom thou lovest / Walk upon the winds with lightness" (II.v.68–69). Then, without so much as a comma for preparation, that "lightness" turns to loss, and the dizzy soul lacks the assistance Peter had when he failed to walk on water: "Till they fail, as I am failing / Dizzy, lost . . . yet unbewailing!" (II.v.70–71). Thus the goddess's star is sign not so much of the lover's rescue from desire as his reinscription by it.

For the moment, though, bedazzling feeling obscures these tensions—even contradictions—between a love-filled and a desire-filled subject. Asia's soul (which is to say Prometheus', hers being his), described as an "enchanted Boat" (II.v.72) and the boat in turn as "the boat of my desire" (II.v.94)—her soul structured, then, as desirous in its essence—has come to harbor in "realms where the air we breathe is Love" (II.v.95).

NOTES

1. A. M. D. Hughes notes a number of instances that show the continuing presence of Luxima's image virtually throughout Shelley's work: "Shelley remembered this book [*The Missionary*] when he wrote of Cythna bursting through the soldiers and priests to die with Laon at the stake, of Asia waiting in the paradise of the 'Indian Caucasus,' the mountain girdle of Cashmere, and in *Epipsychidion* of the pleasure-house in the deep woodland. Luxima, with all her tenderness, her delicate speech, her long dusk hair and 'dove-like eyes,' her 'bright and etherial form,' is a frequent type in Shelley's verse from *Alastor* onwards" (*Nascent Mind*, 91–92).

2. Moved by her love of liberty the woman makes a journey to a "vast and peopled city . . . / Which was a field of holy warfare then" (I.xliv.388–89), as Wollstonecraft did to Paris, and like her returns disconsolate when "those hopes had lost the glory of their youth" (I.xliv.394 [*CW* I, 269]). In a chronological sequence that parallels Wollstonecraft's, the woman then describes her feelings in scenes that evoke those described in *Letters Written During a Short Residence in Sweden, Norway, and Denmark:* "In lonely glens, amid the roar of rivers, / When the dim nights were moonless, have I known / Joys which no tongue can tell" (I.xlvi.406–8 [*CW* I, 270]).

3. Hillman also notes that while Jung's "basic definition" has reference only to the psyche, it is reinforced by this biological speculation: "The anima is presumably a psychic representation of the minority of female genes in a man's body" [Jung 11, 48]. Anima, Hillman judges, "thus becomes the carrier and even the image of 'wholeness' . . . since she completes the hermaphrodite both psychologically and as representative of man's biological contrasexuality" ("Anima" 99).

4. Consider, for example, the restrictions effected by Promethean appropriativeness on a supposedly universal drama: this is a universal history without a single woman subject or, for that matter, a single non-Western one. Commenting on the significance of *Prometheus Unbound* as a drama including history, Curran writes:

> As man's original benefactor in Greek mythology, Prometheus stands at the fountain-head of western civilization. His consort rules over the east, for—in the opinion of Varro cited by many commentators—Asia, the wife of Iapetus, gave her name to the continent. To unite Prometheus and Asia in a symbolic drama is to join numerous contraries, including those associated with the principal cultures of the ancient world: the intellect, objectivity, productivity of the west and the emotional subtlety, intuitiveness, and meditative retirement of the east. (*Annus Mirabilis* 46)

But in a play that takes white masculinity not only as the human norm but as the only fully operative subjectivity, the action represents not the joining of contraries but the assimilative process whereby masculine Western subjects appropriated all of Western history and colonized the globe. That this summary of the "plot" works against Shelley's actual intention goes without saying. My point is that Shelley's play, by which he hopes to project an ideal society and a reordering of human history, acts out in its fantasies the human injustices it means to rectify. Its mimetic function is thus not utopian but diagnostic.

5. Frazer writes: "The Egyptians called it [Sirius] Sothis, and regarded it as the star of Isis, just as the Babylonians deemed the planet Venus the star of Astarte. To both peoples apparently the brilliant luminary in the morning sky seemed the goddess of life and love come to mourn her departed lover or spouse and to wake him from the dead" (VI,34–35).

6. See also Stern's comment on the centrality of the gaze to the formation of an interactive subjectivity:

> We have found that, during feeding, mothers spend about 70 percent of the time facing and looking at their infants. Accordingly, what he [sic] is most likely to look at and see is his mother's face, especially her eyes. . . . Thus the arrangement of anatomy, normal positioning, and visual competence dictated by natural design all point to the mother's face as an initial focal point of importance for the infant's early construction of his salient visual world, and a starting point for the formation of his early human relatedness. (*The First Relationship* 36)

7. Rajan's commentary bears on my interpretation of this interchange: "The logocentric concept of the 'written soul' resolves the paradox . . . that in order to preserve vision one must fix it in writing, but that writing is always external and supplemental to what it transmits. The process of moving beyond the linguistic sign to the language of the eyes suggests to us how the reader too can break the hermeneutic circle by moving beyond a grammatical and semiological reading that decenters vision to a psychological reading that allows us unmediated access to the inner core of the work" (325).

8. See Jane Harrison's statement in the introduction to *Themis:* "I saw that . . . Dionysus, with every other mystery god, was an instinctive attempt to express what Professor Bergson calls *durée,* that life which is one, indivisible and yet ceaselessly changing" (viii).

9. Shelley, plagued at times in his life by bouts of sleepwalking (Medwin 27, 90, 271), would have had a personal interest in the subject, and surely he discussed somnambulism in both its forms with John Polidori, Byron's physician, during the summer of 1816. Somnambulism had been the topic of Polidori's medical thesis (M. Shelley, *Frankenstein* 227), and Polidori visited Dr. Odier in Geneva to discuss problems relating to somnambulism only days before the "ghost story" sessions of mid-June 1816 that gave rise to *Frankenstein* (225) and Polidori's *Vampyre* (Polidori 119–20).

Somnambulism of the specifically magnetic variety also figures in the climactic incident of those ghost story sessions: Shelley's hysterical reaction to Byron's recitation of verses from "Christabel." In the very last stanza of part one, after the lines that (in the manuscript version Byron would have quoted) describe Geraldine's bosom as "lean and old and foul of hue," Geraldine hypnotizes Christabel, saying:

> In the touch of this bosom there worketh a spell,
> Which is lord of thy utterance, Christabel!
> Thou knowest to-night and wilt know to-morrow,
> This mark of my shame, this seal of my sorrow.
>
> (Coleridge, *Poems* 224–25)

Polidori's account states only that "L[ord] B[yron] repeated some verses of Coleridge's 'Christabel' of the witch's breast; when silence ensued, and Shelley suddenly shrieking and putting his hand to his head, ran out of the room with a candle" (128). Commentators on this incident usually refer primarily to the description of Geraldine's breasts in the second-to-last stanza of the first part of the poem as the source of Shelley's fright, but it stands to reason that Byron recited the last stanza as well before the "silence" that gave way to Shelley's screams. There Geraldine ascribes mesmeric power to her bosom, not her eyes, but the displacement involved in the lines themselves makes Shelley's hallucinatory vision, while looking at Mary, of "a woman he had heard of who had eyes instead of nipples" (Polidori 128) a strong response to the poem, to be sure, but one with textual justification.

10. Freud postulates two forms of libido: ego-libido, which is narcissistic and takes the ego itself as love-object, and object-libido, which is "anaclitic," or attaching, and seeks its fulfillment in another ("On Narcissism," in *Standard Edition XIV*, 87–88).

11. The direction of the magnetic energy also contradicts Shelley's own experience, since he himself seemed to get the most benefit from being magnetized by women: specifically Mary Shelley and Jane Williams (Medwin 269–70). For the latter he wrote "From a Magnetic Lady to her Patient." The speaker in the poem is imagined as Jane herself, and one stanza in particular equates psychic and sexual commingling, with the suggestion that both mirror the intrauterine symbiosis of mother and fetus:

> Like a cloud big with a May shower
>   My soul weeps healing rain
> On thee, thou withered flower.—
> It breathes mute music on thy sleep,
>   Its odour calms thy brain—
> Its light withing thy gloomy breast
> Spreads, like a second youth again—
> By mine thy being is to its deep
>   Possess.—
>
> (Chernaik 258)

12. Deleuze gives special notice to the role of eyes and hands in transmitting the magnetic fluid: "Although the magnetic fluid escapes from all the body, and the will suffices to give it direction, the external organs, by which we act, are the most proper to throw it off with the intention determined by the will. For this reason, we make use of our hands and of our eyes to magnetize" (24).

13. Figure 8 gives striking graphic evidence of the differing emphases attached to particular senses at different points in the play. This graph was produced through a text retrieval system created by Academic Information Resources (AIR) at Stanford Uni-

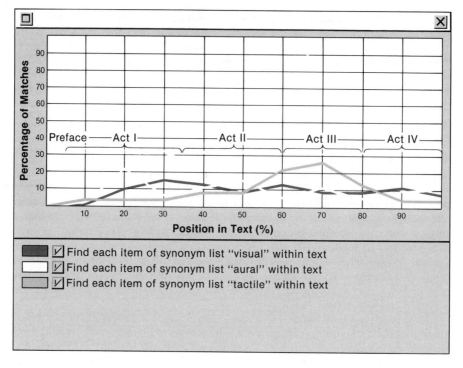

Fig. 8. Graph created by the Searcher computer program to chart patterns of imagery in *Prometheus Unbound* (*Produced by Academic Information Resources, Stanford University*)

versity. I am particularly grateful to Malcolm Brown and Alison Reid for their help in producing it.

At several points I relate infant transmodal experience as described by Stern to Shelley's use of synesthetic imagery, but the subject deserves a much fuller study that would build on the foundation provided by Glenn O'Malley's *Shelley and Synesthesia*. O'Malley's research into seventeenth- and eighteenth-century speculation on synesthesia shows its connection with doctrines of "sympathy" (19); also, with acknowledged indebtedness to Erika von Erhardt-Siebold's work on synesthesia, O'Malley notes that "synesthetic motifs dominate contexts in which Shelley describes millennial or quasi-mystical states of being" (14).

14. Drummond's sentence on the ear as cavern, with its allusion to Dionysus, tyrant of Sicily, whom Plato vainly attempted to bring to philosophic wisdom, must have caught Shelley's particular attention: "When Dionysus listened in the cavern, which was called his *ear,* it served as an organ for the tyrant, while it was he alone, who was perceptive of sound. Now as Dionysus heard, and not the cavern; so the mind hears, and not the ear" (122).

15. Fernald uses the word "motherese" to describe the baby talk of a caretaker to an infant because at the time research in this area limited itself to the interactions of mothers and their babies. Her own more recent research shows, however, that across languages men's and women's speech patterns are remarkably consistent during interaction with infants (Fernald et al., "A Cross-Language Study" 491).

16. I am indebted here to Andrea Nye's discussion of Wittgenstein in "The Unity of Language" (98).

17. William Ulmer has also noted the salience of allusions to the Oedipus legend in *Prometheus Unbound* (80–85) and discusses (though on different terms from mine) the drama's strategies for liberating Prometheus from Oedipal guilt.

18. A Victorian autobiographical sketch of Taylor in *Fraser's Magazine* (November 1875) describes, for instance, the Platonist's horror at receiving a letter in 1788 from the Marquis of Valady, who described himself as a "Pythagorean" and, taking Taylor's agreement for granted, asserted that "the philosophic doctrine of community should be extended to the conjugal relations" (Raine and Harper, eds. 127).

19. The metonymic connection between Demogorgon and the uroboros, the "snake-like Doom coiled underneath his throne" (*SPU* II.iii.97), creates another link between Demogorgon and Pan. Constantin Volney considers both the "emblem of Pan (the great whole)" and the uroboros as representations of the idea that "God" is "being, effect, and cause, agent and patient, moving principle and thing moved, having for law the invariable properties that constitute fatality" (142; cf. Hartley 529).

20. Robert Hartley, though approaching the topic from a different, more strictly historical, perspective, makes a similar point (528–35), and Jerrold Hogle describes Asia's descent as a "reinitiation" (189).

21. When discussing the very definition of the Greek word *mysteria*, Walter Burkert notes that it is best revealed by "the established Latin translation of *mysteria*, *myein*, *myesis* as *initia*, *initiare*, *initiatio*, which brought the word and the concept of 'initiation' into our language. Following this line, we find that mysteries are initiation ceremonies" (*Ancient Mystery Cults* 7–8).

22. John Chailley mentions that, in addition to the undoubted fact that Mozart was an initiated Mason, there is a widespread misapprehension that he was also one of the Illuminati—a rumor that H.D. could very easily have heard and that may have triggered this connection. Also, Mozart's allegiance to Masonry, celebrated through *The Magic Flute,* may explain the surprising parallels between that work and *Prometheus Unbound.* Curran, describing Shelley's pleasure in opera (i.e., "lyrical drama"), writes, "Jupiter exits through the same trapdoor as Don Giovanni," and adds, "However, the opera that might most have justified the ritualistic conception of *Prometheus Unbound,* Mozart's *Magic Flute,* was unknown to him, and, indeed, not produced in England until some years after he left" (*Annus Mirabilis* 232).

23. I am using "metaphysical" with Linda Alcoff's meaning when she writes:

> There are questions of importance to human beings that science alone cannot answer (including what science is and how it functions), and yet these are questions that we cannot usefully address by combining scientific data with other logical, political, moral, pragmatic, and coherence considerations. . . . Metaphysical problems are problems that concern factual claims about the world (rather than simply expressive, moral, or aesthetic assertions, e.g.) but are problems that cannot be determined through empirical means alone. (429)

24. Hogle does not refer specifically to Delphi in discussing this passage but makes associated connections between Asia as a Maenad, "half-Dionysian in her generation of natural fecundity," and as "a variation of Virgil's Cumaean Sibyl," besides being transformed into "the prophetic figure of Liberty" (185).

25. William Blake's version of the same historical process takes the form of the story, told in a number of different ways, of Urizen's assertion of dominance among the Four Zoas. The consequences, as Blake has Urizen describe them in this passage from *The Four Zoas,* come very close to Shelley's:

> I will walk forth thro those wide fields of endless Eternity
> A God & not a Man a Conqueror in triumphant glory
> And all the Sons of Everlasting shall bow down at my feet
>
> First Trades & Commerce & armed vessels he builded laborious
> To swim the deep & on the Land children are sold to trades
> Of dire necessity still laboring day & night till all
> Their life extinct they took spectre form in dark despair
> And slaves in myriads in ship loads burden the hoarse sounding deep
> Rattling with clanking clains the Universal Empire groans
>
> (392)

Or, in the analysis of Horkheimer and Adorno:

> In class history, the enmity of the self to sacrifice implied a sacrifice of the self, inasmuch as it was paid for by a denial of nature in man for the sake of domination over non-human nature and over other men. This very denial, the nucleus of all civilizing rationality, is the germ cell of a proliferating mythic irrationality: with the denial of nature in man not merely the *telos* of the outward control of nature but the *telos* of man's own life is distorted and befogged. (54)

26. One could say that the uroboros was Shelley's "totem" as well, or at least was the one that Byron assigned him by giving him "the Snake" as his nickname (Holmes 672–73). Byron wrote in jesting explanation: "Goethe's Mephistofeles calls the Serpent who tempted Eve '*my Aunt the renowned Snake*' and I always insist that Shelley is nothing but one of her Nephews—walking about on the tip of his tail" (*Letters and Journals* IX, 81).

27. I suggest this as a possible strategy because it was one that Shelley favored in his interactions with women. In the events leading up to his elopement with Harriet Westbrook, for instance, she, not he, became the initiator. Shelley wrote to Hogg: "Her father has persecuted her in a most horrible way, & endeavours to compel her to go to school. She asked my advice . . . & in consequence of my advice *she* has thrown herself upon *my* protection!" (*L* I, 131; author's emphasis). Similarly, Mary Godwin, not Shelley, is described as the one whose declaration precipitated their love affair: "The sublime & rapturous moment when she confessed herself mine, who has so long been her's in secret cannot be painted to mortal imaginations—" (*L* I, 403).

28. Diodorus Siculus links Isis not only with other Mother Goddesses but also with Dionysus:

> Now I am not unaware that some historians give the following account of Isis and Osiris: The tombs of these gods lie in Nysa in Arabia, and for this reason Dionysus is also called Nysaeus. And in that place there stands also a stele of each of the gods bearing an inscription in hieroglyphs. On the stele of Isis it runs: "I am Isis, the queen of every land. . . . I am she who riseth in the star that is the Constellation of the Dog. (I.27.4–5)

Passages in Sir William Drummond's *Essay on a Punic Inscription*, a work that we know was familiar to Shelley (*L* I, 345), also draw attention both to the ancient identification of the planet with the Mother Goddess and to the relationship between the Goddess and Dionysus. Drummond writes, "We know from Pliny that the star in question was called the star of Juno, of Isis, and of the Mother of the Gods; and we are told by various authors, that Venus was occasionally considered as the same with all of these" (55–56). At another point he observes, "*Osiris* was the same with Bacchus, and Bacchus was styled by eminence *The Father*" (92).

29. Early 1818 or late 1817 is the date accepted as most likely for Shelley's translation of two pastoral pieces, both of which take up the theme of mourning for Adonis or an Adonis-like figure: from Bion, "Fragment of the Elegy on the Death of Adonis," and from Moschus, "Fragment of an Elegy on the Death of Bion" (Webb 69). In Shelley's review of Peacock's *Rhododaphne,* written before he left England in 1818, he alludes to Lucian's *De Dea Syria* (*CW* VI, 273).

Although archaeological and linguistic discoveries in the Middle East and Far East—linked, as the very locutions "Middle" and "Far" betray, to England's rapidly expanding colonialism—placed Shelley in a period of dizzying and at times eccentric but also often brilliant speculation about religious origins, a connection had been made even in ancient times between Adonis and a Semitic cult figure much like him called Tammuz. In the Vulgate, Jerome, translating the passage in Ezekiel (8:13–14) in which the prophet inveighs against the idolatry of the women outside the temple wailing for Tammuz, changes the Semitic name Tammuz to the Greek Adonis. Jerome, in turn, was taking for granted an identification familiar to the Greeks themselves: Walter Burkert describes Adonis as "the clearest example of a Semitic god adopted by the Greeks in the archaic period, and the Greeks knew it" (*Structure and History in Greek Mythology and Ritual* 105).

Shelley's familiarity with a wide variety of Greek sources makes it possible and even likely that he shared the Greeks' awareness of a link between Tammuz and Adonis. He could not possibly, however, have known of a connection stretching back deep into antiquity between the Semitic Tammuz and a young male hero named Dumuzi who figures in the central rituals and the related literature of the Sumerians, a non-Semitic people who flourished in the area of the Tigris-Euphrates basin from 4500 to 1770 B.C. The very existence of such a people was not suspected until more than thirty years after Shelley's death, and translation of the cuneiform texts recording their extraordinary culture has made rapid progress only in recent decades (Kramer, *The Sumerians* 5–32). I am not, therefore, suggesting that even by the most extraordinary intuitive leap Shelley could have had any *firsthand* knowledge of the myth and ritual surrounding the shepherd Dumuzi, the chosen one of the Mother Earth goddess Inanna, but he did know versions of the same legend through the pastoral tradition. Different myths surrounding the passionate love affair and eventual marriage of goddess and shepherd were the subject of countless poems and the basis for yearly fertility rituals. Poems also center on another important series of events, varying in different tellings, about Dumuzi's death—sometimes brought about through the agency of Inanna—his descent to the underworld, and Inanna's rescue of him (Kramer, *The Sacred Marriage Rite* 132; Jacobsen, *Toward the Image of Tammuz* 100–101).

30. Critics give proof of Shelley's success in restricting Asia's role to that of consort by associating her "triumph" not with the ancient legends surrounding the Mother Goddess but with later, much more clearly patriarchal revisions of that myth: the "Biblical figure of the exile, return, and marriage of the bride" (Abrams, *Natural Supernaturalism* 299; Ulmer 79) and "the *hieros gamos* imaged in *Revelation* as the New Jerusalem descending from Heaven as a bride to meet the bridegroom" (Woodman 228).

6

"Where the Split Began" (*Prometheus Unbound*, Act III)

As part of his initial discussion about the aesthetic's social function, Eagleton writes: "At the very root of social relations lies the aesthetic, source of all human bonding. If bourgeois society releases its individuals into lonely autonomy, then only by such an imaginative exchange or appropriation of each other's identities can they be deeply enough united" (24). On the basis of ideas discussed throughout this book, but particularly in the first two chapters, I would modify the first of these sentences to read: "At the very root of social relations (i.e., of the human) lie affect attunement and mimetic responsiveness, source of all human interaction, which make possible the broad range of experiences signified under the term 'aesthetic.'" Later in his argument Eagleton describes the aesthetic as "from the beginning a contradictory, double-edged concept" (28), but in the second sentence quoted here he has not yet taken up that point and leaves the words "exchange" and "appropriation" as seeming moral equivalents. They are clearly not, however, and in the third act of *Prometheus Unbound* Shelley addresses himself to dramatizing the difference between them.

In the first of this act's four scenes, Shelley imagines the denouement Aeschylus believed unimaginable: given no warning about Thetis, Jupiter has sexual relations with her, Jupiterean sexuality serving as paradigm for the appropriative. Jupiter imagines that the "fatal Child, the terror of the Earth" (III.i.19), produced by this union will finally establish his total power over humankind; instead, the Power who appears, describing himself as Jupiter's "child" (III.i.53), is Demogorgon. Helpless before him, Jupiter plummets to the abyss. After a pastoral transition (sc. ii), we witness the unbinding of Prometheus and his reunion with the Oceanides and with Earth (sc. iii). There and in scene four the dialogue and the dramatic action turn on love as a constant, fructifying, nonviolent, and nonviolational exchange, its paradigm a domestic intimacy somewhat reminiscent of Field Place on Shelley's last visit there in June 1814: the father disposed of, while a mother and devoted sisters make up a loving circle surrounding the son.

The Rape of Thetis (Scene i)

Shelley devotes only fifty-one lines to conjuring up for his readers some image of what Jupiter's "Heaven" has been like through the millennia. The first, perhaps most hellish, thing about it is that its ruler is a monologist. A large cast, made up of "Thetis and other Deities," is assembled, but they are props, extras; not one has a line of dialogue. Addressed as "Powers," they function only as vehicles for Jupiter's own power, a process he calls "sharing" (III.i.1).

In contrast "the soul of man," described in a Promethean simile as "like unextinguished fire" (III.i.5), resists such total assimilation, though in a confused and still ineffectual way. With an interestingly Blakean turn, Jupiter describes the source of his ages-long strength as "eldest faith, and Hell's coeval, fear" (III.i.10)—that is, as the process, described by Hogle (89ff.), by which humans alienate their own powers through the concept of an all-powerful Other, empty themselves as the "Powers" of heaven have been emptied, and then live in subservient fear of their own false creation. So the "Father in Heaven" conceived through this "eldest faith" is actually Lord of Hell. As with Dante's Satan and Blake's Urizen, his malevolence expresses itself in images not of fire but of cold: "And though my curses through the pendulous air / Like snow on herbless peaks, fall flake by flake / And cling to it [the soul of man] . . . / It yet remains supreme o'er misery" (III.i.11–13, 16).

As Reiman and Powers point out (*SPP* 180), Jupiter's image of snow piling up "flake by flake" on mountain peaks to describe his gathering power ironically echoes Asia's words on the process by which just perception builds "flake after flake, in Heaven-defying minds / As thought by thought is piled" (II.iii.39–40) and so looks forward to the avalanche of changed perception about to sweep Jupiter down into the abyss. But on its own terms the image also shows the action whereby Jupiterean discourse blanks out all signification except its own. Functioning as the discourse of all those political, religious, legal, and social agencies that serve as conduits of Jupiterean power, its purpose is to make that power seem an inescapable given, certainly, but also, ideally, to make it an acceptable good. Jupiter's snow, in brief, is the blanketing ideology that Shelley describes in "A Philosophical View of Reform": "It is in vain to exhort us to wait until all men shall desire Freedom whose real interest will consist in its establishment. It is in vain to hope to enlighten them whilst their tyrants employ the utmost artifices of all their complicated engine to perpetuate the infection of every species of fanaticism & error from generation to generation." Its soft and constant fall obliterates all the boundaries between separate subjectivities: "Unless the cause which renders them passive subjects instead of active citizens be removed, they will sink with accelerated gradations into that barbaric & unnatural civilization which destroys all differences among men" (*SHC* VI, 1056).

From Jupiter's own admission, an "unextinguish'd fire" in the "soul of man" (III.i.5) has so far prevented that merging of subjectivity into an undifferentiated mass. That fire is Promethean, of course, but also—in the mountain landscape described by Jupiter's extended simile—the allusion conjures up the figure of Demogorgon. Given my adaptation and extension of Matthews's argument so as to link Demogorgon with both repressed sexuality and the spirit of revolution, the "unextinguish'd fire" therefore has sexuality as part of its fuel. Indeed, there is evidence to suggest that Shelley, making an identification that Foucault has shown to be axiomatic by the early nineteenth century (*History of Sexuality* I, 155–56), takes sexuality to be definitive in the structuring of a sense of individual identity.

A marshaling of this evidence must begin with Jupiter's gloating over a "fatal Child," product of his union with Thetis, who will finally smother the unextinguished fire burning on despite the Jupiterean reign of ice and snow:

> Even now have I begotten a strange wonder,
> That fatal Child, the terror of the Earth,
> Who waits but till the destined Hour arrive,
> Bearing from Demogorgon's vacant throne
> The dreadful might of ever living limbs
> Which clothed that awful spirit unbeheld—
> To redescend and trample out the spark . . .
>   (III.i.18–24)

Again, as in the echo of Asia's words "flake on flake," the passage is heavily ironic in that the forthcoming event in no way resembles Jupiter's anticipation of it. Jupiter's own, unironic message also deserves—and has received—scholarly attention, notably from Pulos, who suggests that the "Child" on whom Jupiter rests his hope for total possession of the human spirit "may quite possibly be a symbol for Malthusianism" ("Shelley and Malthus" 120).

With clarity and sweet reason Malthus sets forth his foundational principle: "Population, when unchecked, increases in a geometrical ratio. Subsistence increases only in an arithmetical ratio" (9). The "checks" to population explosion are moral restraint, vice, and misery. Of these the negative ones, vice and misery, take their greatest toll among the poor, whose marginal resources make them most vulnerable when the population level becomes disproportionate to the food supply. It is therefore particularly incumbent on the poor—a matter for them of special "Necessity" within this mathematical schema—to use the "positive" check of moral restraint and/or sexual abstinence: to practice continence before marriage, to marry late, and to observe prolonged periods of abstinence in marriage.

Shelley's diatribe against Malthus in "A Philosophical View of Reform" (where, unnamed, he is characterized as "a priest of course—for his doctrines are those of a eunuch & of a tyrant" [*SHC* VI, 1023]) focuses on these Malthusian dicta against sexual expression among the poor. In its inclusion of all domestic bonds within the sexual, Shelley's description of sexuality as "the single alleviation of their sufferings & their scorns, the one thing which made it impossible to degrade them below the beasts" actually resembles Eagleton's "aesthetic." Shelley makes sexuality the very core of identity, "the last tie by which Nature holds them [the poor] to the benignant earth" and connects it also with those qualities the maternal ideology placed within the purview of the feminine: "all the soothing elevating & harmonious gentlenesses of the sexual intercourse, & the humanizing charities of domestic life which are its appendandages" [sic] (*SHC* VI, 1024). The vehemence of his indignation stems from a proto-Foucauldian insight that the whole area with which the uniqueness of each individual seems most identified can actually be the site of its deepest inscription. The volatility of Demogorgon, however, serves as dramatic parallel to Eagleton's assertion that "the aesthetic as custom, sentiment, spontaneous impulse may consort well enough with political domination; but these phenomena border embarrassingly on passion, imagination, sensuality, which are not always so easily incorporable" (28).

In annotating the text of "A Philosophical View," Reiman feels bound in fairness to point out that Malthus "though a priest was hardly a eunuch (he sired a son and two daughters) or a tyrant" (*SHC* VI, 1023). But read again in the context of act three, scene one of *Prometheus Unbound,* the epithets take on particular doubled significance. As an *instrument* of Jupiter (i.e., of the hegemonic power structure) Malthus, emptied of sexual desire himself and thereby a "passive subject" rather than an "active citizen," advises that others be likewise emptied; he is in that capacity a eunuch and a propagandist or sycophant. As the *image* or microcosm of Jupiter, he is, for reasons to be discussed next, a rapist and a tyrant.

Rape functions in this scene as both metaphor and metonym for Jupiter's tyrannical inscription of vulnerable mirroring subjectivity. The narrated rape of Thetis constitutes the only action in the scene besides that of Jupiter's fall and serves to characterize his whole reign. In a use of ventriloquism as charged with meaning as that in act one when the shade of Jupiter repeats Prometheus' curse, but with a very different dramatic purpose, Shelley has Jupiter so totally appropriate Thetis' speech that the account of the rape is his alone, and her very cry of protest becomes a vehicle for his expression of sadistic pleasure. Through the passage reverberate other versions of a similar event; Jupiter's words comment ironically on Hesiod's admiration for Zeus' cunning in swallowing Metis (*Hesiod* 143) and on Zeus' infiltration of Io's dreaming mind in *Prometheus Bound* (ll. 949–68):

> And thou
> Ascend beside me, veiled in the light
> Of the desire which makes thee one with me,
> Thetis, bright Image of Eternity!—
> When thou didst cry, "Insufferable might!
> God! spare me! I sustain not the quick flames,
> The penetrating presence; all my being,
> Like him whom the Numidian seps did thaw
> Into a dew with poison, is dissolved,
> Sinking through its foundations"—
> (III.i.33–42)

The intertexuality of these lines involves not only classical allusions but thematic connections with two works that Shelley was soon to write, *The*

Cenci and "On Life." The relevant passage from "On Life" is the meditation on the nature of pronouns that have been considered before in other contexts: "The existence of distinct individual minds . . . is likewise found to be a delusion. The words, *I, you, they,* are not signs of any actual difference subsisting between the assemblage of thoughts thus indicated, but are merely marks employed to denote the different modifications of the one mind" (*SPP* 477–78). The perceiving mind is not a Lockean, separate, bourgeois entity cheerfully gathering, filing, and storing impressions. Perceptions invade mind so that one becomes what one experiences. We have acquired signifiers for the process—"introjection," "colonization"—unavailable to Shelley, but his "thread of reasoning" has brought him to the concept.

Now, as Shelley's use of the word "eunuch" to characterize Malthus and as the ravaged body of Prometheus both show, a male subject's castration could represent human vulnerability to impression at least as well as a female subject's rape. Both in this scene of *Prometheus Unbound* and in *The Cenci,* however, Shelley veils and displaces the horror of castration, substituting for it the rape of a powerless and virtuous woman by a syphilitic patriarch whose purpose is to permeate and disease her body while making her mind a mirror and receptacle of his own. That is, like most men of his time and on up to our time, Shelley drew back from imagining psychic vulnerability as universal, preferring to accept guilt for a male sexuality constructed as violent and intrusive if it were also both signifier for and guarantor of impermeable autonomy. The split in the Eagleton passage quoted at the beginning of this chapter between the "lonely autonomy" of "individuals" on the one hand and "exchange or appropriation" among subjectivities on the other is elided by the gendering of one as male, the other as female.

The lines with which Jupiter first addresses Thetis mildly foreshadow the more violent mirroring to come. He moves quickly from satisfaction with Thetis as his mirror to exhibitionist pleasure in using her words of protest to reveal his potency. Central to Thetis' quoted speech, and proof that hers is not an orgasmic cry in any positive sense, is the allusion to a grotesquely horrible incident in Lucan's *Pharsalia* (IX.762–88) in which Sabellus is bitten by a seps. The poison of this serpent dissolves bone itself, reducing his body to a revolting jelly. The image thus carries the thought that syphilitic Jupiter (Crook and Guiton 188) is a universal source of contagion; his mirror in world history is the diseased Count Cenci, who says of his incestuous rape of his daughter, Beatrice, "I will make / Body and soul a monstrous lump of ruin" ([*SPP*] *Cenci* IV.i.94–95).

A similar echo of Thetis' cry appears in Beatrice's maddened screams after her rape. She comes on stage suffering the delusion that blood is pouring into her eyes. The next sensations she describes are schizophrenic: one "self" stands watching, while another experiences a sickening, giddy dissolution. Further images of blood follow, and then (the two selves collapsing into one) evocations of loathsome smells. The most intimate of the senses, smell invades the body even more than hearing does. As image of that penetration

Shelley has these smells assume a visible form in a "clinging, black, contaminating mist" that "glues / My fingers and my limbs to one another, / And eats into my sinews, and dissolves / My flesh to a pollution" (III.i.17–22).

For both Thetis and Beatrice this sense of physical dissolution serves merely as trope for a more appalling fear that subjectivity itself now permanently includes the "penetrating presence" of the rapist Other. This, a horrible but parallel version of Jupiter's plan to make Thetis "one" with himself, is the ultimate suffering that Cenci intends to inflict on his daughter: "She shall become (for what she most abhors / Shall have a fascination to entrap / Her loathing will), to her own conscious self / All she appears to others" (IV.i.85–88). And Cenci almost succeeds. Condemned to die for having murdered him, Beatrice quails before the possibility that after death there will be no God and no Heaven but no oblivion either:

> If all things then should be . . . my father's spirit
> His eyes, his voice, his touch surrounding me;
> The atmosphere and breath of my dead life!
> If sometimes, as a shape more like himself,
> Even the form which tortured me on earth,
> Masked in grey hairs and wrinkles, he should come
> And wind me in his hellish arms, and fix
> His eyes on mine, and drag me down, down, down!
> For was he not alone omnipotent
> On Earth, and ever present?
> (V. iv.60–69)

The fantasy is by no means irrational but, as I have noted, shows a psychologically astute understanding of the fluid nature of subjectivity. Beatrice's stepmother, the loving but ineffectual Lucretia, offers an escape from it through trust in "the tender promises of Christ" and the hope of attaining Paradise. But Shelley's Beatrice can take no comfort from Lucretia's words: "You do well telling me to trust in God, / I hope I do trust in him, In whom else / Can any trust?" (V.iv.87–89). All the action of the play suggests that the answer to her rhetorical question is "in no one—including God." One might even say "especially not in God," since, as Curran points out, "the paternal power in this play is almost mystical, a direct reflection of God's authority and the Pope's" (*Shelley's "Cenci"* 67), and all three are manifestations of the paternal power called Jupiter in *Prometheus Unbound*.

The "sad reality" (*SPP* 237) of the historically based *Cenci* contrasts sharply with the mythic and utopian *Prometheus Unbound*. In the one, having characterized "revenge, retaliation, atonement" as "pernicious mistakes" (*SPP* 240), Shelley dramatizes a situation in which Beatrice's only recourse in the face of subjective dissolution is murder. No Demogorgon rises to her rescue. Indeed, the murder of Cenci itself does not offer a resolution, since it leaves her still in danger of possession by her father's spirit. Only acceptance of death as reunion with the mother exorcises that paternal spirit and makes it possible for Beatrice to die bravely (V.iv.115–18). As I shall shortly discuss, relationship with the mother is of similarly crucial significance in *Prometheus Unbound.*

Also, if one puts aside the kind of *response* to patriarchal appropriation of subjectivity available to the protagonists in the two plays and focuses rather on that appropriation itself, one can see a parallel between the myth and its reflection in history. Both *Prometheus Unbound* and *The Cenci* suggest that the patriarchal assault on subjectivity that seeks finally to appropriate sexuality itself acts as "the last straw" in the cliché, the last snowflake in Shelley's metaphor, which overwhelms Cenci in death, Jupiter in the downfall created by the appearance of Demogorgon.

Crook and Guiton, building on Matthews's association of Demogorgon with the many-headed rebel giant Typhon and on Pulos's theory that the Malthusian fatal Child envisioned by Jupiter turns out to be his doom, offer an interpretation of the conclusion of act three, scene one of *Prometheus Unbound* that I find convincing though incomplete: "Demogorgon can therefore be identified with the force of the proletariat, irresistible because of its 'unvanquishable number' once roused from sleep. The increase in population, held by Malthus to be the reason for keeping the masses in perpetual subservience, is the very means of their self-deliverance" (196).

While true to the political aspect of Shelley's thought, signaled through its applicability to *The Mask of Anarchy,* this reading does not address the closely related problems centered on subjectivity and language. Nor do gender politics enter into it. As prelude to a later consideration of all these, we need to hear one further echo in Thetis' reported speech: the fate of Semele. Like Io, Semele had the misfortune to arouse the ardor of Zeus and the consequent jealousy of Hera. Taking the form of Semele's nurse, Hera persuaded the young woman to ask Zeus, as the favor he had promised, that he come to her in the full panoply of his godhead; doing so, he consumed her by fire. Dionysus, the infant she had conceived, was saved from the fire and carried in Zeus' thigh until he was mature enough to be born.

The evocation of Semele in the line "God! spare me! I sustain not the quick flames" (III.i.39), coupled with Demogorgon's statement to Jupiter "I am thy child, as thou wert Saturn's child" (III.i.54), elides Demogorgon with Dionysus. Abstractly or allegorically described, the process by which Jupiter produces Demogorgon involves a Jupiterean overreaching that attempts the final takeover of the unity in which "each is at once the centre and the circumference" ("On Life," *SPP* 476). The attempt to infiltrate that unity to its depths finds in those depths its nemesis. For the "unity" is in fact a mysteriously shared life—Dionysian, not Jupiterean. Again, a statement of Eagleton's offers a useful gloss: " 'Deep' subjectivity is just what the ruling social order desires, and exactly what it has most cause to fear. If the aesthetic is a dangerous, ambiguous affair, it is because . . . there is something in the body which can revolt against the power which inscribes it; and that impulse could only be eradicated by extirpating along with it the capacity to authenticate power itself" (28).

Utopian Paradigms (Scene ii)

Scenes three and four of act three further explore the nature of this unity, and I shall discuss the topic at length, pausing only to consider before that what purpose scene two serves in the drama. In brief I would say that its principal function is its pastoral form. Structurally, this scene balances act two, scene two, thereby picking up a pastoral motif expressive of the determination to achieve an art that "leads man who cannot now go back to Arcady forward to Elysium" (Schiller, *Naïve and Sentimental Poetry* 153), a purpose that will dominate the drama from this point on. At least complicating, if not hampering, this linear trajectory, however, is the pastoral's tendency toward a regressive or a cyclic vision. Both these complicating tendencies are given particular opportunity to flourish by the scene's setting: "The Mouth of a great River in the Island Atlantis."

As was true in the "forest" scene of act two, scene two, a book-lined study is more truly the locus of the action than the river mouth, and our eyes lift to scan texts by Plato and Bacon on the surrounding shelves. The story of an ancient and powerful civilization centered on the island of Atlantis somewhere west of the Pillars of Hercules appears first in the Platonic dialogues *Timaeus* and *Critias*. The *Timaeus* contrasts luxurious, commercial, slave-holding Atlantis (much resembling Plato's contemporary Athens) with an equitable and moderate Athens of an earlier period. But in *Critias* we learn that at one time the power-mad Atlantans also "bore the burden of their wealth and possessions lightly, and did not let their high standard of living . . . make them lose their self-control" (145). Similarly, in Bacon's *New Atlantis* the admirable people of the island of Bensalem, while expert mariners, "maintain a trade, not for gold, silver, or jewels; nor for silks; nor for spices; nor for any other commodity of matter; but only for God's first creature, which was *Light:* to have *light* . . . of the growth of all parts of the world" (58).

Critias takes up the subject of Athens and Atlantis once again, beginning with a description of Athens in prehistoric times:

> Once upon a time the gods divided up the Earth between them—not in the course of a quarrel. . . . Each gladly received his just allocation, and settled his territories; and having done so they proceeded to look after us, their creatures and children, as shepherds look after their flocks. They did not use physical means of control, like shepherds who direct their flock with blows, but brought their influence to bear on the creature's most sensitive part, using persuasion as a steersman uses the helm to direct the mind as they saw fit and so guide the whole mortal creature. (131–32)

With elegant allusion to his precedent masters in the utopian, Shelley takes up these ideas and images while adding touches of his own, as he has Ocean say:

and from their glassy thrones
Blue Proteus and his humid nymphs shall mark
The shadow of fair ships, as mortals see
The floating bark of the light-laden moon
With that white star, its sightless pilot's crest,
Borne down the rapid sunset's ebbing sea;
Tracking their path no more by blood and groans;
And desolation and the mingled voice
Of slavery and command—but by the light
Of wave-reflected flowers, and floating odours,
And music soft, and mild, free, gentle voices,
That sweetest music, such as spirits love.

                                   (III.ii.23–34)

An extended simile structures the passage: Proteus and his nymphs "mark-ing" the humans' ships that sail above them are compared to human beings noting the "light-laden" moon ship—the crescent moon of the cow-goddess Hathor/Isis bearing the outlined full moon—piloted by the planet Venus. In addition to setting up this parallel, however, the phrase "as mortals see," through the breadth of the term "mortals," shifts the image so that the particu-lar ship noted by Proteus changes into Earth as a spaceship mirroring the moon ship, both piloted by a Venus that as light source needs no sight, being the transcendent focus for all other sight.

The synonym "note" that I have used for "mark" seems adequate until one comes to Shelley's own synonym "tracking," which carries the suggestion that Proteus and his nymphs also have the function of pilots, though unheeded ones in the times just past. The passage thus places the world within a circle of care that extends from the sea's depths up through the heavens. In that circle the former language in which "mirroring" inscribes the slave disappears. In its place is a synesthetic language of difference mingling into harmony, "flow-ers," "odours," "music," and "voices" all blending in a "light" that mirrors the light of the "white star," Venus.

Another Platonic text in which the gods of a former age are compared to shepherds calls for attention because it bears on the significance not only of this scene but also of the one to follow. The description of life in the age of Kronos as it appears in Plato's *Statesman* is one that Jane Harrison describes as "haunted by reminiscences . . . of matrilinear social structure" (*Themis* 496). Its appeal to someone as imbued as Shelley was with the Godwinian form of "anarchy" is also obvious:

> When God was Shepherd there were no political constitutions and no taking
> of wives and begetting of children. For all men rose up anew into life out of
> earth, having no memory of former things. Instead they had fruits without
> stint from trees and bushes; these needed no cultivation but sprang up of
> themselves out of the ground without man's toil. For the most part they
> disported themselves in the open needing neither clothing nor couch, for the
> seasons were blended evenly so as to work them no hurt, and the grass which
> sprang up out of the earth in abundance made a soft bed for them.   (150)

The "Stranger" who gives Socrates and his followers this account concludes it by asking, with heavy irony, "Our present life—said to be under the government of Zeus—you are alive to experience for yourself," and adds: "But which of these makes for greater happiness do you think? Can you give a verdict?" (150). Shelley's challenge as he begins writing scene three is to answer the same questions. He has to make an imagined return to innocence something other than a regression. He also has a problem inherited from his Platonic cyclical model: Is the renewal of human life the start of what eventually will be a repetition?

Mother and Son (Scene iii)

The climactic scene in *Prometheus Unbound,* in that it depicts the very moment of "unbinding," gets off to an awkwardly anticlimactic start. Aeschylus gives eighty-five emotion-packed lines as accompaniment to the "stage business" during which Hephaestus, along with Power and Force, labors over the binding of Prometheus. But the unbinding by Hercules in Shelley's play is performed without a word, and Hercules' opening comment on the feat he has performed seems formulaic: "Thus doth strength / To wisdom, courage, and long suffering love, / And thee, who art the form they animate, / Minister, like a slave" (III.iii.1–4). Still, the contrast between Hercules' attitude here as personified Strength and that of Power and Force in *Prometheus Bound* does help recall the Aeschylean trilogy, as do the stage presences of Hercules and Earth. Appropriately so, for the drama of the scene inheres not in the actions performed on stage so much as in Shelley's situation as a dramatist. The moment has come to transform the Aeschylean "catastrophe" into the vision of a new world order. What will it be?

"It" is essentially two long speeches, one by Prometheus describing a "Cave" (III.iii.10) where he with Asia, Panthea, and Ione will live without parting; the other by Earth describing a "Cavern" (III.iii.124), which she also calls a "Cave," beside a "Temple" (III.iii.175). These allusions create an interpretive crux: Are these two different caves or descriptions of the same one? And whichever way that question is answered—whether this odd quartet, Prometheus and the three Oceanides, is imagined as stay-at-homes in a single cave or as leisured gentry with the diversion of travel between two— there arises the more serious difficulty that the Promethean agon seems to be resolving itself into an eternity of boredom. Dramatically that judgment has to be correct. The excitement charging this crucial scene is not dramatic but altogether lyric: it turns upon the significance to be read into descriptions of the cave(s), and the mixture there of aesthetic and erotic pleasure that was the consolation offered Prometheus in the fourth Spirit's song of act one: feeding "on the aerial kisses / Of shapes that haunt thought's wildernesses" (I.i.741–42).

Prometheus' opening address to Asia after their millennia-long separation scarcely bears out my contention that an erotic dynamism crackles through the language of this scene. True, the two epithets he uses for Asia—"Thou light of life, / Shadow of beauty unbeheld" (III.iii.6–7)—recall with exquisite succinctness the epiphanic moment in which her unveiled presence becomes the veil or atmosphere for the sunlike fire of love "filling the living world" (II.v.26–27) and its return as herald of Prometheus' release. Nonetheless, Prometheus does not address as much as a full sentence to Asia but links her instantly to the "fair sister nymphs" whose love and care were so long his only comfort. The form of his address makes it clear that the promise "Henceforth we will not part" firmly includes Panthea and Ione as part of the household (III.iii.8–10). Drama's generically necessary reifications create some of this awkwardness. As triune aspects of the introjected feminine—specifically, relation through the maternal to body, to language, and to feeling—all three Oceanides belong with a Prometheus healed of inner divisions. Also, Asia's task as reverie, as the memory trace of relationship with the mother, is completed once the memory itself is activated, once Prometheus gets "back of the Muses" to Mnemosyne herself (Duncan 27). This culminating event is about to occur through Prometheus' reunion with Earth.[1]

Rationally, if not romantically, Prometheus' first concern is a dwelling for his ménage, and his opening words on the subject—"There is a Cave"—should be "heard" on the mind-stage of this closet drama as somewhat tentative and reminiscent in tone, but growing more assured as the recollection of physical details recreates a past experience of happiness:

> There is a Cave
> All overgrown with trailing odorous plants
> Which curtain out the day with leaves and flowers
> And paved with veined emerald, and a fountain
> Leaps in the midst with an awakening sound;
> From its curved roof the mountain's frozen tears
> Like snow or silver or long diamond spires
> Hang downward, raining forth a doubtful light;
> And there is heard the ever-moving air
> Whispering without from tree to tree, and birds
> And bees; and all around are mossy seats
> And the rough walls are clothed with long soft grass;
> A simple dwelling, which shall be our own.
>   (III.iii.10–22)

Synesthesia plays some part in the effect of this passage—as in the phrase "raining forth a doubtful light"—but the emphasis on sensual fulfillment comes also through the doubling or tripling of pleasure in the description of each detail. Thus "trailing odorous plants" refresh sight, smell, and feeling; the floor of veined emerald appeals simultaneously to sight and touch, and so on. Only taste seems neglected, though the dramatic placing of "And bees" metonymically calls up honey. Though complex in this fashion, the pleasures described are also simple. The dazzle of "emerald," "silver," and "diamond" enriching the dwelling shines out of the natural surroundings. The setting, including the abundant grass, thus recalls Plato's fantasy of the age of Kronos.

Shelley must now address the question posed in *Politicus:* how are those favored with a life passed in beautiful natural surroundings with all their physical needs met to use their time? A certain insecurity about the answer may lie behind Shelley's overdependence on a passage from *King Lear* as he starts out:

> Where we will sit and talk of time and change
> As the world ebbs and flows, ourselves unchanged—
> What can hide man from Mutability?—
> And if ye sigh, then I will smile, and thou
> Ione, shall chant fragments of sea-music,
> Until I weep, when ye shall smile away
> The tears she brought, which yet were sweet to shed.
>
> (III.iii.23–29)

For convenience let me set down the haunting lines from *King Lear* to which this passage obviously and repeatedly alludes:

> No, no, no, no! Come, let's away to prison.
> We two alone will sing like birds i' th' cage.
> When thou dost ask me blessing, I'll kneel down
> And ask of thee forgiveness. So we'll live,
> And pray, and sing, and tell old tales, and laugh
> At gilded butterflies, and hear poor rogues
> Talk of court news; and we'll talk with them too—
> Who loses and who wins; who's in, who's out—
> And take upon's the mystery of things,
> As if we were God's spies; and we'll wear out,
> In a wall'd prison, packs and sects of great ones,
> That ebb and flow by th' moon.
>
> (V.iii.8–19)

Return to infant joys is a theme that links both passages. The difficulty is that the context of Lear's speech sweeps in with his echoed words to trouble the vision of Prometheus' unchanging happiness at its very inception. Prometheus' plan to "sit and talk of time and change / . . . ourselves unchanged" echoes Lear's "and we'll wear out, / In a wall'd prison packs and sets of great ones / That ebb and flow by th' moon," but with heart-aching difference. Lear and Cordelia are about to experience the final mutability of death. Prometheus' exemption from such change gives an unpleasantly fatuous ring to "What can hide man from Mutability?" And while the Promethean group's pleasure in both sighing and smiling over human life's transience has the doctrines of "sensibility" as its rationale, their exquisitely complex enjoyments seem contemptibly trifling when made so closely parallel to Lear's desire to reenact the pain of repentance in order to reexperience the joy of reconciliation. A further difference lies in the dynamics of the infant play itself. The "we" of Lear's speech—himself and Cordelia—share a condition of wise childhood, while the "I" and "ye" of Prometheus' fantasy take on some of the character of an infant with adoring baby-sitters.

In short, barely twenty-five lines after the release of Prometheus, the difference in his symbolic function begins to create serious difficulties. Chained to the precipice, a suffering god, Prometheus served from age to age as image—thus mirror—of suffering humankind; released to the fulfilled existence appropriate to a god, he becomes the "form"—still "mirror" but only as ideal image—of a humanity in the Godwinian process of growing toward an ever-unreachable perfection. The split between the eternal ideal and humans' actual situation opened up by the line "What can hide man from Mutability?" threatens to make Prometheus fade, dissolve, become irrelevant: "Thou wast not born for death, eternal Prometheus!"

This problem diminishes if attention turns from the alienating difference between mortal and god to the pattern of relationship offered by the divine mirror, the important topic taken up in the lines that follow:

> We will entangle buds and flowers, and beams
> Which twinkle on the fountain's brim, and make
> Strange combinations out of common things
> Like human babes in their brief innocence;
> And we will search, with looks and words of love
> For hidden thoughts each lovelier than the last,
> Our unexhausted spirits, and like lutes
> Touch'd by the skill of the enamoured wind,
> Weave harmonies divine yet ever new,
> From difference sweet where discord cannot be.
>   (III.iii.30–39)

If the setting is Platonic, the activities are Schillerean and Marcusean. Pleasure in things mutable which disregards their mutability for imaginative and playful wonder in their transient being, their constant metamorphoses: this is one important source "Of Painting, Sculpture, and rapt Poesy / And arts, though unimagined, yet to be" (III.iii.55–56). In the former world, Jupiter's rape of Thetis and appropriation of her speech served as the paradigm for all human relationships refracted through culture's arts, sciences, and social institutions. The image replacing it carries the infant's polymorphous perversity over into an eroticism at the heart of language: pleasure in exploring the Other's difference and pleasure in finding a shared means of understanding and communicating difference makes speech not the inscription of the dominant on the enslaved but the constant rediscovery through language of the inexhaustible potential in all common yet unique experience; so "words of love" bring forth—create—previously "hidden thoughts" in a process that constantly enlarges the range and depth of human perception.[2]

The trope that Prometheus uses to describe the centrality of this cave offers the strongest suggestion that all the actions and interactions in it are performed under the sign of the Mother Goddess:

> And hither come, spread on the charmed winds
> Which meet from all the points of Heaven, as bees
> From every flower aerial Enna feeds

At their known island-homes in Himera,
The echoes of the human world, which tell
Of the low voice of love, almost unheard,
And dove-eyed pity's murmured pain and music,
Itself the echo of the heart, and all
That tempers or improves man's life, now free.
(III.iii.40–48)

His simile transforms the cave into Jacob Bryant's "hive of Venus," the home, resource, and source of care for a human race who all might now be "called Melittae" (Bryant 373) in that all manifest the spirit of the beneficent goddess. Also, while Himera, like Enna, was an actual place in Sicily, the name evokes Himeros, personified Desire that, with Eros, attended Aphrodite when she rose from the sea (Hesiod 95).[3] The allusion to the soil of "aerial Enna," torn up by Pluto's chariot when he rose up from under it to ravish Kore, but now whole and flower-strewn once more, underscores the contrast I have already noted between the maternal spirit and one of rapacious, tyrannical, paternal power. The imagined scene thus parallels the fantasy so prominent in the contemporary literature directed toward women of a pastoral haven in which a devoted mother models and inculcates sympathy.

The eroticism made culturally so salient in the relation between mother and infant becomes "acted out," as it were, when Prometheus, having described the cave and sent the Spirit of the Hour to proclaim deliverance, turns at last to address his mother. This is the moment of Prometheus' reunion with her—reunion on terms that the Aeschylean drama could not allow. Once accomplished, it ends his story. Kissing the ground, Prometheus says, "And thou, O Mother Earth!—" (III.iii.84).

Although Shelley denies Asia any line of greeting in return, he fills the response of Earth with erotic power. Her first line leaps to round out Prometheus' unfinished one:

> I hear—I feel—
> Thy lips are on me, and their touch runs down
> Even to the adamantine central gloom
> Along these marble nerves—'tis life, 'tis joy,
> And through my withered, old and icy frame
> The warmth of an immortal youth shoots down
> Circling.
>
> (III.iii.84–90)

Ambiguities, particularly the double meanings of the phrase "the warmth of an immortal youth," make it impossible to distinguish between the thrill of an infant's and a lover's lips as Earth describes her sensations. "Warmth" refers to temperature, but in Shelley's time carried connotations also of male sexual arousal (*OED* XIX, 915); "youth" signifies a period of one's life or a young person, usually male. So the phrase suggests both that Earth feels herself restored to the warm, animated body of her youthful prime and that the semen of a young lover fructifies her body.

In the lines that follow the figure of Earth/Themis in her past mourning for Prometheus elides with that of Demeter, whose grief over Kore's loss made winter of the world. But eroticized maternal breast-feeding as paradigmatic of all relationship continues to dominate the language in a way not usual in the more agrarian images associated with Demeter. The lines are a reprise of Earth's first dialogic interchange with Prometheus in the opening action of the drama, and they place great emphasis, as did the earlier ones, on the way in which the "nurse's soul" enters the child. Under the patriarchal rule of Jupiter, the alienated mother nursed the whole world into alienation; under the new order, the mother-son dyad restored, creatures nourished in loving relationship will similarly nourish one another because their "souls" are relational. Malthusian doctrine, product of one reared on the scarce fare of a despondent Earth, will seem absurd to those whose bountiful nurture makes axiomatic the idea that goods of all kinds should be shared:

> Henceforth the many children fair
> Folded in my sustaining arms—all plants,
> And creeping forms, and insects rainbow-winged
> And birds and beasts and fish and human shapes
> Which drew disease and pain from my wan bosom,
> Draining the poison of despair—shall take
> And interchange sweet nutriment.
>   (III.iii.90–96)

The astonishing word "interchange" placed contextually, as it is here, within the doctrine of the nurse's soul entering the child opens up a positive understanding of the fluidity of pronouns discussed in "On Life" as the true inscription of life's unity. We all, so to speak, breast-feed one another, and all thereby exchange "soul" so that "the existence of distinct individual minds . . . is . . . a delusion" ("On Life," *SPP* 477). This thought comes not as a terrifying revelation of Jupiterean inscription and appropriation but as awareness of universal relationship paradigmatically linked to the relationship between mother and nursing child. As a new insight into the nature of the psychic interchange at the core of subjectivity, it has the potential to transform our understanding of all social relationships and the character of all our social institutions.

With such a theme the pyrotechnics of Shelleyan "transference," in Hogle's locution, become even more startling in the lines that follow. Themis/ Earth elides again, this time with the Maenads, the nursing mothers who form the *thiasos* of Dionysus, when she says: "To me / Shall they [her many children] become like sister-antelopes / By one fair dam, snowwhite and swift as wind / Nursed among lilies near a brimming stream" (III.iii.96–99).

The simile fuses Judeo-Christian and Greek allusions to achieve its strong erotic impact; through this intertextuality the mother antelope to whom Earth compares herself heightens rather than subsumes the evoked image of a woman's form. One verbal echo is to the Song of Songs—"Your two breasts are two fawns, / twins of a gazelle, / that feed among the lilies" (4:5)—in which the simile leads us to "see" the beloved's breasts as deer and also, redoubling the tactility of the image, as deer feeding at those breasts. Meanwhile also the juxtaposition of "snowwhite" and "swift as wind" with "nursed" calls up associations with the Bacchae as described by Euripides, the "Wild White Women . . . / whose fleet limbs darted arrow-like" (ll. 664–65) through the forest: "And one a young fawn held, and one a wild / Wolf cub, and fed them with white milk, and smiled / In love" (ll. 699–701).

The sense of a connection, indeed a conflation, between the Maenads and the Mother Goddess is not peculiar to Shelley. In *The Bacchae* the members of the *thiasos* themselves chant of the relation between their rituals and those that go back to Crete, where Rhea hid the infant Zeus from Kronos:

> Hail thou, O Nurse of Zeus, O Caverned Haunt,
>> Where fierce arms clanged to guard God's cradle rare
> For thee of old some crested Corybant
>> First woke in Cretan air,
> The wild orb of our orgies,
>> Our Timbrel.

> (ll. 120–25)

When commenting on this passage, Jane Harrison, in language that itself shows the inscription of the same maternal ideology as that established by the time of Shelley's birth, writes: "The Maenads are the mothers and therefore the nurses of the holy child; only a decadent civilization separates the figures of mother and nurse." Within a few paragraphs Harrison makes a further statement linking mother, lover, and (implicitly) mourner as different manifestations of the same goddess, a "natural" connectedness that Earth herself is about to verbalize: "It is not hard to see that, given women worshippers and a young male god grown to adolescence, the relation of son to mother might be conceived as that of lover to bride. We find the same misunderstanding of matriarchal conditions in the parallel figures of Adonis and Attis" (*Themis* 39, 41). We saw earlier that a further "parallel" structures the myth of the young shepherd whose intimate connectedness with natural process makes him a guardian spirit after his early death. Serenely, then, and with the same image that Shelley would soon use as a source of comfort at Beatrice Cenci's death, Earth concludes her paean to human life circled round by her beneficence by saying: "And death shall be the last embrace of her / Who takes the life she gave, even as a mother / Folding her child, says, 'Leave me not again!' " (III.iii.105–7).

At this point Asia interposes with a single—and somewhat awkward— comment on a speech that will then continue unbroken to the end of the scene: "O mother! wherefore speak the name of death? / Cease they to love and move and breathe and speak / Who die?" (III.iii.108–10). With others on stage as listening onlookers only, Earth's speech begins in dialogue with Prometheus, but, significantly, Shelley does not ascribe the lines to him. To do so would be to signal a potential rift between Prometheus and his mother. Asia, the questioner of act two, must take on the role again, though for her, too, the role is inappropriate. A human's but not a goddess's question, her interruption, like Prometheus' earlier mention of "Mutability," betrays an underlying problem, a stubborn knot in this denouement.

For the moment, however, it serves to elicit from Earth the gnomic and hieratic words: "Death is the veil which those who live call life; / They sleep—and it is lifted" (III.iii.113–14). Read prosaically, the lines convey the biological truism that the life processes of organisms can rightly be conceived of as their continual impulsion toward death; but spoken by Earth they have a revelatory grandeur celebrating her mystery: she is Life/Death, Veil/Revelation, Constancy/Mutability, Alpha/Omega.

Lest the exchange with Asia create an ambiguity about the identity of the central participants in this colloquy, Earth readdresses Prometheus—"And Thou!"—and, echoing with a slight change his earlier phrase, she continues, "There is a Cavern . . ." (III.iii.124). But with much more specificity about geographic location, Earth makes it clear that the cave his memory was groping for is at Delphi, once sacred to her, wrested from her by the Olympians, and now hers once again.

Three classical accounts, all of them familiar to Shelley, give different versions of the oracle's history: the Homeric *Hymn to Apollo,* the opening of *The Eumenides,* and a choral recitation in Euripides' *Iphigenia in Tauris* (Parke and Wormell I, 3). I have already noted the Aeschylean version: the oracle, at first a shrine of the Mother Goddess, passed peacefully to Phoebus Apollo as a present from Phoebe. The Homeric hymn obscures mention of any conflict altogether. Apollo, seeking "a glorious temple to be an oracle for men," finds the perfect place at "Crisa beneath snowy Parnassus." He lays out his temple there, and at a spring beside it bravely slays a she-serpent that had been creating havoc in the neighborhood (Hesiod 345). Pytho, the name of the site, alludes to the serpent's rotting corpse. Only the serpent's sex gives any suggestion that "she" is a totemic stand-in for the Mother Goddess—though, with the serpent as one of the Mother Goddess's common attributes or signs (Harrison 281–82), that subtext is clear enough. And the medium for messages for the oracle, always a woman, had the ceremonial name of Pythia.

Euripides' account alludes both to the slaying of the serpent and to the Mother Goddess's original ownership of the oracle, making the point, however, that the transition to Apollo was by no means peaceful. The Chorus also links the cult of Dionysus with that of the Mother Goddess. Leto, mother of Apollo and Diana, brought her infants from their birthplace in Delos to Parnassus, the mountain above Delphi "on whose heights / Bacchus shouting holds his rites" (ll. 1241–42). In this version an enormous (male) dragon guarded the shrine; while yet a child, Phoebus slew this beast "and seized the shrine" (ll. 1251). In revenge for this theft, Earth troubled those seeking counsel from the oracle with frightening and deceptive dreams. Apollo complained to Zeus, who put an instant stop to these bizarre visions, and from that time the shrine has redounded to the glory of the young god.

In *Prometheus Unbound* Earth's account jibes with that of Euripides, except for a striking change in its conclusion. The oracle at Delphi, once wrested from her, functioned from that point on as a destructive influence:

There is a Cavern where my spirit
Was panted forth in anguish whilst thy pain
Made my heart mad, and those who did inhale it
Became mad too, and built a Temple there
And spoke and were oracular, and lured
The erring nations round to mutual war
And faithless faith, such as Jove kept with thee.
(III.iii.124–30)

While giving more information about the locus and significance of Prometheus' "Cave," her words also identify the cave/cavern with "the realm of
Demogorgon" as Panthea describes it at the beginning of act two, scene
three—the "pair" to this scene, as act three, scene two was to the second
scene in the previous act. In Panthea's account also "the oracular vapour"
causes false prophecies that bring "contagion to the world" (II.iii.4, 10).[4] The
"meaning" of Delphi is, therefore, most intimately tied into the "meaning" of
Prometheus Unbound and warrants much closer critical attention than it has
so far received.

Even had Shelley been able to make his way to Greece and travel there
freely, he could not have seen Delphi. The Danish archaeologist Peter
Brøndsted, a visitor to the area in 1810 and 1811, wrote: "The wretched little
village of Kastri in many ways renders it difficult to survey the whole site, and to
be able to get a satisfactory plan of Delphi one would have to begin by pulling
down many of its huts" (quoted in Poulsen 44). In the 1890s, after years of
negotiations, French archaeologists excavated Delphi; Jane Harrison was using
their very new findings when she wrote *Themis*. So "Delphi" to Shelley was
necessarily a text, or a conflation of texts, but particularly the text of Pausanias'
Description of Greece, by far the most detailed ancient source though not
always an accurate one. One must, then, on the mind's feet, make the walk to
Delphi as Shelley did, with prolix Pausanias as guide and companion.

Starting from the plain at Chaeronea, Pausanias ascends to Panopeus, four
miles from Daulis (V, 222), where he stops to comment that Athenian women
called Thyiads (alluded to again in the description of Delphi itself) made
Panopeus one of the "dancing grounds" on their way to join Delphian women
on Mount Parnassus "and there hold orgies in honour of Dionysus." Panopeus
is also the site of a small shrine housing an image claimed by some to be
Aesculapius, by others to be Prometheus. The latter position takes strength
from the presence of two huge stones lying near the edge of the ravine: "Their
colour is that of clay . . . and they smell very like the flesh of a man. They say
that these stones are remains of the clay out of which the whole race of man
was moulded by Prometheus" (I, 503).

Turning south after Daulis and skirting the eastern slope of Mount Parnassus, Pausanias comes after five miles to the place where three roads—from
Daulis, from Delphi, and from Thebes—meet at what is called the Cleft Way.
Pausanias allows himself a guide's deprecatory joke about the "memorials of
the woes of Oedipus . . . left all over Greece" (I, 505), but in fact this route
from Daulis to Delphi does not encounter the Cleft Way; Pausanias has made

shifts and adjustments of landscape in order to include it. So Frazer could point out by going over the ground himself (Pausanias V, 231), but for Shelley, dependent on Pausanias, the Oedipal link to Delphi was made even more dramatic than it is.

Taking the Delphi fork up the slopes of Parnassus, Pausanias turns discussion to the oracle's history. With agnostic evenhandedness he sets down two theories: a short version of the Aeschylean peaceable transfer—"Earth resigned her share to Themis, and Themis made a present of it to Apollo"—and a "rationalist" version, stemming from Diodorus Siculus, that "shepherds feeding their flocks lit upon the oracle, and . . . were inspired by the vapour, and prophesied at the prompting of Apollo" (I, 505). Pausanias' transmission of the vapor theory is one of several pieces of evidence that he did not himself enter the Pythia's sanctuary, for inhalation of vapors had no actual part in the procedure for consulting the oracle (Parke and Wormell 20–24). The theory had had wide acceptance from the time of Roman domination onward, however, and Shelley's allusion both to the "oracular vapour" fuming from Demogorgon's "mighty portal" (II.iii.4,2) and to Earth's panting forth her anguish through the "breath" of the Cavern (III.iii.131) suggests that he took the presence of intoxicating vapors as factual. Shelley's use of the word "Cavern" in conjunction with these vapors points specifically to Lucan's description of the Pythia in *Pharsalia*—a work that, as I discussed earlier, helped shape the concept of Demogorgon—as an important source. There the Pythia enters a "vast cavern" in which vapors filtering up from a chasm drive her into a frenzy (V. 161–74).

When Pausanias' account turns to the different temples that have been built on the site of the oracle, his allusions bear in interesting ways on Prometheus' recollections of "a Cave." "The most ancient temple of Apollo was made of laurel," states Pausanias, not far from the truth if "temple" is linked metonymically to the religious observances practiced within it. On the evidence of the *Homeric Hymn to Apollo,* E. W. Parke and D. E. W. Wormell suggest that "the god's communication . . . was probably recognized in the rustling of the leaves which the priests claimed to understand" (3). Prometheus remembers "the ever-moving air / Whispering without from tree to tree" (III.iii.18–19).

The image of bees that figures so prominently in Prometheus' recollection of the cave has an echo in Pausanias' mention of the second temple, which, "the Delphians say . . . was made by bees out of wax and feathers." Pausanias grows huffy over a third possibility: "As to the story that they made a temple out of the fern that grows on the mountains by twining the stalks together while they were still fresh and green, I do not admit it for a moment" (I, 506). Shelley seems to have disagreed, for he has Prometheus remember the "rough walls" as "clothed with long soft grass" (III.iii.21). The passage from Plato's *Politicus,* as I mentioned earlier, is another relevant source, but the beds of grass described there are not as close a parallel as these fern walls.

Pausanias continues with a detailed description of the treasures sent as thanks offerings to the oracle. His account gives a gloss for the "Praxitelean shapes" that Earth describes in the culminating lines of her speech (III.iii.165), and we will return to it there. At this point one last parallel between the cave described by Prometheus and Pausanias' description of Delphi should be noted. Pausanias gives further evidence that he was not privileged to enter the innermost sanctuary of the temple when he writes that the spring named Cassotis near the shrine "goes down underground and inspires the women with the spirit of prophecy in the shrine of the god" (I, 536). In fact, the excavations at Delphi have shown that the sanctuary enclosed no spring, but, like the vapor, its presence was widely accepted as a fact. The "foun-tain" that leaps in the cave Prometheus describes acts as a further sign that Earth's cavern and Prometheus' cave are a single place: the inner sanctum at Delphi, the *omphalos* of the world, the "seat" of Demogorgon, an area sacred to Mother Earth.[5]

Rather offhandedly, just before mentioning the spring Pausanias points out a "small stone" outside the temple. It is clearly a significant object, though, for "on this stone they pour oil every day, and at every festival they put unspun wool on it." Pausanias concludes the matter with a deprecatory explanation of what that importance is taken to be: "There is also a notion that this stone was given to Cronus instead of the child, and that Cronus spewed it out again" (I, 536). Pausanias does not use the word *omphalos* with reference to the stone, but from other classical sources such as the passage from Varro discussed in the last chapter Shelley would have known that this stone signified Delphi's position as the center of the earth (Harrison 396). Varro, as we saw, writes of the stone as grave marker for the body of the Python. He does not mention the holy of holies at Delphi as site of the grave of Dionysus and center for his worship for the several months of each year during which Apollo absented himself, as it were, but again other classical sources would have made Shelley well aware of these linked symbolisms (Parke and Wormell 11).

While Shelley places no stone of this kind in his description of the cave/cavern, we have already seen it as the "throne" of Demogorgon with the "snake-like Doom" coiled under it (II.iii.97). Demogorgon—called "the ser-pent of being" in an early draft of act three, scene three (*SHC* VI, 1024)—is at once masculine and in his snake form the manifestation of the Mother God-dess, of Themis/Earth, whose name means "Doom" (Harrison 483). Varro's quibble over whether centrality lies in the navel or the genitals thus takes on hermeneutic as well as hermetic significance: the generative line from phallus to umbilicus is the center of human life and sign of the sexuality that acts as the source of humans' "unextinguished fire" (III.i.5).

When Earth moves, then, into the associative, synesthetic discourse that has functioned throughout the play as her sign or leitmotif, the place of which she is speaking gives a further mythic dimension to the connectedness or interpenetration operative in the language itself. Words such as "serpent" and "ivy" become signifiers not only for natural objects but also for presences and processes manifested through them. Most significantly, the passage has as its organizing trope the breath of Earth:

Which breath now rises as among tall weeds
A violet's exhalation, and it fills
With a serener light and crimson air
Intense yet soft the rocks and woods around;
It feeds the quick growth of the serpent vine
And the dark linked ivy tangling wild
And budding, blown, or odour-faded blooms
Which star the winds with points of coloured light
As they rain through them, and bright, golden globes
Of fruit, suspended in their own green heaven;
And, through their veined leaves and amber stems,
The flowers whose purple and translucid bowls
Stand ever mantling with aerial dew,
The drink of spirits; and it circles round
Like the soft waving wings of noonday dreams,
Inspiring calm and happy thoughts, like mine
Now thou art thus restored . . . This Cave is thine.

                                    (III.iii.131–47)

The phrase "drink of spirits" (l. 144) focuses the theme of these lines on spirit as drink, on Earth's breath as the fluid infusing and connecting all life. So this description of the cave as the dwelling place of Prometheus has thematic links with Panthea's dream vision of his transformed body (II.i.61–89). This spirit breath is also a feminine influence, the customary meaning of that word intensified through its ancient astrological signification: "an ethereal fluid thought to flow from the stars and to affect the language of men" (*OED* VII, 939). As I noted in Chapter 2, the word was the standard one used in conduct books to describe mothers' socialization of children.

The literary associations called up by the phrase "as among tall weeds / A violet's exhalation" (ll. 131–32) reinforces the feminine nature of the influence, already implicit through its identification with Earth's breath. The synesthetic word "violet," especially as closely associated as it is with "light" (l. 133), calls up Wordsworth's Lucy, "a violet by a mossy stone." But unlike Lucy's influence, which suggests the asexual purity of a pre-Victorian angel, the atmosphere or current emanating from Earth is "serene" and "soft" yet also "intense" and arousingly "crimson" (ll. 133–34).

Through the placing of the words, as well as the visual images and mythic connotations they evoke, a description of vegetation like that of the intertwined ivy and serpent vine becomes, in a montagelike metamorphosis, phallus penetrating the tangle of pubic hair. The eroticism of these lines carries over into the ones that follow. On first reading the "serpent vine" and the ivy appear to be "tangling wild" together; only as one reads further does one see that "wild" may modify "vine" and "ivy" but may also modify "blooms" (l. 137). The pollen from the blooms changes synesthetically to "points of coloured light" and then to "rain" (ll. 138–39), with connotations of semen.

While the passage owes something to Darwin's *Botanic Garden,* the spirit of its eroticism is very different.[6] The waggishness of Darwin's implicit or explicit comparisons has no part in the intensity with which Shelley's lines suggest an interconnectedness between human creativity—both physical and imaginative—and the fruitfulness of vegetation. In 1811 Shelley had heard John Abernathy lecture on the "sympathy" between different parts of the body and among all bodies created by a "subtle substance of a quickly power-fully mobile nature" which "appears to be the life of the world" (Crook and Guiton 70). Like the related ideas of Mesmer, this theory has affinities with the sympathetic magic of the ancients in which human copulation mirrors a universal fecundating process and thereby fosters the fertility of all forms of animal and vegetable life. Or, reversing perspective, one could say that the burgeoning of creativity of any kind manifests this process. Shelley's image for it, drawing on the wealth of mythic and pastoral material most familiar to us when rendered as the story of Venus and Adonis, is the reunion of Prometheus and Earth.

The words "it circles round" (l. 144), with "spirit" from many lines earlier—"where my spirit / Was panted forth in anguish" (III.iii.124–25)—and "breath" (l. 131) as well as "the drink of spirits" (l. 144) all as referents for "it," themselves make a circle of Earth's speech. For what gives her "breath" its beneficent power? When separated from Prometheus, she has told us, her "spirit" transmitted madness, violence, and death (III.iii.124–30). This new circling, interpenetrating power arises, therefore, not from her alone but from her as she feels the circling warmth created by the touch of Prometheus' lips (III.iii.84–90). Her two long speeches between that point and her gift to Prometheus of the cave (III.iii.147) function as a delicate, elegant, metaphoric, and nonliteral yet nonetheless erotic fantasy of "union" between mother and son as the source of beneficent life—a union for which *both* maternal breast-feeding and the interchanges of lovemaking serve simul-taneously as metaphors.

The allusions to signs of a Dionysian presence have already suggested at several points in the play that Prometheus elides with Dionysus as well as with the Adonis figures of the pastoral tradition. As we have seen, the worship of Dionysus flourished at Delphi, and Earth makes explicit a connec-tion between Dionysus and Prometheus when she has the group's itinerary back to her cavern follow that of Dionysus' legendary progress from Asia to Greece. She instructs their guide to lead them "beyond the peak / of Bacchic Nysa, Maenad-haunted mountain / And beyond Indus and its tribute rivers" (III.iii.153–55).

The whereabouts of Nysa were and are uncertain, there being an *embarras de richesse* among towns of that name (Lemprière 508–9), but sources agree on what occurred there: the nymphs of Nysa, nurses of the infant Dionysus, raised him to manhood, and the city was the eastern center of his cult. They were, therefore, the first of the Maenads or Thyades who form the *thiasos* of the god. Earth's allusion to Nysa thus not only draws attention to a Dionysian aspect of Prometheus but also implies a parallel between Dionysus with his *thiasos* and Prometheus with the Oceanides. For to think of the latter commu-nity as that of a lord or sultan with his harem, as seems possible, misconceives Shelley's thought, or at least his conscious purpose: such a parallel would give the Promethean group precisely the Jupiterean sexual character explicitly repudiated in the first scene of act three. The nurse-mothers, lovers, followers of Dionysus are, by contrast, celebrators of a shared communal life. Classicists late in the nineteenth century were more explicit on this point than Shelley, but their analyses have the same classical sources as his fantasy. Jane Harrison writes: "Bacchic religion is still based on the collective emotion of the *thiasos*. Its god is a projection of group-unity. Dr. Verrall in his essay on the *Bacchants of Euripides* hits the mark in one trenchant, illuminating bit of translation. 'The rapture of the initiated,' he says, 'lies essentially in this: "*his soul is congregationalized*" ' " (48). As we saw in Chapter 3, Shelley's insistent need for mothering from the women who were his lovers made the Dionysian pattern for sexual relationships a deeply compatible fantasy; and it conformed, however paradoxically, both with Godwin's blandly rational ideas of perfected social mores as he described them in the first edition of *Political Justice* (II, 851–53) and with sentimentalism's insistence on shared "soul" (McGann 31). (Let me add, however, that if we are to judge by the experience of the many women drawn in as participants in Shelley's personal *thiasos*, its improvement over the harem pattern is, in strictly liberatory terms, moot.)

The group, Earth says, is coming near the end of its journey when it starts "up the green ravine, across the vale" (III.iii.158), the phrases suggesting the Parnassian landscape around Delphi that her earlier words would lead us to expect. As she continues, however, we discover that the temple she describes is not the one attached to the Delphic oracle but the temple of Prometheus many miles away in Athens:

> Beside the windless and chrystalline pool
> Where ever lies, on unerasing waves
> The image of a temple built above,
> Distinct with column, arch, and architrave
> And palm-like capital, and overwrought,
> And populous with most living imagery—
> Praxitelean shapes, whose marble smiles
> Fill the hushed air with everlasting love.
> It is deserted now, but once it bore
> Thy name, Prometheus; there the emulous youths
> Bore to thine honour through the divine gloom
> The lamp, which was thine emblem . . . even as those
> Who bear the untransmitted torch of hope
> Into the grave across the night of life . . .
> And thou hast borne it most triumphantly
> To this far goal of Time . . . Depart, farewell.
> Beside that Temple is the destined Cave.
>
> (III.iii.159–75)

As we saw in the liberties Pausanias took with the actual location of the Cleft Way, the words of a text can defy geography. Like a film text, they can easily place the Delphic cave beside the Athenian altar to Prometheus, upgrading the altar to a temple in the process, as Shelley does here. The question involves not the possibility of the juxtaposition but what it achieves. In search of an answer, with Pausanias again as guide, we must explore the Promethean altar and its environs as we did Delphi. The thirtieth chapter in the first book of Pausanias' *Description of Greece* brings together three sites: the Academy, a tree-filled area just outside the walls of the ancient city, where Plato taught and near which he is buried; the altar of Prometheus in the Academy, scene of the torchbearers' race; and "a place called Colonus Hippius ('horse knoll'), said to be the first spot in Attica to which Oedipus came" (I, 47).

The lines "even as those / Who bear the untransmitted torch of hope / Into the grave across the night of life" refer specifically to the runner Euchidas, who died after carrying the sacred fire at full speed from Delphi to Plataea in one day (Plutarch II, 277). But their even more poignant reference is to the dying Oedipus. When Oedipus and his daughter Antigone make their way to the grove at Colonus and ask whom the ground is sacred to, they are told by a passerby that no one may live in it, that it is sacred to the Eumenides, "daughters of darkness and mysterious earth" (l. 40). Their informant also tells them that "in it the fire-carrier / Prometheus has his influence" (ll.55–56). So, in their beginnings and their endings the stories of Prometheus and Oedipus converge. Near Delphi each performed the act that would pit him against a patriarchal order; near Colonus both have transcended that order. Prometheus is celebrated in the race that, in the opinion of most Aeschylus scholars, was the third and culminating play of the trilogy, *Prometheus Purphoros* (Winnington-Ingram 188–89), and in Shelley's version did not submit to Jupiter before achieving that apotheosis; Oedipus' secret resting place in the grove of the Eumenides, where "the underworld / Opened in love the unlit door of earth" (ll. 1662–63), guarantees the continued prosperity of Athens (ll. 1518–35).

Pausanias mentions only an altar, not a temple in Athens dedicated to Prometheus. For the description of a temple "populous" with "Praxitelean shapes," Pausanias' catalogue of the treasures gathered at Delphi was to some extent a resource. His pages, however, read more like an inventory of goods than a celebration of gods and serve rather as evidence for the "mutual war / And faithless faith" that Earth says characterized Olympian power at Delphi than as model for a vision of perfected human society.[7]

For the temple of his new world, then, Shelley turned rather to his own imagination's rebuilding of the classical ruins that so moved him in Pompeii and at Rome (Reiman, "Roman Scenes" passim). Informing his description also is that third, Platonic presence in the Academy. The Platonic doctrine of eternal Forms along with its transmutation into the mystical neo-Platonic dictum "The world below is as the world above" structures the multiple reflections of the passage. We first "see" not the temple itself but its reflection in a calm pool, while the lines "Where ever lies, on unerasing waves, / The image of a temple built above" carry the suggestion that the temple reflected is itself a reflection, and thus that the scene is the mirror of a mirroring central to human life. Touches of rhyme—"waves"/"architrave," "above"/"love"—add verbal echoes to the visual ones.

The smiles of the "Praxitelean shapes" initiate still another form of mirroring. The allusion to them serves as reprise of Asia's words in act two—"till marble grew divine, / And mothers, gazing, drank the love men see / Reflected in their race" (II.iv.82–84)—and so refers again to Johann Winckelmann's theory that the Greeks placed beautiful statues in the rooms of pregnant women so that they would bear beautiful children (I, 288). The "marble smiles" of these statues shape the bodies and psyches of unborn children when mothers drink in this love manifested as beauty. With these images of a perfected world, Earth's speech and the scene end. There remains the more difficult task of showing this idea in action.

The Dipsas of Desire (Scene iv)

When comparing Prometheus and the Oceanides to Dionysus and the Nysae, I made no mention of their guide, the Spirit "in the likeness of a winged child"—a male child, one gathers from the pronoun Earth uses in referring to him (III.iii.149). She calls him her "torch-bearer": *purphoros,* a Promethean epithet. Her only other introductory comment informs us that the torch he bears is his love for Asia, extinguished in the past but now renewed: "Who let his lamp out in the old time, with gazing / On eyes from which he kindled it anew / With love which is as fire, sweet Daughter mine, / For such is that within thine own" (III.iii.149–52).

The list of characters for scene four further identifies this torchbearer as "the Spirit of the Earth," but Panthea, in answering Ione's question about his identity, makes it clear that besides being Purphoros he is Phosphoros, the male aspect or attendant or emanation of the planet/goddess Venus: "It is the delicate spirit / That guides the earth through Heaven. From afar / The populous constellations call that light / The loveliest of the planets" (III.iv.6–9). And again his central characteristic is his love for Asia, described now in terms that echo those that Prometheus used in act one to describe his own former relation to her. There Prometheus spoke of himself as "drinking life from her loved eyes" (I.i.123); Panthea says that "before Jove reigned" the Spirit "loved our sister Asia, and it came / Each leisure hour to drink the liquid light / Out of her eyes" (III.iv.15–18). The metaphor of breast-feeding, with eyes displacing breasts, is obvious in both passages but underlined in the Spirit's case by the fact that he calls Asia "Mother, dearest Mother" (III.iv.24).

Casually, recollecting the way in which the Spirit verbalized its pleasure in this "liquid light," Panthea recalls, "It said it thirsted / As one bit by a dipsas" (III.iv.18–19). The image, drawn again from Lucan's *Pharsalia,* is just as horrific in its way as the earlier comparison between Jupiter's phallus and "the Numidian seps" (III.i.40). Mention of both snakes occurs in a long passage describing the sufferings endured by Cato's men in the Libyan desert during the civil wars. So—as was appropriate in Jupiter's "Heaven" but seems jarring in this context, a scene placed outside Prometheus' idyllic cave—the associations called up by the simile are of Caesar's assassination by his political "sons" and of ensuing violence inflicted and endured within a deadly natural setting. Then there is the nature of the suffering itself. The consequence of the bite was maddening, unslakable thirst. In the Lucan passage the bitten soldier clawed at the sand in his desperate search for water, gulped seawater, and finally opened "his swollen veins with his sword . . . [to] fill his mouth with the blood" (IX.755–60). The image of the dipsas, then, conveys unassuageable, violent, and self-destructive desire. If such an emotion arose "before Jove reigned," its appearance was a sign that the reign was imminent.

In any event, the Spirit's joyful greeting to Asia takes such frustration as past and projects a future of "infant joy" resembling the one in Prometheus' description of life in their cave:

> Mother, dearest Mother;
> May I then talk with thee as I was wont?
> May I then hide mine eyes in thy soft arms
> After thy looks have made them tired of joy?
> May I then play beside thee the long noons
> When work is none in the bright silent air?
> (III.iv.24–29)

Asia answers soothingly, "I love thee, gentlest being, and henceforth / Can cherish thee unenvied" (III.iv.30–31). "Unenvied" can modify either "I" or "thee" or both, but this ambiguity is not as puzzling as the word itself. Who was in the earlier time—as opposed to "henceforth"—the envier? If the envy included both of them, if it was envy of their relationship, why did that envier feel envy? The text offers only the clue of Asia's further words—"Thy simple talk once solaced, now delights" (III.iv.32)—to suggest that they did have meetings, if troubled and inadequate ones, during the Jupiterean period. Now she gives assurance that whoever or whatever in the past found their intimacy enviable and made its continuance impossible is no longer operative. No need to fear the return of that dipsas thirst, frustrated Oedipal desire. Oedipus is laid to rest.

The child Spirit, delighted as in the past to explore on its own if assured of her constant presence on his return, tells Asia of the "happy changes" (III.iv.84) occurring in all human interactions and in the natural environment, a fulfillment of the love, health, and harmony that Earth promised in the previous scene. He concludes by reiterating his joy in their reunion: "We meet again, the happiest change of all" (III.iv.85). But Asia takes the discussion into a startling new direction, shifting the tone of their meeting. The language shifts as well into a distinctly Shakespearean mode:

Asia

> And never will we part, till thy chaste Sister
> Who guides the frozen and inconstant moon
> Will look on thy more warm and equal light
> Till her heart thaw like flakes of April snow
> And love thee.

> *Spirit of the Earth*
>
> What, as Asia loves Prometheus?
>
> *Asia*
>
> Peace, Wanton—thou art yet not old enough.
> Think ye, by gazing on each other's eyes
> To multiply your lovely selves, and fill
> With sphered fires the interlunar air?
>
> *Spirit of the Earth*
>
> Nay, Mother, while my sister trims her lamp
> 'Tis hard I should go darkling—
>
>   (III.iv.86–96)

More telling then certain words—"wanton," "darkling," "inconstant moon"—that give a Shakespearean quality to this interchange is the imagined situation itself: a dialogue charged with sexual innuendo between an older woman—or women—and a precocious male child.[8] In Shelley's dialogue, as is often the case in Shakespeare's, Asia initiates the "wantonness" she treats later with mock protest by turning the discussion to the Spirit's future marriage—apparently, in the fashion of great courts, already arranged. Stung by her cheerfulness in the face of this separation, the Spirit of the Earth alludes insinuatingly to the sexual relationship between Asia and Prometheus. Unstated but perfectly obvious in his question is envy of a sexual rival. In replying, Asia gives no recognition to the real source of his emotion but addresses herself to the supposed topic, his eventual union with the Moon. At the same time she mocks his undeveloped sexual powers and thereby delivers on the father's behalf the threat of sexual castration under which the son must submit: he is not to desire her; his reward for suppressing that desire will (in time) be his own possession of a female whom he can forbid to his son, and so on.

The Spirit of the Earth's harsh response suggests that prostitution will soon reappear in the vicinity of the Promethean cave. Also, the unusual word "darkling" and the rhythm of the phrase in which it appears recall the warning of Lear's Fool:

>   For you know, nuncle,
>   "The hedge-sparrow fed the cuckoo so long
>   That it had it head bit off by it young."
> So, out went the candle, and we were left darkling.
>   (I.iv.211–14)

The castrative revenge taken in turn by children in response to paternal tyranny, with Gloucester's blinding and Lear's madness as exempla, becomes the Spirit's theme and threat. No wonder that Asia is relieved to change the subject by exclaiming over the arrival of the Spirit of the Hour. Prometheus, passive through this interchange, now admits a sense of anticlimax, as if talk about the new order were already a burden, when he says in greeting, "We feel what thou hast heard and seen—yet speak" (III.iv.97).

Behind his words one senses Shelley's own fatigue at describing a world freed from the encircling power of tyrannous institutions to take the linear course of Godwinian perfectibility. The task involved not the excited capture of a fresh inspiration but the laborious revision of material worked through at length in earlier poems, particularly in section eight of *Queen Mab* and in canto nine of *Laon and Cythna*. With stubborn gallantry Shelley returns to the labor of verbalization because, as he writes most movingly in "A Philosophical View of Reform," the process of imagining one's purpose fulfilled serves as necessary beginning to its fulfillment. Writing about equality in possessions as the goal toward which "it is our duty to tend," he continues: "We derive tranquillity & courage & grandeur of soul from contemplating an object which is, because we will it, & may be, because we hope & desire it, & must be if succeeding generations of the enlightened sincerely & earnestly seek it" (*SHC* VI, 1044).

Used as a gloss of the scene we have just witnessed between Asia and the Spirit of the Earth, this passage from "A Philosophical View of Reform" shows the magnitude of Shelley's utopian difficulty. In Earth's aria in the previous scene, Shelley could lyrically convey the feeling of reunion with "the mother" that he sees as effecting a transformation in all forms of life on the planet. But the only dramatization of that feeling, its only acting out, is the exchange between Asia and the Spirit of the Earth. That quickly becomes a replaying of the Oedipal scenario that was the given of Shelley's own upbringing. It provides no grand and tranquillizing pledge of something new; worse, contemplation of it reinscribes the old order as inescapable. Something of the gloom of this failure may underlie the fatigue in Prometheus' words and, even more signifi-cantly, may help to explain why these and Asia's exclamation are the last words spoken by them in the drama. Shelley cannot imagine their life together or the social world this union would mirror. He cannot create an object for contempla-tion that can then be willed into actual human existence.

When Shelley, himself dissatisfied with the three-act version of the drama, returned to it to add act four, in the opinion of Reiman and Powers he "broadened the scope of his most ambitious work from a myth of the renova-tion of the human psyche to a renewing of the whole cosmos" (*SPP* 130). I think myself that the former of these two projects was the harder task. Imagin-ing the earth and moon joyously and harmoniously aspin presents nothing like the difficulty involved in imagining a world of harmonious, just, and equable human beings. Shelley admits as much in act four when, averting his gaze from all specific human interactions, he solaces himself in the total appropria-tiveness granted through a constructed universal: "Man, oh, not men! a chain of linked thought, / Of love and might to be divided not" (IV.i.394–95). I can fully agree with Woodman that this "Man" is indeed "the Androgyne."[9]

The conclusion of the Spirit of the Hour's long speech, the last lines of the play as Shelley first conceived it, summarize the scenes and events the Spirit has just described:

> The painted veil, by those who were, called life,
> Which mimicked, as with colours idly spread,

All men believed and hoped, is torn aside—
The loathsome mask has fallen, the man remains
Sceptreless, free, uncircumscribed—but man:
Equal, unclassed, tribeless and nationless,
Exempt from awe, worship, degree,—the King
Over himself; just, gentle, wise—but man:
Passionless? no—yet free from guilt or pain
Which were, for his will made, or suffered them,
Nor yet exempt, though ruling them like slaves,
From chance and death and mutability
The clogs of that which else might oversoar
The loftiest star of unascended Heaven
Pinnacled dim in the intense inane.

(III.iv.190–204)

Striking first of all is the echo of Earth's line from the previous scene "Death is the veil which those who live call life" (III.iii.114), though with a very different meaning. *This* veil is that of false ideology that made desire for happiness, empowerment, and freedom a means for maintaining human adherence to corrupt and enslaving institutions. But while the sense conveyed is different, the verbal echo itself recalls the troubling ideas raised earlier in Prometheus' question "What can hide man from Mutability?" (III.iii.25) and Asia's interjection "O mother! wherefore speak the name of death?" (III.iii.108).

The next jarring note comes in the sudden buckle "—but man" after the forward stride of "Sceptreless, free, uncircumscribed." Considered positively, the phrase simply clarifies the point that the humankind here envisioned does not transcend human potential as we know it. Through their placement, however, both here and three lines down, the words become the alarm of a muffled drum beat, and "but" changes its signification from "still" to "only" and "insufficiently." At last in lines 200–201 the unspoken thought forces itself to the surface: even in this attempt to imagine a world growing ever more perfect, one can never imagine away "chance and death and mutability." One can only imagine them ruled like slaves. But how imagine that? By envisioning the eternal pattern for man, man's ideal man, ruling them.

I deliberately use the male noun here but with a gendered not a generic meaning because the "clogs" being ruled are traditionally associated with the feminine. So if the ideal man, the pattern of man, is to rule them men must rule women.[10] Through this oversoaring, in short, a Jupiterean Prometheus, as such a pattern for man, swallows Metis. He swallows Earthson Prometheus on his Caucasian pinnacle, and with all the stars he swallows Venus, Earthson's star.

In the last three lines the obvious and true referent for the participial phrase "Pinnacled dim in the intense inane" is "star." At the same time, the powerful enjambment after "oversoar" makes the phrase appear to refer to "that which else might oversoar"—the human ideal described earlier. Read that way the last line conveys an image of Jupiter/Prometheus pinnacled above all the heavens as "Monarch of Gods and Dæmons" (I.i.1). "Pinnacled" suggests that he is bound once again, not this time as rebel and victim but as Jupiterean power maintaining control over the clog-slaves of chance, death, and mutability, through constant, vigilant denial of his actual situation. And the inane, the formless void of infinite space, when designated as "intense"—that is, as "stretched"—becomes a gigantic womb about to give birth to "bright and rolling Worlds" (I.i.2) of Oedipal subjectivities, all bearing his inscription.

NOTES

1. The difference between Woodman's reading of *Prometheus Unbound* as culminating in "the constellated androgyne that is the union of Asia and Prometheus" (247) and my reading of it as a reexperiencing of relationship with the mother allows us to view the conflation of Asia and Earth in different ways. In this scene I have the sense that Asia becomes in some way assimilated to Earth, with Earth dominant, while Woodman takes Earth to be "Asia's veil"; at its lifting, she becomes one with Asia (245).

2. Other passages in Shelley's work serve as glosses on this one and bring at least associative evidence to suggest that the erotic relation between mother and infant has the function of a theme on which all other (positive) forms of love play variations. In *Laon and Cythna* the cave in which Cythna gives birth to a daughter also has a fountain. Mother and infant play by enjoying "the swift lights which might that fountain pave"; in the following stanza Cythna describes a stage prior to the infant's acquisition of speech in phrases reminiscent of "the looks and words of love" in the passage under discussion:

> Methought her looks began to talk with me;
> And no articulate sounds, but something sweet
> Her lips would frame,—so sweet it could not be,
> That it was meaningless; her touch would meet
> Mine, and our pulses calmly flow and beat
> In response while we slept; and on a day
> When I was happiest in that strange retreat,
> With heaps of golden shells we two did play,—
> Both infants, weaving wings for time's perpetual way.
> (VII.xxi.181–89, [CW I, 399–40])

In "Alastor" the image of a wind-harp becomes associated with accession to language through the mother-infant relationship. The Narrator, addressing the "Mother of this unfathomable world," says: "And moveless, as a long-forgotten lyre / Suspended in the solitary dome / Of some deserted and mysterious fane, / I wait thy breath, Great Parent" (ll.42–45).

3. In a note to the "Letter to Maria Gisborne" Shelley identifies Himeros as "a synonym of Love" (*SPP* 321).

4. E. W. Parke and D. E. W. Wormell in their history of Delphi note as "a notorious fact in antiquity" that "Apollo's oracular responses were crooked and ambiguous" (40).

5. Eagleton's description of the "territory" of the aesthetic applies also to the area within what Shelley calls "the human mind" ('Preface' to *PU*, in *SPP* 133), for which this cave serves as image: "That territory is nothing less than the whole of our

sensate life together—the business of affections and aversions, of how the world strikes the body on its sensory surfaces, of that which takes root in the gaze and the guts and all that arises from our most banal, biological insertion into the world" (13). I would disagree only with the epithet "banal" for a process so crucial, so much the focus of ideological interests, and so little understood as "our biological insertion into the world."

6. Carl Grabo identifies "crimson air" (l. 133) as nitrous gas (*Newton Among Poets* 189–90). To quotations from Priestley and Davy attesting to that color, Grabo adds these lines from Darwin's *Botanic Garden:* "As woos Azotic Gas the virgin Air, / And veils in *crimson clouds* the yielding Fair, / Indignant fire the treacherous courtship flies, / Waves his light wings and mingles with the skies" (II, ll. 147–50; Grabo's emphasis).

7. Pausanias writes, for instance: "The treasury of the Thebans [at Delphi] was built with the spoils of war, and so was the treasury of the Athenians. . . . But I do not know whether the Cnidians built their treasury to commemorate a victory or to display their wealth" (I, 515).

8. Act two, scene one of *The Winter's Tale* serves as the best example.

9. Woodman is less judgmental than I when evaluating the social usefulness, if you will, of androgynous fantasies but does take note of a difficulty. He writes: "The vision of a selfsustaining cosmos revolving in an ecstasy of love for itself, which is none other than the 'bound or outward circumference' of man united with his feminine soul, is the achievement of Shelley's final act." Then, the left hand taking what the right hand gave, he adds, "The solipsistic dangers inherent in his androgynous vision should, I think, be apparent" (247).

10. See Bordo passim.

Conclusion

To say that "the nurse's soul will enter the child" is to recognize, at least implicitly, that "soul" is a postuterine *donnée,* a social not an essential or natural given. Using the word "soul" with this meaning, I judge that Shelley had an Oedipal soul. That is, in Shelley's society, with the taboo against mother-son incest strongly operative, child-rearing practices were effectively if not consciously designed to make the mother the forbidden object of desire. The obsessive and highly eroticized focus on women's breasts and the erotic implications present in the admonitions for breast-feeding cast a sexual aura over the interactions of mother and infant, whether or not a mother actually fed the baby herself. Then insistence on the mother's constant and participatory presence made that presence the one thing needful for the infant's well being and her absence or her necessary attention to another child the worst possible betrayal. At the same time, within the newly "affective" family the mother was most decidedly the father's possession. The argument that infants were not reading this literature or aware of these fashions misses the point that infants—quickly children—imbibe the attitudes of their caretakers. The centrality of mimesis to human development ensures that, as Girard comments: "The object of desire is indeed forbidden. But it is not the 'law' that forbids it, as Freud believes—it is the person who designates the object to us as desirable by desiring it himself" (*Things Hidden* 295).

Once the family scenario had instilled deeply ambivalent feelings toward both parents, boys of Shelley's class were abruptly denied the maternal presence by being sent to boarding school, there to bond with others of their own gender and to reject the mother who had committed the final betrayal in ordering or acquiescing to their banishment. I am not saying that this fanning of an Oedipal passion that demanded in consequence a suitably stern repression was a fully conscious project on the part of those who implemented it; I am looking rather at the pragmatic effects. Judith Butler's comments on Kristeva's revision of the Lacanian infancy narrative offer an illuminating insight. She writes: "Because Kristeva restricts herself to an exclusively *prohibitive* conception of the paternal law, she is unable to account for the ways in

267

which the paternal law *generates* certain desires in the form of natural drives. . . . Indeed, repression may be understood to produce the object it comes to deny. That production may well be an elaboration of the agency of repression itself" (93; author's emphasis). The "object" produced in this case is the desiring subject, the soul of desire created through repression of the Oedipal wish. As such a soul, Shelley paid homage to the goddess of love experienced as desire.

Shelley, it is true, did not conform to the usual pattern of these souls. Under "ideal" circumstances the son, having been led to desire the mother and having found himself denied both by the paternal fiat and by her desire for the father (so by a combination of paternal dominance and maternal betrayal), reacts by identifying admiringly with the father. That bonding is then strengthened and further socialized by a similar pattern of sexual excitation and repression at boarding school and results in a homoerotic but homophobic, heterosexual but misogynist man well fitted for the manifold duties and endeavors of a growing empire. Had Shelley been this typical product, he would in time have taken his father's seat in Parliament and functioned in it with more intelligence and more drive than his father, because he was a more gifted and more intense personality, but with the same principles and purposes.

But Shelley did not maneuver the boat of his desiring soul through the Oedipal straits along the designated channel. The dynamics of the Shelley household offer possible reasons for what must still be understood as an imponderably overdetermined outcome: perhaps his mother's desire for his father was not sufficient or wholehearted enough to make her a credible betrayer; perhaps his father was not dominant enough to be a focus for admiring identification. Also, Shelley seems to have stayed home longer, as well as in a more mother-identified way, than the "system" found optimal. In any case, when sent to boarding school, he did not make the customary adaptation, reacting instead with outrage against the school's violent, hierarchical, masculine world. All the rest of his life he remained similarly in rebellion against the patriarchal authority deployed through the political, economic, religious, and social institutions of his country. *Prometheus Unbound* is his most ambitious attempt to express that rebellion: to analyze the strategies that are ineffective in any attempt to overturn entrenched power, to rescind them, and to imagine a new and radical social reordering through a narrative that would also serve as that society's utopian paradigm.

Having experienced sexual frustration as a—perhaps *the*—principal effect of patriarchal control, but having also learned that aggressive defiance mirrors the aspect of its opponent, Shelley sought in *Prometheus Unbound* to imagine a nonconfrontational release of tabooed sexual energies linked to fantasies of a peaceable matriarchate. In Eagleton's terms, Shelley attempts to use the "double-edged" aesthetic, designed to internalize repression, as the basis for "a community of subjects . . . linked by sensuous impulse and fellow feeling rather than by heteronomous law" (28). In making that attempt, he, like others (such as Marcuse) with similar intentions, showed himself unaware of all the ramifications of power. Again Butler, who is working off Foucauldian insights and who cites Marcuse's *Eros and Civilization* as an exemplum (72), offers a gloss: "One way in which power is both perpetuated and concealed is through the establishment of an external or arbitrary relation between power, conceived as repression or domination, and sex, conceived as a brave but thwarted energy waiting for release or authentic self-expression" (95). In other words, the ramifications of power extend to the cave of Demogorgon/ the Promethean Delphic cave; indeed, they *create* the cave and connive at its use as a "ludic space" (Mitchell 428) for the cathartic release of revolutionary energies.

In fact, the drama enacted there will itself always and necessarily be Oedipal as long as society accepts the attitudes toward subjectivity implicit in the thought that the nurse's soul will enter the child. These attitudes persist. In Heinz Lichtenstein's psychoanalytic version of them we are told that "while the mother satisfies the infant's needs, in fact creates certain specific needs, which she delights in satisfying, the infant is transformed into an organ or an instrument for the satisfaction of the mother's unconscious needs" (207). As such an instrument, or as a mere receptacle of "soul," the infant mirrors appropriativeness, not exchange. Then, too, when this "soul" is pouring into an infant who is conceptualized as a nonsubject from the unconscious of a woman constructed as having only marginal subjectivity, the infant becomes both an instrument for and a mirror of the mother's desire—desire not for the father but for what the father has: Lacan's "phallus," the full subjectivity that gives him the right to appropriate her.

There is a further difficulty: to think of using sexuality as a force to overcome power is to share the Jupiterean instrumental view of sexuality. *And this instrumentality in attitude necessarily presupposes the possession of power over sexual desire.* As the conclusion of act three of *Prometheus Unbound* reveals, the subject of desire, still identified with power, desires above all the power over desire, for desire makes one vulnerable to "chance and death and mutability," and the true desideratum is invulnerability. One can also see that the dynamic between a male worshiper and the maternal goddess experienced as liberated desire will not conduce to the liberation of women. Control over women, on the contrary, gives at least some assurance that one controls desire.

Foucault's statement on the nature of soul highlights the consequences of having an Oedipal soul. In *Discipline and Punish* he writes: "It would be wrong to say that the soul is an illusion or an ideological effect. On the contrary, it exists, it has a reality, it is produced permanently around, on, within, the body by the functioning of a power that is exercised on those that are punished" (29). In discussing this and other related statements by Foucault, Butler adds as commentary: "In Foucault's terms, the soul is not imprisoned by or within the body, as some Christian imagery would suggest, but 'the soul is the prison of the body' " (135).

Prison discipline is an extreme form of socialization, but *as* a form of socialization it is on a continuum with child rearing. So considered, Foucault's statement repeats in only slightly different language the thought that the nurse's soul enters the child and adds the further comment that the child raised to be an Oedipal soul is imprisoned within the Oedipal. Shelley's goddess, as goddess of desire and thereby as agency or channel for maintenance of a system of power, imprisons him through the conflation of desire with love and then the denigration of desire/love under the mirroring will to power.

At this point, however, one must allow a very different view about soul to be heard—that of Bakhtin. The soul built "around, on, within" the infant's—or, for that matter, the prisoner's—body is not always or totally or necessarily a prison, if one believes Bakhtin.

Like Foucault, Bakhtin describes soul as imposed on the body by an outside agent or agents. With the socialization of infants as his specific context he writes, "The soul descends upon me—like grace upon the sinner, like a gift that is unmerited and unexpected" (101), and "the soul is spirit the way it looks *from outside,* in the other" (100; author's emphasis). The "other" referred to here is the mother, and this liberatory soul is the gift of the socializing maternal: "The biological life of an organism becomes value only in *another's* sympathy and compassion with that life (motherhood)" (55; author's emphasis). The interaction between "sympathy and compassion" on the one hand and the struggles of a "biological organism" on the other gets fuller description in this passage:

> Words of love and acts of genuine concern come to meet the dark chaos of my inner sensation of myself. They name, direct, satisfy, and connect it with the outside world—as with a response that is interested in me and in my need. And as a result, they give plastic form, as it were, to this boundless, "darkly stirring chaos" of needs and dissatisfactions, wherein the future dyad of the child's personality and the outside world confronting it is still submerged and dissolved. (50)

Translated into the discourse of developmental psychology, Bakhtin's words describe the process whereby the affect attunement of the care giver(s) creates in an infant that primary narcissism that transforms the desirous chaos of infant need into outgoing or answering love; this experience of participatory exchange leads to the exchange involved in language and finally to all possible forms of creativity. As presider over the process of socialization conceptualized in these terms, Shelley's goddess is the goddess of relationship whose countless children, patterning themselves on her, "take / And interchange sweet nutriment" (*PU* III.iii.95–96).

The objection can well be brought forward, with my own earlier Foucauldian analysis of socialization processes as evidence, that Bakhtin's is a rosily sentimentalized picture, with strong overtones of the very ideology of motherhood I have been describing as conscripted for patriarchal purposes. True; and as the simplest preliminary to my own thinking about the beneficent spirit ideally present in the socialization of children for the modeling of ideal human community, I would say this spirit must be assigned no specific gender or, for that matter, number. But the relevance of Bakhtin's analysis of Shelley's thinking is the topic before us here; and as such an ideal, rather than merely sentimental, view of the socialization process Bakhtin's analysis offers a necessary balance to the excessive pessimism of Foucault's, or at least to the pessimism of my extrapolation from his image of soul as prison. However frequent the incidence of "failed attunement," and however dark the reasons for those failures, one must allow the possibility, indeed the actuality, of countless instances when soul is a gift rather than a prison. As shown in the quotation from Earth—along with others noted in the foregoing chapters—Shelley's goddess presides over the exchange of soul as gift, and this aspect of her bears continuing thought.

More problematic than Bakhtin's strong accentuation of the positive when he describes interaction between mothers and their infants is his disregard of the access of both to full subjectivity. He also takes insufficient note of the terrors inherent in the nature of the interaction itself. When Bakhtin writes "It is his mother's loving embraces that 'give form' to [the child] axiologically" (50), the context presupposes that the self-valuation received by the child is positive, but it could just as easily be negative. Also, the care giver's capacity to lean in upon the child, involving a psychic interaction also present in hypnosis, can induce psychosis if pushed too far. And since the infant's malleability to the caretaker's gaze and voice remains in adult susceptibility to hypnosis, the vulnerable nature of the psyche cannot be taken to have a clear cutoff point.

This vulnerability is at its most fearsome when one person can deny being vulnerable, can indeed assert invulnerability while making the other's vulnerability manifest. Elaine Scarry, describing the experience of torture, uses "world" as Shelley does in "On Life" to mean "whatever we call that which we are and feel" (*SPP* 474). She writes: "The torturer's questions—asked, shouted, insisted upon, pleaded for—objectify the fact that he has a world . . . a world whose asserted magnitude is confirmed by the cruelty it is able to motivate and justify. Part of what makes his world so huge is its continual juxtaposition with the small and shredded world objectified in the prisoner's answers" (36).

As the description of the rape of Thetis in *Prometheus Unbound* and the treatment of rape in *The Cenci* both show, Shelley fully grasped the potential horror in the openness of each human's world to the intrusive and appropriative presence of another. A further instance of this awareness appears in "On Life." As Shelley moves toward the point at which the fragment breaks off, his repeated phrase "Nothing exists but as it is perceived" makes a turn toward the meaning "No subjectivity exists but as that subjectivity is perceived," because "the existence of distinct individual minds . . . is . . . found to be a delusion" (*SPP* 477). That thought in turn brings him to the verge of a "dark abyss" (*SPP* 478).

In this last instance, it is true, Shelley avoids final confrontation with an idea that I have said he "fully grasped." And in the rape scenes of *Prometheus Unbound* and *The Cenci*, as in the analogous if totally positive moment in which Panthea dreams herself hypnotized by Prometheus, Shelley adopts his—and our—culture's strategy of assigning vulnerability to women while appropriating a fictitious but pragmatically effective invulnerability for men.

Indeed, Shelley's positive affirmation of the idea that "the difference is merely nominal between those two classes of thought which are vulgarly distinguished by the names of ideas and of external objects" (*SPP* 477) does not involve as clear and dramatic a visualization as the negative ones I have mentioned, but it can be extrapolated from his use of the pastoral. Through the topos of a relationship between the Mother Goddess and a son/lover, Shelley superimposes the paradigm of affect attunement between mother and infant on the metaphoric relation (once the interwoven system of "correspondences") between the "world" of external natural forms and the "world" of what "we are and feel."

Timothy Webb suggests that it was "the personification of Nature" in the elegies of Bion and Moschus that led Shelley to translate them. Noting that Shelley even exaggerates the instances of the pathetic fallacy to be found in these poems, Webb adds: "In his defence it should be pointed out that for him the link between man and nature was no mere literary device but an intimation of mystic communion, an adumbration of the essential unity of all things" (70).

Taking a look at the historical context is a first step toward a better understanding of the nature of this "mystic communion." It seems likely that Shelley, along with huge numbers of his contemporaries, gave credence to something like Abernethy's "subtle substance" as an actual fluid creating universal "sympathy" (Crook and Guiton 70). It is true that this particular reification of "the essential unity of all things" no longer gains the same general assent. But the nature of the communion adumbrated by this circling fluid can be demystified. Interpreted psychologically and socially, though not thereby without metaphysical implications as well, an intimation of mystic communion like the one to be found in Earth's speech after her reunion with Prometheus is a meditation on human vulnerability as historically fearsome but potentially salvific.

When the goddess of love as relationship is denied, the connectedness of humans with one another, most dramatically experienced as the ability to inscribe one another, continues to function, but only as a source of "disease and pain." The return of the goddess of love as relationship, made possible by the renunciation of the will to power along with the myth of the invulnerability of power, and by an according of the status of a separate yet interdependent subjectivity to all, will create an interchange of "sweet nutriment" to shape human bodies and human souls, which is to say their attitudes toward themselves as bodies, in the way described by Bakhtin: "This love that shapes a human being from outside throughout his life—his mother's love and the love of others around him—this love gives body to his inner body, and . . . make[s] him the possessor of that body's potential value—a value capable of being actualized only by another human being" (51).

Commenting further on Shelley's translation of Bion and Moschus, Webb writes: "The poems would also have attracted Shelley because they dealt with a theme which obsessed him from *Alastor* to *Adonais*—the untimely death of a gifted young man" (70). As we have seen, that young man has as chief among his gifts the love of the Mother Goddess. Within the Oedipal scenario she, as source of his hopeless desire, lures her poet-lover to his dissolution and the silencing of all language. But when the goddess is experienced as relationship, the great pastoral myth has a completely different meaning. The love between the goddess and the ever-dying, ever-reborn poet stands in metaphoric, indeed typological, relation to the production of language, dramatizing the process in which language—born from the matrix of unmediated experience that it mediates and thus kills, mourns, and revives transformed—becomes the human soul: prison or gift according to its human uses.

Death and chance and mutability are all synonyms for this profoundly erotic but nongenital change or exchange, this "turning" in its Celtic root, that incorporates experience as language. The poet's vulnerability to death signifies a privileged awareness of that moment of turning; but the poet (who, in my gloss of the legend is assigned no gender) acts as representative for the universal human vulnerability that is the necessary precondition for the exchange at the heart of language.

Shelley's poetic and social manifesto in "A Philosophical View of Reform" raises only the question whether a universal acceptance of universal vulnerability can be imagined with sufficient clarity to make it an object for contemplation that will in turn produce the "tranquillity & courage & grandeur of soul" (*SHC* VI, 1044) necessary to transform it into lived reality. I raise but I cannot resolve that question.

Works Cited

"The Abandoned Infant: A Tale." *The Lady's Magazine* 25 (1794): 119–20.

Abrams, M. H. *Natural Supernaturalism: Tradition and Revolution in Romantic Literature.* New York: Norton, 1971.

"Account of the Arrival, and Ceremony of Nuptials of Her Royal Highness, the Princess of Wales." *The Lady's Magazine* 26 (1795): 155–58.

"Account of the City of *Palmyra.* Collected from Various Authors." *La Belle Assemblée* 3.34 (1808): 154–59.

Aeschylus. *Eumenides.* Trans. E. D. A. Morshead. In *Complete Greek Drama.* Ed. Whitney J. Oates and Eugene O'Neill, Jr. 2 vols. New York: Random House, 1938: 271–307.

———. *Prometheus Bound.* Trans. James Scully and C. J. Herington. New York: Oxford UP, 1975.

Alcoff, Linda. "Cultural Feminism Versus Post-Modernism: The Identity Crisis in Feminist Theory." *Signs: Journal of Women in Culture and Society* 13 (1988): 405–36.

Allen, Don Cameron. *Mysteriously Meant.* Baltimore: Johns Hopkins UP, 1970.

Alpers, Paul. *The Singer of Eclogues.* Berkeley: U of California P, 1979.

"Anna Marie Stanhope." *La Belle Assemblée* 3.35 (1808): 1.

Anzaldúa, Gloria, ed. *Making Face, Making Soul: Haciendo Caras.* San Francisco: Aunt Lute Foundation Books, 1990.

Anzieu, Didier. "L'Enveloppe Sonore du Soi." *Nouvelle Revue de Psychanalyse,* no. 13 (Spring 1976): 161–80.

Armstrong, Nancy. *Desire and Domestic Fiction: A Political History of the Novel.* New York: Oxford UP, 1987.

Aveling, Edward, and Eleanor Marx. *Shelley's Socialism.* West Nyack, NY: Journeyman, 1975.

Babbitt, Irving. *Rousseau and Romanticism.* Cleveland: Meridian Books, 1955; rpt. of 1919 edition.

Bachelard, Gaston. *The Poetics of Reverie.* Trans. Daniel Russell. Boston: Beacon, 1971.

Bachofen, Johann. *Myth, Religion, and Mother Right.* Princeton: Princeton UP, [1967].

Bacon, Francis. *The Great Instauration; and, New Atlantis.* Ed. J. Weinberger. Arlington Heights, IL: AHM Publishing, [1980].

Bailblé, Claude. "Programmation de l'Écoute, (1)." *Cahiers du Cinéma,* no. 293 (1978): 53–54.

Baker, Carlos. *Shelley's Major Poetry: The Fabric of a Vision.* Princeton: Princeton UP, 1948.

Bakhtin, Mikhail. *Art and Answerability.* Ed. Michael Holquist. Trans. Vadim Liapunov. Austin: U of Texas P, 1990.

Barbauld, Anna Letitia. *Hymns in Prose for Children.* London: J. Johnson, 1787.

———. *The Female Speaker.* London: J. Johnson, 1811.

Barnhart Dictionary of Etymology. Ed. Robert K. Barnhart. New York: H. W. Wilson, 1988.

Barruel [Augustin de]. *Memoirs, Illustrating the History of Jacobinism.* 4 vols. London: T. Burton, 1797–98.

Barthell, Edward E., Jr. *Gods and Goddesses of Ancient Greece.* Coral Gables, FL: U of Miami P, 1971.

Beck, Evelyn Torton, ed. *Nice Jewish Girls.* Trumansburg, NY: Crossing, 1982.

Behrendt, Stephen C. *Shelley and His Audiences.* Lincoln: U of Nebraska P, 1989.

Bell, Susan Groag, and Karen M. Offen. *Women, the Family, and Freedom: The Debate in the Documents.* 2 vols. Stanford: Stanford UP, 1983.

Benjamin, Jessica. *The Bonds of Love: Psychoanalysis, Feminism, and the Problem of Domination.* New York: Pantheon, 1988.

Benveniste, Émile. *Problems in General Linguistics.* Coral Gables, FL: U of Miami P, 1971.

Berg, William. "Daphnis and Prometheus." *Transactions of the American Philological Association* 96 (1965): 11–23.

Bernstein, Basil. "Social Class, Speech Systems, and Psychotherapy." *British Journal of Sociology* 15 (1964): 54–64.

Bettelheim, Bruno. *Symbolic Wounds.* New York: Collier Books, 1962.

Blake, William. *The Poetry and Prose of William Blake.* Ed. David V. Erdman. Garden City, NY: Doubleday, 1970.

Bonnard, Augusta. "The Primal Significance of the Tongue." *International Journal of Psycho-Analysis* 41 (1960): 301–7.

Borch-Jacobsen, Mikkel. *The Freudian Subject.* Stanford: Stanford UP, 1988.

———. *Lacan: The Absolute Master.* Stanford: Stanford UP, 1991.

Bordo, Susan. "The Cartesian Masculinization of Thought." *Signs: Journal of Women in Culture and Society* 11 (1986): 439–56.

Bowles, John. "Selection from *Reflexions Political and Moral at the Conclusion of the War.*" *The Lady's Magazine* 33 (1802): 583–85.

Branca, Patricia. *Silent Sisterhood.* London: Croom Helm, 1975.

Brisman, Susan. " 'Unsaying His High Language': The Problem of Voice in *Prometheus Unbound.*" *Studies in Romanticism* 16 (1977): 51–86.

Brown, Nathaniel. *Sexuality and Feminism in Shelley.* Cambridge, MA: Harvard UP, 1979.

Brown, Sarah. *Letter to a Lady on the Best Means of Obtaining the Milk.* London, 1777.

Bruns, Gerald. *Modern Poetry and the Idea of Language.* New Haven: Yale UP, 1974.

Bryant, Jacob. *A New System, or an Analysis of Ancient Mythology.* 3 vols. London: T. Payne, 1775.

Buchan, William. *The New Domestic Medicine . . . to which now is first added . . . his Advice to Mothers.* Ed. William Nisbet. London: Thomas Kelley, 1809.

Bulkin, Elly, et al. *Yours in Struggle: Three Feminist Perspectives on Anti-Semitism and Racism.* Brooklyn: Long Haul, 1984.

Burke, John. *A Genealogical and Heraldic History of the Extinct and Dormant Baronetcies of England, Ireland, and Scotland.* 2nd ed. London: John Russell Smith, 1844.

Burkert, Walter. *Structure and History in Greek Mythology and Ritual.* Berkeley: U of California P, 1979.

———. *Greek Religion.* Cambridge, MA: Harvard UP, 1985.

———. *Ancient Mystery Cults.* Cambridge, MA: Harvard UP, 1987.

Butler, Judith. *Gender Trouble: Feminism and the Subversion of Identity.* New York: Routledge, 1990.

Byron, George Gordon. *Byron's Letters and Journals.* Ed. Leslie A. Marchand. 12 vols. London: John Murray, 1973–1982.

Cadogan, William. *An Essay upon Nursing and the Management of Children from Their Birth to Three Years of Age.* London: J. Roberts, 1750.

Cameron, Kenneth Neill. *The Young Shelley.* London: Macmillan, 1950.

———. *Shelley: The Golden Years.* Cambridge, MA: Harvard UP, 1974.

Cameron, Kenneth Neill, et al., eds. *Shelley and His Circle: 1773–1822.* 8 vols. Cambridge, MA: Harvard UP, 1961–1986.

Campbell, Joseph. *The Hero with a Thousand Faces.* Princeton: Princeton UP, 1971.

Campe, Joachim Heinrich. *Reise durch England und Frankreich.* [*Travels Through England and France*] (1804). Ed. P. Baensch. Breslau: Priebatsch [1927].

———. "Selections from Travels in England." *La Belle Assemblée* 1.2 (1806): 66–68.

Chailley, John. *The Magic Flute, Masonic Opera.* Trans. Herbert Weinstock. London: Gollancz, 1972.

Chernaik, Judith. *The Lyrics of Shelley.* Cleveland: Case Western Reserve UP, 1972.

Child, Lydia Maria. *The Mother's Book,* 2nd ed. Boston: Carter, Hendee and Babcock, 1831.

Chion, Michel. *La Voix au Cinéma.* Paris: Éditions de l'Étoile, 1982.

Chodorow, Nancy. *The Reproduction of Mothering.* Berkeley: U of California P, 1978.

Chodorow, Nancy, and Susan Contratto. "The Fantasy of the Perfect Mother." In *Rethinking the Family: Some Feminist Questions.* Ed. Barrie Thorne and Marilyn Yalom. New York: Longman, 1982.

Clark, J. C. D. *English Society, 1688–1832.* Cambridge: Cambridge UP, 1985.

[Clementina]. "On the Difference Between the Sexes." *The Lady's Magazine* 34 (1803): 341–43.

Cliff, Michelle. *Claiming an Identity They Taught Me to Despise.* Watertown, MA: Persephone, 1980.

Coleridge, Samuel Taylor. *The Poems of Samuel Taylor Coleridge.* Ed. Ernest Hartley Coleridge. London: Oxford UP, 1912.

———. *Collected Letters of Samuel Taylor Coleridge.* Ed. Earl Leslie Griggs. 6 vols. Oxford: Clarendon, 1956–1971.

———. *The Notebooks of Samuel Taylor Coleridge.* Ed. Kathleen Coburn. 3 vols. Princeton: Princeton UP, 1957–73.

Complete Baronetage. 5 vols. Exeter: William Pollard, 1904.

Conacher, D. J. *Aeschylus' "Prometheus Unbound": A Literary Commentary.* Toronto: U of Toronto P, 1980.

Cott, Nancy. "Passionlessness: An Interpretation of Victorian Sexual Ideology." *Signs: Journal of Women in Culture and Society* 4 (1978): 219–36.

"Countess of Harrington." *La Belle Assemblée* 3.36 (1808): 1.

Coward, Rosalind. "Julia Kristeva in Conversation with Rosalind Coward." *Institute of Contemporary Arts Documents* (November 1983): 22–27.

Crompton, Louis. *Byron and Greek Love: Homophobia in Nineteenth-Century England.* Berkeley: U of California P, 1985.

Crook, Nora, and Derek Guiton. *Shelley's Venomed Melody.* Cambridge: Cambridge UP, 1986.

Cunnington, Willet. *English Women's Clothing in the Nineteenth Century.* London: Faber and Faber, 1937.

Cunnington, Willet, and Phillis Cunnington. *The History of Underclothes.* London: Michael Joseph, 1951.

Curran, Stuart. *Shelley's "Cenci."* Princeton: Princeton UP, 1970.

———. *Shelley's Annus Mirabilis.* San Marino, CA: Huntington Library, 1975.

———. *Poetic Form and British Romanticism.* New York: Oxford UP, 1986.

Darnton, Robert. *Mesmerism and the End of the Enlightenment in France.* Cambridge, MA: Harvard UP, 1968.

———. *The Great Cat Massacre and Other Episodes in French Cultural History.* New York: Basic Books, 1984.

Darwin, Erasmus. *Zoonomia, or The Laws of Organic Life.* 2 vols. London: J. Johnson, 1794–96.

———. *A Plan for the Conduct of Female Education in Boarding Schools.* East Ardsley, England: S. R. Publishers, 1797.

———. *The Botanic Garden.* New York: Garland, 1978.

Davidoff, Leonore, and Catherine Hall. *Family Fortunes.* London: Hutchinson, 1987.

Debrett, John. *The Baronetage of England.* 2 vols. London: F. C. and J. Rivington, 1808.

De Galitzin, Baris. "Diogenes and Glycere." *Lady's Monthly Museum* 4 (1800): 346–50.

Deleuze, Joseph. *Practical Instruction in Animal Magnetism.* Trans. Thomas C. Hartshorn. New York: Appleton, 1843.

Detienne, Marcel, and J.-P. Vernant. *Cunning Intelligence in Greek Culture and Society.* Hassocks, England: Harvester, 1978.

Dinnerstein, Dorothy. *The Mermaid and the Minotaur.* New York: Harper and Row, 1976.

Diodorus of Sicily. *The Library of History.* Trans. C. H. Oldfather. 10 vols. Cambridge, MA: Harvard UP, 1933.

Doane, Mary Anne. "The Voice in the Cinema: The Articulation of Body and Space." *Yale French Studies,* no. 60 (1980): 33–50.

Douglas, Mary. *Natural Symbols: Explorations in Cosmology.* New York: Pantheon, 1982.

Dowden, Edward. *The Life of Percy Bysshe Shelley.* 2 vols. London: Kegan Paul, Trench, 1886.

Drummond, Sir William. *Academical Questions.* London: Cadell and Davies, 1805.

———. *An Essay on a Punic Inscription.* London, 1810.

Duncan, Robert. "The H.D. Book, Part I: Chapter 2." *Coyote's Journal* 8 (1967): 27–35.

Durham, Margery. "The Mother Tongue: *Christabel* and the Language of Love." In *The (M)other Tongue.* Ed. Shirley Nelson Garner et al. Ithaca: Cornell UP, 1985.

Eagleton, Terry. *The Ideology of the Aesthetic.* Oxford: Basil Blackwell, 1990.

Edgeworth, Maria. *Practical Education.* 3 vols. 2nd ed. London: J. Johnson, 1801.

———. *Continuation of Early Lessons.* Boston: Bradford and Read, 1815.

"Edict Against the Use of Stays." *Lady's Monthly Museum* 4 (1800): 393.

"Editors' Note." *La Belle Assemblée* 1.3 (1806): 121.

Emerson, Caryl. "The Outer Word and Inner Speech: Bakhtin, Vygotsky, and the Internalization of Language." *Critical Inquiry* 10 (1983): 245–64.

Ensor, George. *The Independent Man.* London: J. Johnson, 1806.

"An Essay upon Female Education." *Lady's Monthly Museum* 1 (1798): 51–56.

Euripides. *Bacchae.* Trans. Gilbert Murray. In *Complete Greek Drama.* Ed. Whitney J. Oates and Eugene O'Neill, Jr. 2 vols. New York: Random House, 1938.

———. *Iphigenia in Tauris.* Trans. Robert Potter. In *Complete Greek Drama.* Ed. Whitney J. Oates and Eugene O'Neill, Jr. 2 vols. New York: Random House, 1938.

"Fashion." *La Belle Assemblée* 2.16 (1807): 196.

Favret, Mary. "The Idea of Correspondence in British Romantic Literature." Ph.D. diss. Stanford, 1988.

Felman, Shoshana. *Jacques Lacan and the Adventures of Insight.* Cambridge, MA: Harvard UP, 1987.

Fenn, Lady Eleanor [Mrs. Lovechild]. *The Rational Dame, or Hints Towards Supplying Prattle for Children.* London: Baldwin, Craddock and Joy, 1784.

———. *The Infant's Friend: A Spelling Book.* London: E. Newberry, 1797.

———. *Parsing Lessons for Young Children.* London, n.p., 1798.

———. *The Mother's Grammar.* London: John Marshall, [1798?].

———. *Rational Sports, In Dialogues Passing Among the Children of a Family.* Boston: Cummings and Hilliard, 1814.

Fernald, Anne. "Perceptual and Affective Salience of Mother's Speech to Infants." In *The Origins and Growth of Communication.* Ed. Lynne Feagans et al. Norwood, NJ: Ablex, 1984.

Fernald, Anne, et al. "A Cross-Language Study of Prosodic Modifications in Mothers' and Fathers' Speech to Preverbal Infants." *Journal of Child Language* 16 (1989): 477–501.

Fine, Reuben. *Narcissism, the Self, and Society.* New York: Columbia UP, 1986.

Fogel, Aaron. "Coerced Speech and the Oedipus Complex." In *Rethinking Bakhtin: Extensions and Challenges.* Ed. Gary Saul Morson and Caryl Emerson. Evanston: Northwestern UP, 1989: 173–96.

Foucault, Michel. *Discipline and Punish: The Birth of the Prison.* Trans. Alan Sheridan. New York: Pantheon, 1977.

———. *The History of Sexuality.* Vol. 1. Trans. Robert Hurley. New York: Pantheon, 1978.

Frazer, James. *The Golden Bough: A Study in Magic and Religion.* 12 vols. London: Macmillan, 1911.

Freud, Sigmund. *The Standard Edition of the Complete Works of Sigmund Freud.* Trans. James Strachey. 24 vols. London: Hogarth, 1957.

Fry, Paul H. "Made Men: A Review Article on Recent Keats and Shelley Studies." *Texas Studies in Literature and Language* 21 (1979): 433–54.

Gallagher, Catherine. *The Industrial Reformation of English Fiction, 1832–1867.* Chicago: Chicago UP, 1985.

Garland, J. A. ["Jorrocks"]. *The Private Stable.* Boston: Little, Brown, 1899.

Garner, Shirley Nelson, Claire Kahane, and Madelon Sprengnether, eds. *The (M)other Tongue: Essays in Feminist Psychoanalytic Interpretation.* Ithaca: Cornell UP, 1985.

Garvie, A. F. *Aeschylus' "Supplices": Play and Trilogy.* Cambridge: Cambridge UP, 1969.

Gaull, Marilyn. *English Romanticism: The Human Context.* New York: Norton, 1988.

[Gelpi], Barbara Charlesworth. *Dark Passages: The Decadent Consciousness in Victorian Literature.* Madison: U of Wisconsin P, 1965.

———. "The Politics of Androgyny." *Women's Studies* 2 (1974): 151–60.

"Georgiana, Duchess of Devonshire." *Lady's Monthly Museum* 31 (1800): 241.

Gilbert, Sandra M. "Life's Empty Pack: Notes Toward a Literary Daughteronomy." *Critical Inquiry* 11 (1985): 355–84.

Girard, René. *Deceit, Desire, and the Novel.* Trans. Yvonne Freccero. Baltimore: Johns Hopkins UP, 1965.

———. *Violence and the Sacred.* Trans. Patrick Gregory. Baltimore: Johns Hopkins UP, 1972.

———. *Things Hidden since the Foundation of the World.* Trans. Stephen Bann and Michael Metteer. Stanford: Stanford UP, 1987.

Gisborne, Thomas. *An Enquiry into the Duties of the Female Sex.* London: T. Caddell, Jr., and W. Davies, 1797.

———. "On the Female Character." *The Lady's Magazine* 34 (1803): 254–56.

Godwin, William. *An Enquiry Concerning Political Justice.* 2 vols. London: G. G. J. and J. Robinson, [1793].

Grabo, Carl. *"Prometheus Unbound": An Interpretation.* Chapel Hill: U of North Carolina P, 1935.

———. *A Newton Among the Poets.* New York: Cooper Square, 1968.

Gray, Thomas. *The Poetical Works of Gray and Collins.* Ed. Austin Lane Poole. 3rd ed. Oxford: Oxford UP, 1937.

Gregory, R. L. "Origin of Eyes and Brains." *Nature* 213 (1967): 369–72.

Griffith, Elizabeth, trans. *Memoirs of Ninon De L'Enclos.* Philadelphia: T. H. O. Palmer, 1806.

Griffith, Mark. *The Authenticity of "Prometheus Bound."* Cambridge: Cambridge UP, 1977.

Griffith, Mark, ed. Introduction. *Prometheus Bound* by Aeschylus. Cambridge: Cambridge UP, 1983.

H.D. [Hilda Doolittle]. *Tribute to Freud.* Boston: David R. Godine, 1974.

Halperin, David. "The Forebears of Daphnis." *Transactions of the American Philological Association* 113 (1983): 183–200.

———. *Before Pastoral: Theocritus and the Ancient Tradition of Bucolic Poetry.* New Haven: Yale UP, 1983.

Hamilton, Elizabeth. *Letters on the Elementary Principles of Education.* 2 vols. 3rd American ed. Boston: S. H. Parker, 1825.

Harrison, Jane Ellen. *Themis.* Cambridge: Cambridge UP, 1912.

Hartley, Robert A. "The Uroboros in Shelley's Poetry." *JEGP* 73 (1974): 524–542.

Hellerstein, Erna O., Karen M. Offen, and Leslie Parker Hume, eds. *Victorian Women.* Stanford: Stanford UP, 1981.

"Her Majesty, Queen Charlotte." *La Belle Assemblée* 2.13 (1807): 1.

Herington, C. J. *The Author of "Prometheus Bound."* Austin: U of Texas P, 1970.

Hesiod. *Homeric Hymns and Homerica.* Trans. Hugh G. Evelyn-White. Rev. ed. Cambridge: Cambridge UP, 1936.

Hibbert, Christopher. *George IV, Regent and King, 1811–1830.* New York: Harper & Row, 1973.

Hildebrand, William H. "A Look at the Third and Fourth Spirit Songs: *Prometheus Unbound,* I." *Keats-Shelley Journal* 20 (1971): 87–99.

———. "Naming Day in Asia's Vale." *Keats-Shelley Journal* 32 (1983): 190–203.

Hill, John ["Juliana-Susannah Seymour"]. *On the Management and Education of Children*. New York: Garland, 1985.

Hillman, James. *The Myth of Analysis*. Evanston: Northwestern UP, 1972.

———. "Anima." *Spring* (1973): 19–130.

Hirsch, Marianne. "Mothers and Daughters." *Signs: Journal of Women in Culture and Society* (1981): 200–222.

Hoeveler, Diane Long. *Romantic Androgyny: The Women Within*. University Park: Pennsylvania State UP, 1990.

Hogg, Thomas Jefferson. *The Life of Percy Bysshe Shelley*. 2 vols. London: J. M. Dent and Sons, 1933.

———. *Memoirs of Prince Alexy Haimatoff*. London: Folio Society, 1952.

Hogle, Jerrold E. *Shelley's Process*. New York: Oxford UP, 1988.

Hollander, Anne. *Seeing Through Clothes*. New York: Viking, 1978.

Holmes, Richard. *Shelley: The Pursuit*. New York: E. P. Dutton, 1975.

Holquist, Michael. "The Politics of Representation." In *Allegory and Representation*. Ed. S. J. Greenblatt. Baltimore: Johns Hopkins UP, 1982.

Holquist, Michael, and Katerina Clark. *Mikhail Bakhtin*. Cambridge, MA: Harvard UP, 1984.

Homans, Margaret. *Bearing the Word*. Chicago: U of Chicago P, 1986.

Horkheimer, Max, and Theodor W. Adorno. *Dialectic of Enlightenment*. Trans. John Cumming. New York: Continuum, 1982.

Houston, Mathilda. *A Woman's Memories of World-Known Men*. 2 vols. London: F. V. White, 1883.

Hughes, A. M. D. *The Nascent Mind of Shelley*. Oxford: Clarendon, 1947.

Hughes, A. M. D., ed. *Shelley: Poems Published in 1820*. Oxford: Clarendon, 1910.

Hughes, Daniel J. "Potentiality in *Prometheus Unbound*." *Studies in Romanticism* 2 (1963): 107–26.

Hungerford, Edward B. *Shores of Darkness*. New York: Columbia UP, 1941.

Hunt, Leigh. *Lord Byron and Some of His Contemporaries*. 2 vols. London: Henry Colburn, 1828.

Ingpen, Roger. *Shelley in England*. 2 vols. Boston: Houghton Mifflin, 1917.

Jack, Lawrence Pearsall. *Life and Letters of Stopford Brooke*. London: J. Murray, 1917.

Jacobsen, Thorkild. *Toward the Image of Tammuz*. Ed. W. L. Moran. Harvard Semitic Studies 21. Cambridge, MA: Harvard UP, 1970.

———. *The Treasures of Darkness: A History of Mesopotamian Religion*. New Haven: Yale UP, 1976.

Jardine, Alice. *Gynesis: Configurations of Woman and Modernity*. Ithaca: Cornell UP, 1985.

Jeaffreson, John. *The Real Shelley*. 2 vols. London: Hurst and Blackett, 1885.

Joukovsky, Nicholas A. "Peacock Before Headlong Hall: A New Look at His Early Years." *Keats-Shelley Memorial Bulletin* 36 (1985): 1–40.

Jung, C. G. *Collected Works*. 20 vols. 2nd ed. Ed. Herbert Read et al. Princeton: Princeton UP, 1966–1979.

Kahn, Coppélia. "The Hand That Rocks the Cradle: Recent Gender Theories and Their Implications." In *The (M)other Tongue: Essays in Feminist Psychoanalytic Interpretation*. Ed. Shirley Nelson Garner, Claire Kahane, Madelon Sprengnether. Ithaca: Cornell UP, 1985.

Keach, William. *Shelley's Style*. London: Methuen Books, 1984.

Keats, John. *The Letters of John Keats, 1814–1821*. Ed. Hyder Edward Rollins. 2 vols. Cambridge, MA: Harvard UP. 1958.

Kessel, Marcel. "The Mark of X in Claire Clairmont's Journal." *PMLA* 66 (1951): 1180–83.

Kittler, Friedrich A. *Discourse Networks, 1800/1900.* Trans. Michael Metteer with Chris Cullen. Stanford: Stanford UP, 1990.

Klein, Melanie. *The Selected Melanie Klein.* Ed. Juliet Mitchell. New York: Free Press, 1986.

Kramer, Samuel Noah. *The Sumerians: Their History, Culture, and Character.* Chicago: U of Chicago P, 1963.

———. *The Sacred Marriage Rite: Aspects of Faith, Myth, and Ritual in Ancient Sumer.* Bloomington: Indiana UP, 1969.

Kristeva, Julia. *Desire in Language.* New York: Columbia UP, 1980.

———. *The Powers of Horror.* Trans. Leon S. Roudiez. New York: Columbia UP, 1982. Trans. of *Pouvoirs de l'Horreur.* Paris: Seuil, 1980.

———. "Histoires d'Amour—Love Stories." *Institute of Contemporary Arts Documents* (November 1983): 18–21.

———. *Revolution in Poetic Language.* New York: Columbia UP, 1984. Trans. of *La Révolution du Langage Poétique.* Paris: Seuil, [1974].

———. *Tales of Love.* Trans. Leon S. Roudiez. New York: Columbia UP: 1987. Trans. of *Histoires d'Amour.* Paris: Denoel, 1983.

Lacan, Jacques. *Écrits.* Trans. Alan Sheridan. New York: W. W. Norton, 1977.

———. *The Four Fundamental Concepts of Psycho-Analysis.* New York: Norton, 1978.

———. *Feminine Sexuality.* Ed. Juliet Mitchell and Jacqueline Rose. London: Macmillan, 1982.

"The Ladies' Toilette or Encyclopedia of Beauty." *La Belle Assemblée* 1.2 (1806): 79.

Laing, R. D. *The Politics of the Family and Other Essays.* New York: Vintage, 1972.

Langbauer, Laurie. "Motherhood and Women's Writing in Mary Wollstonescraft's Novels." In *Romanticism and Feminism.* Ed. Anne K. Mellor. Bloomington: Indiana UP, 1988.

Langdon, Stephen Herbert. *Semitic: The Mythology of All Races.* 13 vols. Boston: Marshall Jones, 1916–32.

Laslett, Peter, and Richard Wall. *Household and Family Past Time.* Cambridge: Cambridge UP, 1972.

Laver, James. *Dress: How and Why Fashions in Men's and Women's Clothes Have Changed During the Past Two Hundred Years.* London: John Murray, 1950.

Lemaire, Anika. *Jacques Lacan.* London: Routledge and Kegan Paul, 1977.

Lemprière, John. *A Classical Dictionary.* 1st American ed. from the 6th London ed. New York: Samuel Campbell, 1809.

"Letter from Paris." *The Lady's Magazine* 32 (1801): 630–31.

Lewis, C. S. *The Discarded Image.* Cambridge: Cambridge UP, 1964.

Lewis, Judith Schneid. *In the Family Way: Childbearing in the British Aristocracy, 1760–1860.* New Brunswick, NJ: Rutgers UP, 1986.

"The Libertine Reclaimed." *The Lady's Magazine* 26 (1795): 159–60.

Lichtenstein, Heinz. "Identity and Sexuality: A Study of Their Interrelationship in Man." *Journal of the American Psychoanalytic Association,* 9 (1961): 179–260.

Lloyd-Jones, Hugh, trans. *The "Eumenides" by Aeschylus.* Englewood Cliffs, NJ: Prentice-Hall, 1970.

Locke, John. *Two Treatises of Government.* Ed. Peter Laslett. Cambridge: Cambridge UP, 1988.

———. *Some Thoughts Concerning Education.* Oxford: Clarendon, 1989.

Locock, Charles, ed. *The Poems of Percy Bysshe Shelley.* London: Methuen, 1911.

Longaker, John Mark. *The Della Cruscans and William Gifford: The History of a Minor Movement in an Age of Literary Transition.* Philadelphia: U of Pennsylvania P, 1924.

Lower, Mark Antony. *The Worthies of Sussex.* Lewes: G. P. Bacon, 1865.

Lucan. *Pharsalia.* Trans. J. D. Duff. 2 vols. Cambridge, MA: Harvard UP, 1928.

Lucretius. *De Rerum Natura.* Trans. H. A. J. Munro. Cambridge: D. Bell, 1886.

Macfarlane, Alan. *Marriage and Love in England: Modes of Reproduction, 1300–1840.* Oxford: Basil Blackwell, 1986.

"Madame de Genlis." *La Belle Assemblée* 2.17 (1807): 230–31.

Mahler, Margaret. *The Psychological Birth of the Human.* New York: Basic Books, 1975.

Maine, Sir Henry. *Ancient Law.* London: J. M. Dent and Sons, 1917.

Malthus, Thomas Robert. *On Population.* Ed. Gertrude Himmelfarb. New York: Modern Library, 1960.

Marcuse, Herbert. *Eros and Civilization: A Philosophical Inquiry into Freud.* Boston: Beacon, 1966.

Marks, Lawrence E. *The Unity of the Senses: Interrelations Among Modalities.* New York: Academic, 1978.

Marlowe, Christopher. *The Complete Works of Christopher Marlowe.* 2 vols. Ed. Fredson Bowers. Cambridge: Cambridge UP, 1973.

Massey, Marilyn C. *Feminine Soul: The Fate of an Ideal.* Boston: Beacon, 1985.

"Maternal Antipathy, Contrasted with Filial Piety." *Lady's Monthly Museum* 2, n.s. (1815): 263–64.

Matthews, G. M. "A Volcano's Voice in Shelley." *ELH* 24 (1957): 191–228.

McGann, Jerome J. " 'My Brain is Feminine': Byron and the Poetry of Deception." In *Byron: Augustan and Romantic.* Ed. Andrew Rutherford. London: Macmillan, 1990.

Medwin, Thomas. *The Life of Percy Bysshe Shelley.* London: Oxford UP, 1913.

Meister, Henry. *Letters Written During a Residence in England* [excerpts]. *The Lady's Magazine* 31 (1800): 132–33.

Mellor, Anne K. *Mary Shelley.* New York: Routledge, 1988.

Mellor, Anne K., ed. *Romanticism and Feminism.* Bloomington: Indiana UP, 1988.

"Memoir of Caroline Matilda, Queen of Denmark." *La Belle Assemblée* 4.37 (1808): 105–7.

Milton, John. *The Poems of John Milton.* Ed. John Carey and Alastair Fowler. London: Longman, 1968.

Mitchell, Juliet. "Femininity, Narrative, and Psychoanalysis." In *Modern Criticism and Theory: A Reader.* Ed. David Lodge. London: Longman, 1988.

Moir, John. *Female Tuition; or an Address to Mothers on the Education of Daughters. A New Edition.* London: Murray and Highley, [1817].

Moore, Thomas. *Letters and Journals of Lord Byron with Notices of His Life.* 2 vols. London: J. Murray, 1830.

Moraga, Cherríe, and Gloria Anzaldúa, eds. *This Bridge Called My Back.* Watertown, MA: Persephone, 1981.

More, Hannah. *The Works of Hannah More.* 9 vols. London: H. Fisher, 1840–1844.

Morson, Gary Saul, and Caryl Emerson. *Mikhail Bakhtin: Creation of a Prosaics.* Stanford: Stanford UP, 1990.

Morson, Gary Saul, and Caryl Emerson, eds. *Rethinking Bakhtin: Extensions and Challenges.* Evanston: Northwestern UP, 1989.

Moss, William. *An Essay on the Management, Nursing, and Diseases of Children.* London: W. N. Longman, 1794.

Nelson, James. *An Essay on the Government of Children.* London: R. and J. Dodsley, 1756.

Neumann, Erich. *The Origins and History of Consciousness.* Trans. R. F. C. Hull. Princeton: Princeton UP, 1969.

The New Jerusalem Bible. New York: Doubleday, 1985.

Newton, Judith Lowder. *Women, Power, and Subversion: Social Strategies in British Fiction, 1778–1860.* Athens: U of Georgia P, 1981.

Nietzsche, Friedrich. *The Birth of Tragedy and The Case of Wagner.* Trans. Walter Kaufmann. New York: Vintage, 1967.

Notopoulos, James A. *The Platonism of Shelley.* Durham: Duke UP, 1949.

The Nurse's Guide. London: J. Brotherton, 1729.

Nye, Andrea. " 'A Woman Clothed with the Sun': Julia Kristeva and the Escape from/to Language." *Signs: Journal of Women in Culture and Society* 12 (1987): 664–86.

———. "The Unity of Language." *Hypatia* 2 (1987): 95–111.

O'Malley, Glenn. *Shelley and Synesthesia.* [Evanston]: Northwestern UP, 1964.

"On Modern Taste and Style." *The Lady's Magazine* 34 (1803): 375.

Ong, Walter J., S.J. *Interfaces of the Word: Studies in the Evolution of Culture and Consciousness.* Ithaca: Cornell UP, 1977.

Otto, Walter F. *Dionysus: Myth and Cult.* Trans. Robert B. Palmer. Bloomington: Indiana UP, 1965.

Owenson, Sydney. *The Missionary* (1811). Delmar, NY: Scholars' Facsimiles & Reprints, 1981.

Oxford Classical Dictionary. 2nd ed. Oxford: Clarendon, 1970.

Oxford English Dictionary. Ed. J. A. Simpson and E. S. C. Weiner. 2nd ed. Oxford: Clarendon, 1989.

Paltock, Robert. *The Life and Adventures of Peter Wilkins.* Ed. Christopher Bentley. London: Oxford UP, 1973.

Parke, E. W., and D. E. W. Wormell. *The Delphic Oracle.* 2 vols. Oxford: Basil Blackwell, 1956.

Pateman, Carole. *The Sexual Contract.* Stanford: Stanford UP, 1988.

Pater, Walter. *Three Major Texts (The Renaissance, Appreciations, and Imaginary Portraits).* Ed. William E. Buckler. New York: New York UP, 1986.

Pausanias. *Description of Greece.* Trans. James Frazer. 6 vols. London: Macmillan, 1898.

Peacock, Thomas Love. *The Works of Thomas Love Peacock.* Ed. H. F. B. Brett-Smith and C. E. Jones. 10 vols. London: Constable, 1924–34.

Peck, Walter E. *Shelley, His Life and Work.* Boston: Houghton Mifflin, 1927.

Pennington, Lady Sarah. *A Mother's Advice to Her Absent Daughters.* New York: Garland, 1986.

Percival, Thomas. *A Father's Instructions.* London: J. Johnson, 1784.

Pestalozzi, Johann Heinrich. *Leonard and Gertrude.* London: S. Hazard, 1800.

Pick, Franz, and René Sédillot. *All the Monies of the World: A Chronicle of Currency Values.* New York: Pick Publishing, 1971.

Plato. *Republic.* Trans. Benjamin Jowett. New York: Modern Library, 1946.

———. *Timaeus and Critias.* Trans. H. D. P. Lee. London: Penguin, 1971.

Plato's Statesman. Trans. J. B. Skemp. London: Routledge and Kegan Paul, 1952.

Plotinus. *Enneads.* Trans. A. H. Armstrong. 7 vols. Cambridge, MA: Harvard UP, 1984.

Plutarch. *Plutarch's Lives.* Trans. Bernadotte Perrin. 11 vols. London: William Heinemann, 1914.

Polidori, John. *The Diary of Dr. John William Polidori, 1816.* Ed. William Michael Rossetti. London: E. Matthews, 1911.

Pollock, Linda A. *Forgotten Children.* Cambridge: Cambridge UP, 1983.

Poovey, Mary. *The Proper Lady and the Woman Writer.* Chicago: U of Chicago P, 1984.

Pottle, Frederick. "The Role of Asia in the Dramatic Action of Shelley's *Prometheus Unbound.*" In *Shelley: A Collection of Critical Essays.* Ed. George M. Ridenour. Englewood Cliffs, NJ: Prentice-Hall, 1965.

Poulsen, Frederik. *Delphi.* Trans. G. C. Richards. London: Gyldendal, [n.d.].

"Princess Sophia." *La Belle Assemblée* 2.13 (1807): 3.

"The Princess of Wales." *Lady's Monthly Museum* 31 (1800): 1–3.

Pulos, C. E. "Shelley and Malthus." *PMLA* 68 (1952): 113–24.

———. *The Deep Truth: A Study of Shelley's Scepticism.* Lincoln: U of Nebraska P, 1962.

Quayle, Eric. *Early Children's Books: A Collector's Guide.* Newton Abbot, Devon, England: David and Charles, 1983.

Ragland-Sullivan, Ellie. *Jacques Lacan and the Philosophy of Psychoanalysis.* Urbana: U of Illinois P, 1986.

Raine, Kathleen, and George Mills Harper, eds. *Thomas Taylor the Platonist: Selected Writings.* Princeton: Princeton UP, [1969].

Rajan, Tilottama. "Deconstruction or Reconstruction: Reading Shelley's 'Prometheus Unbound.' " *Studies in Romanticism,* no. 23 (Fall 1984): 317–38.

Reiman, Donald H. "Roman Scenes in *Prometheus Unbound* III.iv." *Philological Quarterly* 46 (1967): 69–78.

———. "Introduction." In Charlotte Dacre. *Hours of Solitude.* 2 vols. in 1. New York: Garland, 1978.

———. *Intervals of Inspiration.* Greenwood, FL: Penkevill, 1988.

"Review of *A Voyage to the East Indies* and *The Works of Sir William Jones.*" *The Lady's Monthly Museum* 30 (1799) 477–80.

Rich, Adrienne. *Of Woman Born.* New York: Norton, 1976.

Richardson, Alan. "Romanticism and the Colonization of the Feminine." In *Romanticism and Feminism.* Ed. Anne K. Mellor. Bloomington: Indiana UP, 1988.

Robinson, Paul A. *The Freudian Left: Wilheim Keich, Géza Róheim, Herbert Marcuse.* New York: Harper and Row, 1969.

Rogers, Neville. *Shelley at Work.* 2nd ed. Oxford: Clarendon, 1967.

———. "An Unpublished Shelley Letter." *Keats-Shelley Memorial Bulletin* 24 (1973): 20–24.

Rolleston, Maud. *Talks with Lady Shelley.* London: G. G. Harrop, 1925.

Romm, May E. "The Unconscious Need to Be an Only Child." *Psychoanalytic Quarterly* 24 (1955): 331–42.

Rosolato, Guy. "La Voix: Entre Corps et Langage." *Revue Française de Psychoanalyse* 38. 1 (1974): 75–94.

Rousseau, Jean-Jacques. *Julie ou la Nouvelle Héloïse.* Paris: Éditions Garnier Frères, 1952.

———. *On the Origin of Language.* Trans. John H. Moran and Alexander Gode. New York: F. Ungar, [1966].

———. *Emile: or, On Education.* Trans. Allan Bloom. New York: Basic Books, 1979.

Roustang, François. *Dire Mastery.* Baltimore: Johns Hopkins UP, 1982.

Ryerson, Alice. "Medical Advice on Child Rearing, 1550–1900." *Harvard Educational Review* 31 (1961): 302–23.

Said, Edward. *Orientalism.* New York: Vintage Books, 1979.

St. Clair, William. *The Godwins and the Shelleys.* London: Faber, 1989.

———. "The Impact of Byron's Writings: An Evaluative Approach." In *Byron: Augustan and Romantic.* Ed. Andrew Rutherford. London: Macmillan, 1990.

Sawyer, Paul. "Ruskin and the Matriarchial Logos." In *Victorian Sages and Cultural Discourse: Renegotiating Gender and Power.* Ed. Thaïs E. Morgan. New Brunswick: Rutgers UP, 1990.

Scarry, Elaine. *The Body in Pain: The Making and Unmaking of the World.* New York: Oxford UP, 1985.

Schapiro, Barbara A. *The Romantic Mother.* Baltimore: Johns Hopkins UP, 1983.

Schiller, Friedrich von. *Naïve and Sentimental Poetry.* Trans. Julius A. Elias. New York: Frederick Ungar, 1966.

———. *On the Aesthetic Education of Man.* Ed. and trans. Elizabeth M. Williamson and L. A. Willoughby. Oxford: Clarendon, 1967.

Scott, Walter Sidney, ed. *The Athenians.* London: Golden Cockerel, 1943.

Shakespeare, William. *Complete Works.* Ed. David Bevington. Rev. ed. Glenview, IL: Scott, Foresman, [1973].

"Shawls." *La Belle Assemblée* 1.1 (1806): 64.

Shelley, Lady Jane, ed. *Shelley Memorials.* London: Smith, Elder, 1859.

Shelley, Mary. *Frankenstein.* Ed. James Reiger. Chicago: U of Chicago P, 1974.

———. *The Letters of Mary Wollstonecraft Shelley.* Ed. Betty T. Bennett. 3 vols. Baltimore: Johns Hopkins UP, 1980–1988.

———. *The Journals of Mary Shelley, 1814–1844.* Ed. Paula K. Feldman and Diana Scott-Kilvert. 2 vols. Oxford: Clarendon, 1987.

Shelley, Percy Bysshe. *Shelley's Prose; or The Trumpet of a Prophecy.* Ed. David Lee Clark. Albuquerque: U of New Mexico P, 1954.

———. *Prometheus Unbound: A Variorum Edition.* Ed. Lawrence Zillman. Seattle: U of Washington P, 1960.

———. *The Letters of Percy Bysshe Shelley.* Ed. Frederick L. Jones. 2 vols. Oxford: Clarendon, 1964.

———. *The Complete Works of Percy Bysshe Shelley.* Ed. Roger Ingpen and Walter E. Peck. New York: Gordian, 1965.

———. *Shelley's "Prometheus Unbound": The Text and the Drafts.* Ed. Lawrence John Zillman. New Haven: Yale UP, 1968.

———. *Shelley's Poetry and Prose: Authoritative Texts, Criticism.* Ed. Donald H. Reiman and Sharon B. Powers. New York: Norton, 1977.

———. *Bodleian MS. Shelley e.4.* Ed. P. M. S. Dawson. *The Bodleian Shelley Manuscripts.* Vol. 3. New York: Garland, 1987.

———. *The Poems of Shelley.* Ed. Geoffrey Matthews and Kelvin Everest. New York: Longman, 1989.

———. *The "Prometheus Unbound" Notebooks: A Facsimile of Bodleian MSS. Shelley e.1, e.2, and e.3.* Ed. Neil Fraistat. *The Bodleian Shelley Manuscripts.* Vol. 9. New York: Garland, 1991.

Silverman, Kaja. *The Subject of Semiotics.* New York: Oxford UP, 1983.

———. "Fragments of a Fashionable Discourse." In *Studies in Entertainment: Critical Approaches to Mass Culture.* Ed. Tania Modleski. Bloomington: Indiana UP, 1986.

———. *The Acoustic Mirror: The Female Voice in Psychoanalysis and Cinema.* Bloomington: Indiana UP, 1988.

Slater, Philip. *The Glory of Hera.* Boston: Beacon, 1971.

Smith, Bonnie. *The Women of Lille Bourgeoisie.* Rochester, NY: U of Rochester P, 1975.

Smith, Paul. *Discerning the Subject.* Minneapolis: U of Minnesota P, 1988.

Sophocles. *Oedipus at Colonus.* Trans. Robert Fitzgerald. In *The Complete Greek Tragedies.* Ed. David Grene and Richmond Lattimore. 3 vols. Chicago: U of Chicago P, 1959.

———. *Oedipus the King.* Trans. David Grene. In *The Complete Greek Tragedies.* Ed. David Grene and Richmond Lattimore. 3 vols. Chicago: U of Chicago P, 1959.

Spenser, Edmund. *The Faerie Queene.* Ed. Thomas P. Roche, Jr. New Haven: Yale UP, 1978.

Spitz, René A. "The Primal Cavity." *Psychoanalytic Study of the Child* 10 (1955): 215–40.

Steele, Valerie. *Fashion and Eroticism.* New York: Oxford UP, 1985.

Steinthal, Heymann. "The Original Form of the Legend of Prometheus." In *Mythology Among the Hebrews and Its Historical Development.* Ed. Ignaz Goldhizer. Trans. Russell Martineau. New York: Cooper Square Publishers, 1967.

Stern, Daniel. *The First Relationship.* Cambridge, MA: Harvard UP, 1977.

———. "Affect Attunement." In *Frontiers of Infant Psychiatry.* Vol. 2. Ed. J. D. Call, E. Galenson, and R. L. Tyson. New York: Basic Books, 1985.

———. *The Interpersonal World of the Infant.* New York: Basic Books, 1985.

Stone, Lawrence J. *The Family, Sex, and Marriage in England, 1500–1800.* London: Weidenfeld and Nicolson, 1977.

Sunstein, Emily W. *Mary Shelley: Romance and Reality.* Boston: Little, Brown, 1989.

Synopsis of the Contents of the British Museum. London: R. and J. Dodsley, 1814.

Taunton, Thomas Henry. *Portraits of Celebrated Racehorses of the Past and Present Centuries.* 4 vols. London: Sampson Low, Marston, Searle & Rivington, 1887.

Taylor, Anne. *Practical Hints to Young Females, on the Duties of a Wife, a Mother, and a Mistress of a Family.* Boston: Wells and Lilly, 1816.

"Three Years After Marriage: A Tale from the French of M. Imbert." *Lady's Monthly Museum* 38 (1808): 28–32.

Todorov, Tzvetan. *Mikhail Bakhtin: The Dialogical Principle.* Trans. Wlad Godzich. Minneapolis: U of Minnesota P, 1984.

"The Triumph of Patience and Virtue." *Lady's Monthly Museum* 30 (1799): 389–90.

Trotter, Thomas. *A View of the Nervous Temperament.* London: Longman, 1807.

Trumbach, Randolph. *The Rise of the Egalitarian Family.* New York: Academic, 1978.

"The Unfeeling Father: A Fragment." *Lady's Monthly Museum* 33 (1803): 383–84.

Ulmer, William A. *Shelleyan Eros: The Rhetoric of Romantic Love.* Princeton: Princeton UP, 1990.

Vallas, Stacey. "Embodying the Unspeakable in Melville, Hawthorne, and Davis." Ph.D. diss. Stanford, 1991.

Varro, Marcus Terentius. *On the Latin Language.* Trans. Ronald G. Kent. 2 vols. Cambridge, MA: Harvard UP, 1938.

Veeder, William. *Mary Shelley and "Frankenstein"—The Fate of Androgyny.* Chicago: U of Chicago P, 1986.

Volney, Constantin. *The Ruins, or, Meditations on the Revolutions of Empires; and the Law of Nature.* New York: Peter Eckler, 1890.

Von Mücke, Dorothea. *Virtue and the Veil of Illusion: Generic Innovation and the Pedagogical Project in Eighteenth-Century Literature.* Stanford: Stanford UP, 1991.

Vygotsky, Lev Semenovich. *Thought and Language.* Trans. and ed. Alex Kozulin. Cambridge, MA: MIT Press, 1986.

Waldoff, Leon. "The Father-Son Conflict in 'Prometheus Unbound': The Psychology of a Vision." *Psychoanalytic Review* 62 (1975): 79–96.

Ward, Humphrey, and W. Roberts. *Romney: A Biographical and Critical Essay with a Catalogue Raisonné of His Works.* 2 vols. London: Thomas Agnew and Sons, 1904.

Wasserman, Earl R. *Shelley: A Critical Reading.* Baltimore: Johns Hopkins UP, [1971].

Webb, Timothy. *The Violet in the Crucible: Shelley and Translation.* Oxford: Clarendon, 1976.

Wecklein, Nikolaus, ed. *The "Prometheus Bound" of Aeschylus.* Boston: Ginn, [1891].

Werkmeister, Lucy. *A Newspaper History of England, 1792–1793.* Lincoln: U of Nebraska P, 1967.

White, Newman Ivey. *Shelley.* 2 vols. New York: A. A. Knopf, 1940.

Wilde, Oscar. *Intentions and The Soul of Man.* London: Methuen, 1908.

Wilden, Anthony. *The Language of the Self.* Baltimore: Johns Hopkins UP, 1968.

Wilkins, W. H. *A Queen of Tears: Caroline Matilda, Queen of Denmark and Norway.* 2 vols. New York: Longmans, Green, 1904.

Wilson, Milton. *Shelley's Later Poetry.* New York: Columbia UP, 1959.

Winckelmann, Johann. *History of Ancient Art.* 4 vols. in 2. New York: Ungar [1969].

Winnington-Ingram, R. P. *Studies in Aeschylus.* Cambridge: Cambridge UP, 1983.

Wittgenstein, Ludwig. *Philosophical Investigations.* Trans. G. E. M. Anscombe. Oxford: Basil Blackell, 1958.

Wollstonecraft, Mary. *The Female Reader.* London: J. Johnson, 1789.

———. *Original Stories from Real Life.* London: J. Johnson, 1791.

———. *A Vindication of the Rights of Woman.* Ed. Charles W. Hagelman, Jr. New York: W. W. Norton, 1967.

———. *Letters Written During a Short Residence in Sweden, Norway, and Denmark.* Ed. Carol H. Poston. Lincoln: U of Nebraska P, 1976.

Woodbridge, Robert. *The Pad.* London: J. Parsons, 1793.

Woodman, Ross. "The Androgyne in 'Prometheus Unbound.' " *Studies in Romanticism,* no. 20 (Summer 1981): 225–47.

Woolf, Virginia. *To the Lighthouse.* London: Hogarth, 1927.

———. "Professions for Women." In *Death of the Moth and Other Essays.* London: Harcourt, Brace, 1943.

Wordsworth, William. *The Prelude; or Growth of a Poet's Mind* (text of 1805). Ed. Ernest de Selincourt. London: Oxford UP, 1970.

———. *The Prose Works of William Wordsworth.* Ed. W. J. B. Owen and Jane Worthington Smyser. 3 vols. Oxford: Clarendon, 1974.

Wormhoudt, Arthur. *The Demon Lover: A Psychoanalytic Approach to Literature.* Freeport, NY: Books for Libraries Press, 1968.

Yeats, William Butler. *The Collected Poems of W. B. Yeats.* New York: Macmillan, 1957.

Index